HOW TO GET A JOB IN SOUTHERN CALIFORNIA

How to Get a Job in Southern California

Robert Sanborn and Naomi Sandweiss

SURREY BOOKS
CHICAGO

HOW TO GET A JOB IN SOUTHERN CALIFORNIA

Published by Surrey Books, Inc., 230 E. Ohio St., Suite 120, Chicago, IL 60611.

Copyright © 1997 by Surrey Books, Inc. All rights reserved, including the right to reproduce this book or portions thereof in any form, including any information storage and retrieval system, except for the inclusion of brief quotations in a review.

This book is manufactured in the United States of America.

6th Edition.   1   2   3   4   5

Library of Congress Cataloging-in-Publication data:
Sanborn, Robert, 1959–
    How to get a job in Southern California/ Robert Sanborn and Naomi Sandweiss.— 6th ed.
        p.   cm. — (The Insider's guide series)
    Rev. ed. of: How to get a job in Southern California/Thomas M. Camden, Jonathan Palmer. 5th ed. 1995.
    Includes bibliographical references and index.
    ISBN 1-57284-009-9
    1. Job hunting—California, Southern—Directories. 2. Job vacancies—California, Southern—Directories. 3. Business enterprises—California, Southern—Directories. 4. Vocational guidance—California, Southern—Directories. I. Sandweiss, Naomi. II. Camden, Thomas M., 1938-1995 How to get a job in Southern California. III. Title. IV. Series.
HF5382.75.U62C217   1997   96-39365
650.14'09794'9—dc21   CIP

AVAILABLE TITLES IN THIS SERIES—$16.95
How To Get a Job in Atlanta
How To Get a Job in Chicago
How To Get a Job in The New York Metropolitan Area
How To Get a Job in The San Francisco Bay Area
How To Get a Job in Seattle/Portland
How To Get a Job in Southern California

Single copies may be ordered directly from the publisher. Send check or money order for book price plus $4.00 for first book and $1.50 for each additional book to cover insurance, shipping, and handling to Surrey Books at the above address. For quantity discounts, please contact the publisher.

Editorial production by Bookcrafters, Inc., Chicago.
Cover and book design by Joan Sommers Design, Chicago.
Illustrations by Mona Daly.
Typesetting by On Track Graphics, Inc., Chicago.
"How To Get a Job Series" is distributed to the trade by Publishers Group West.

Acknowledgments

Robert Sanborn wishes to thank his personal support system: Ellen Sanborn and Virginia Elisabet, wife and daughter respectively. Naomi Sandweiss wishes to thank her research assistant, Larissa Pickens, and the people who offered support and encouragement: Dan Sandweiss, husband, Stanley and Rosalia Feinstein, parents, Debbie Feinstein, sister, and Rebecca Mattson, friend and colleague. Additional thanks go to publisher Susan Schwartz and managing editor Gene DeRoin.

We also wish to acknowledge the seminal contributions of Thomas M. Camden, Editor Emeritus.

NAMES AND ADDRESSES CAN CHANGE

The authors and editors have made every effort to supply you with the most useful, up-to-date information available to help you find the job you want. Each name, address, and phone number has been verified by our staff of fact checkers. But offices move and people change jobs, so we urge you to check before you write or visit. And if you think we should include information on companies, organizations, or people that we've missed, please let us know.

The publisher, authors, and editors make no guarantee that the employers listed in this book have jobs available

DROP US A LINE

Among the new features in this edition are "Dear Dr. Bob" letters—short notes from job seekers or workers like yourself, recounting their experiences. For this feature to be a success, we need your input. So if you have any interesting stories to share with your fellow job hunters, write to us in care of Surrey Books. We cannot guarantee publication, and letters will not be returned. Send your letters to:

> Dear Dr. Bob, Job Hunting Stories
> c/o Surrey Books
> 230 E. Ohio St., Suite 120
> Chicago, IL 60611

JOB HUNTING?

These books, covering 6 major markets, can help you achieve a successful career

HOW... to get the job you want: Each book gives you more than 1,500 major employers, numbers to call, and people to contact.

WHERE... to get the job you want: How to research the local job market and meet the people who hire.

PLUS... how to use local networks and professional organizations; how to choose a career; advice on employment services; how to sell yourself in the interview; writing power resumes and cover letters; hundreds of names and numbers, many available nowhere else!

ORDER FORM

Please send the following at $16.95 each

___ **HOW TO GET A JOB IN ATLANTA**

___ **HOW TO GET A JOB IN CHICAGO**

___ **HOW TO GET A JOB IN NEW YORK**

___ **HOW TO GET A JOB IN SAN FRANCISCO**

___ **HOW TO GET A JOB IN SEATTLE/PORTLAND**

___ **HOW TO GET A JOB IN SOUTHERN CALIFORNIA**

Enclosed is my check/money order for $_____

☐ Visa ☐ MasterCard ☐ AmEx ☐ Discover

_____
CARD NUMBER

_____
EXP. DATE

_____
SIGNATURE

_____
NAME

_____
ADDRESS

_____
CITY   STATE   ZIP

_____
PHONE

For Easier Ordering Call 1-800-326-4430

Send check or money order, and include $4.00 for first book and $1.50 for each additional book to cover insurance, shipping and handling to: Surrey Books, 230 E. Ohio St., Suite 120, Chicago, IL 60611. Or call toll-free: 1-800-326-4430. Allow 2-4 weeks for delivery. Satisfaction Guaranteed or your money back.

Contents

1 ONE/SO YOU WANT TO GET A JOB IN SOUTHERN CALIFORNIA
How this book can help. Preparing for the job search. Using local and business newspapers. Using the Internet. Career trends in Southern California. Ten best places to work, fastest growing companies, and largest employers in Southern California. Using Chambers of Commerce.

21 TWO/CHOOSING A CAREER
Self-exploration and assessment. Professional testing. Career counseling. Career assistance from colleges and universities. Social service agencies that can help in the career search. Career changing. Starting your own business. Resources for women and minorities. Career strategy book list.

42 THREE/IF I CAN'T FIND A JOB, SHOULD I GO BACK TO SCHOOL?
When to go back to school. How education relates to income. Getting organized for graduate school. Selecting a graduate school. Vocational, trade, and continuing education programs. On-line education.

54 FOUR/THE 10-STEP JOB SEARCH
(1) Know where you're going. (2) Research the job market: libraries, directories, trade magazines, job-listing publications and telephone hot lines, Internet resources. (3) Organize your search. (4) Network. (5) Be persistent. (6) Prepare your resume. (7) Distribute your resume. (8) Use career resources: lists of employment agencies, executive search firms, social service and government agencies, career consultants, college career centers, career fairs, World Wide Web job links. (9) The "killer" interview. (10) Evaluating job offers.

97 FIVE/NETWORK, NETWORK, NETWORK: THE BEST JOB-SEARCH TECHNIQUE
The six myths of networking. Step-by-step guide to networking. The information interview. Networking etiquette. Networking resources in Southern California: a list of more than 125 professional organizations, trade groups, clubs, and societies.

116 SIX/DEVELOPING THE PERFECT RESUME
The basics of a good resume. Choosing a resume format. Sample resumes. Resume checklist. Using the computer to design your resume. List of professional resume preparers. The cover letter with examples. Cybertips and books on resume and cover letter writing.

133 SEVEN/THE KILLER INTERVIEW
Six steps to a killer interview: (1) Preparation. (2) Dressing right. (3) The first impression. (4) Expressing yourself. (5) Asking questions. (6) The aftermath. 15 toughest interview questions—and how to answer them. 9 interview styles to watch for. Tips on interviewing. Cybertips and books on interviewing.

154 EIGHT/SUMMER, TEMPORARY, AND PART-TIME JOBS
Tips for summer-job seekers. Six-step system for finding summer jobs. Summer job hunting on the Internet. Top summer internship programs. Temporary/part-time jobs, with list of employment agencies. Books on the subject.

164 NINE/HOW TO HANDLE A NEW JOB AND WORKPLACE
The first day on the job: do's and don'ts. Adjusting to the job. Maintaining good relations with the boss. Creativity and innovation in your career. Romance in the office. Keeping your career on the high road and your network alive.

172 TEN/WHERE SOUTHERN CALIFORNIA WORKS
Names, addresses, phone numbers, and contact names (where possible) of more than 1,500 major employers, by industry. Professional organizations that can furnish information; industry magazines and directories. Candid interviews and helpful hints.

306 Employers Index

323 General Index

one

So You Want To Get a Job in Southern California

You've decided to get a job in one of the most dynamic and diverse areas of the country. As the second largest metropolitan area in the United States, Southern California provides numerous opportunities for job seekers. Whether you are entertaining a career in Hollywood, engineering employment opportunities in San Diego, or surfing the Internet for a job on the Coast, Southern California can be exciting and rewarding. This book will help you find the job you're looking for.

How This Book Can Help

There are, of course, other books about finding jobs and about aspects of the job search such as resume writing and interviewing. This book is a little different. We have taken an approach that will make your Southern California job search easier and, hopefully, successful.

How is this book any different from the rest? First, we are local. We have inside information on the job market and things unique to the job search in Southern California, which includes Los Angeles, San Diego, and Orange County. Second, this book combines job-search information from the World Wide Web with conventional information on how to conduct a job search. Once you have access to the Internet, you will see how your search for a career can be made easier with a wealth of information at your fingertips. Finally, this Insider's Guide is coauthored by an expert on the local job market and a national career guru; the information you'll get is cutting edge and proven effective. This book is designed to help you find *and land* the best job for you.

Before You Arrive

Preparation is a key to any job search, and this is especially true if you are relocating to Southern California. If you're from out of town, you'll want to learn as much about the area as possible. This will help ease the transition to your new home and allow you to concentrate on your job search. This chapter will give you a head start on learning about the region and its job market.

Much of this chapter is devoted to surveying the vast array of media sources that can help you gain a better knowledge of the area. But for some readers, the first step in the job search might be to figure out their best career options. In other words, you might need to revisit the old "what do I want to do when I grow up?" question. Choosing a career direction early on will help you focus on which industries to target. Chapter 2 will help you get that part of your search behind you.

The Southern California Job Search

As unique as the area is, it is no different from any other place in the world when it comes down to finding a job. It takes work and perseverance. Chapter 4 outlines the ten steps for seeking and securing a job. From networking to interviewing, all steps in the process are important. Chapter 5 highlights one of the most important and proven activities of the search for a career: networking. Chapter 6 will help you get your resume in shape, and Chapter 7 gets you ready to ace the interview. Chapter 8 will help if you are looking for a summer or temporary job. And Chapter 10 is our exclusive listing of major employers in Southern California, complete with addresses, phone numbers, and contacts where available.

Going to a new region to look for a job is much different from being a tourist. You'll face not only the challenges of getting to know a new place but you'll face the task of carving a niche for yourself as well. Getting a head start on researching the area and employers will make your search much easier.

Using Local Newspapers

Learning more about Southern California and all it has to offer should be one of the more interesting and enjoyable parts of your preparation. There are a number of local publications that can help you learn more about the area and, of course, provide insight into the local job market.

Local newspapers are an excellent place to begin. As you start your job search, it is important to read the want ads for more than job vacancies. The classifieds can give you an idea of who the key employers are in your field and which ones are growing.

MAJOR NEWSPAPERS IN SOUTHERN CALIFORNIA

Los Angeles Times
Times Mirror Square
Los Angeles, CA 90053
(213) 237-5000
http://www.latimes.com/HOME/
The *Los Angeles Times* publishes a daily separate business section and special supplements featuring information on careers, higher education, and employers. The Sunday edition with full classified ads goes on sale at grocery stores and major newsstands after 12:00 p.m. on Saturday and contains the largest classified ad section in the metropolitan area.

San Diego Union-Tribune
P.O. Box 191
San Diego, CA 92112
(619) 299-4141
http://www.uniontrib.com/aboutut/
Daily business coverage with special workweek features on Mondays. The Sunday edition runs full classified ads. Also, check the Web page for an on-line listing of advertised positions.

OTHER SOUTHERN CALIFORNIA NEWSPAPERS

Investor's Business Daily
12655 Beatrice St.
Los Angeles, CA 90066
(310) 448-6000
Covers regional business and economic news.

La Opinion
411 W. 5th St.
Los Angeles, CA 90013
(213) 896-2152
Southern California's largest Spanish-language paper. Published daily.

Long Beach Press-Telegram
604 Pine Ave.
Long Beach, CA 90804
(310) 435-1161
Daily.

Orange County Register
625 Grand Ave.
Santa Ana, CA 92701
(714) 835-1234
Daily.

Pasadena Star-News
525 E. Colorado Blvd.
Pasadena, CA 91109
(818) 578-6300

Making the move to Southern California?
Check out the following resources to help you get acquainted with the area.

Curbside LA: An Offbeat Guide to the City of Angels From the Pages of the Los Angeles Times, Celilia Rasmussen, Los Angeles Times Syndicate, Los Angeles, CA.

Features descriptions of Los Angeles movie locations, jogging paths, book nooks, romantic spots, special libraries, unusual museums, and more.

Los Angeles Access, ACCESS Press, New York, NY. Offers suggestions on cultural activities, restaurants, parks/recreation, architecture, and shopping within 17 Southern California areas, including Los Angeles and Orange County.

Newcomer's Handbook for Los Angeles, First Books, Inc., Chicago, IL. Information on neighborhoods, housing, utilities, and other helpful resources to help you get settled in.

San Diego Access, ACCESS Press, New York, NY. Organized by San Diego neighborhoods, this book offers suggestions on recreational and cultural activities within San Diego, La Jolla, and surrounding areas.

The Big Picture: Business Magazines and Newspapers

The general business climate affects the local job market, no matter what career field you are in. You should keep abreast of changing trends in the economy, both regional and national. The following publications can help.

NATIONAL PUBLICATIONS

The Wall Street Journal
Western Edition
6500 Wilshire Blvd.
Los Angeles, CA 90048
(213) 658-6464
http://wsj.com
The *Journal* is the nation's leading newspaper for news about the business community. The paper publishes annual reports on careers and small business. In addition, the *Journal* publishes the *National Business Employment Weekly,* which includes the classified ad sections of the paper's four regional editions. The jobs here are generally targeted to mid- to upper-level managers. Editorials about the business community are also included as well as articles on the job-search process, including resume writing, interviewing, networking, changing jobs, relocating, and entrepreneurial options.

Business Week
1221 Avenue of the Americas
New York, NY 10020
(212) 997-1221
Published weekly, this magazine will keep you informed as to key happenings in

the business world. Special issues include: Industry Outlook (24 key industries; January), Corporate Scoreboard (ranks companies in selected industries; March), Hot Growth Companies/Best Small Companies (May), and Best Business Schools (October).

Forbes
60 5th Ave.
New York, NY 10011
(212) 620-2200
Publishes 26 issues/year. Special issues include: The Annual Report on American Industry (January), Top 500 U.S. Companies (April), International 500 (July), 800 Top U.S. Corporate Executives (personal and compensation information; May), 200 Best Small U.S. Companies (November), and 400 Largest Private Companies in the U.S. (December).

Fortune
Time-Life Building
1271 Avenue of the Americas
New York, NY 10020-1301
(212) 586-1212
Publishes 27 issues/year. Special issues include: 18-Month Economic Forecast (January and July), America's Most Admired Corporations (February), U.S. Business Hall of Fame (profiles selected business leaders; March), Fortune 500: Largest U.S. Industrial Corporations (April), Service 500 (June), Global 500: U.S. and Foreign Corporations (July), Fastest Growing 100 Public Companies (October), Pacific Rim Survey (October), and Best Cities for Business (November).

Inc.
38 Commercial Wharf
Boston, MA 02110
(617) 248-8000
Published monthly. Special issues include: Best Cities for Starting a Business (April), 100 Fastest Growing Public Companies (May), and 500 Fastest Growing Private Companies (October).

Money
Time-Life Building
1271 Avenue of the Americas
New York, NY 10020-1301
(212) 522-1212
Published monthly. Annual September issue (Best Places to Live) is especially insightful for those thinking of relocating.

Working Mother
Lang Communications
230 Park Ave.
New York, NY 10169
(212) 551-9500

Monthly publication. Special October issue features a list of the best 100 companies for working mothers.

Working Woman
342 Madison Ave.
New York, NY 10173-0008
(212) 309-9800
This monthly publication is a great resource for professional women. Special issues include: Salary Survey (January), Top 50 Women in Business (May), Top 25 Careers for Women (July), and Ten Women to Watch (November).

REGIONAL PUBLICATIONS

Inland Empire Business Journal
8560 Vineyard Ave., Suite 306
Rancho Cucamonga, CA 91730
(909) 484-9765
Monthly publication focusing on business news in the communities located between Los Angeles and Palm Springs.

Investor's Business Daily
12655 Beatrice St.
Los Angeles, CA 90066
(310) 448-6000
Covers regional business and economic news.

Los Angeles Business Journal
5700 Wilshire Blvd., Suite 170
Los Angeles, CA 90036
(213) 549-5225
Weekly publication focusing on news and business trends in the Los Angeles area. Compiles an annual Los Angeles "Book of Lists" ranking companies in 60+ industries.

Orange County Business Journal
4590 MacArthur Blvd., Suite 100
Newport Beach, CA 92660
(714) 833-8373
Weekly publication focusing on business news and trends in Orange County. In addition, annual "Book of Lists" ranks over 950 companies.

San Diego Business Journal
4909 Murphy Canyon Road, Suite 200
San Diego, CA 92123-5381
(619) 277-6359
Published weekly. Features San Diego business news and trends. Publishes annual "Book of Lists" ranking organizations in 40+ industries.

You know you're job hunting in Southern California when...
despite warm weather and an apparent lack of seasons, you observe seasonal changes in dress. Southern Californians typically don't wear light-colored summer suits to interviews in January or February. In these months, darker clothing colors predominate. Many people find that tropical weight wool is a good fabric choice for the region.

The Internet

One of the key features of this book is the inclusion of numerous World Wide Web (WWW) addresses to help you learn about the local area and jump start your job search. If you have never used cyberspace or the WWW, don't worry. In most cases it's as simple as point and click. Surfing the Internet is an excellent way to stay up-to-date on career opportunities and techniques. The Internet provides access to volumes of information and numerous contacts, all without leaving your desk.

To get started you'll need a computer, modem, and software to give you Internet access. You'll probably find it most convenient to have your own computer, but if you don't, fear not. Friends, universities, and cybercafes can provide you access to the Internet so you can join the millions now "on-line."

The "information superhighway" is really a worldwide link-up of computers and computer networks. All WWW addresses start with the letters http:// . Following this will usually be a long string of characters—often words or abbreviations—with no spaces in between. When you type that "address" into the Web browser on your computer (Netscape, Internet Explorer, Mosaic, or something similar), you will be linked with the organization listed.

There are many articles and books about the Web and how to access it. We will let you explore those on your own. However, we would like to give you an idea of the type of information the Web addresses provide. For example, there are places to get career counseling, learn about careers, post your resume, find information on companies, and view the types of positions they have open. You should note the cost of each Internet-access service (America On-Line, Prodigy, or others) and other charges before signing up for any service. In addition, there are career services on the Net that will offer you some free service with hopes that you will buy others. Keep in mind that many of the best sites and homepages are free.

Let's get you started with some WWW addresses that can provide information about Southern California itself, careers, and the local scene.

CYBERINFO ABOUT SOUTHERN CALIFORNIA

Anaheim/Orange County Visitor's Bureau
http://www.anaheimoc.org/
Includes Anaheim attractions, events, transportation and weather information.

California Virtual Tourist
http://www.research.digital.com/SRC/virtual-tourist/California.html
Features links to California tourist attractions, government, education and other on-line resources.

San Diego Convention & Business Bureau
http://www.sandiego.org/
Visitor's guide and detailed clickable map of the San Diego area.

San Diego Online
http://www.sandiego-online.com/
Maintained by *San Diego Magazine*. Features local attractions, calendar of events, local restaurant poll.

San Diego Source
http://www.sddt.com/
News and information on government, education, business, and more. Sponsored by the *San Diego Daily Transcript*.

Southern California CityNet
http://www.city.net/countries/united_states/california/southern_california
Links to 93 cities and 6 counties within Southern California.

State of California Home Page
http://www.ca.gov/
Provides information about California, including tips on moving into the State. Includes links to state government agency Web sites.

Virtually Los Angeles
http://www.virtually.com/los_angeles/
Resources include business and real estate listings, restaurants.

You know you're job hunting in Southern California when....
you schedule interviews between 10:00 a.m. and 2:00 p.m. to avoid the rush hour. Most Southern California job hunters won't be caught without their map books—invaluable tools for navigating Southern California's freeways and surface streets. Before you leave for your interview, check out the traffic situation on-line.

Southern California Real Time Traffic Report
http://www.scubed.com/caltrans/transnet.html
Provides up-to-the-minute information on freeway driving.

CYBERRESOURCES FOR YOUR JOB SEARCH

Try a few of these sites on the World Wide Web to get an overview of the job search and how the Internet might help. Many of these sites will give you a multitude of other links to continue honing your job-hunt skills.

http://www.cs.purdue.edu/homes/swlodin/jobs.html
Provides a comprehensive list of major job sites including:

Adams Online
http://www.adamsonline.com/

America's Employers
http://www.americasemployers.com/
Tips on job-search correspondence, job listings, company databases.

America's Help Wanted
http://helpwanted.com/

America's Job Bank
http://www.ajb.dni.us
An increasingly large collection of actual jobs posted at state Job Service offices nationwide. Over 100,000 jobs were available in a recent week.

Business Job Finder (Ohio State University College of Business)
http://www.cob.ohio-state.edu/dept/fin/osujobs.htm
A well-organized and comprehensive collection of accounting, finance, and consulting career resources on the Internet.

Career Action Center
http://www.GATENET.com/cac/
A good page with links to other career-related resources.

The Career Channel
http://riceinfo.rice.edu:80/projects/careers/
A lot of links to other career sites, as well as material on all aspects of careers and the job search, from Rice University's Career Center.

Career Magazine
http://www.careermag.com/careermag/
Internet links and career information.

Career Mosaic
http://www.careermosaic.com/cm/
Includes information on hot companies, new products and technology, benefits and employee programs, and other career-related facts.

CareerNet (Career Resource Center)
http://www.careers.org
Thousands of job, employer, and career-reference Web links. Also maintains a growing database, including employers, professional associations, government jobs, educational resources, career counselors, self-employment resources, career events, and more.

Career Path
http://www.careerpath.com
Access to classified job listings for nationally read newspapers including the *Los Angeles Times*.

The Catapult
http://www.jobweb.org/catapult/
An excellent page, with links to many other useful career-related Internet resources.

College Grad Job Hunter
http://www.collegegrad.com/
Job listings, advice on how to negotiate a job offer, conduct a job search.

Employment Opportunities and Job Resources (Margaret Riley)
http://www.jobtrack.com/jobguide/
One of the most highly respected collections of career-resource links, with extensive advice on using the Internet's resources in the career-search process.

Interactive Employment Network
http://www.espan.com
Provides current resources for the job seeker, salary guides, advice from career specialists, and job listings (mostly in technical fields).

Job Center
http://www.jobcenter.com/home.html

JobHunt (Dane Spearing at Stanford University)
http://rescomp.stanford.edu/jobs.html
A well-organized list of major Internet career-resource links.

Job Web
http://www.jobweb.com

Monster Board, The
http://www1.monster.com:80/home.html/
Post a resume to the Internet, learn about employers and job openings.

NationJob Online
http://www.nationjob.com/

Online Career Center
http://www.occ.com
A highly respected Internet jobs resource. OCC is a non-profit employer association, providing a database, job and resume files, company information and profiles, and on-line search software for both employers and applicants.

Rennsselaer Polytechnic Institute (Career Resource Homepage)
http://www.rpi/edu/dept/cdc/homepage.html
An excellent collection of career resource links maintained by the R.P.I. Career Development Center.

United States Department of Labor
http://ww.dol.gov/
The latest job-related news and issues.

RECOMMENDED BOOKS FOR THE ON-LINE JOB SEARCH

Gonyea, James. *The On-line Job Search Companion.* New York, NY: McGraw-Hill,1994. A complete guide to hundreds of career-planning and job-hunting resources available via your computer.

Goodwin, M., D. Cohn, and D. Spivey. *Net Jobs: Use the Internet to Land Your Dream Job.* New York, NY: Michael Wolff Publishing, 1996. Provides web addresses of major companies, classifieds, and career and job-search information.

Hahn, Harley, and Rick Stout. *The Internet Yellow Pages.* Berkeley, CA: Osborne McGraw-Hill,1994. Provides listing of where to search for ads or post your resume.

Kennedy, Joyce Lain, and Thomas J. Morrow. *Electronic Resume Revolution.* New York, NY: John Wiley & Sons,1994. Provides resume information and resources via the Internet.

Kennedy, Joyce Lain. *Hook Up, Get Hired!* New York, NY: John Wiley & Sons,1995. Provides job-search information via the Internet.

Rittner, Don. *The Whole Earth On-line Almanac: Info from A to Z.* New York, NY: Brady Publishing,1993. Describes bulletin boards and on-line services along with phone numbers.

Career Trends in Southern California

Southern Californians have a knack for reinventing themselves. After weathering several years of layoffs, restructuring, and natural disasters, the economic forecast for Southern California is once again sunny. Many of the Southern California companies hardest hit by earlier downturns have since diversified and revived their operations. For example, Rockwell International, one of the largest employers in Southern California, shifted its focus from aerospace to high-growth areas such as modems, semiconductors, and automotive components.

The $20 billion entertainment industry continues to create Southern California employment opportunities. According to one report, during 1995, the industry added 36,000 jobs to the local economy. In particular, digital filmmakers and computer imaging graphics companies are expanding rapidly. Indeed, UCLA forecasters anticipate the greatest growth in the software development, multimedia, television, amusement, and recreation fields.

International trade is also a major player in the Southern California job market. The combined ports of Los Angeles and Long Beach are the busiest in the country.

The telecommunications industry has played a major role in reviving San Diego's economy. According to a *Los Angeles Times* report, 70 telecommunications companies have generated tens of thousands of jobs in San Diego since 1990. Telecommunication companies such as Qualcomm Inc. and Pacific Communication are expanding at such a rapid pace that their hiring can't keep pace.

In Orange County, job development is expected to outpace population growth. According to Cal State Fullerton's Center for Demographic Studies, most new job creation will be in the health care/health products, financial services, retail/wholesale trade, and high-tech manufacturing fields.

Ten Best Places To Work In Southern California

Amgen
1840 Dehavilland Drive
Thousand Oaks, CA 91320
(805) 447-1000
Staffing Department: P.O. Box 2569, Thousand Oaks, CA 91319
jobs@amgen.com
http://amgen.bio.com/
Founded in 1980, Amgen is the largest biotechnology firm in the world. Career opportunities are available in research, process development, quality control, management information systems, marketing, finance, and human resources. Amgen's employees enjoy a campus-like atmosphere featuring an on-site fitness center, child-care center, dry cleaner, and credit union. Other benefits of employment at Amgen include reimbursement for relevant coursework and a minimum of 10 days vacation per year. The company has been cited by *Working Mother* magazine as one of the best employers for working mothers. Amgen utilizes an electronic database system to review resumes. Applicants are encouraged to submit resumes via e-mail at the address above.

ARCO
515 S. Flower St.
Los Angeles, CA 90071
(213) 486-3511

Vice President, Human Resources: John Kelly
http://www.arco.com/
ARCO is one of the largest oil companies in the United States, employing over 23,000 worldwide. ARCO has been cited as one of the most "family-friendly" companies in America. Some employees receive full tuition for graduate education. In 1995, retirees and employees determined where more than 50% of ARCO's philanthropic grants were distributed.

California Institute of Technology
Human Resources
Mail Stop 101-06
Pasadena, CA 91125
(818) 395-4661
Job hotline: (818) 395-4660
http://caltech.edu
Founded in 1891, Caltech maintains an excellent reputation among American universities, consistently ranked as one of the finest science and engineering colleges in the nation. Caltech also manages the Jet Propulsion Lab (JPL) and seven other off-campus astronomical, seismological, and marine biology facilities. 1,714 employees work on-campus and 6,000 are employed at the nearby JPL site. You don't have to be a professor to work at Caltech; positions are available for engineers, administrative and clerical staff, and tradespeople. Benefits to employees include a child-care center, free workouts at University athletic facilities, and access to concerts, lectures, and other on-campus events. In addition, some employees even enjoy special perks, such as access to massages on Fridays. According to Tina Lowenthal, Senior Negotiator in the Purchasing Department, the atmosphere at Caltech is relaxed. "My manager gives us freedom and autonomy but at the same time, she supports us 110%." When we asked what she enjoyed most about Caltech, Tina said, "I like the fact that I'm working among some of the greatest scientific minds in the world."

Disney, The Walt, Company
500 S. Buena Vista St.
Burbank, CA 91521
(818) 560-1000
Job hotline: (818) 558-2222
http://www.disney.com
Many job seekers are attracted to the Disney empire. In addition to their well-known theme parks, Disney manages entertainment, consumer products, and sports team operations in Southern California. In 1996, the Walt Disney Company was recognized by *Fortune* magazine as America's top entertainment organization. According to many within the Disney organization, the work environment here is intense. Positions exist within Disney's corporate administration, consumer products, studio, store, Imagineering, and Disneyland divisions.

Fluor Corporation
3333 Michelson Drive
Irvine, CA 92730
(714) 975-2000
Job hotline: (714) 975-5253
The Fluor Corporation provides engineering and construction services worldwide. Fluor was recognized in 1996 as the number one engineering and construction company in the United States by *Fortune* magazine. Fluor hires engineering, clerical, data processing, finance, telecommunications, and administrative personnel.

Getty, J. Paul, Trust
401 Wilshire Blvd., Suite 900
Santa Monica, CA 90401
(310) 458-2003
Job hotline: (310) 451-6556
http://www.getty.edu/getty.html
The J. Paul Getty Trust, a private non-profit foundation, manages Malibu's J. Paul Getty Museum, five institutes, and a grant program that supports the visual arts. The Getty Center, open to the public in 1997, will house all of the programs of the Trust, including a second museum. Positions are available in clerical/administrative areas, conservation, research, accounting, technical/computer, security, buildings and grounds, library, education, and public affairs.

Mattel
Corporate Staffing M1-0108
333 Continental Blvd.
El Segundo, CA 90245
(310) 252-2000
If the toy business sounds like fun, you might be interested in opportunities at Mattel. Mattel produces well-known products such as the Barbie doll, Hot Wheels, and See 'n Say Learning Toys. Ranked by *Working Mother* magazine as one of the top 100 companies for working mothers, Mattel provides on-site child care. All resumes are scanned electronically; make sure yours is formatted accordingly (see Chapter 6).

Odetics
1515 S. Manchester Ave.
Anaheim, CA 92802
(714) 774-5000
Job hotline: (714) 774-5000, ext. 6718
Vice President, Human Resources: Linda Krumme
http://www.odetics.com/index.html
Odetics makes products that "automate, store, retrieve, process, and communicate all kinds of information." Named as one of the 100 best companies to work for in America, Odetics works to foster an atmosphere of energy and enjoyment. Opportunities include positions in sales/marketing, commercial design, production, and software engineering.

Patagonia
259 W. Santa Clara St.
Ventura, CA 93001
(805) 643-8616
Job hotline: (805) 667-4614
http://www.patagonia.com
Founded in the late 1960s by a group of surfers and climbers, Patagonia has been making outdoor clothing one mile from the beach ever since. Patagonia employees are serious about the outdoors. They run the company's Guide Line, an outdoor information service. Patagonia is also committed to environmental preservation and restoration efforts. Of all sales, 1% go to such causes. Patagonia is known for the high quality of life it offers employees, including an on-site child-care center. The company has been cited among the 10 best companies to work for in America by *Working Mother* magazine. Recent job listings include opportunities for designers, fabric lab personnel, and sample makers.

TBWA/Chiat Day
340 Main St.
Venice, CA 90291
(310) 314-5000
Human Resources: Tammi Martray
http://www.chiatday.com/web/ (under construction)
http://www.chiatday.com/web/index_orig.html
The philosophy of Chiat Day is best expressed in the words of its founder, Jay Chiat, "You can't force someone to do great work or be innovative; you can create an environment where that is more likely to happen." Chiat Day, the Southern California advertising agency founded in 1968, aims to do just that. Rather than using assigned offices, employees check out computers, phones, meeting rooms, work stations, and other office equipment as needed. One employee describes the atmosphere as "a cross between a think tank and a Turkish bazaar." In 1995, Chiat Day was purchased by TBWA, a large international advertising conglomerate. Both organizations put a positive spin on the merger, heralding the creative potential of the combination of cultures. In addition to their work, Chiat Day employees are committed to community service, supporting such causes as Heal the Bay and the Pediatric Aids Foundation.

You know you're job hunting in Southern California when....
you have to dial up to eight different area codes in your job search. As one of the nation's largest metropolitan areas, Southern California is continually adding new area codes. The greater Los Angeles area alone uses the 213, 310, 818, and 562 prefixes.

Ten Fastest Growing Companies in Southern California

Based on our research and reports from the local media, the fastest growing companies in Southern California are, in alphabetical order:

Aames Financial Corporation
3731 Wilshire Blvd., 10th Floor
Los Angeles, CA 90010
(213) 351-6100
Employment Coordinator: Meredith Hauger
Human Resource Director: Nanette Duff Sullivan
Mortgage lending and brokerage services.

All American Communications
808 Wilshire Blvd.
Santa Monica, CA 90405
(310) 656-1100
http://165.121.1.145/
Produces and distributes television programs and records. The television show *Baywatch* is among their claims to fame.

Davidson & Associates
19840 Pioneer Ave.
Torrance, CA 90503
(310) 793-0600
Job hotline: (310) 793-0599
Human Resources: Melanie Doell
http://www.davd.com
Founded in 1985, over 700 Davidson & Associates employees produce education and entertainment software. Positions exist in technical support, finance, programming, customer service, advertising, quality assurance, and production.

HomeTown Buffet
9171 Town Center Drive, Suite 575
San Diego, CA 92122
(619) 546-9096
Hiring: Cindy Bezella
http://www.buffet.com/
Family restaurant chain with 90+ properties nationwide. Subsidiary of CKE Restaurants, which also operates Carl's Jr., JB's, and Galaxy Diner eateries. Restaurant management opportunities available.

Pairgain Technologies
14402 Franklin Ave.
Tustin, CA 92680
(714) 832-9922
Job hotline: (714) 730-3255
Human Resource Director: Sheryll Straight
http://www.pairgain.com
Designs, manufactures, and markets advanced communication systems.

Established in 1988, Pairgain employs 400. Positions available within the engineering, sales, accounting, operations, and corporate communications areas.

PIMCO
700 Newport Center Drive
Newport Beach, CA 92660
(714) 640-3011
Assistant Vice President: Peggy Schmidt
PIMCO manages mutual funds and offers institutional and individual investment advice. Its parent company is Pacific Mutual, the largest life and health insurance company based in California.

Qualcomm Incorporated
6455 Lusk Blvd.
San Diego, CA 92121
(619) 587-1121
Job hotline: (619) 658-5627
Human Resource Staffing
http://www.qualcomm.com
Qualcomm manufactures wireless communications systems. Established in 1985, the company has over 6,000 employees. According to a *Los Angeles Times* report, payroll is growing by an average of 200 employees per month. Qualcomm hires staff for a variety of positions within the engineering, technical support, management, finance, sales/marketing, manufacturing, and administrative areas.

Quarterdeck Corporation
13160 Mindanao Way, 3rd Floor
Marina del Rey, CA 90292
(310) 309-3700
http://quarterdeck.com
Develops, markets, and supports telecommunications and Internet software.

Tenet Healthcare Corporation
3820 State St.
Santa Barbara, CA 93105
(805) 563-7000
Human Resource Director: Jim Ferrier
Operates 70 U.S. Hospitals, long-term care, rehabilitation, and psychiatric facilities.

Watson Pharmaceuticals
P.O. Box 1900
311 Bonnie Circle
Corona, CA 91718
(909) 270-1400
Vice President: George Leischer
Founded in 1984, Watson Pharmaceuticals manufactures and sells generic medications. According to a *Los Angeles Times* report, sales have grown five-fold since 1991. Watson has 350 employees.

Ten Largest Employers in Southern California

Based upon our research and reports from local media, the largest employers in Southern California are, in alphabetical order:

Disney, The Walt, Company
500 S. Buena Vista St.
Burbank, CA 91521
(818) 560-1000
Job hotline: (818) 558-2222
http://www.disney.com
Employees: 71,000; 17,000 in California
Disney manages theme park, entertainment, consumer product, and sports team operations.

Dole Food Company
5795 Lindero Canyon Road
Westlake Village, CA 91361
(818) 874-4000
Job hotline: (818) 874-4999
http://www.dole5aday.com/dole.html
Employees: 43,000 worldwide; 7,300 in California
Dole has food operations worldwide. Positions available in the following areas: administration, sales, marketing, accounting/finance, operations.

Fluor Corporation
3333 Michelson Drive
Irvine, CA 92730
(714) 975-2000
Job hotline: (714) 975-5253
Employees: 41,600 worldwide; 3,300 in California
Engineering and construction services. Fluor hires engineering, clerical, data processing, finance, telecommunications, and administrative personnel.

Hilton Hotels
9336 Civic Center Drive
Beverly Hills, CA 90210
(310) 278-4321
Job hotline: (310) 205-7692
Hiring: Christine Koslowski
http://www.hilton.com/
Employees: 44,000 worldwide; 7,200 in California
Hilton operates hotel and gaming establishments in the United States and worldwide. Opportunities within the corporate office exist for clerical, sales/marketing, purchasing, and development staff.

Hughes Aircraft Company
Human Resources Center
P.O. Box 80028

Los Angeles, CA 90080
(310) 658-7200
Employees: 77,000 total
Electronics and communications manufacturer. Products include satellite-based telecommunications equipment, air traffic control systems, and automotive electronics.

Litton Industries
21240 Burbank Blvd.
Woodland Hills, CA 91367
(818) 598-5000
Human Resource Director: Nancy Gaymon
Employees: 29,000 worldwide; 6,000 in California
Electronics, engineering, and manufacturing.

Northrop Grumman
1840 Century Park East
Los Angeles, CA 90067
(310) 553-6262
Job hotline: (310) 942-5001
Corporate Staffing Director: Robert Navarro
Employment Manager: Ms. Mickey Leong
http://www.northgrum.com
Employees: 37,300 total; 22,000 in California
Defense contractor. Manufactures military equipment, aircraft parts, and electronic systems.

Pinkerton's
15910 Ventura Blvd. Suite 900
Encino, CA 91436
(818) 380-8800
Human Resource Manager: Joanne McGuff
Employees: 45,000 worldwide; 7,200 in California
Consulting, investigative, and security services.

Rockwell International
2201 Seal Beach Blvd.
Seal Beach, CA 90740
(310) 797-3311
Job hotline: (310) 797-5627
http://www.rockwell.com
Employees: 82,000 total; 20,000 in California
After the decline in aerospace contracts, Rockwell reinvented itself and now makes most of its profits manufacturing modems, semiconductors, and automotive components.

Tenet Healthcare
3820 State St.
Santa Barbara, CA 93105

(805) 563-7000
Human Resource Director: Jim Ferrier
Operates hospitals, long-term care, rehabilitation, and psychiatric facilities.

You know you're job hunting in Southern California when....
while you're searching for the perfect job, you have the opportunity to generate income as a game show contestant. Many nationally syndicated shows are taped during the day in the Los Angeles area. Auditions are typically required to secure a spot. Check the *Los Angeles Times* classifieds under "Entertainment-TV Contestants" for listings.

Using Chambers of Commerce

Most chambers of commerce publish material that is helpful to newcomers or anyone who wants to be better informed about a community, and Southern California chambers of commerce are no exception. They have free or nominally priced brochures and maps that provide much of what you'll want to know about area businesses, city services, transportation, public schools, utilities, and entertainment. Additionally, many chambers publish lists of professional organizations and other networking options within the region as well as directories and publications pertaining to Southern California.

Chambers of commerce focusing on minorities are listed at the end of Chapter 2.

Anaheim Chamber of Commerce
100 S. Anaheim Blvd., Suite 300
Anaheim, CA 92805
(714) 758-0222

Greater San Diego Chamber of Commerce
402 W. Broadway, Suite 1000
San Diego, CA 92101-3585
(619) 232-0124
Publishes welcome package that includes information on housing, education, cost of living.

Irvine Chamber of Commerce
17200 Jamboree Road, Suite A
Irvine, CA 92714
(714) 660-9112

Long Beach Area Chamber of Commerce
1 World Trade Center, Suite 350
Long Beach, CA 90831
(310) 436-1251

Los Angeles Area Chamber of Commerce
350 S. Bixel St.
Los Angeles, CA 90051
(213) 580-7500
Serves Los Angeles, Orange, Riverside, San Bernardino, and Ventura counties.

Pasadena Chamber of Commerce and Civic Association
117 E. Colorado Blvd., Suite 100
Pasadena, CA 91105
(818) 449-5419

Choosing a Career

Choosing a career or making a decision about which direction you wish to take in the world of jobs is certainly important, but it also can be one of the most difficult processes we go through in life. Ever since we learned to speak as two-year-olds, aunts, uncles, and other assorted adults have asked us, "What do you want to be when you grow up?" Now we ask ourselves that same question. So how do we choose that career, anyhow?

The first step in choosing a career is to learn who you are and what you want. In other words, start with self-assessment. We've outlined a few tools for you to use in assessing yourself and your abilities. It is important to remember that it is very difficult to get a job if you do not know what you want to do. Self-assessment will enable you to start with a goal in mind. After you figure out who you are, it is much easier to find a compatible career.

A Few Facts about Career Decision Making

According to a recent Gallop poll, most people don't have goals when starting to think about the job search. No real planning goes into what is arguably the most important decision of their lives. The poll shows that:
- 59% of us work in an area or career in which we never planned to work.
- 29% of us are influenced by another person to go into a career. It's like the advice given to Dustin Hoffman in *The Graduate*. Someone says, "Plastics—that's where you should be. Try working in plastics." So we consider plastics.
- 18% of us fall into jobs by chance. You're looking for a job in banking and someone mentions that they know of a job in consulting. Sure you're willing to look at it. Next thing you know, you're a consultant.
- 12% of us took the job because it was available. You're walking by the local GAP store and see a "management trainee" sign. You take it!

This same Gallop poll indicated that we fail to properly assess ourselves and our career options. If we had to do it over, the poll indicates, 65% of the American public would get additional information on career options early on. Other polls show that up to 80% of the working public is dissatisfied with one or more aspects of their career and have seriously considered changing.

All of these facts and figures certainly bode poorly for those who jump into a career haphazardly. And, conversely, the statistics bode well for those who delve into a little career exploration before taking the plunge. This is especially true in light of the fact that the average American emigrates through seven to ten jobs and three to four careers in a lifetime. Thus, we will probably need to assess ourselves more than once as our own life changes with the changing job market. Self-assessment is a tool we will use throughout our professional lives.

Strategies in Self-Exploration

Practically everyone wants a job that provides personal satisfaction, growth, good salary and benefits, a certain level of prestige, and a desirable location. But unless you have a more specific idea of the kind of work you want, you probably won't find it. You wouldn't take off on your big annual vacation without some kind of destination in mind. Given that your job will take up much more of your time than your vacation, a little planning is certainly in order.

There are several strategies that can help you learn who you are. Among them are talking with friends and family, self-assessing, and getting help from a career professional.

Friends and family sometimes know you better than you think. They can also provide great support throughout the job search. Try the self-assessment exercises in this chapter, then discuss your results with those who know you best. They may have some insight that you overlooked. However, it is important to follow your own desires and not the dreams of family and friends when choosing a career.

Everyone can benefit from a thorough self-appraisal. The insight gained from self-appraisal is valuable not only in deciding on a career but also in articulating this knowledge in the resume and interviewing process. Perhaps you want to be a little more scientific in your appraisal of yourself. Try career testing. Professionals in vocational planning have literally dozens of tests at their disposal designed to assess personality and aptitude for particular careers.

Getting Started with Self-Assessment

What follows is a list of highly personal questions designed to provide you with insights you may never have considered and to help you answer the Big Question, "What do I want to do?"

To get the most from this exercise, write out your answers. This will take some time, but it will force you to give each question careful thought. The more effort you put into this exercise, the better prepared you'll be for the tough questions you'll be asked in any job interview. The exercise also can be the basis for constructing a winning resume—a subject we'll discuss in more detail in Chapter 6.

QUESTIONS ABOUT ME

Here are some questions to get you started. The answers will indicate what kind of person you are. Be honest. Take as much time as necessary.
1. Describe yourself in less than 500 words. Address these questions: Do you prefer to spend time alone or with other people? How well disciplined are you? Are you quick-tempered? Easygoing? Do you prefer to give orders or take orders? Do you tend to take a conventional, practical approach to problems? Or are you imaginative and experimental? How sensitive are you to others?
2. What accomplishment are you most proud of?
3. What are the most important things you wish to accomplish?
4. What role does your job play in those achievements?
5. Why do you (or don't you) want your career to be the most important thing in your life?
6. What impact do you have on other people?
7. Describe the kind of person others think you are.
8. What role does money play in your standard of values?
9. What do you enjoy most/dislike most?
10. What do you want your life to be like in 5 years?
11. What are your main interests?

What Job Attributes Do You Value Most?

After answering the above questions, it is important to match the job attributes you value to your career. Job burnout usually happens when people are in jobs that don't allow them to do and get the activities and rewards they want. But job satisfaction will occur if a person follows his or her motivations into a career. The following ranking will assist you in beginning to match the job attributes you value with careers that are in step with them.

Rank the following in order of importance to you:
- Leadership
- Creativity
- High Salary
- Helping Others
- Variety
- Physical Activity
- Self-development
- Recognition

- Job Security
- Competition
- Taking Risk
- Working with My Mind
- Prestige
- Independence

Once you've ranked the above, you should begin to get an idea of what's important to you. Compare your priorities to those of the workplace in your potential career/job. Values of the workplace can be determined in several ways. One method is to interview current employees of the company. Another is to research the company through articles and publications to determine its values and beliefs.

QUESTIONS ABOUT MY JOB

Questions about your job can also help in your self-assessment.
1. Describe *in detail* each job you have had. Begin with your most recent employment and work back toward graduation. Include your title, company name, responsibilities, salary, achievements and successes, failures, and reason for leaving. If you're a recent college graduate and have little or no career-related work experience, you may find it helpful to consider your collegiate experience, both curricular and extracurricular, as your work history for questions 1, 2, 3, 7, 8, 9, and 10.
2. What would you change in your past, if you could?
3. In your career thus far, what responsibilities have you enjoyed most? Least? Why?
4. How hard are you prepared to work?
5. What jobs would allow you to use your talents and interests?
6. What have your subordinates thought about you as a boss? As a person?
7. What have your superiors thought about you as an employee? As a person?
8. If you have been fired from any job, what was the reason?
9. Does your work make you happy? Should it?
10. What do you want to achieve by the time you retire?

Answering these questions will help clarify who you are, what you want, and what you realistically have to offer. They should also reveal what you don't want and what you can't do. It's important to evaluate any objective you're considering in light of your answers to these questions. If a prospective employer knew nothing about you except your answers to these questions, would he think your career objectives were realistic?

One way to match who you are with a specific career is to refer to the *Dictionary of Occupational Titles (DOT)*. The *DOT* is an encyclopedia of careers, covering hundreds of occupations and industries. For the computer buff, *The Perfect Career* by James Gonyea (3444 Dundee Rd., Northbrook, IL 60062) has a database of over 600 occupations for IBM and compatibles.

Professional Testing

As mentioned earlier, professionals in career counseling (see list below) have literally dozens of tests at their disposal designed to assess personality and aptitude for particular careers. Here are a few of the most commonly used career tests.

Strong Interest Inventory
This test looks at a person's interests to see if they parallel the interests of people already employed in specific occupations. It is used chiefly as an aid in making academic choices and career decisions. It continues to be one of the most researched and highly respected counseling tools in use.

Myers-Briggs Type Indicator
This test is based on Carl Jung's theory of perception and judgment and is a widely used measure of personality dispositions and preferences. Used in career counseling, it helps to identify compatible work settings, relate career opportunities and demands to preferences in perception and judgment, and gain insight into personality dimensions, all of which provide the opportunity for greater decision-making ability.

16 PF (Personality Factor) Questionnaire
This test measures 32 personality traits of a normal adult personality along 16 dimensions. Used frequently in counseling, the computerized printout and narrative report show how personality traits may fit into various career fields.

Career Counseling

Although the terms are often used synonymously, there is a difference between a career counselor and consultant. Most professionals use the title "counselor" if they have an advanced degree in psychology, counseling, social work, or marriage, family, and child counseling and are licensed by the state.

Need a list of certified counselors?
The National Board for Certified Counselors provides a list of professional "certified career counselors" in local areas. Certification requires a master's degree and three years of supervised counseling experience. For further information call (800) 398-5389.

Professionals who are not licensed often call themselves "career consultants." This field attracts people from a variety of backgrounds, education, and levels of competency. It's important, then, to talk to others who have used a given service before committing yourself.

Because most career counseling and consulting firms are private, for-profit businesses with high overhead costs, they usually charge more for testing than local colleges or social service agencies, which are listed later in this chapter.

What can you expect from a career counselor? For one thing, counselors offer an objective viewpoint. One licensed professional career counselor puts it this way: "You may not be able to discuss everything with family, friends, and especially coworkers if you happen still to be working. A trained professional can serve as a sounding board and offer strategies and information that you can't get elsewhere. We can essentially help a person become more resourceful."

This particular career counselor usually spends four sessions with individuals who want to establish a sense of direction for their careers. Here's what sessions cover:

- Exploring problems that have blocked progress and considering solutions.
- Establishing career objectives and determining strengths and areas to work on.
- Writing a career plan that outlines a strategy to achieve goals.
- Preparing an ongoing, self-directed plan to explore career goals.

"A counselor should help people develop methods and a framework on which to base continual exploration about what they want from a career, even after they are employed," our counselor friend says.

All too often people look for "quick fixes" in order to get back to work, she says. "In haste, they may not take time to reflect on where their career is going, to make sure they look for a job that will be challenging and satisfying."

What follows are a few counselors and consultants who may be able to help you in your job search. Keep in mind, though, that a listing in this book does not constitute an endorsement of any consulting firm or testing service. Before embarking on a lengthy or expensive series of tests, try to get the opinion of one or more persons who have already used the service you're considering. Many of the counselors listed below are certified by the National Board for Certified Counselors. For a free referral to a career counselor, contact the California Registry of Professional Counselors at 2555 E. Chapman Avenue Suite 201, Fullerton, CA 92631, (714) 871-6460.

CAREER COUNSELORS AND CONSULTANTS IN SOUTHERN CALIFORNIA

Baron, Judith Kaplan
6046 Cornerstone Court West, Suite 208
San Diego, CA 92121

(619) 558-7400
Board-certified career counselor, Assistant Director, America On-Line Career Center.

Career Ambitions Unlimited
25411 Cabot Road, Suite 105
Laguna Hills, CA 92653
(714) 770-2675

Career Development Services
7434 Herschel Ave., #5
La Jolla, CA 92037
(619) 456-0775
Vocational testing, career counseling.

Career Planning Center
1623 S. La Cienega Blvd.
Los Angeles, CA 90035
(310) 273-6633
Non-profit organization featuring job resource center, counseling, skill assessment, computer training.

Cooper, Gwendalle
9392 Grossmont Blvd.
La Mesa, CA 91941
(619) 463-9664
Board-certified career counselor.

Elliott, Myrna
Pathfinder Associates
1420 N. Claremont Blvd., #106A
Claremont, CA 91711
(909) 624-9372
Board-certified career counselor.

Forty Plus Orange County Office
23172 Plaza Pointe Drive, Suite 285
Laguna Hills, CA 92653
(714) 581-7990
Non-profit, self-help employment service for experienced professionals in career transition.

Forty Plus San Diego Office
8845 University Center Lane
San Diego, CA 92122
(619) 450-4440

Forty Plus of Southern California
3450 Wilshire Blvd., Suite 510
Los Angeles, CA 90010
(213) 388-2301
http://web.sirius.com/"40plus/

Roth, Sheldon
16944 Ventura Blvd., #26
Encino, CA 91316
(818) 501-2243
Board-certified career counselor.

SinClair, Bonnie
7801 Mission Center Court, Suite 200
San Diego, CA 92108
(619) 296-7065
Board-certified career counselor.

Sinsheimer, Joan
301 W. Huntington Drive, Suite 209
Arcadia, CA 91007
(818) 445-4160
Board-certified career counselor.

Sommerstein & Associates Career Consultants
24520 Hawthorne Blvd., Suite 110
Torrance, CA 90505
(310) 373-4249
Offices also in Brentwood.

Women at Work
50 N. Hill Ave., Suite 300
Pasadena, CA 91106
(818) 796-6870
Non-profit organization offering support groups, job listings, resource library, workshops and counseling to men and women.

Women's Focus
210 W. Main St., Suite 204
Tustin, CA 92680
(714) 731-8992
Serves men and women, providing career counseling, corporate outplacement, and career marketing assistance.

CYBERTIPS FOR CAREER TESTING AND COUNSELING

Try this site to determine your Myers-Briggs (MBTI) type and to get more information on your MBTI personality type:

http://sunsite.unc.edu/jembin/mb.pl

For more information on personality types try:

http://www.yahoo.com/Science/Psychology/Personality/

Career Action Center, http://WWW.GATENET.COM/cac/ offers extensive services in interest and skills testing, test interpretation, and career counseling. **America On-Line** and **eWorld** both provide career information and on-line career counseling services.

Career Assistance at Colleges and Universities

Students often don't realize how much help is available through college and university career and placement centers. Career and placement centers provide assistance in choosing a program of study as well as career testing to current students. After graduation, many colleges and universities continue to work with alumni through their career centers. Check with your school and others to find out what's available and who is eligible for assistance.

While most colleges and universities don't permit the general public to use their counseling and placement services, some will offer programs to the public for a fee. The extent of assistance varies from campus to campus.

Some colleges and universities offer non-credit and credit courses as well as special lectures and seminars to help individuals prepare for the job hunt and explore options in the work world. In recent years, schools also have offered more practical courses that are designed to help individuals acquire job skills or brush up on ones they already have.

Try on a career with an internship

Internships are more popular today than ever before—with both new grads and seasoned workers interested in changing careers. It's a form of on-the-job training that lets both you and your employer determine your potential in a specific work environment.

If you're about to graduate, check the career services office at your college, where lists of available internships usually abound. If you're already in the workforce, get in touch with the same office at the college you attended or try the career offices in nearby colleges. When applying, be sure to stress what you can offer an organization and express your enthusiasm for the field.

For more information, look into these resources:

America's Top 100 Internships, Mark Oldman and Samer Hamadeh (Princeton Review).

Internships 1997 (Peterson's Guides, Princeton, NJ).

Internships Leading to Careers (The Graduate Group, West Hartford, CT).

Job Finder series, Daniel Lauber (Planning/Communications Publishers, River Forest, IL).

National Association for Interpretation (Ft. Collins, CO), call (303) 491-6784 for free Dial-an-Intern service.

National Directory of Internships (National Society for Experiential Education, Raleigh, NC).

SOUTHERN CALIFORNIA COLLEGES OFFERING CAREER GUIDANCE

The International Association of Counseling Centers accredits college and university counseling centers and provides regional referrals. Contact them at 101 S. Whiting St., Suite 211, Alexandria, VA 22304, (703) 823-9840 for further information. Also, keep in mind that there is a cooperative career planning arrangement among the University of California branches. If you are a UC graduate, call the closest career planning office for more information on services. Please note that some of the following universities only offer services to their own students and alumni.

California State University, Fullerton
Career Development and Counseling
Fullerton, CA 92634
(714) 773-3121
Offers counseling, recruiting opportunities, and job fairs. Alumni are charged a nominal fee for services.

California State University, Los Angeles
Career Planning and Placement
Los Angeles, CA 90032
(213) 343-3280
Offers on-campus recruiting and specialized job fairs for students including an Education and a Law Enforcement Expo. Alumni are charged an annual fee for services.

California State University, Northridge
Career Center
Northridge, CA 91330
(818) 885-2381
Offers counseling, recruiting, and job fairs throughout the year to students. Alumni must register and pay an annual fee.

San Diego State University
Career Services
San Diego, CA 92182
(619) 594-6851
Offers Business, Engineering & Sciences, Summer Jobs, Health, Nursing, Social Services, Law Enforcement, Education, and Multicultural job fairs for students.

University of California, Irvine
Career Planning and Placement
Irvine, CA 92717
(714) 856-4642
Offers counseling, recruiting, and job fairs for students including a Technical Career Fair. Alumni may register to be on the waiting list for on-campus interviewing.

University of California, Los Angeles (UCLA)
Career Center
Los Angeles, CA 90095
(310) 206-1915
Offers recruiting, career connections, career days for students. Alumni may use services for 3 months after graduation at no cost.

University of California, Los Angeles Extension
10995 LeConte Ave.
Los Angeles, CA 90024
(310) 825-2934
Offers counseling and career library to community members.

University of California, San Diego
Career Services Center
La Jolla, CA 92093
(619) 534-3750
Offers individual assistance, job fairs to students, including a Multicultural Job Fair in January.

University of California San Diego Extension
9500 Gilman Drive
La Jolla, CA 92093
(619) 534-8296
Provides testing, career counseling, Internet access, computerized career library. Fee required.

Women's Opportunities Center
University of California, Irvine
Irvine, CA
(714) 824-7128
Open to community members, both women and men. Offers career counseling/testing, workshops, support groups, job listings. Fee required.

Social Service Agencies Offering Career Assistance

Unlike independent career counselors and consultants, social service agencies are not-for-profit. They offer a wide range of services, from counseling and vocational training to job placement and follow-up—and their services are either low cost or free. Keep in mind, though, that a listing in this book does not constitute an endorsement of any agency.

LOS ANGELES AGENCIES

Chicana Service Action Center
134 E. 1st St.
Los Angeles, CA 90012
(213) 253-5959
Provides job training and vocational rehabilitation services.

Goodwill Industries of Southern California
342 San Fernando Road
Los Angeles, CA 90031
(213) 223-1211
Employment, training, and job placement for disabled adults.

Jewish Vocational Service
6505 Wilshire Blvd., Suite 303
Los Angeles, CA 90048
(213) 655-8910
Main location. Three other Los Angeles locations. Offers nonsectarian workshops, job support groups, job listings, career testing and counseling. Sliding fee scale.

Los Angeles Gay & Lesbian Community Services Center
1625 N. Schrader Blvd.
Los Angeles, CA 90028
(213) 993-7480
Offers job postings, employment services.

Santa Monica YWCA
Aware Advisory
2019 14th St.
Santa Monica, CA 90405
(310) 452-3833
Provides vocational testing and counseling.

Southern California Indian Center
3600 Wilshire Blvd., Suite 226
Los Angeles, CA 90057
(213) 387-5772
Placement services, job-search training.

Urban League of Los Angeles
3450 Mt. Vernon
Los Angeles, CA 90080
(213) 299-9660
Provides employment services, sponsors annual job fair. Call to register for an orientation session.

Women Helping Women
543 N. Fairfax Ave.
Los Angeles, CA 90036
(213) 655-3807
Job clubs and career workshops for women.

ORANGE COUNTY AGENCIES

Catholic Charities
Employment Services
2301 W. Lincoln Ave., Suite 112

Anaheim, CA 92801
(714) 635-5230
Free employment services.

Goodwill Industries/Orange County
410 N. Fairview Road
Santa Ana, CA 92701
(714) 547-6308 x324
Provides job training and placement to disabled adults.

Orange County Urban League
12391 Lewis St., Suite 102
Garden Grove, CA 92640
(714) 748-9976
Offers employment assistance, sponsors job fairs focused on minority hiring.

Orange Resource Center
City of Orange
210 N. McPherson St.
Orange, CA 92665
(714) 633-2753
Offers free job-placement services.

SAN DIEGO AGENCIES

Deaf Community Services of San Diego
3788 Park Blvd.
San Diego, CA 92103
(619) 497-2811
Interpreting, job-placement services.

Occupational Training Services
8799 Balboa Ave., Suite 100
San Diego, CA 92123
(619) 560-0411

San Diego Career Center Network
8401 Aero Drive
San Diego, CA 92123
(619) 974-7620
Provides career assessment, job-skills training, job-search assistance.

San Diego Consortium & Private Industry Council
1551 4th Ave., Suite 600
San Diego, CA 92101
(619) 238-1445

San Diego Job Corps
1325 Iris Ave.
Imperial Beach, CA 91932
(619) 429-8500

San Diego Regional Occupational Program
6401 Linda Vista Road
San Diego, CA 92111
(619) 292-3758
Job training and free public education.

Career Change: Reality Bites

One morning you wake up, put on your $200 sunglasses, and head to work in your new Lexus. When you get to the office the doors are locked. To your surprise a sign on the door says "Filed for Bankruptcy." At this point you are probably saying, "I must be dreaming." Well, in today's work world, downsizing, mergers, and cost-cutting are all real—and sometimes reality bites!

Dramatic setbacks can often be your best opportunity for considering a career change. However, most people changing careers tend to believe they lack the skills for another career field. Maybe and maybe not. Self-assessment, defining your aptitudes and values, and possibly vocational testing can assist you in deciding on a career change.

There are three main reasons why people change careers:

1. A desire for a better fit among occupation, interests, and values is the primary reason that managers and professionals change careers. People want more career satisfaction and are usually willing to change careers to get it. Those who were coerced into that first career either by parents, misguided ambition, or lack of career information are highly likely to be dissatisfied. In time, they seek change.
2. Job loss. People that are laid off or fired make up a significant portion of those deciding to change careers rather than just replace the job that was lost. Appropriately, it is these people who may experience depression in their search because they feel they have been forced into the change.
3. A smaller group of career changers comprise those who at mid-career decide to turn a passion or hobby into an occupation.

The ability to transfer your skills is crucial in a career change. Many people feel their experience is only relevant to the previous job. In reality, most skills may be applied to a wide variety of jobs. Below are a number of commonly transferable skills. How many do you have?

administering	distributing
analyzing	editing
assisting	gathering
calculating	instructing
creating	monitoring

motivating
operating
organizing
persuading
planning
problem-solving

recommending
researching
speaking
supervising
trouble-shooting
writing

From customer service to fund-raising

After working for a year in customer service for a large retail chain, Sharon decided to make a career change when the company was faced with financial difficulties and had to downsize. Having been a music major in college, Sharon was not sure if she had acquired enough useful job skills to transfer into a new career. She became interested in a fund-raising job at a local university when one of her business contacts mentioned an opening in the development office.

"I volunteered for the annual telefund-raising campaign at the university to find out if I could handle development activities. I discovered that I really enjoyed the work. Best of all, many of my skills from my previous job, especially in communication, writing, and computer literacy, were well suited for it. I interviewed for the job and got it, with the additional help of a recommendation from my business contact."

Starting Your Own Business

Perhaps your self-assessment results lead you away from employment altogether and toward starting your own business. If so, a wealth of information is provided through the **U.S. Small Business Administration**, which provides free information on a variety of topics, including loan programs, tax preparation, government contracts, and management techniques. Although simple questions can be answered by telephone, you'll learn more by visiting one of their offices to meet with staff members or volunteers from **SCORE** (Service Corps of Retired Executives). SCORE is a federally funded organization of retired executives who volunteer their time and expertise to assist small business owners. Their Southern California offices are located at:

330 N. Brand Blvd., Suite 190
Glendale, CA 91203
(818) 552-7272

485 N. Garey Ave.
Pomona, CA 91769
(909) 622-1256

200 W. Santa Ana Blvd., #700
Santa Ana, CA 92701
(714) 550-7420

550 W. C St.
San Diego, CA 92101
(619) 557-7252

SMALL BUSINESS WEB SITES

U.S. Small Business Association
http://www.sbaonline.sba.gov

Southern California New Business Association
http://www.catalog.com/rmg/scnba.htm
Non-profit organization founded to help new business people promote, network, and develop business strategies.

CALIFORNIA SMALL BUSINESS DEVELOPMENT CENTERS

The following small business development centers provide free one-on-one consulting, business training, and licensing assistance in Southern California.

Accelerate Technology
Small Business Development Center
Irvine
(714) 509-2990

Eastern Los Angeles County
Small Business Development Center
Pomona
(909) 629-2247

El Monte
Outreach Center
El Monte
(818) 459-4111

Export Small Business Development
Center of Southern California
Los Angeles
(213) 892-1111

Inland Empire
Small Business Development Center
Riverside
(909) 781-2345

Northern Los Angeles
Small Business Development Center
Van Nuys
(818) 373-7092

Orange County
Small Business Development Center
Santa Ana
(714) 647-1172

San Diego Chamber of Commerce
Small Business Development Center
La Jolla
(619) 453-9388

Southwestern College
Small Business Development &
International Trade Center
Chula Vista
(619) 482-6391

Southwest Los Angeles County
Small Business Development Center
Torrance
(310) 787-6466

OTHER SMALL BUSINESS RESOURCES

Business Innovation Center
3350 Market St.
San Diego, CA 92102
(619) 685-2949

California Business Incubation Network
Non-profit association assists small businesses with affordable space, marketing, support services. Membership fee charged.
350 S. Grand Ave.
Los Angeles, CA 90071
(619) 237-0559

Business Resources for Women and Minorities

The following resources for women and minorities may also be of help. Refer to the networking organizations listed in Chapter 5 for additional support groups and information.

The most comprehensive listing of women's organizations in Southern California is published by the Los Angeles City Commission on the Status of Women, City Hall East, Room 550, 200 N. Main Street, Los Angeles, CA 90012. The 150-page directory lists local women's organizations across a wide variety of categories including education, child care, counseling, employment, health, and many more. The Commission can be reached at (213) 485-6533.

The following selection of organizations provide assistance specific to women-owned and minority-owned enterprises.

Asian American Economic Development Enterprises
216 West Garvey Ave., Unit E
Monterey Park, CA 91754
(818) 572-7021
Coordinates Asian Career Transition job conferences.

Black Business Association
3550 W. Wilshire Blvd., Suite 816
Los Angeles, CA 90062
(213) 299-9560

Black Business Chamber of Commerce, Orange County
1202 Civic Center Drive West, Suite 205
Santa Ana, CA 92703
(714) 547-2646

Chinese-American Chamber of Commerce, Orange County
8907 Wamer Ave.,#225
Huntington Beach, CA 92647
(714) 848-0043

Hispanic Business Association
P.O. Box 2367
Anaheim, CA 92804
(714) 535-5899

Hispanic Chamber of Commerce of Orange County
116-A West 4th St., #5
Santa Ana, CA 92701
(714) 953-4289

Los Angeles Urban League
5414 Crenshaw Blvd.
Los Angeles, CA 90043
(213) 292-8111

National Association of Women Business Owners
1804 W. Burbank Blvd.
Burbank, CA 91506
(818) 843-7348

Vietnamese Chamber of Commerce
9938 Bolsa Ave., Suite 216
Westminster, CA 92683
(714) 839-2257

Women in Business
7060 Hollywood Blvd., Suite 614
Los Angeles, CA 90048
(213) 461-2936

WOMEN'S WEB SITES

http://www.sbaonline.sba.gov/womeninbusiness/
is the SBA's homepage for women in business. Links are provided to the National Women's Business Council and other related sites.

http://www.intac.com/~kgs/bbpw/meta.html
lists sites related to businesswomen's issues and organizations, employment, and more.

http://www.igc.apc.org/womensnet/
links you to services and resources for women.

Great Books to Help You Figure Out Your Life

People who are entering the job market for the first time, those who have been working for one company for many years, and those who are considering a career change can usually use a little more help than we have supplied here, and certainly the more help the better. To get that little extra boost, we can refer you to some excellent books. If you have access to college resources, be sure to take advantage of the career libraries as well as the counseling and career planning services that are available on most campuses.

CAREER STRATEGY BOOKS

Baldwin, Eleanor. *300 Ways to Get a Better Job.* Holbrook, MA: Adams Publishing, 1991.

Beatty, Richard H. *Get the Right Job in 60 Days or Less.* New York: John Wiley & Sons, 1991.

Bolles, Richard N. *The Three Boxes of Life and How to Get Out of Them.* Berkeley, CA: Ten Speed Press, 1981.

Bolles, Richard N. *What Color Is Your Parachute?* Berkeley, CA: Ten Speed Press. The bible for job hunters and career changers, this book is revised every year and is widely regarded as one of the most useful and creative manuals on the market.

Clawson, James G., et al. *Self Assessment and Career Development.* Englewood Cliffs, NJ: Prentice-Hall, 1991. A very thorough guide with self-assessment worksheets and a good bibliography.

Dubin, Judith A., and Melonie R. Keveles. *Fired for Success.* New York: Warner Books, 1990.

Harkavy, Michael. *One Hundred One Careers: A Guide to the Fastest Growing Opportunities.* New York: John Wiley & Sons, 1990.

Jackson, Tom. *Guerrilla Tactics in the Job Market.* New York: Bantam Books, 1991. Filled with unconventional but effective suggestions.

Krannich, Ronald L. *Change Your Job, Change Your Life: High Impact Strategies for Finding Great Jobs in the 90's.* Manassas, VA: Impact Publications, 1994.

Levinson, Harry. *Designing and Managing Your Career.* Boston: Harvard University Press, 1989.

Morin, William J., and Colvena, James C. *Parting Company: How to Survive the Loss of a Job and Find Another Successfully.* San Diego, CA: HBJ, 1991.

Munschauer, John L. *Jobs for English Majors and Other Smart People.* Princeton, NJ: Peterson's Guides, 1991.

Petras, Kathryn and Ross. *The Only Job Hunting Guide You'll Ever Need.* New York: Fireside, 1995.

Roper, David H. *Getting The Job You Want . . Now!* New York: Warner Books, 1994.

Washington, Tom. *Complete Book to Effective Job Finding.* Bellevue, WA: Mount Vernon Press, 1992.

Weinstein, Bob. *Resumes Don't Get Jobs: The Realities and Myths of Job Hunting.* New York: McGraw-Hill Inc., 1993.

Yate, Martin. *Knock 'Em Dead.* Holbrook, MA: Adams Publishing, 1995.

If you're **still in college or have recently graduated,** the following books will be of particular interest:

Briggs, James I. *The Berkeley Guide to Employment for New College Graduates.* Berkeley, CA: Ten Speed Press, 1984.

Holton, Ed. *The M.B.A.'s Guide to Career Planning.* Princeton, NJ: Peterson's Guides, 1989.

La Fevre, John L. *How You Really Get Hired: The Inside Story from a College Recruiter.* New York: Prentice-Hall, 1993.

Richardson, Bradley G. *Jobsmarts for Twentysomethings.* New York: Vintage Books, 1995.

Steele, John, and Marilyn Morgan. *Career Planning & Development for College Students and Recent Graduates.* Lincolnwood, IL: National Textbook Co., 1991.

Tener, Elizabeth. *Smith College Guide: How to Find and Manage Your First Job.* New York: Pflume, 1991.

For those involved in a **mid-life career change,** here are some books that might prove helpful:

Anderson, Nancy. *Work With Passion: How to Do What You Love for a Living.* Rafael, CA: New World Library, 1995.

Birsner, E. Patricia. *The Forty-Plus Job Hunting Guide: Official Handbook of the 40-Plus Club.* New York: Facts on File, 1990.

Byron, William J. *Finding Work Without Losing Heart: Bouncing Back from Mid-Career Job Loss.* Holbrook, MA: Adams Publishing, 1995.

Holloway, Diane, and Nancy Bishop. *Before You Say "I Quit": A Guide to Making Successful Job Transitions.* New York: Collier Books, 1990.

Logue, Charles H. *Outplace Yourself: Secrets of an Executive Outplacement Counselor.* Holbrook, MA: Adams Publishing, 1995.

Stevens, Paul. *Beating Job Burnout: How to Turn Your Work into Your Passion.* Lincolnwood, IL: VGM Career Horizons, 1995.

For workers who are **nearing retirement age** or have already reached it, here are some books that might be useful:

Kerr, Judy. *The Senior Citizen's Guide to Starting a Part-Time, Home-Based Business.* New York: Pilot Industries, 1992.

Morgan, John S. *Getting a Job After Fifty.* Blue Ridge Summit, PA: TAB Books, 1990.

Ray, Samuel. *Job Hunting After 50: Strategies for Success.* New York: John Wiley & Sons, 1991.

Strasser, Stephen, and John Sena. *Transitions: Successful Strategies from Mid-Career to Retirement.* Hawthorne, NJ: Career Press, 1990.

And for people with **disabilities,** these titles could prove helpful:

Rabbi, Rami, and Diane Croft. *Take Charge: A Strategic Guide for Blind Job Seekers.* Boston: National Braille Press, 1990.
Pocket Guide to Federal Help for Individuals with Disabilities. Clearinghouse on the Handicapped, Washington, DC: U.S. Department of Education, 1989. Discusses the many types of federal help for disabled job seekers. Useful and concise, only $1.

For **women and minority groups** in the workforce, these titles will be of interest:

Berryman, Sue E. *Routes Into the Mainstream: Career Choices of Women & Minorities.* Columbus, OH: Continuing Educational Training Employment, 1988.
Betz, Nancy E., and Louise Fitzgerald. *The Career Psychology of Women.* Orlando: Academic Press, 1987.
Lunnenborg, Patricia. *Women Changing Work.* New York: Bergin & Garvey Publishers, 1990.
Nivens, Beatrice. *The Black Woman's Career Guide.* New York: Anchor Books, 1987.
Thompson, Charlotte E. *Single Solutions—An Essential Guide for the Single Career Woman.* Brookline Village, MA: Branden Publishing, 1990.

three

If I Can't Find a Job, Should I Go Back to School?

"I'm having a real hard time finding a job. Maybe I'll just go back to school." The rationale seems logical: more schooling equals better job. The facts, however, don't always show the "more schooling" route to be the best one, as we will discuss below. Sometimes, however, getting another degree or a bit more education can make the difference between a job and a great career.

When To Go Back to School

Admittedly, additional education can enhance your marketability. But as you weigh the pros and cons of committing time and money to the classroom, you should never consider additional education a panacea for all of your career woes.

A myth people want to believe is that an advanced degree, a different degree, or even a bit more education will automatically translate into a better job. People considering law school or an MBA frequently fall prey to this myth. The reality is that the job market is very tight, especially for lawyers, and employers are reluctant to hire people who may have entered a particular field on a whim and don't have any real long-term commitment to the profession. It is less risky for employers to hire someone with a proven track record than someone with a new advanced degree. Those pursuing graduate work in the liberal arts, not wishing to teach, are also in for a big surprise when they realize that they often end up in the same predicament they were in upon graduating with a B.A.: undecided upon a career and having very few options.

Despite the negatives, though, there are several good reasons for returning to school for additional education. These include:

To Acquire Additional Skills.
If you find that your skills are not keeping pace with the demands of your career, you may consider returning to school. Learning accounting, computer systems, or a foreign language, for example, may be the boost your career needs.

To Prepare for a Career Change.
Frequently, job changers will realize that they want to leave their current field altogether. If after talking with a career counselor, assessing your goals, and weighing your options, you decide that a career change is the right choice, additional education—a different degree—may be a requirement.

To Advance in Your Career.
For certain fields, such as investment banking, an MBA is necessary to advance. In other fields, the standards for additional education may be more subtle. Another degree or merely additional coursework toward a degree may translate into a salary increase or consideration for a promotion.

Some people may be intimidated at the thought of acquiring additional education because they associate it with spent time and money. In reality, professional education can take many forms and carry a wide range of price tags. Other options to graduate school with varying cost-benefit trade-offs include community college courses, evening classes at a university, professional training for certification, or even executive education programs offered by many business schools. The bottom line is that when you consider additional education, do not limit your thinking only to formal degree programs at a university.

Tips on Considering Additional Schooling

There are many issues to consider before returning to school. First, determine how an additional degree or professional training will fit into your long-term goals. As you prepare to invest money, time, and energy on education, it is essential to know how you will benefit one year, five years, or even ten years later. Additionally, in order to select your best educational alternative, you must be able to articulate what benefit it will offer your career.

Second, many graduate schools require work experience before you can apply. For example, top business schools require two years of work experience. Thus, it is important to be familiar with the requirements of your proposed field of study.

Third, ask yourself whether you've really done your homework when weighing alternatives. Your watchword should be research. If you are changing career fields, avoid any post-degree surprises by researching the market, employment trends, and major employers. When evaluating professional training programs, be sure you have researched the schools to know who is offering accredited and respected courses. Make your decisions based on facts and figures and not on the suggestions of well-meaning friends and family members—and certainly not on the advice of admission representatives from graduate schools.

Finally, the biggest obstacle to returning for more education may be yourself. Saying that you're too old, you don't want to invest the money, or you don't want to take time off from your current job may merely be excuses to justify your refusal to take the plunge. Alternatively, you may have valid reasons for staying put for the time being. Be honest with yourself; only you can decide.

Law school at sixty—you're never too old!
One of our favorite stories is about a man who decided at the age of 60 to go to law school. "That will take three years," his friends and family moaned. "You'll be 63!" "So what?" Ed replied. "If I don't go to law school, in three years I'll still be 63." In Ed's way of thinking, he couldn't put three years to better use than to accomplish a lifelong goal.

In considering additional education, ask yourself, "If I do not choose to pursue additional education now, will I be satisfied with my career progress in a year?...five years?" This may be the best measure of how you might benefit from additional education.

Education and Income

Most of us have heard of the guy down the street who flunked out of college or failed to complete high school and is now a millionaire. *Forbes* magazine listed Bill Gates, a Harvard dropout, the founder of Microsoft computers, as the world's richest individual in 1995. Howard Hughes flunked out of Rice University and still managed to gain genius status and amass an empire. The fact is that there are many such success stories among the not-so-educated.

What we don't hear are stories about the many failures. According to the Bureau of the Census, when salaries of all working people over the age of 25 were examined, on average those with the most education had the highest annual incomes. People who failed to enter high school averaged a salary of $15,223 a year. These figures include those with large amounts of experience. Those with less than a high school diploma but with some high school education increased on average to $18,012 per year, and high school graduates earned $23,410 per year.

In terms of income, even some college education is better than none. Americans who have completed some college average incomes of $27,705. Those completing a bachelor's or four-year degree earn an average of $35,900 per year, some $12,000 higher per year than the high school graduate.

Finally, there are those that strive for more than a bachelor's degree. For those who complete graduate, professional, or other college work beyond the bachelor's, the extra education will garner them an average of $43,032 per year. This will, of course, vary with the type of graduate study pursued. Law or medical school will almost certainly give you a higher income than one year of graduate study in a less marketable area.

Dear Dr. Bob
I recently heard that a doctor who is a general practitioner makes on average $117,000 a year and that internal medicine specialists make $181,000 a year. Should I change careers to become a doctor? Signed, Curious Career Changer

Dear Curious Career Changer
Certainly, becoming a doctor can seem like a wonderful choice. The drama of the emergency room, a good salary, knowing that you're making a difference in people's lives. However, you should consider the hard work, high cost, and many years it takes to become a doctor. Since there are three times as many applicants as there are slots for med school, I recommend exploring all your options in the medical field.

First, make sure that the health field is the field you are most interested in, then look into all the options. Options such as medical physics, physicians, assistants, pharmacy, and occupational and physical therapy are a few alternatives in the health field that may be a good fit and more time and cost effective for you.

However, don't do anything drastic! Being in medicine isn't exactly what you see on TV. You ought to talk to a few real health professionals or a career counselor before leaping into anything.

Getting Organized for Graduate School

If you decide that graduate or professional school is definitely what you need in your life and you've weighed the pros and cons, then get ready for the graduate school application process, which can be "The Nightmare on Elm Street." However, organization can make your life much easier and good preparation can eventually land you in the school of your choice. Here are some tips to help you:

- Request application materials around September of the year prior to the year you want to enroll.
- Know each school's application timeline (exam results, application due date, etc.).
- Establish a time frame for yourself, setting goals to complete tests and prepare paperwork and other relevant information well before the actual due date.
- Take practice tests, and learn what to expect on the tests, how answers are scored, whether you lose points for wrong answers, and so on.
- Take the actual tests.
- Forward exam results to selected schools.
- Get transcripts from schools attended.
- Obtain letters of recommendation.
- Write essays.
- Use certified mail to deliver materials to schools. This insures receipt of the materials by the school.
- Visit schools you are interested in attending, if possible.

Preparing for graduate school admissions tests

Graduate schools, law schools, and medical schools all require test scores before admitting anyone. The standardized tests include the GMAT (Graduate Management Admission Test), LSAT (Law School Admission Test), and MCAT (Medical College Admission Test). Prep courses can help ready you for these tests. Such courses help familiarize you with the contents of the tests and question types. They also offer strategies of test taking to help you improve your scores. Below are two services that provide test preparation courses.

Kaplan (1-800-KAP-TEST)
Princeton Review (1-800-2-REVIEW)

Selecting a Graduate School

Selecting a graduate school requires much consideration before committing money and two to three years of your life. The task of making the best selection in a graduate school is one that will have a significant impact on subsequent job placement, starting salary, and career potential. Here are some criteria to help in evaluating potential graduate schools: the school's reputation, both academically and among the employment community; curriculum, specialization(s), geographic location, department size, selectivity of admissions, faculty reputations and areas of expertise, and level of financial aid/support for students.

CYBERTIPS ON GRADUATE SCHOOLS

The Career Channel
http://riceinfo.rice.edu:80/projects/careers/
Provides information on graduate school application deadlines; rankings of top professional, medical, and graduate schools; test prep courses; and test examples.

CollegeNET
http://www.collegenet.com
Find information about colleges and universities in Southern California and throughout the U.S. including Web addresses.

Educational Testing Service
http://www.ets.org/
Provides test dates for SAT, GRE, GMAT, and teaching tests.

Graduate & Professional Schools from the University of Virginia
http://minerva.acc.virginia.edu/~career/grdsch.html

Jobtrak
http://www.jobtrak.com/gradschool_docs/gradschool.html
Offers advice on grad school: applying, testing, and financing; also has links to grad school sites by topic.

Law School Admissions Council
http://www.lsac.org
Information on the LSAT, Annual Law School Forum dates.

MBA Explorer
http://www.gmat.org
Links to 200 business schools, financial aid information, GMAT registration.

Peterson's Guide to Graduate and Professional Study
http://www.petersons.com/graduate/gsector.html
Links to over 1,500 universities on the Net that offer grad programs; arranged by geography.

Financial Aid Web Sites
If you're wondering how you're going to pay for graduate school, check out the following sites to learn about financial aid resources.

Financial Aid Information Page
http://www.finaid.org/
Provides links to sources of financial aid information.

Scholarships and Fellowships Database
http://www.cs.cmu.edu/~finaid/html/fellowships.html

FURTHER EDUCATION IN SOUTHERN CALIFORNIA

Below is a partial list of graduate programs in Southern California. All of the following programs are nationally or regionally accredited.

Art Center College of Design
1700 Lida St.
Pasadena, CA 91103
(818) 396-2373
Nationally ranked programs in fine arts. Awards Bachelor's and Master's degrees.

California Institute of the Arts
24700 McBean Parkway
Velencia, CA 91355
(805) 255-1050
http://www.calarts.edu
Nationally ranked programs in film and fine arts. Offers certificates, Bachelor's and Master's degrees.

California Institute of Technology
1201 E. California Blvd.
Pasadena, CA 91125
(818) 395-6326
http://www.caltech.edu
Top-ranked programs in chemistry, computer science, geology, mathematics, and physics. Awards Bachelor's, Master's, and Doctoral degrees.

California School of Professional Psychology
1000 S. Fremont Ave.
Alhambra, CA 91803
(213) 483-7034
Offers Doctoral degrees.

Claremont Graduate School
150 E. 10th St.
Claremont, CA 91711
(909) 621-8069
http://www.cgs.edu/
Programs in business administration, fine arts, psychology, and education. Awards Master's, Doctor's, and teaching credentials.

College of Osteopathic Medicine
309 E. 2nd St., College Plaza
Pomona, CA 91766
(909) 623-6116
Offers Master and Doctor of Osteopathic Medicine degrees.

If I Can't Find a Job, Should I Go Back to School? 49

Otis/Parsons School of Art and Design
2401 Wilshire Blvd.
Los Angeles, CA 90057
(213) 251-0500
Nationally ranked fine arts program. Offers Bachelor's and Master's degrees.

Postbaccalaureate Premedical Program
Scripps College
1030 Columbia Ave.
Claremont, CA 91711
(909) 621-8764
15-month post-baccalaureate medical school preparation program.

Southern California College of Optometry
2575 Yorba Linda Blvd.
Fullerton, CA 92631
(714) 870-7226
Doctor of Optometry program.

University of California, Irvine
Irvine, CA 92717
(714) 856-5011
http://www.uci.edu
Nationally ranked medical school, programs in theater and English.

University of California, Los Angeles (UCLA)
405 Hilgard Avenue
Los Angeles, CA 90024
(310) 825-4321
http://www.ucla.edu
Nationally ranked law school, business school, programs in engineering, nursing, dentistry, social work, health administration/public health, chemistry, physics, mathematics, geology, computer science, economics, psychology, sociology, English, film, history, political science, architecture, theater, and fine arts.

University of California, San Diego
9500 Gilman Drive
La Jolla, CA 92093
(619) 534-1193
http://www.ucsd.edu/
Medical school, nationally ranked programs in biology, geology, psychology, mathematics, economics, physics, engineering, theater, and political science.

University of Southern California
Graduate and Professional Studies
Los Angeles, CA 90089
(213) 743-2311
Nationally ranked law, business, social work, pharmacy, computer science, film, and music programs. Social work, engineering, urban and regional planning, business administration, education.

Vocational/Trade Schools in Southern California

If you need to update your skills, such as computing or accounting, you may want to consider an apprenticeship program. An apprenticeship program is less costly than a full-time graduate program and may provide just the current skills you need.

If you want to try a new career such as chef, travel agent, or medical assistant, vocational schools can provide the skills necessary. Below are a few resources for vocational schools in Southern California.

Academy Pacific Travel College
1777 N. Vine St.
Hollywood, CA 90028
(213) 462-3211

Epicurean School of Culinary Arts
8759 Melrose Ave.
Los Angeles, CA 90069
(213) 659-5990
Professional chef's training course.

Fashion Careers of California College
1923 Morena Blvd.
San Diego, CA 92110
(619) 275-4700

Gemological Institute of America
1660 Stewart St.
Santa Monica, CA 90406
(310) 829-2991

Los Angeles Floral Career Center
755 Wall St.
Los Angeles, CA 90014
(213) 892-0230

Los Angeles Trade-Technical College
400 W. Washington Blvd.
Los Angeles, CA 90015
(213) 744-9058

Nova Institute of Health Technology
3000 S. Robertson Blvd.
West Los Angeles, CA 90034
(310) 840-5777
Programs also in Whittier, Ontario, and Long Beach.

Pacific Travel Trade School
3807 Wilshire Blvd., 3rd Floor

Los Angeles, CA 90010
(213) 427-1040

San Diego Golf Academy
12520 High Bluff Drive, Suite 180
San Diego, CA 92130
(619) 794-2810

Shiatsu Massage School of California
2309 Main St.
Santa Monica, CA 90405
(310) 396-4877

TWA Travel Academy
1543 Shatto St.
Los Angeles, CA 90017
(213) 413-7510

Continuing Education Programs in Southern California

Many professionals opt to take short courses in specific technology to stay abreast of their field. Some fields, such as nursing, require a certain amount of coursework each year to maintain a license. And for all of us, education is a personally enriching lifelong process. Whatever the reason, there are many good continuing education classes being offered. Below are a few schools providing continuing education courses.

Art Center at Night
1700 Lida St.
Pasadena, CA 91103
(818) 396-2319
Classes in design, advertising.

California State Polytechnic University/Pomona
3801 W. Temple Ave.
Pomona, CA 91768
(909) 869-2288
Certification programs, credit and non-credit courses in fields including construction, computers, engineering, equine studies, human resource management, business administration, and English.

UCLA Extension
P.O. Box 24901
Los Angeles, CA 90024
(310) 825-9971
http://www.unex.ucla.edu
Certification, credit, and non-credit courses including architecture, legal programs, writing, humanities, engineering, education, computers, entertainment

studies, and performing arts. Courses offered at the Westwood campus, Universal City Walk, World Trade Center, the Third Street Promenade in Santa Monica, and on-line.

University of California, Irvine Extension Program
P.O. Box 6050
Irvine, CA 92716
(714) 824-5414
Coursework in many fields including multimedia, graphic design.

University of California, Riverside Extension Program
Riverside, CA 92521
(800) 442-4990

University of California, San Diego
Extended Study Programs
9500 Gilman Drive
La Jolla, CA 92093
(619) 534-3400
Classes are offered in the downtown, north county, and La Jolla areas.

On-line Education

No need to pack those bags or leave your job and friends to head off for school. Today's technology brings the teachers, ideas, books, and dialogue to the student electronically. The advantages are that correspondence study is dependable, low cost, and can be done anywhere. Still it is important to check out what credits, degree, or credentials you may receive. Additionally, consider all costs associated with on-line education and don't forget to inquire about financial aid.

Although on-line education is convenient, some people may not do well outside a typical classroom environment where you see the teacher and take part in dialogue. Think about the kind of study environment that works best for you. It is also important to note that the field of on-line education is constantly changing, and new possibilities certainly will pop up after the publication of this book.

If you would like to learn more about on-line or long-distance learning programs, the following books and organizations can assist you:
- The National University Continuing Education Association (NUCEA) provides comprehensive guides to long-distance learning ranging from correspondence programs to programs delivered through various electronic media. These guides are:
- *Peterson's Guide to Independent Study.* Princeton, NJ: Peterson's Guides, 1992.
- *The Electronic University: A Guide to Long-distance Learning Programs.* Princeton, NJ: Peterson's Guides, 1993.

Did you know that you can also take courses offered by certified teachers and professional experts on-line? Typical courses offered include: History, English, Sociology, Languages, Math, Science, the Arts, and Computer Science. However, no college credit or certificates are awarded for these courses. For further information contact The Electronic University Network (Sarah Blackmun, Director of Instruction, 1977 Colestin Road, Hornbrook, CA 96044, (415) 221-7061). This network consists of organizations that work with groups of colleges to provide long-distance learning programs.

COLLEGE COURSES ON THE WEB

http://www.petersons.com:8080/
Has pages under construction on schools offering continuing education, vocational schools, electronic courses, and executive development programs.

http://www.then.com/
Cooperates with UCLA Extension to provide on-line courses.

http://www.caso.com/iuhome.html
North American on-line course offerings.

four

The 10-Step Job Search

Almost everything can be broken down into steps. The job search is no different. If you take the process one step at a time and follow our basic rules, you are more likely to find a job. As you begin, it is important to remember that you are in control, and in the end it is you who must land the job. To get there you need to be proactive; companies will not come looking for you. Rather, you have to search out the companies, the jobs, and the people that are in a position to hire.

The 10-Step Job Search
1. Know Thyself—Where Are You Going?
2. Research the Job Market.
3. Organize Your Search.
4. Network.
5. Persistence and Follow-Up.
6. Prepare Your Resume.
7. Mail Your Resume.
8. Use Your Career Resources.
9. The Killer Interview.
10. Make Sure This Is the Job for You.

Step 1: Know Thyself—Where Are You Going?

Hopefully, Chapter 2 has set you on the right path to choosing a career. To get somewhere you need to decide where it is you are going, what you want to do, and what you are capable of doing. Other items to assess include the characteristics of your ideal work environment, the type of experience you wish to gain from the job, and how much money you intend to make. To a large extent, your happiness with your job coincides with how closely it meets your needs and motivates you.

Once you've answered these questions you will be able to articulate why you are interviewing for a particular position and why you are right for that position.

Step 2: Research the Job Market

The alarm clock rings, and you slowly get out of bed and head downstairs for your morning jolt of java along with the want ads from the daily paper. Tempted to read the comics, you resist the urge and resume your job search with the want ads. After all, this is how people find jobs. Wrong! According to *Forbes* magazine, only about 10 percent of professional and technical people find their jobs through want ads.

Your best bet is *not* to send a resume to every ad in the paper. Instead, try to identify who's hiring and where the opportunities may be. How do you learn these things? Research.

Libraries

Libraries provide vast amounts of resources for job searching, ranging from company information (ranking, annual sales, product information, number of employees, who's running the show) to resume writing guides, business newspapers and magazines, salary statistics, and, of course, directories such as *Standard and Poor's Register of Corporations, Directors, and Executives*. To save precious time in your research, the reference desk is invaluable in locating materials for your job search.

Local university and community college libraries may also offer resources for job seekers. Many local schools have reference libraries that are well equipped with career resource information and job directories that you can use even if you are not an alumnus. Some libraries also offer vocational testing and career guidance, often in conjunction with the school's career planning office.

TOP THREE BUSINESS LIBRARIES

The three most useful libraries, each housing a wealth of information on business and career resources, are:

Los Angeles Public Library
Central Library
630 W. 5th St.
Los Angeles, CA 90071
(213) 228-7000 General Information
(213) 238-7100 Business & Economics
Internet access
http://www.lapl.org

The Business and Economics section is located on Lower Level One of the Tom Bradley Wing. Resource guides include "Researching a Public Company."

Rosenfeld Business Library
Anderson School of Business
University of California, Los Angeles (UCLA)
Los Angeles, CA 90095
(310) 825-3138
http://www.anderson.ucla.edu/resources/library/libhome.htm
Resources available to the general public, although some materials are restricted. UCLA Extension students can purchase a library card for a nominal fee. 147,000 volumes.

City of San Diego Central Library
820 E St.
San Diego, CA 92101
(619) 236-5800
http://www.sannet.gov/public-library/
Internet access in every branch.

OTHER LIBRARIES WITH JOB-RESOURCE COLLECTIONS:

Anaheim Public Library
Central Library
500 W. Broadway
Anaheim, CA 92805
(714) 254-1880
Test and Employment section, Internet access.

Fullerton Public Library
Main Library
353 W. Commonwealth Ave.
Fullerton, CA 92632
(714) 738-6326
Career Center, job listings, Internet access.

Long Beach Public Library
Main Library
101 Pacific Ave.
Long Beach, CA 90822
(310) 570-7500
Internet access.

Pasadena Public Library
Central Library
285 E. Walnut St.
Pasadena, CA 91101
(818) 405-4052
http://www.ci.pasadena.ca.us/library.html
Internet access.

Directories

Directories provide you with corporate structures, company financial figures, company rankings, best companies to work for, best places to live, who's making what salary, and top careers. When you're beginning your homework, whether you're researching an entire industry or a specific company, there are four major directories with which you should be familiar.

OUR FOUR FAVORITE DIRECTORIES

The Directory of Corporate Affiliations (National Register Publishing, New Providence, NJ) is an organized business reference tool covering public and private businesses in the U.S. and throughout the world. This six-volume directory allows the user to examine the parent company and all subsidiaries of the parent company, categorized by geographic area or S.I.C. (Standard Industrial Classification) codes that identify the company's product or service. If you want to know the corporate reporting structure, the company's subsidiaries, or the company's banking, legal, or outside service firms, this is the directory to use.

Standard and Poor's Register of Corporations, Directors, and Executives (Standard and Poor's Publishing, 25 Broadway, New York, NY 10004) is billed as the "foremost guide to the business community and the executives who run it." This three-volume directory lists more than 50,000 corporations and 70,000 officers, directors, trustees, and other bigwigs.

Each business is assigned an S.I.C. number. Listings are indexed by geographic area and also by S.I.C. number, so it's easy to find all the companies in a local area that produce, say, industrial inorganic chemicals.

You can also look up a particular company to verify its correct address and phone number, its chief officers (that is, the people you might want to contact for an interview), its products, and, in many cases, its annual sales and number of employees. If you have an appointment with the president of XYZ Corporation, you can consult *Standard and Poor's* to find out where he or she was born and went to college—information that's sure to come in handy in an employment interview. Supplements are published in April, July, and October.

Ward's Business Directory of U.S. Private and Public Companies (Gale Research Inc., New York, NY) is the leading source for hard-to-find information on private companies. This six-volume publication lists more than 142,000 companies in alphabetic, geographic, and industry arrangements. It also provides rankings and analyses of the industry activity of leading companies. If you want to determine parent/subsidiary relationships, merger and acquisition positions, or general information on private and public companies, this is the directory to use.

The **Million Dollar Directory** (Dun & Bradstreet, 3 Century Drive, Parsippany, NJ 07054) is a three-volume listing of approximately 160,000 U.S. businesses with a net worth of more than half a million dollars. Listings appear alphabetically, geographically, and by product classification and include key personnel. Professional and consulting organizations such as hospitals and engineering services, credit agencies, and financial institutions other than banks and trust companies are not generally included.

So much for our favorite directories. The following listings contain more than 40 additional directories and guides, most with a local focus, that may come in handy. Many of these, as well as other directories, are available at area libraries.

NATIONAL/REGIONAL DIRECTORIES:

Adweek Directories
Adweek Agency Directory
1515 Broadway, 12th Floor
New York, NY 10036
Includes directories of ad agencies and public relations firms as well as guides to media, advertising, and marketing services.

The African-American Almanac
Gale Research Co.
835 Penobscot Bldg.
Detroit, MI 48226-4094
Lists of civil rights organizations; African-Americans in law, politics; highly capitalized black companies; publishers and journalists, and more. Includes contact information and biographies where applicable. A resource for African-American history. Arranged in chapters by major subjects.

The Almanac of American Employers: A Guide to America's 500 Most Successful Large Corporations
Contemporary Books
180 N. Michigan Ave.
Chicago, IL 60601
Alphabetical profiles of major corporations including information about benefits, job turnover, and financial stability.

Book Publishing Career Directory
Gale Research Co.
835 Penobscot Bldg.
Detroit, MI 48226
Covers over 300 U.S. and Canadian publishers and 300 publishing trade organizations offering entry-level positions. Includes names, addresses, phone numbers, contacts, book specialties, and employment information.

California Almanac
Pacific Data Resources

P.O. Box 4397
Santa Barbara, CA 93103
California statistics and information.

California Association of Hospitals Membership Directory
California Association of Hospitals
P.O. Box 1100
Sacramento, CA 95812
Listings of hospitals by California city.

California Colleges and Universities
California Postsecondary Education Commission
1020 12th St., 3rd Floor
Sacramento, CA 95814
Profiles California colleges and courses of study within the state.

California's High Tech Companies
Database Publishing Company
P.O. Box 70024
Anaheim, CA 92825-0024
(714) 778-6400
Contains nearly 10,000 companies in industries including computers, electronic components, instrumentation, software development, chemicals, machinery, robotics, office equipment, and research facilities.

California Manufacturers Register
Database Publishing Company
P.O. Box 70024
Anaheim, CA 92825-0024
(714) 778-6400
Lists 27,000 top California manufacturing firms.

California Public School Directory
California Department of Education
721 Capitol Mall
Sacramento, CA 95814
Lists primary and secondary schools within California counties.

Career Guide: Dun's Employment Opportunities Directory
Dun and Bradstreet
3 Century Drive
Parsippany, NJ 07054
Employment information on companies with at least 1,000 employees, including hiring practices and disciplines hired geographically.

College Placement Annual
National Association of Colleges and Employers Directory
62 Highland Ave.
Bethlehem, PA 18017
Occupational needs of more than 2,300 corporations and government employers.

Consultants and Consulting Organizations Directory
Gale Research Co.
835 Penobscot Bldg.
Detroit, MI 48226
Descriptions of 20,000 firms and individuals involved in consulting, indexed geographically.

Corporate Technology Directory
Corporate Technology Information Services
1 Market St.
Wellesley Hills, MA 02181
Profiles of high-technology corporations including address, phone, ownership, history, brief description, sales, number of employees, executives, and products. Indexed by company names, geography, technology, and product.

Dictionary of Occupational Titles
U.S. Dept. of Labor
200 Constitution Ave., N.W.
Washington, DC 20210
Occupational information on job duties and requirements; describes almost every conceivable job.

Directories in Print, Thirteenth Edition
Gale Research Co.
835 Penobscot Bldg.
Detroit, MI 48226-4094
This is a directory of directories. It is an annotated guide to over 14,000 directories published worldwide, including business, industry, professional, scientific, entertainment, recreation, and cultural listings. Includes electronic databases.

Directory of Minority Arts Organizations
Civil Rights Division, National Endowment for the Arts
1100 Pennsylvania Ave., N.W., Room 812
Washington, DC 20506
Almost 1,000 performing groups, presenters, galleries, art & media centers, literary organizations, and community centers with significant arts programming that have leadership and constituency that is predominantly Asian-American, African-American, Hispanic, Native American, or multiracial.

Directory of Women-Owned Businesses
National Association of Women Business Owners
2000 P St., N.W., Suite 511
Washington, DC 20036
Free directory lists women-owned businesses by state; describes products and services.

Dun and Bradstreet State Sales Guide
Dun and Bradstreet
430 Mountain Road
New Providence, NJ 07974

Covers all businesses in each state that are included in Dun and Bradstreet's "Reference Book."

Encyclopedia of Associations
Gale Research Co.
835 Penobscot Bldg.
Detroit, MI 48226-4094
Five volumes, each containing over 16,000 listings for American associations limited in activity to regional, state, and local levels. Does not duplicate entries in *Encyclopedia of Associations: National Organizations*. Includes extensive information on each organization. Also available on CD-ROM, diskette, magnetic tape, computer printout, or as mailing label list.

Encyclopedia of Associations: National Organizations of the U.S.
Gale Research Co.
835 Penobscot Bldg.
Detroit, MI 48226-4094
Approximately 23,000 non-profit U.S. membership organizations of national scope divided into industry classifications. Includes extensive information on each organization. Also available on CD-ROM, diskette, magnetic tape, computer printout, or as mailing label list.

Encyclopedia of Business Information Sources
Gale Research Co.
835 Penobscot Bldg.
Detroit, MI 48226-4094
Lists each industry's encyclopedia, handbooks, indexes, almanacs, yearbooks, trade associations, periodicals, directories, computer databases, research centers, and statistical sources.

Engineering, Science, and Computer Graduates: Peterson's Job Opportunities
Peterson's Guides
202 Carnegie Center
P.O. Box 2123
Princeton, NJ 08543-2123
Lists specific companies within these industries.

Environmental Engineering Selection Guide
American Academy of Environmental Engineers
130 Holiday Court, Suite 100
Annapolis, MD 21401
A directory to engineering firms and educational institutions employing Board Certified Specialists.

Fortune Double 500 Directory
Time, Inc.
Rockefeller Bldg., Rockefeller Center
New York, NY 10020
Lists the 500 largest and the 500 second-largest industrial corporations, along with the 500 largest commercial banks, utilities, life insurance companies, diver-

sified financial companies, retailers, transportation companies, and diversified services.

Gale Directory of Publications
Gale Research Co.
835 Penobscot Bldg.
Detroit, MI 48226-4094
Lists national, local, and trade magazines alphabetically and by state.

Gale Directory of Publications and Broadcast Media
Gale Research Co.
835 Penobscot Bldg.
Detroit, MI 48226-4094
Lists 35,000 publications and broadcast stations as well as the feature editors of major daily newspapers.

Grocery Commercial Food Industry Directory
GroCom Group
P.O. Box 10378
Clearwater, FL 34617
Profiles 2,500 manufacturers, wholesalers, brokers, distributors, and other suppliers of food and beverage products and food industry-related products.

Harbinger File
Harbinger Communications
50 Rustic Lane
Santa Cruz, CA 95060
Directory of government agencies, companies, citizen's groups, and governmental education programs concerned with energy and environmental issues. Alphabetical listing includes address, phone, contact name, brief description, funding source, publications, and key issues. Indexed by major categories and key descriptions.

Hispanic Media & Markets Source
Standard Rate & Data Service
3004 Glenview Road
Wilmette, IL 60091
Hispanic-targeted media, including radio and television stations, newspapers, consumer and business publications, outdoor advertising, and direct mail lists. Arranged by type of media.

Hoover's Guide to the Top Southern California Companies
The Reference Press
P.O. Box 140375
Austin, TX 78714
http://www.hoovers.com
Profiles Southern California companies, includes history, key competitors.

Hoover's Handbook of American Companies
The Reference Press
P.O. Box 140375
Austin, TX 78714
http://www.hoovers.com
Profiles 450 major public and private companies. Includes company histories and a list of key competitors.

International Advertising Association Membership Directory
International Advertising Association
342 Madison Ave.
New York, NY 10017
Covers 3,200 member advertisers, advertising agencies, media, and other firms involved in advertising. Arranged geographically and by function or service.

Job Openings—Publication #510K
Consumer Information Center, Dept. G
Pueblo, CO 81009
Free 80-page booklet, revised monthly, highlights occupations with large numbers of openings and indicates where they are located.

Job Seeker's Guide to Private and Public Companies
Gale Research Co.
835 Penobscot Bldg.
Detroit, MI 48226-4094
Lists over 15,000 firms, including products and services, size, human resource contacts, and application procedures.

Los Angeles Sourcebook
Bernardo Press
16496 Bernardo Center Drive
San Diego, CA 92128
Lists Los Angeles professional, social, and civic organizations.

National Directory of Addresses and Telephone Numbers
Omnigraphics Inc.
2500 Penobscot Bldg.
Detroit, MI 48226
Includes names, addresses, phone numbers, and fax numbers of national corporations, financial institutions, colleges and universities, government agencies, and other businesses and organizations.

The National Directory of Magazines
Oxbridge Communications
150 5th Ave.
New York, NY 10011
Profiles magazines by interest categories; includes key staff names, circulation, and description. Cross-indexed by subject. Indexed alphabetically by title.

National Directory of Minority-Owned Business Firms
Business Research Services
4201 Connecticut Ave., N.W.
Washington, DC 20008
Lists company name, size, description, and address.

National Directory of Women-Owned Business Firms
Business Research Services
4201 Connecticut Ave., N.W.
Washington, DC 20008
Lists company name, size, description, and address.

National Trade & Professional Associations of the United States
Columbia Books
1212 New York Ave., N.W., Suite 207
Washington, DC 20005
Alphabetical profiles of associations including address, phone, affiliations, history, publications, meetings, and annual budget. Indexed by subject, geography, budget, and acronym.

Occupational Outlook Handbook
U.S. Bureau of Labor
200 Constitutional Ave., N.W.
Washington, DC 20210
Describes what people do in their jobs, training and education needed, earnings, working conditions, and employment outlook.

O'Dwyer's Directory of Public Relations Firms
J. R. O'Dwyer & Co.
271 Madison Ave.
New York, NY 10016
Describes 2,200 public relations firms in the U.S., their key personnel, local offices, and accounts; indexed geographically.

Orange County Commerce and Industry Directory
Database Publishing Company
P.O. Box 70024
Anaheim, CA 92825-0024
(714) 778-6400
Profiles 6,500 Orange County-based companies.

Orange County Sourcebook
Bernardo Press
16496 Bernardo Center Drive
San Diego, CA 92128
Orange County professional, social, and civic organizations.

Peterson's Job Opportunities in Engineering and Technology
Peterson's Guides
202 Carnegie Center
P.O. Box 2123
Princeton, NJ 08543
Describes 800 government agencies, technical firms, and manufacturers that hire engineers, computer scientists, and physical scientists.

Recording Industry Sourcebook
Mix Publications
6400 Hollis St., Suite 10
Emeryville, CA 94608
National directory of the recording industry, including record labels, production agencies, and industry associations.

San Diego Sourcebook
Bernardo Press
16496 Bernardo Center Drive
San Diego, CA 92128
Lists San Diego professional, social, and civic organizations.

Sheldon's Retail Directory
Phelon, Sheldon & Marsar
15 Industrial Ave.
Fairview, NJ 07022
Directory of the largest department stores, women's specialty stores, chain stores, and resident buying offices. Geographical listings plus alphabetical index.

Southern California Business Directory
Database Publishing Company
P.O. Box 70024
Anaheim, CA 92825-0024
(714) 778-6400
Includes listings for over 15,000 manufacturers and 11,000 service businesses. Includes listings of company owners and minority and female-owned companies.

Ward's Business Directory of U.S. Private and Public Companies
Gale Research Co.
835 Penobscot Bldg.
Detroit, MI 48226-4094
Covers nearly 85,000 privately owned companies, representing all industries.

Trade Magazines

Every industry or service business has its trade press—that is, editors, reporters, and photographers whose job it is to cover an industry or trade. You should become familiar with the magazines of the industries or professions that interest you, especially if you're in the interviewing stage of your job search. Your prospective employers are reading the trade magazines; you should too.

Many of the magazines we've included are available at the libraries listed earlier in this chapter. Most of the following magazines have editorial offices in the area, reporting area news about the people and businesses in their industry. The majority carry local want ads and personnel changes. Additional trade magazines are listed in Chapter 10 under specific career categories. For a complete listing of the trade press, consult the *Gale Directory of Publications and Broadcast Media* (formerly the *Ayer Directory of Publications*) at the library.

REGIONAL TRADE MAGAZINES

Advertising Age
6500 Wilshire Blvd.
Los Angeles, CA 90048
(213) 651-3710

Adweek Western Edition
BPI Communications
5055 Wilshire Blvd., 7th Floor
Los Angeles, CA 90036
(213) 525-2270

American Cinematographer
P.O. Box 2230
Los Angeles, CA 90078
(213) 876-5080

Animation Magazine
28024 Dorothy Drive
Agoura Hills, CA 91301
(818) 991-2884

Architectural Digest
6300 Wilshire Blvd.
Los Angeles, CA 90048
(213) 965-3700

Back Stage West
5055 Wilshire Blvd., 6th Floor
Los Angeles, CA 90036
(213) 525-2356

Billboard (BPI)
5055 Wilshire Blvd.
Los Angeles, CA 90036
(213) 525-2270

California Apparel News
Apparel News Group
110 E. 9th St., Suite A-777
Los Angeles, CA 90079
(213) 627-3737

California Real Estate Journal
Daily Journal Corporation
915 E. 1st St.
Los Angeles, CA 90012
(213) 229-5300

Computer Technology Review
West World Productions
924 Westwood Blvd., #650
Los Angeles, CA 90024
(310) 208-1335

Daily Variety
5700 Wilshire Blvd., Suite 120
Los Angeles, CA 90036
(213) 857-6600

Data Processing Digest
P.O. Box 1249
Los Angeles, CA 90078
(213) 851-3156

Entertainment Law Reporter
2210 Wilshire Blvd., #311
Santa Monica, CA 90403
(310) 892-9335

Gems & Gemology
Gemological Institute of America
1660 Stewart St.
Santa Monica, CA 90404
(310) 829-2991

Hollywood Reporter
5055 Wilshire Blvd., Suite 600
Los Angeles, CA 90036
(213) 876-1000

Los Angeles Magazine
11100 Santa Monica Blvd., 7th Floor
Los Angeles, CA 90025
(310) 477-1181

Music Connection Magazine
4731 Laurel Canyon Blvd.
North Hollywood, CA 91607
(818) 755-0101

Radio & Records
10100 Santa Monica Blvd., 5th Floor
Los Angeles, CA 90067
(310) 788-1625

San Diego Magazine
4206 Westpoint Loma Blvd.
San Diego, CA 92110
(619) 225-8953

Screen Actor
7065 Hollywood Blvd.
Hollywood, CA 90028
(213) 856-6650

Simulation
P.O. Box 17900
San Diego, CA 92177
(619) 277-3888

Job Listings

Cover all your bases and respond to promising job advertisements in your field. The following resources contain only job listings and job-related information.

Art Calendar
Box 199
Upper Fairmont, MD 21867
(410) 651-9150
http://www.artspeaks.com/art_life/calendar/art_calendar.html
11 issues/year. Profiles opportunities for visual artists.

Art Job
Western States Arts Federation
236 Montezuma Ave.
Santa Fe, NM 87501
(505) 988-1166
Semi-monthly. Includes internships and administrative positions.

ArtSEARCH
Theatre Communications Group
355 Lexington Ave.
New York, NY 10017
(212) 697-5230
Semi-monthly. Lists jobs in a wide range of performing arts; also includes internships.

Association for Experiential Education Jobs Clearinghouse
2305 Canyon Blvd., Suite 100
Boulder, CO 80302
(303) 440-8844
Monthly. Lists jobs in outdoor adventure and environmental education.

Athletics Employment Weekly
RDST Enterprises
RR2, Box 140

Carthage, IL 62321
(217) 357-3615
Weekly. Lists openings for directors, coaches, and assistants.

Aviso
American Association of Museums
1225 I St., N.W., Suite 200
Washington, DC 20005
(202) 289-1818
Monthly. Jobs in museums, galleries, and archives.

Back Stage West
1515 Broadway, 14th Floor
New York, NY 10036
(212) 764-7300
Weekly. West Coast edition. Focused on performing arts opportunities. Includes casting information for film, television, and stage.

California Job Journal
Job Journal, Inc.
1800 Tribute Road
Sacramento, CA 95815
(916) 925-0800
Weekly. Display ads for California companies.

Career Opportunity News
Garrett Park Press
P.O. Box 190
Garret Park, MD 20896
(301) 949-2553
Semi-monthly. Includes job trends, statistics, and news.

Chronicle of Higher Education
Department E
1255 23rd St., N.W.
Washington, DC 20037
(800) 347-6969
http://chronicle.com/
Weekly. Jobs in colleges and universities.

Chronicle of Philanthropy
Department E
1255 23rd St., N.W.
Washington, DC 20037
(800) 347-6969
Bi-weekly. Jobs in fund-raising and development.

Community Jobs
Access/Networking in the Public Interest
50 Beacon St.
Boston, MA 02108

(617) 720-5627
Monthly. Job opportunities with non-profit and social-change organizations.

Current Jobs in Writing, Editing & Communication
P.O. Box 40550
Washington, DC 20016
(703) 506-4400
Monthly. Section on West Coast publishing, writing, and communications jobs.

Earthwork Hotline
Student Conservation Association
P.O. Box 550
Charlestown, NH 03603
(603) 543-1700
Monthly. Positions in environmental advocacy, administration, policy, education, and research. Also includes networking calendar.

Entertainment Employment Journal
P.O. Box 7383
Van Nuys, CA 91409
(800) 335-4335
2 times/month. Jobs and internships with entertainment employers.

Environmental Career Opportunities
P.O. Box 560
Standardsville, VA 22973
(202) 861-0592
Monthly. Lists 80-120 positions in each issue including environmental policy, advocacy, consulting, research, teaching, internships, seasonal positions, and more.

Equal Employment Opportunity Career Journal
CASS Recruitment Publications
1800 Sherman Ave.
Evanston, IL 60201
(847) 475-8800
3 times/yr. Articles, recruitment ads, and job listings.

International Career Employment Opportunities
P.O. Box 305
Standardsville, VA 22973
(804) 985-6444
Bi-weekly. Private, government, and non-profit positions in the U.S. and overseas.

Legal Employment Newsletter
Pacific Edition
P.O. Box 36601
Grosse Point, MI 48236
(313) 961-2023
Features California legal positions as well as other public sector opportunities.

National Ad Search
(800) 992-2832
http://www.nationaladsearch.com/
Weekly. Professional and management jobs listed in the nation's newspapers. Newspaper or Web subscriptions available.

National Business Employment Weekly
Dow Jones & Company
420 Lexington Ave.
New York, NY 10170
(212) 808-6792
http://www.enews.com/magazines/nbew
Weekly. Lists professional and management jobs as well as articles on job-search strategies and salaries. Non-profit job listings every first and third week.

National Human Services and Liberal Arts Careers
KB Enterprises
13137 Penndale Lane
Fairfax, VA 22033
(703) 378-0439
Weekly. Jobs and internships in education, social services. Section on West Coast opportunities.

Opportunity NOC's
The Management Center
870 Market St., Suite 800
San Francisco, CA 94102
(415) 362-9735
Bi-weekly. Lists jobs within California non-profit organizations.

The Source
Rachel PR Services
500 N. Michigan Ave., Suite 1920
Chicago, IL 60611
Monthly. Features employment opportunities in advertising, PR, marketing, and journalism. Includes industry-specific executive recruiters, job banks, job hotlines, and trade associations.

Southern California Broadcasters Association Job Alerts
5670 Wilshire Blvd., Suite 910
Los Angeles, CA 90036
(213) 938-3100
Weekly. Job and internship listings for television and radio stations throughout Southern California.

Technical Employment News
PCI
12416 Hymeadow Drive
Austin, TX 78750

(512) 250-9023
Weekly. Engineering and technical service jobs.

Variety
5700 Wilshire Blvd., Suite 120
Los Angeles, CA 90036
(213) 8577-6600
Daily. Covers the latest in the entertainment industry. Includes a television and cable production chart and a classified ad section.

Voice-Based Job Hot Lines

"Let your fingers do the walking!" Just dial any one of the numerous telephone job banks and listen to the taped recordings that describe available positions and how to apply. Many are available at no charge other than what you might spend for the telephone call. Some company-oriented job information lines include:

Advanced Tissue Sciences (619) 450-5854
ABC Productions (310) 557-4222
Air Touch Cellular (714) 222-8888
Allied Signal (310) 512-2012
Amgen (800) 446-4007
Andersen Consulting (213) 614-7579
ARCO (213) 486-3345
Atlantic Records (310) 205-7450, ext. 8
AT&T (800) 858-5417
Bank of America, Orange County (714) 254-6071
California Community College Job Bank (209) 579-0840
California Federal Bank (213) 930-6712
California Institute of Technology (818) 395-4660
California State University, Fullerton (714) 773-3385
Capitol Records (213) 871-5763
CBS Entertainment Productions (213) 852-2008
Children's Hospital and Health Center (619) 576-5880
Claremont Colleges (909) 607-7373
Coast Savings Financial (818) 316-8730
ComStream Corporation (619) 657-5085
Coopers & Lybrand (213) 356-6440
Cubic Corporation (619) 505-1540
Cytel Corporation (619) 552-2733
Davidson & Associates (310) 793-0599
Deloitte & Touche (213) 688-5222
Disneyland Hotel (714) 781-4407
Disney, Walt (818) 558-2222
Dole Food Company (818) 874-4999
Downey Financial Corporation (714) 509-4310
E! Entertainment Television (213) 954-2666
Fluor Corporation (714) 975-5253
Fountain Valley Regional Hospital (714) 979-8108
GDE Systems, Inc. (800) 545-0506
Geffen Records (310) 278-9010, ext. 2
Gensia (619) 622-3821
Gen-Probe (619) 625-8666
Great Western Financial Corporation (800) 367-3411
GTI Corporation (619) 537-2500, ext. 424
Hanna Barbera Productions (213) 969-1262

Harbor-UCLA Medical Center (310) 222-3241
Health Net (818) 593-7236
Hilton Hotels Corporation (310) 205-7692
Horizons Technology (619) 292-8860, ext. 855
Huntington Memorial Hospital (818) 397-8504
Imperial Bancorp (310) 417-5433
IT Corporation (714) 660-5434
KABC Television (310) 557-4222
Kaiser Permanente Medical Center (213) 857-2615
Kaiser Permanente Pasadena (818) 405-3280
Kaiser Permanente San Diego (619) 528-3071
KCAL Television (213) 960-3770
KCET Television (619) 953-5236
Ketchum Los Angeles (800) 894-0611
KGTV Television (619) 237-6250
Knobble Martens Olson & Bear (714) 721-2929
Knowledge Adventure (818) 246-7330
KNSD Television (619) 467-7605
KPBS Television (619) 594-5703
KPMG Peat Marwick (213) 955-8880
La Jolla Pharmaceutical (619) 452-6600
Long Beach Memorial Medical Center (310) 933-3399
Los Angeles Cellular (310) 403-8519
Los Angeles Times (800) LATIMES, ext. 75700
MCA/Universal (818) 777-5627
MGM (310) 449-3569
Molecular Biosystems (619) 824-2290
Mycogen Corporation (619) 453-7812
NBC Studios (818) 840-4397
Northrop Grumman Corp. (310) 942-5001
O' Melveny & Myers (213) 669-6662
Palomar Medical Center (619) 739-3950
Patagonia (805) 667-4614
Paul Hastings Janofsky & Walker (213) 683-5015
Pepsi Cola West (310) 527-3333
Presto Foods (818) 810-1775, ext. 5912
Qualcomm Inc. (619) 658-JOBS
Samuel Goldwyn Company (310) 284-9229
Sanwa Bank (213) 896-7214
Scripps Clinic (619) 554-8400
Selzer Caplan Wilkens & McMahon (619) 685-3127
Seven Up Royal Crown Bottling (213) 267-JOBS
Sony Electronics (619) 673-2600
Sony Pictures (310) 280-4436
Spelling Entertainment Group (213) 634-3700
St. Joseph Hospital (714) 744-8557
St. Jude Medical Center (714) 992-3925
Stac Electronics (619) 794-4739
State of the Art (714) 753-4080
Twentieth Century Fox (310) 369-2804
University of California, Irvine Medical Center (714) 456-5744
University of California, Los Angeles (UCLA) (310) 794-0890
University of California, San Diego Medical Center (619) 682-1001
University of Southern California (213) 740-4728
Vical Inc. (619) 646-1143
Warner Brothers (818) 954-5400
Western Medical Center (714) 480-5234
Wonderware (800) 541-6930

Job Research on the Internet

Just about any type of information can be accessed by computer today. Journals, occupational outlooks, professional magazines, and business and financial information are easy to access. It's also easy to tap into news groups providing information on job openings in a particular field, discussions of the job market in a specific area, and workplace and employment-related issues. Also see "Cyber Resources for Your Job Search" in Chapter 1. For a longer list of Internet job resources, see the section on "Internet Job Listings" farther on in this chapter.

The following WWW addresses provide general information on library programs, references and abstracts from journals and books, and much more. For links to over 1,000 libraries, go to:
http://wunsite.berkely.edu/Libweb/
or

Libraries on the Web
http://weber.u.washington.edu /~tdowling/libweb/usa.html
which provides an extensive list of national and international library Web sites.

California State Library
http://www.library.ca.gov/california/State_Library/

California State University, Fullerton
http://ccgopher.fullerton.edu/admin/library/csuf.htm

California State University, Long Beach
http://www.csulb.edu/~libweb/

California State University, Los Angeles
http://web.calstatela.edu/library/

Los Angeles Public Library
http://www.lapl.org

San Diego Public Library
http://www.sannet.gov/public-library/

University of California, Irvine
http://www.lib.uci.edu/

University of California, Los Angeles (UCLA)
http://www.library.ucla.edu/

University of California, San Diego
http://www.ucsd.edu/library/index.html

University of Southern California (USC)
http://www.usc.edu/Univ/U_Libraries.html

RECOMMENDED READING

Dixon, Pam, and Sylvia Tiersten. *Be Your Own Headhunter Online.* New York: Random House, 1995.

Kennedy, Joyce Lain. *Hook Up, Get Hired! The Internet Job Search Revolution.* New York: John Wiley & Sons, 1995.

Small Companies

Today's job market has changed. Big business is no longer the biggest employer. Today, 80% of new jobs created in the United States are by small and medium-sized firms that are four or five years old.

Small and medium-sized businesses, those that employ less than 500 people, are good bets for employment opportunities. These companies are expected to expand. Small businesses employ 48% of the American workforce. Two-thirds of all first jobs come from these growing businesses. The big boys of business may still provide better benefits and pay to their employees, but they only manage to provide 11% of the jobs sought by first-time job seekers.

Searching for jobs with small businesses is not, however, as easy as the traditional job search at the large corporation. Small business is less likely to advertise for a position, use an agency, or post a listing at a local college. They generally use the networking method of knowing someone who knows someone. Thus, you may need to be creative when searching out small companies. Use your resources, such as Chambers of Commerce and Small Business Centers (see Chapter 2) to help you in your search.

RECOMMENDED READING

Colton, Kitty, and Michele Fetterolf. *1995: A Job Seeker's Guide to America's 2000 Little-known, Fastest-Growing High-Tech Companies.* Princeton, NJ: Peterson's Guides, 1994.

Step 3: Organize Your Search

The most difficult part of any job search is getting started. The next most difficult is staying organized. Preparing a resume, sending it out, scheduling interviews, and returning phone calls is enough to cause anyone to grab for the extra-strength aspirin! Organize your job search and you'll have fewer headaches.

Don't Get Caught Without Your Daily Planner

Have you ever noticed how many people carry around those little black "Daily Planners"? In this case, what's good for the crowd is also good for you, the job searcher. You need to keep a written record of every person you contact in your job search and the results of each contact. This will prevent a job lead from falling through the cracks. It may even come in handy for future job searches.

Your Daily Planner should serve as a way of organizing your efforts for greatest efficiency. Much of your job search will be spent developing your network of contacts. Still, you should allocate a portion of each week for doing research on companies that interest you and for pursuing other means of contacting employers.

As you go through your contacts and begin to research the job market, you'll begin to identify certain employers in whom you're interested. Keep a list of them. For each one that looks promising, start a file that contains articles on the company, its annual report, product brochures, company profile, and any other interesting information. Every so often, check your "potential companies" list against your planner to insure that you stay in contact with them.

Step 4: Network

While Chapter 5 will give you the essentials of networking, it is important to remember that it's "who you know" that gets you ahead in the job search. Professional organizations are a great source for networking and gleaning vital information about employment. Get involved in organizations in your field of interest to keep abreast of opportunities as they become available. And don't forget to stay abreast of the business world in general through business magazines and newspapers (see Chapter 1 for listings).

If you are just starting your network, use the information interview (see Chapter 5) to find out more about a particular career field and to acquaint yourself with professionals in that field. People like to hire individuals they know, so the more potential employers you meet, the better your odds for landing a job.

Dear Dr. Bob
Is there job-search etiquette I should know about?—Proper Etiquette Job Searcher

Dear Proper Etiquette Job Searcher
As everywhere else, there exists proper etiquette in the job search. For example, the telephone is a wonderful tool by which an assertive job seeker can make contact with employers and follow-up on job applications and leads. However, reminding the employer of your interest in a position is not tantamount to badgering him or her into interviewing you. Follow every letter you mail with a phone call, but allow ample time for the employer to receive and review your credentials. One to two weeks is the usual rule of thumb.

Manic Monday mornings are a particularly unpleasant time for employers to receive phone calls. A better time is between 10 a.m. and 2 p.m. Tuesdays, Wednesdays, or Thursdays. And always check to see if you have called at a convenient time.

The fax machine can be a dangerous beast and should be used cautiously by the job searcher. Certainly it does offer instant communication with an employer. But unsolicited faxes are annoying to employers. Not only does it tie up the fax line and use expensive paper but it is likely that the hiring authority will not even see it. However, my advice is to fax only when requested to do so by a hiring authority.

Finally, treat the potential employer with the utmost respect. Be sure to keep meetings at the time you both agreed on. Follow up with a thank-you letter, reiterating your qualifications and thanking your host for his time. Try to keep everyone in your network informed of your status in the job search.

Step 5: Persistence and Follow-Up

Persistence is one of the key strategies in the job search. Whether you are pursuing job leads, sending out resumes, scheduling interviews, or contacting a hiring authority, you need to be persistent. The passive job searcher relies upon the want ads as his or her only source of job leads. The persistent job searcher is proactive, using resources such as networking groups, newspapers, professional organizations, and directories. The passive job searcher will accept "no" without questioning or pursuing the hiring authority. The persistent job searcher will make a few more calls. Being persistent can help you accomplish the ultimate goal—landing the job.

Persistence is also a state of mind. It's important to remain enthusiastic, to keep going, and to make calls. It is only too easy for the job searcher to lose energy and conveniently forget to make those important follow-up calls. Remember you most likely are just one of many applicants for a job, and persistence is the key to success. Plenty of rejection will probably come your way. It is up to you to keep going and put rejection behind you.

Follow-up all promising contacts with calls and letters. Whether you're networking or actually talking with someone in a position to hire you, it is important to stay in touch with whomever can assist you in your job search. If someone takes the time to give you a lead, it is only proper for you to inform the individual of the outcome.

Follow-up resumes with a phone call to ensure that your resume was received. It is impossible to get an interview if your resume got lost in the mail. Likewise, a thank-you note after an interview will keep your name foremost with the interviewer and less likely to be lost in the shuffle.

Our "silent" president speaks
Nothing in this world can take the place of persistence. Talent will not; nothing is more common than unsuccessful men with great talent.

Genius will not; unrewarded genius is almost a proverb.

Education will not; the world is full of educated derelicts.

Persistence and determination alone are omnipotent.
—*Calvin Coolidge*

Step 6: Prepare Your Resume

Writing a good resume and a cover letter to accompany it is important in marketing yourself and lining up interviews. Chapter 6 goes into detail on resume writing. It is important to remember that this step can be crucial to your other steps.

Remember that most resumes get about 20 seconds of the employer's time. Therefore, it is vital to keep the resume to one page and skimmable enough to grab the reader's attention. The following guidelines should help you develop a well-written resume:
- Tailor your resume to the potential job as much as possible.
- Information should be easy to skim and locate.
- Length should be one page and no more than two.
- Proofread your final version; then have someone else proofread it.
- The overall appearance should be professional.
- Printing should be done on a laser printer.

A cover letter should always accompany your resume. The purpose of the cover letter is to persuade the employer to read your resume and invite you for an interview. The cover letter should be sent to a specific person. It should be brief but provide enough information to entice the employer. The following information should be in the cover letter:
- The first paragraph should identify who you are, whether you were referred by someone, and what your objective is.
- The second paragraph is your chance to sell yourself. It should tell the employer why you are good for the company and what you can offer. Use facts and figures to describe your qualifications.

- The last paragraph is where you request an interview and state how you will follow up with the employer.

The cover letter and the resume are often the *first impression the employer will have of you*. Do your best in preparing them!

Step 7: Mail Your Resume

When sending your resume out, the Personnel Department is probably not your best target since their job is to screen out rather than welcome applicants. Understand that Personnel or Human Resources can help your career once you're in the company. However, your best initial target is the decision-maker who is the "hiring authority."

Mass Mailing

A common job-search technique is to research a list of companies and send off as many resumes and cover letters as possible. Then you wait for your hard work and many dollars in postage to pay off with a call back and an interview. Sometimes mass mailings work, but mostly they don't. We recommend the targeted mailing technique.

Targeted Mailing

A targeted mailing is one that focuses only on companies with jobs you know you are qualified for and in which you have names of specific hiring authorities. Most importantly, in a targeted mailing you must be prepared to follow-up with phone calls.

In doing your research about prospective companies you have come up with the names of many that you are interested in working for. Prioritize these companies and target the top 15—those you are most interested in. Send these a resume and carefully written cover letter directed to the individual who can help or hire you. Follow-up with a phone call. When you take a company off your list, add a new one.

Various directories and networking contacts will help you come up with names of individuals who could be in a position to help or hire you. Or a phone call to the company can sometimes secure the name of the right person to mail to. Never be afraid to mail letters to more than one person at a firm, especially at some of the larger companies, where the more people who see your resume and are in a position to do something about it, the better.

A targeted mailing cannot work without follow-up phone calls. Let the employer know you will be calling so that the resume remains on his or her desk, and make sure you call within 10 to 14 days after you send the letter.

Although we make this sound easy, contacting the hiring authority could require talking with two or three people in order to determine who the decision-maker is. It could take many phone calls and much follow-up, but don't get discouraged. The important thing is to get your resume in front of the right person and away from the resume graveyard.

Treat the secretaries/assistants with all the respect possible since they are essentially gatekeepers. They often have the power to grant or deny you access to a hiring authority. Getting off on the right foot with the secretary enhances your chances of talking directly with the more influential person. Treating the secretary/assistant as a professional is crucial since he or she often knows everything going on in the office and can give you access to the boss.

Step 8: Use Your Career Resources

Finding a good job is difficult and today the traditional job search is insufficient. You need to use every resource available, including employment agencies, executive search firms, social service agencies, government agencies, career consultants, college career centers, career fairs, and the Internet. Let's examine all of these.

Employment Agencies

Your first impulse may be to turn the job hunt over to a professional employment service. However, if you're a recent college graduate or offer no special or high-demand skills, employment agencies can be less than helpful. Those that specialize in temporary jobs are even less likely to lead you to your dream job. We recommend taking charge of your own job search since you know yourself and your goals better than anyone else. If you do decide to use employment services, become familiar with their operations and limitations. This will save you a lot of time, effort, and possibly money.

Employment agencies act as intermediaries in the job market between buyers (companies with jobs open) and sellers (people who want jobs). Agencies are paid either by the employer or the worker for placing people. Find out the total cost beforehand and how the fee is handled.

Employment agencies seldom place a candidate in a job that pays more than $50,000 a year. Most employment agencies concentrate on support jobs rather than middle or upper-management positions.

If you decide to use an agency, be sure it's a reputable firm. Ask people in your field to recommend a quality agency, and consult the Better Business Bureau to see if there have been any complaints about the agency you're considering. In California, employment agencies are no longer regulated by the State. Most important, read the contract thoroughly, including all the fine print, before signing anything. Remember, the agency is loyal to its source of income—usually the company. Finally, the job-search strategies an agency provides are all outlined in this book and you can implement most of them yourself.

A listing in this book does not constitute an endorsement of any agencies or firms. Before using a service, try to get the opinion of one or more people who have already used the service you're considering. You can also contact the following:

Better Business Bureau
P.O. Box 970
Colton, CA 90324
900-225-5222 (Fee charged)
http://www.colton.bbb.org
Serves Los Angeles, Orange, Riverside & San Bernardino counties.

San Diego Better Business Bureau
5050 Murphy Canyon, Suite 110
San Diego, CA 92123
(619) 496-2131
http://www.sddt.com/~bbb

Better Business Bureau via the Net
http://www.igc.apc.org/bbb/
This is the homepage of the Better Business Bureau. It offers a geographic directory of offices, list of publications, reliability reports on businesses, scam alerts, and more.

Below is a list of some local employment agencies, including their areas of specialty where possible.

SELECTED SOUTHERN CALIFORNIA EMPLOYMENT AGENCIES

Abigail Abbott Staffing Services
660 W. 1st St.
Tustin, CA 92680
(714) 731-7757
(619) 542-1310
Clerical, business administration, technical.

Accountants Exchange Personnel Services
5455 Wilshire Blvd.
Los Angeles, CA 90036
(213) 933-7411

The Affiliates
1901 Avenue of the Stars, Suite 350
Los Angeles, CA 90067
(310) 557-2334
Legal positions.

American Mobile Nurses
12730 High Bluff Drive, #400
San Diego, CA 92130
(619) 792-0711
Nurse placement.

Apple One Employment Services
5638 Mission Center Road, Suite 103
San Diego, CA 92108

Chosen Few Personnel Services
911 Wilshire Blvd., Suite 1880
Los Angeles, CA 90017
(213) 689-9400
Specializes in legal and financial support staff.

Excel Health Services
3420 S. Bristol., Suite 310
Costa Mesa, CA 92626
(714) 545-0500
Health care, nursing.

Lab Support
21660 E. Copley Drive, Suite 330
Diamond Bar, CA 91765
(909) 612-1070
San Diego: (619) 299-4811
Specializes in science placement.

Robert Half International
1901 Avenue of the Stars

Los Angeles, CA 90067
(310) 286-6800
Additional locations in Torrance, City of Industry, and Newport Beach.

Search West
1888 Century Park East, Suite 2050
Los Angeles, CA 90067
(310) 284-8888
Additional locations in Orange, Ontario, and Westlake Village.

Source EDP
4510 Executive Drive, Suite 200
San Diego, CA 92121
(619) 552-0300
Engineering, finance, accounting, computer personnel.

Source Finance
1 Park Plaza, Suite 560
Irvine, CA 92714
(714) 553-8115
Specializes in accounting and finance personnel.

Therapists Unlimited
3131 Camino del Rio N., Suite 370
San Diego, CA 92108
(619) 285-0942

Executive Search Firms

Executive search firms are paid by companies to locate people with specific qualifications to meet a precisely defined employment need. Most reputable executive search firms belong to an organization called the Association of Executive Recruiting Consultants (AERC). A search firm never works on a contingency basis. Only employment agencies do that. Because the company has to pay a large fee, they may opt to forgo using an executive search firm during hard times.

Yet, if you choose to use an executive search firm, as specialists who know the market they can be very helpful in providing advice and leads. Keep in mind that you are only useful to the search firm if there is an assignment that matches your background and qualifications exactly.

Dear Dr. Bob

I have recently graduated and was considering using an executive search firm to simplify my job search. What do you recommend?—Recently Confused Graduate

Dear Recently Confused Graduate

Unless you are middle to upper-management, the search firm will not be interested in helping you. Since the search firm looks for candidates with highly developed skills in a particular area, your experience may seem inadequate compared to the candidate with 15 years of work history. For the present time, try the techniques in this book to land a job on your own.

Below is a list of local executive search firms, including their areas of specialty. For a full listing of executive search consultants, see *The Directory of Executive Recruiters* (Kennedy Publications, Fitzwilliam, NH).

SOUTHERN CALIFORNIA EXECUTIVE SEARCH FIRMS

Computer Professionals Unlimited
5942 Edinger Ave., Suite 113
Huntington Beach, CA 92649
(714) 891-1244
Specializes in software development.

Eastridge Environmental Search
P.O. Box 33745
San Diego, CA 92163
(619) 260-2043
Environmental health and safety professionals.

Fortune Personnel Consultants
5300 W. Century Blvd., Suite 208
Los Angeles, CA 90045
(310) 410-9662

Heidrick and Struggles
300 S. Grand Ave., Suite 2400
Los Angeles, CA 90071
(213) 625-8811

Intech Summit Group
5057 Shoreham Place, Suite 280
San Diego, CA 92122
(619) 452-2100
Specializes in health care, human resources, high-tech.

Korn-Ferry International
1800 Century Park East, Suite 900
Los Angeles, CA 90067
(310) 552-1834

Paul Ray Company
2029 Century Park East, Suite 1000
Los Angeles, CA 90067
(310) 557-2828

Russell Reynolds Associates
333 S. Grand Ave., 42nd Floor
Los Angeles, CA 90071
(213) 489-1520

Ward Howell
16255 Ventura Blvd., Suite 400
Encino, CA 91436
(818) 905-6010

Social Service Agencies with Job Resources

Unlike professional employment agencies, career consultants (see farther on), and executive search firms, social service agencies are not-for-profit. They offer a wide range of services, from counseling and vocational testing to job placement and follow-up—and their services are either low cost or free. Below is a list of social service agencies in the area.

One-stop shopping for social services
There are hundreds of social service agencies in Southern California. To help you find the services, fees, and client qualifications that meet your specific needs, check out the Los Angeles, Orange, and San Bernardino County Social Service Directories. These directories are organized by topic area. Address, phone, fees (if any), qualification

requirements, and description of services offered are listed. These directories are particularly useful for finding programs for people with disabilities, hearing or sight impairments, veterans, immigrants, displaced homemakers, and others with specific needs.

LOS ANGELES SOCIAL SERVICE AGENCIES

Chicana Service Action Center
134 E. 1st St.
Los Angeles, CA 90012
(213) 253-5959
Provides job training and vocational rehabilitation services.

Goodwill Industries of Southern California
342 San Fernando Road
Los Angeles, CA 90031
(213) 223-1211
Employment, training, and job placement for disabled adults.

Jewish Vocational Service
6505 Wilshire Blvd., Suite 303
Los Angeles, CA 90048
(213) 655-8910
Main location. Three other Los Angeles locations. Offers nonsectarian workshops, job-support groups, job listings, career testing and counseling. Sliding fee scale.

Los Angeles Gay & Lesbian Community Services Center
1625 N. Schrader Blvd.
Los Angeles, CA 90028
(213) 993-7480
Offers job postings, employment services.

Santa Monica YWCA
Aware Advisory
2019 14th St.
Santa Monica, CA 90405
(310) 452-3833
Provides vocational testing and counseling.

Southern California Indian Center
3600 Wilshire Blvd., Suite 226
Los Angeles, CA 90057
(213) 387-5772
Placement services, job-search training.

Urban League of Los Angeles
3450 Mt. Vernon
Los Angeles, CA 90080
(213) 299-9660
Provides employment services, sponsors annual job fair. Call to register for an orientation session.

Women Helping Women
543 N. Fairfax Ave.
Los Angeles, CA 90036
(213) 655-3807
Job clubs and career workshops for women.

ORANGE COUNTY SOCIAL SERVICE AGENCIES

Catholic Charities
Employment Services
2301 W. Lincoln Ave., Suite 112
Anaheim, CA 92801
(714) 635-5230
Free employment services.

Goodwill Industries/Orange County
410 N. Fairview Road
Santa Ana, CA 92701
(714) 547-6308 x324
Provides job training and placement to disabled adults.

84 How To Get a Job

Orange County Urban League
12391 Lewis St., Suite 102
Garden Grove, CA 92640
(714) 748-9976
Offers employment assistance, sponsors job fairs focused on minority hiring.

Orange Resource Center
City of Orange
210 N. McPherson St.
Orange, CA 92665
(714) 633-2753
Offers free job placement services.

SAN DIEGO SOCIAL SERVICE AGENCIES

Deaf Community Services of San Diego
3788 Park Blvd.
San Diego, CA 92103
(619) 497-2811
Interpreting, job placement.

Occupational Training Services
8799 Balboa Ave., Suite 100
San Diego, CA 92123
(619) 560-0411

San Diego Career Center Network
8401 Aero Drive
San Diego, CA 92123
(619) 974-7620

Provides career assessment, job-skills training, job-search assistance.

San Diego Consortium & Private Industry Council
1551 4th Ave., Suite 600
San Diego, CA 92101
(619) 238-1445

San Diego Regional Occupational Program
6401 Linda Vista Road
San Diego, CA 92111
(619) 292-3758
Job training and free public education.

Government Agencies with Job Resources
Many job seekers do not take advantage of the free job listings offered by the city, county, and state. Call or stop in the following offices and check out the local listings.

SELECTED CALIFORNIA EMPLOYMENT DEVELOPMENT DEPARTMENTS

Anaheim
900 E. Gene Autry Way
Anaheim, CA 92805
(714) 978-7421

Fullerton
233 E. Commonwealth Ave.
Fullerton, CA 92632
(714) 680-7800

Garden Grove
12661 Hoover St.
Garden Grove, CA 92642
(714) 897-3699

San Fernando
1520 San Fernando Road
San Fernando, CA 91340
(818) 365-4637

Torrance
1220 Engracia Ave.
Torrance, CA 90501
(310) 782-2163

West Covina
933 S. Glendora Ave.
West Covina, CA 91790
(818) 962-7011

West Los Angeles
10829 Venice Blvd.
Los Angeles, CA 90034
(310) 280-2830

LOCAL GOVERNMENT EMPLOYMENT OFFICES

City of Los Angeles
Personnel Department
700 E. Temple St., Room 100
Los Angeles, CA
(213) 847-9424
http://www.ci.la.ca.us/dept/PER/index.htm

City of San Diego
Employment Information Office
202 C St.
San Diego, CA 92101
(619) 236-6467

County of San Diego
Department of Human Resources
1600 Pacific Hwy., Room 207
San Diego, CA 92101
(619) 531-5764

San Diego Job Corps
1325 Iris Ave.
Imperial Beach, CA 91932
(619) 429-8500

Career Consultants

Career consultants vary greatly in the kind and quality of the services they provide. Some may offer a single service, such as vocational testing or preparing resumes. Others coach every aspect of the job search and stay with you until you accept an offer. The fees vary just as broadly and range from $100 to several thousand dollars. You, not your potential employer, pay the fee.

A qualified career consultant can be an asset to your job search. But no consultant can get you a job. A consultant can help you focus on an objective, develop a resume, teach you to research the job market, decide on a strategy, and provide interviewing techniques. But in the end, the consultant can't interview for you. You are responsible.

The only time you should consider a consultant is after you've exhausted all the other resources we've suggested here and still feel you need expert and personalized help with one or more aspects of the job search. The key to choosing a career consultant is knowing what you need and verifying that the consultant can provide it.

Check references. A reputable firm will gladly provide them. Check the Better Business Bureau and get referrals from friends who have used a consultant. Before signing anything, ask to meet the consultant who will actually provide the services you want. What are their credentials? How long have they been practicing? What does the consultant promise? What is required from you? How long can you use the consultant's services? Be sure to shop around before selecting a consultant. Refer to Chapter 2 for a list of possible counselors.

College Career Centers

If you are in college and are not acquainted with your school's career center, make a point to stop by and check out the services available. Colleges and universities usually provide services to their alumni and members of the local community also.

There is more to a college career center than just job postings. It's a great resource for building your network, researching the job market, and seeking counseling to establish a career strategy. And most colleges and universities also offer services such as vocational testing and interpretation and the use of the resource library to the general public. Refer to Chapter 2 for a listing of local colleges and universities and the career services provided to students, alumni, and the general public.

Career Fairs

Another job-search resource that can help is the ubiquitous career fair. Career fairs are the shopping malls for job searchers. Employers line up to market their companies and job opportunities. Job searchers browse the aisles, often stopping when a particularly glitzy brochure or big company name catches their eye. And like the shopping mall, employers want to sell, sell, sell their opportunities while job searchers want to snatch up great deals.

Career fairs are a job shopper's delight. The large number of employers in one place makes it easy to research many companies. Additionally, career fairs afford the job searcher a chance to meet face to face with company representatives, often an advantage for people who make a better impression in person than on paper. Finally, at some career fairs candidates can actually interview for jobs with prospective employers during the event.

Career fairs are most often advertised in the classified section of the newspaper. Professional associations will also frequently receive announcements. Colleges and universities often sponsor career fairs and post announcements of these and other events. Some coordinators of career fairs will even put up billboards and advertise on television.

As more and more employers rely on career fairs to meet qualified applicants, the savvy job searcher must be comfortable attending these events. These few tips will help you more effectively use a career fair.

- Prior to the fair, get a list of the companies attending in order to begin researching potential employers. Knowing what a company does allows you to use the precious few minutes you will have with a company representative to sell yourself rather than ask basic questions about the company's products.
- Plan a strategy. Use your research to prioritize the companies you want to talk with. Sequence the companies according to which companies you must, without a doubt, talk with before the end of the fair.
- Arrive early the day of the fair in order to scope out the facilities and meet with company representatives before lines get too long. Familiarize yourself with the location of employers, the flow of traffic, and the layout of the building.

- Avoid wasting time in long lines to talk to big-name employers, even if they have great company give-away goodies. Smaller employers and their representatives will have less traffic, which means that you may be able to spend more time talking with him or her and making a positive impression.
- Take the initiative in approaching employers. Prepare a short two-to-three-minute "infomercial" about yourself so that you can quickly acquaint employers with your background. Have a list of questions ready for employers so that you don't have to suffer angst while trying to decide what to say to him or her.
- Bring lots of resumes and be prepared to leave them with any employer who interests you. Before leaving the career fair, revisit your favorite employers and leave your resume with them again to make sure your name does not get lost in the pile.

The shopping mall was created as a convenience to vendors who want lots of consumers and consumers who want lots of vendors in one easy place; the career fair provides the same convenience to job searchers and employers. A successful strategy will help you avoid lost time and hopefully get you inside the company for a proper interview later.

CAREER FAIR ORGANIZATIONS

There is no one-stop-shopping list or single source of information on job and career fairs in Southern California. However, here are some suggestions:

http://www.espan.com/js/jobfair.html
Lists career fairs geographically.

http://www.jobsamerica.com/jalocations.html
Hosts job fairs in conjunction with local urban leagues.

http://199.107.14.123
Newspaper-sponsored job fairs nationwide.

http://www.jobweb.org/cfairsr.htm
Lists college career fairs, searchable by state.

http://www.vjf.com/
Virtual job fair.

Los Angeles Times
(213) 237-5000
Sponsors annual job fair. Look for promotions/special supplements in the *Los Angeles Times*.

Orange County Urban League
(714) 748-9976
Sponsors job fairs focusing on minority hiring.

Urban League of Los Angeles
(213) 299-9660
Sponsors annual Career Connections job fair, usually in the fall.

Westech Career Expo
(408) 970-4970
Produces high-tech job fairs in Los Angeles and other California cities.

Internet Job Listings

Use the Net as another source of job listings. Below are a few places to begin; you can surf the Net and find many others.

WORLD WIDE WEB JOB-SEARCH SOURCES

America's Job Bank
http://www.ajb.dni.us/
Federal program listing 500,000 openings. May eventually include the jobs posted with state unemployment offices nationwide.

Big Book
http://www.bigbook.com/
Search nationwide *Yellow Pages* by city, state, industry, or company name.

Business Job Finder
http://www.cob.ohio-state.edu/~fin/osujobs/htm
Industry descriptions and company links in finance, accounting, and management.

Career Channel
http://riceinfo.rice.edu:80/projects/careers/
Rice University lists jobs, links, and a wealth of other job-search information.

Career Connections
http://www.employmentedge.com/employment.edge/
Specializes in professional career placement throughout the U.S.

Career Magazine
http://www.careermag.com/careermag/
A comprehensive resource that includes job-opening database, employer profiles, articles, and news to assist in the career search and career forums.

CareerNet
http://www.careers.org/
A good source, with links to many other job-listing organizations.

CareerPath
http://www.careerpath.com
Los Angeles Times (and five other major dailies) classifieds.

CareerWeb
http://www.cweb.com/
Job seekers can browse worldwide career opportunities, including the *Wall Street Journal National Business Employment Weekly.*

Catapult
http://www.jobweb.org/catapult/catapult.htm
Serves as a starting point for career-service practitioners and students, covering topics from resumes to job listings.

Employment Opportunities and Resume Postings—EINet
http://galaxy.einet.net/
A guide to worldwide information and services.

E-Span
http://www.espan.com/
Provides a searchable database of high-tech job openings as well as a wide variety of resources for the job seeker.

Help Wanted
http://www.webcom.com/
On-line employment services.

JobCenter
http://www.jobcenter.com
Matches job searcher's skills with employer's needs.

Job Hunt Meta-List
http://rescomp.stanford.edu/jobs.html

JobTrak
http://www.jobtrak.com/
Database of employment opportunities open to students and alumni of registered colleges. Free to job seekers.

JobWeb
http://www.jobweb.org
National Association of Colleges and Employers. Primarily targeted at college students, JobWeb offers career planning and employment information, job-search articles, and job listings.

Monster Board
http://www.monster.com/
Companies around the country list jobs along with employer profiles. Search for jobs by location, industry, company, and discipline.

Online Career Center
http://www.occ.com/
Includes job listings from over 300 U.S. companies. Browse by job title, company name, or geographic region.

PursuitNet Jobs
http://www.tiac.net/users/job
Job-search service matches skills and desires with compatible jobs in the U.S.

Recruiters Online Network
http://www.onramp.net
Recruiters, employment agencies, search firms, and employment professionals share business opportunities and job postings.

Today's Classifieds
http://www.nando.net/classads/
Internet users can search classifieds by career field.

Top Jobs
http://www.topjobsusa.com/
Database of jobs in the western U.S.

JOB LINKS SPECIFIC TO SOUTHERN CALIFORNIA

California Career & Employment Center
http://webcom/~career/welcome.html
Links to several job databases, including Help Wanted USA.

Federal Government Jobs in California
ftp://ftp.fedworld.gov/pub/jobs/ca.txt

Job Source
http://www.sddt.com/jobsource
High-tech job listings in San Diego.

Los Angeles Times Job Tips/Classifieds
http://www.latimes.com/HOME/CLASS/EMPLOY/
Job tips, advice from career counselors, review *Los Angeles Times* classifieds by key word.

San Diego Jobs
http://www.sandiegojobs.com/
Direct links to San Diego companies.

San Diego Union-Tribune Interactive Job Listings
http://www.uniontrib.com/aboutut/
Search the *Union-Tribune*'s classifieds.

Step 9: The Killer Interview

The killer interview consists of three parts: preparation, success during the interview, and follow-up. We'll highlight key aspects of this process. However, Chapter 7 discusses the interview in greater detail.

Preparation
Before any interview, you need to prepare and practice in order to do the best job possible in selling yourself to the employer. Follow this procedure for best results:
- Identify your strengths, skills, goals, and personal qualities. Self-assessment is crucial to knowing what you have to offer an employer and to conveying it effectively. Try to come up with five unique strengths. Have examples of how you have used them professionally.
- Research the company in order to ask intelligent questions. An interview is suppose to be a dialogue; you want to learn about them just as they want to learn about you.
- Rehearse what you plan to say during the interview. Practice answers to commonly asked questions and determine how you will emphasize your strengths and skills.
- Dress professionally and conservatively. If you make a negative first impression, you may not be fairly considered for the job. Refer to Chapter 7 for dressing tips in the interview.

Success During the Interview
Chapter 7 covers what interviewers are looking for. Below are some additional tips to help you succeed in your interview.
- Arrive on time or ten minutes early. This will ensure you the full amount of time allotted and show that you are enthusiastic about the position.
- The first five minutes of the interview can be extremely important. To start your interview off right, offer a firm handshake and smile, make good eye contact, and say something to break the ice. "Nice to meet you," or something of that sort, should clear your throat nicely and prepare you for more substantive conversation.
- As you begin the interview, be aware of non-verbal behavior. Wait to sit until you are offered a chair. Look alert, speak in a clear, strong voice, try to stay relaxed, avoid nervous mannerisms, and try to be a good listener as well as a good talker.
- Be specific, concrete, and detailed in your answers. The more information you volunteer, the better the employer gets to know you and thereby is able to make a wise hiring decision. But *don't* be longwinded.
- Always have questions for the interviewer.
- Don't mention salary in a first interview unless the employer does. If asked, give a realistic range and add that opportunity is the most important factor for you.
- Offer examples of your work and references that will document your best qualities.
- Answer questions as truthfully as possible. Never appear to be "glossing

over" anything. If the interviewer ventures into ticklish political or social questions, answer honestly but try not to say more than is necessary.
- Never make derogatory remarks about present or former employers or companies. Make sure you look very positive in the interviewer's eyes.

Follow-Up

The following suggestions will help you survive the "awful waiting" time after the interview.

- Don't get discouraged if no definite offer is made or specific salary discussed.
- If you feel the interview isn't going well, don't let your discouragement show. Occasionally an interviewer who is genuinely interested in you may seem to discourage you to test your reaction.
- At the end of the interview, ask when a hiring decision will be made. This is important not only because it reconfirms your interest in the position but also so you'll know when to expect a response.
- Send a thank-you letter to the interviewer: thank him or her for the time and effort; reiterate your skills and qualifications for the position; and make clear your interest in the job.
- Make notes on what you feel you could improve upon for your next interview and on what you feel went particularly well. After all, experience is only valuable to the extent that you're willing to learn from it.
- If offered the position, up to two weeks is a reasonable amount of time to make your decision. All employment offers deserve a written reply, whether or not you accept them.

You will learn a great deal about patience during the waiting period that follows an interview. The important point to remember during this time is that all your hopes shouldn't be dependent on one or two interviews. The job search is continuous and shouldn't stop until you have accepted an offer. Keeping all your options open is the best possible course.

Keep in contact with the company if they haven't responded by the date they indicated in the interview. Asking the status of your application is a legitimate question. This inquiry should be stated in a manner that is not pushy but shows your continued interest in the company.

Step 10: Make Sure This Is the Job for You

Start celebrating! You have received a job offer after working so diligently on the job search. But before you accept or decline, consider the offer carefully. Make sure the details of the offer are clear; preferably, get them in writing. Details should include starting date, salary and benefits, location, job description and responsibilities, and the date by which you must respond. Evaluating a job offer can be both exciting and difficult. We have provided the following information to assist you in making a job decision.

Negotiating Salary

Be aware of what other people in similar positions are making before accepting any offer. The *Occupational Outlook Handbook,* put out by the U.S. Department of Labor every two years, cites salary statistics by field. Another good source of information is *The American Almanac of Jobs and Salaries* by John Wright, published by Avon. Professional societies and associations frequently provide this sort of information too. It's one more good reason to belong to one.

When negotiating salary, proceed with care to prevent jeopardizing a positive relationship with your new employer. Here are some points in negotiating salaries:

- Be prepared with salary research before discussing any figures.
- Approach the session with trust and a willingness to compromise.
- Know when to stop. Don't push your luck.
- Be open to substituting other benefits in exchange for a higher salary.

The end result should be that both parties are happy with the outcome.

For advice on how to get the salary you want, we recommend these books:

BOOKS ON SALARY NEGOTIATION

Chapman, Jack. *How to Make $1000 a Minute.* Berkeley, CA: Ten Speed Press, 1987.

Chastain, Sherry. *Winning the Salary Game: Salary Negotiation For Women.* New York: John Wiley & Sons, 1980.

Fisher, Roger, and William Levy. *Getting to Yes: Negotiating Agreement Without Giving In.* New York: Penguin Books, 1992.

Kennedy, Marilyn Moats. *Getting the Job You Want & The Money You're Worth.* American College of Executives, 1987.

Krannich, Ronald L., and Rae. *Salary Success: Know What You're Worth and Get It.* Woodbridge, VA: Impact Publications, 1990.

Compare the Offers on Paper

Don't blindly accept the first offer you receive. You've put a great deal of effort in the job search, so spend a little more time in comparing the relative merits of each offer. Below is a sample checklist to assist you in this endeavor. The idea is to list the factors that you consider important in any job, and then assign a rating for how well each offer fills the bill in each particular area.

We've listed some factors that should be considered before accepting any offer. Some may not be relevant to your situation. Others that we've left out may be of great importance to you. So feel free to make any additions, deletions, or changes you want. Assign a rating (1 being the lowest and 5 the highest) for each factor under each offer. Then total the scores.

The offer with the most points is not necessarily the one to accept. The chart doesn't take into account the fact that "responsibilities" may be more important to you than "career path," or that you promised yourself you'd never punch a time clock again. Nevertheless, looking at the pros and cons of each offer in black and white should help you make a much more methodical and logical decision.

Factor	Offer A	Offer B
Responsibilities	_____	_____
Company reputation	_____	_____
Salary	_____	_____
Vacation leave	_____	_____
Insurance/Pension	_____	_____
Profit sharing	_____	_____
Tuition reimbursement	_____	_____
On-the-job training	_____	_____
Career path advancement	_____	_____
Company future	_____	_____
Product/service quality	_____	_____
Location (housing market, schools, transportation)	_____	_____
Boss(es)	_____	_____
Co-workers	_____	_____
Travel	_____	_____
Overtime	_____	_____
Other _____	_____	_____
TOTAL POINTS	_____	_____

Evaluating Job Offers

A job involves more than a title and salary. Before you accept any offer, be sure you understand what your responsibilities will be, what benefits you'll receive besides salary (insurance, profit sharing, vacation, tuition reimbursement, etc.), how much overtime is required (and whether you'll be paid for it), how much travel is involved in the job, who your supervisor will be, how many people you'll supervise, and where the position could lead (do people in this position get promoted?). In short, find out anything and everything you can to evaluate the offer.

The cost of living is essential in comparing job offers in different cities. The difference in the cost of living can mean living like royalty in Houston or struggling in New York, even if the salaries offered seem relatively close. To compare cost of living, check the Consumer Price Indexes provided by the Bureau of Labor Statistics.

It seems obvious that it's unwise to choose a job solely on the basis of salary. Consider all the factors, such as your boss and colleagues and the type of work you'll be doing, before making any final decision.

Corporate Cultures
Every company has a different corporate culture (philosophies and management style) and some fit better with your own personality than others. Thus it is important to research the company's culture in your career search. Specific companies are discussed in the following books:

Kanter, Rosabeth Moss, and Barry A. Stein. *Life in Organizations.* New York: Basic Books, 1979.
Levering, Robert, and Milton Moskowitz. *The 100 Best Companies To Work For In America.* New York: Doubleday, 1993.
Peters, Thomas J., and Robert H. Waterman, Jr. *In Search of Excellence.* New York: Warner Books, 1982.
Peters, Thomas J., and Nancy Austin. *Passion for Excellence.* New York: Random House, 1985.
Plunkett, Jack. *The Almanac of American Employers.* Boerne, TX: Corporate Jobs Outlook, 1994.

It is also possible to decipher a company's culture during the interview. The following are factors worth examining:
- What is the environment like? Look at the appearance of the office, the company newsletter, brochures, and bulletin boards.
- Who is on board? How does the company greet strangers, what kind of people work for them, and why is the company a success (or failure)?
- How are employees rewarded? Look at the benefits, awards, compensation, and recognition given to employees.
- What is the fashion statement? Look at the dress code. Are there different dress styles for levels of employment?
- How do people spend their time? Look at the ambience of the workplace and what an average day is like.
- How do managers behave? Look at the history of the company, how things get done, and the management style.

Is the Job a Dream or a Nightmare?
Dream jobs sometimes do turn into nightmare employment. It happens all the time. How do you avoid this possibility? Look for the eight danger signs of the "job from hell."

Financial problems and corporate turmoil. Prospective employees rarely do financial or management research on a company in which they are interested. It will behoove you to find out if the firm is financially sound and if there has been much turmoil within the company.

Layoffs indicate danger. Many companies try to convince new employees that recent layoffs will have no affect on their position. Don't believe it! A good indication of a job about to go bad is that mass layoffs have recently occurred.

Recent mergers or acquisitions can be another danger signal. Companies that have bought or merged with another company are usually trying to reduce expenses. And the easiest way for the corporate world to reduce expenses is to cut employees and reorganize. The chances of you working in the position you interviewed for will diminish with reorganization. Being new, you may also be one of the first to be laid off or transferred.

Word on the street. What is the informal word about your new potential workplace? Word of mouth is often a good source of inside information about the reality of working for a particular company. Try to eliminate gossip and scuttlebutt from those who are naturally and overly negative. But if a general consensus exists that a company is not good to its employees or that people are unusually unhappy, carefully weigh your decision.

Turnover within your position. How many people have worked in your new position during the last couple of years? Is your particular job one that experiences a great deal of turnover? High turnover should alert you to the possibility that either the job is horrible and no one can stand it or that no one is really capable of doing this job, including you. Percentages show that those who take jobs with high turnover rates are very likely to become a statistic as well.

Elusive or vague job description. A key danger signal is the absence of or vagueness in your job description. Look for a job where the duties are known up front. It's fine for some things about a job to be determined later, and you certainly want your responsibilities to be increased, but don't take a job in which you are not sure what your primary duties will be or to whom you will report.

"Bad boss" potential. Don't discount the boss's influence on your job performance or your satisfaction within a job. Most employees spend more waking time with a boss than with their spouse. Try to meet your boss before you accept the job and ask yourself if you are ready to live with him or her on a daily basis. As we have mentioned before, your boss should be a role model. He or she should help you grow and develop in your career. If you have doubts about your boss, you should have doubts about the job.

That gut feeling. Finally, you can never discount that deep-down feeling you get about your job offer. Even when the pay and benefits are great, you still might have mixed emotions about a particular job. Explore those emotions and find out why they are "mixed." They may be more than a premonition.

Even if a job looks like a winner, if you see one or more of these danger signs, do a little more research before you accept. Don't wind up a major loser.

Network, Network, Network: The Best Job-Search Technique

What's the difference between knowing a lot of people and having an influential network? If you're a smart job searcher, you will realize that knowing a lot of people is just the start. It is the process of staying in touch with people and building strong connections that creates an influential and powerful network. While the old axiom "it's not what you know but who you know" may be an overstatement for all job searches, savvy job seekers combine ingenuity and creativity to use who they know to help them find jobs in which they can use what they know.

For many people, networking has a negative connotation. It implies cocktail parties, insincere conversation, and golf games with people you don't really like. In reality, however, job networking is simply asking people you know for information about careers and employment. You may already be networking and not know it!

The Six Myths of Networking

In order to encourage more networking, let's start by debunking some common myths.

MYTH #1: People get jobs through ads and other formal announcements. The truth is that fewer than 20 percent of available jobs are ever advertised. The majority of jobs are in the "hidden job market." Mark S. Granovetter, a Harvard sociologist, reported to *Forbes* magazine that informal contacts, or networks, account for almost 75 percent of successful job searches. Agencies find about 9 percent of new jobs for professional and technical people, and ads yield about another 10 percent.

If those figures don't convince you to begin networking, how about these. A recent study found that employers preferred using networks to hire new employees because it reduced recruiting costs and decreased the risks associated with hiring a new, unknown employee. Furthermore, people who use networking are generally more satisfied with the job they land and tend to have higher incomes.

MYTH #2: Networking is so effective, you can ignore more traditional means of job searching, such as responding to ads. This is simply not true. As important as networking is to your job search, you will shorten the time you spend looking for a job if you use more methods. The average job seeker only uses a few of the available job-search techniques. No wonder job searches take so long! Networking complements your other techniques, not replaces them. Don't put all your eggs in one basket; use as many options as possible.

MYTH #3: Networking is only effective for people who are very assertive. If you were asking people for jobs, this might be true. However, networking is just asking people for information for your job search, which requires you to be polite but not overly assertive.

If you are uncomfortable contacting people, start your network with people you know well or with whom you have some connection: you go to the same church, you are both members of the same alumni association, etc. Talking with friends and family is less intimidating than approaching strangers. Networking in friendly territory will help you develop confidence in your approach and know what questions to ask.

MYTH #4: The job hunter's most important networking contacts within a company are in the HR department. If you limit your network to human resources personnel, you will be waiting a long time for a job. Only one person in four gets their job by relying strictly on personnel offices. Human resources people are there to help others hire. Find those "others."

The purpose of networking is to talk to as many people as possible. Sometimes people only tangentially related to the hiring process can provide you with valuable information about your industry, tips on companies that may be hiring, or names of other contacts.

MYTH #5: No one knows enough people to network effectively. Most people know an average of 200 people. Even if only 20 people you know can help you with your job search, those 20 can refer you to 400 additional people, and your network has taken off.

Certainly if you're moving to a new town, your list of contacts will be small. You must act to develop it. Find out about your local alumni association, join a church, join professional associations, and attend as many social functions as possible. Meet people!

MYTH #6: Once you've found a job, there is no need to keep up with your network. Absolutely false. Write a thank-you note immediately after meeting with someone who was helpful with your job search. Once you've landed a job, let your network know and periodically touch base with them.

Networking as a waiter

Eric, a recent college graduate, was interested in getting a job in the very competitive field of advertising. While waiting for interviews to roll in, he waited tables at a local pub in order to pay the bills.

One night, several months and part-time jobs after graduation, Eric struck up a conversation with a group of people that had stopped by after work. After learning that they worked for a large advertising agency, Eric told them about his job search, collected their business cards, and contacted the office the following week. Eric's personality, resume, and samples impressed the office staff so much that they invited him for an interview. He got the job.

Step-by-Step Guide to Networking

To begin the networking process, draw up a list of all the people you know who might help you gain access to someone who can hire you for the job you want. Naturally, the first sources, the ones at the top of your list, will be people you know personally: friends, colleagues, former clients, relatives, acquaintances, customers, and club or church members. Just about everyone you know, whether or not he or she is employed, can generate contacts for you.

Don't forget to talk with your banker, lawyer, insurance agent, dentist, and other people who provide you with services. It is the nature of their business to know lots of people who might help you in your search. Leave no stone unturned in your search for contacts. Go through your holiday-card list, college yearbook, club membership directories, and any other list you can think of.

The next step is to expand your network to include new people who can help you. The easiest way to do this is to ask each of the people you do know for the names of two or three other people who might be helpful in your job search.

Professional organizations are another resource. If you are changing careers, you should view professional organizations as essential to your job search. Most groups meet on a regular basis and are an excellent way to contact other people in your field. Some professional associations offer placement services to members. Many chambers of commerce publish directories of the professional and trade associations that meet in your area. Local business magazines and newspapers also publish times and locations for meetings of professional associations.

Your college alumni association is another resource to expand your network. Alumni club meetings provide opportunities to catch up on happenings with your alma mater and meet other professionals in your area. Additionally, some schools maintain alumni databases for the express purpose of networking. This is a valuable resource for both seasoned professionals and recent college grads looking for a job lead and a friendly face. Still other alumni associations offer resume referral services that you can join for a small fee.

The Information Interview

There are situations, however, when your existing network simply won't be adequate. If you're changing careers, you may not know enough people in your new field to help you. If you've just moved to a new area, your network may still be in Iowa. Your situation may require you to creatively build a new network. One of the best techniques for doing this is the "information interview."

Information interviewing is a technique for developing contacts by interviewing people for job-search information. This technique acknowledges that names of contacts are easy to find but relationships that can help you find a job require additional action on your part.

First, telephone or write to possible contacts whom you've identified through lists of acquaintances, professional associations, your alumni organization, or simply a cold call. Explain that you are very interested in his or her field, and arrange a twenty-minute appointment. Be very clear that you are not asking him or her for a job but only for information. Also, never ask new people out to lunch. It is too time consuming and lunch isn't as important to the business person as it may be to the job searcher. Don't give someone a reason to turn you down. Twenty minutes is enough time for you to get information without imposing on your host.

The information interview is the time to ask your contact questions about the field, the job market, and job-hunting tips. Ask your contact to review your resume and make recommendations about how to present yourself or fill in gaps in your experience. Most importantly, ask your contact for the names of two or three other people to talk with, thus expanding your network. And always follow up with a thank-you letter.

QUESTIONS TO ASK IN AN INFORMATION INTERVIEW

Job Function Questions
What do people with a job like yours do?
What does your typical day consist of?
What do you like/dislike about your work?
Who are the key people in your field?
What skills are necessary for your position?

Company Questions
What has been the major achievement of this organization?
How often do you interact with top management?
What trends do you foresee for this organization and in the field?
What is the company's corporate culture like?
Who are your major competitors?

Career Field Questions
What is the growth potential in your field for the next five years?
What journals or magazines should I read?
What professional organizations do you recommend?
Who else would you recommend that I talk with?

Information interviews not only help build your network but they can identify career paths, potential employers, worthwhile professional associations, and weaknesses in your work or educational background. Most importantly, learning to glean information is a skill that will serve you throughout your life.

Example of an Information Interview Letter

Rich Smith
6613 Barron
Irvine, CA 92714
(714) 555-3367

April 11, 1997

Dr. David Hart
President
Environmental Research

Dear Dr. Hart:

Dr. Young, with whom I have studied these past two years, suggested that you might be able to advise me of opportunities in the environmental engineering field.

I am about to graduate from the university with a B.S. in civil engineering, and I am a member of Phi Beta Kappa. For two of the last three summers, I have worked as an intern with the Air Pollution Control Association.

I am eager to begin work and would appreciate a few minutes of your time to discuss trends in environmental research and, as a newcomer, gain the benefit of your advice regarding a career. Exams are finished on June 6, and I would like to arrange a meeting with you shortly thereafter. I look forward to hearing from you and in any case will be in touch with your office next week.

Sincerely,

Rich Smith

Information interview letter tips:
- Keep it short and direct.
- Tell enough about yourself to demonstrate that you are sincere and qualified.
- Always conclude with a date when you'll call, and always call if they haven't called you by that date.

Admittedly, networking will not work in every situation. No amount of networking will help you land a job for which you do not have the minimum qualifications. Nor will networking work if you try to meet with people at a much higher professional level than your own. A CEO will likely be unwilling to help someone looking for an entry-level position. You can also make people unwilling to help you by being pushy and demanding. But if you avoid these pitfalls, you should develop a great network.

Do You Know Your Networking Net Worth?

To determine the net worth of your networking ability, take the following quiz to assess how you approach people at professional meetings, social events, and community functions. For each statement, circle Y for yes or N for no.

Y N 1. I belong to at least one professional or trade association in which I can meet people in my field.

Y N 2. In the past year, I have used my contacts to help at least two people meet someone of importance to them.

Y N 3. In the last month, I have attended at least two functions in order to meet people who are potential professional contacts.

Y N 4. When I meet new professional contacts, I ask them for a business card and make notes on the back about our conversation.

Y N 5. When asked, "What kind of job are you looking for?" I can answer in two sentences or less.

Y N 6. I keep in touch with former classmates and workmates.

Y N 7. I have given colleagues information to help them solve a problem.

Y N 8. I always know at least 25 professionals in my field well enough to call and say, "Hi, this is (my name)," and they know who I am.

Y N 9. When attending professional or social functions, I introduce myself to new people and show interest in their careers.

Y N 10. I am involved in at least one community or social organization outside work.

Count how many times you circled Y, then analyze your score:

0-4   You can make your job search easier by learning the basics of networking.

5-8   You can give and get even more out of your professional networks.

9-10 You're well on your way to feeling the power of networking in your job search!

Networking Etiquette

There are, of course, many ways in which to network, and for each method you must know the rules, or the etiquette, of networking.

On the Telephone. Since the purpose of networking is to establish a personal relationship with people who can help you with your job search, you will find that the telephone is more effective than letters to contact people. When calling, clearly state the purpose of your call and explain how you found the person's name and telephone number. Be sensitive about the time you call. In one study, employers indicated that Monday mornings and Friday afternoons were the worst times to try to reach them, for obvious reasons. The best times to call business people, this same survey said, are Tuesdays, Wednesdays, and Thursdays between 10:00 a.m. and 2:00 p.m.

The Twenty-Minute Meeting. When you make an appointment to meet with someone for information, many of the same rules apply as when interviewing for a job. Arrive a few minutes early; bring a copy of your resume; and be prepared with questions to ask. It is best not to ask to meet someone for the first time over lunch.

Thank-You Notes. The thank-you note is more than just a polite gesture. A well-written thank-you note enhances your credibility with your interviewee. In your thank-you note, reiterate key points of your conversation and explain how you intend to act on your contact's advice. Include a copy of your resume for his or her files. Make sure that your contact has your correct phone number and address so that he or she can contact you with additional information.

Networking On-line. On-line computer services can help you expand your network to mind-boggling numbers. Many of the main on-line services such as CompuServe and America On-line have discussion groups that can be useful for job searchers. Prodigy offers a careers bulletin board that is another way to do information interviews.

One caution, however, about using these services. Be careful about providing too much personal information such as your address, phone number, social security number, and so on, because you never know who is lurking on the Net. Additionally, people can easily misrepresent themselves, and you may not be corresponding with whom you think you are.

E-mail has become commonplace in the corporate world and presents another way to make networking contacts. "Netiquette," or etiquette on the Net, however, suggests that this is not always the best way to conduct informational exchanges. It is, however, a great way to confirm appointments and send thank-you notes.

CYBERTIPS ON NETWORKING

A few sources for networking on the Net include:

http://www.espan.com/
Interactive Employment Network
Provides networking advice.

http://www.sirius.com/-40plus/
Forty-Plus Club
Not-for-profit organization of skilled and experienced job-searching executives, managers, and professionals who share their knowledge and skills with each other. A great networking source.

Professional Organization Homepages. Many local and national professional organizations are developing sites on the Internet for their members. Often these include times of meetings and information on job openings or careers in that particular field. Ask your contacts if such sites exist within your field and look them up.

List-Serves. Many professional organizations also maintain list-serves, or e-mail mailing lists that members use to maintain on-going dialogues on issues within the field. This is an excellent way to get up-to-date information and to learn of people who can help you in your job search. Do not, however, ask people for jobs over the list-serve. Find their e-mail address and contact those you are interested in talking to individually.

Networking hangouts

Southern Californians are serious about their recreation. You're just as likely to network on the surf, on the trail, or at a bookstore as at a professional association meeting. Looking for some offbeat, informal, and inexpensive places to network in Southern California? Here are some ideas to get you started.

At the following specialty bookstores you can strike up a conversation with people of similar interests while browsing for books or attending a lecture or book signing.

Beyond Baroque
Literary/Arts Center
681 Venice Blvd.
Venice, CA 90291
(310) 822-3006

Cook's Library
8373 W. 3rd St.
Los Angeles, CA 90048
(213) 655-3141

Sports Books
8302 Melrose Ave.
West Hollywood, CA 90069
(310) 659-4045

Traveler's Bookstore
62 S. Raymond Ave.
Pasadena, CA 91105
(818) 449-3220

If on-line is more your style, check out L.A.'s first on-line coffeehouse.

CyberJava
1029 Abbot Kinney Blvd.
Venice, CA 90291
(310) 581-1300

Networking After You Land the Job

Networking doesn't end when you land the job. Keep people who are part of your network informed about your job search, and let them know when you finally land a job. Periodically touch base and let them know how things are working out with the new job.

Maintaining your network requires that you contribute as much as you receive. After you find your job — or even while you are looking for it — remember that your ideas, information, and contacts can help other people in your network. Often we have to train ourselves to offer such information because we don't think of ourselves as resources.

Sometimes people seem to walk into successful jobs or successful career changes. If you asked them how they did it, they would probably say they were in the right place at the right time. No doubt, some people do just get lucky, but others have high career awareness, or an idea of what their next career move or career change might be. Developing high career awareness means knowing what your next move is, planning for it, knowing who might be involved in helping you, and positioning yourself for it.

In other words, networking should become a part of your life and a part of your plans for your next career move. Knowing people in all types of career areas allows you to keep up with the possibilities and helps you position yourself to take the next step up the career ladder.

BOOKS ON NETWORKING

Numerous books have been written on job searching and networking. Here are a few good ones.

Krannich, R.L. and C.R. *Network Your Way to Job and Career Success.* Manassas, VA: Impact Publications, 1989.

Petras, Kathryn and Ross. *The Only Job Hunting Guide You'll Ever Need.* New York: Fireside, 1995.

Stoodley, Martha. *Information Interviewing: What It Is and How to Use It In Your Career.* Deerfield Beach, FL: Garrett Publishing, 1990.

Network, Network, Network: The Best Job-Search Technique

Networking Resources in Southern California

The following is a list of more than 125 organized groups, ready-made for networking, establishing relationships, and gathering information about career and job opportunities in Southern California.

SELECTED PROFESSIONAL ORGANIZATIONS, CLUBS, TRADE GROUPS, AND NETWORKS

Academy of Country Music
6255 W. Sunset Blvd., Suite 923
Los Angeles, CA 90028
(213) 462-2352

Academy of Motion Picture Arts and Sciences
8949 Wilshire Blvd.
Beverly Hills, CA 90211
(310) 247-3000

Academy of Television Arts and Sciences
5220 Lankershim Blvd.
North Hollywood, CA 91601
(818) 754-2800

Actors Fund of America
5410 Wilshire Blvd., Suite 400
Los Angeles, CA 90036
(213) 933-9244

Advertising Club of Los Angeles
6404 Wilshire Blvd., Suite 1111
Los Angeles, CA 90048
(213) 782-1044

Advertising Club of Orange County
P.O. Box 18197
Santa Ana, CA 92799
(714) 573-2400

Advertising Club of San Diego
5625 Ruffin Road, #130
San Diego, CA 92123
(619) 576-9833

Advertising Production Association of Orange County
P.O. Box 25858
Santa Ana, CA 92799
(714) 252-7939

Air Conditioning and Refrigeration Contractors Association
401 Shatto Place, Suite 103
Los Angeles, CA 90020
(213) 738-7238

Air Transport Association of America
8939 S. Sepulveda Blvd., Suite 408
Los Angeles, CA 90045
(310) 670-5183
Affiliate of Washington, DC-based organization.

Alliance of Motion Picture and Television Producers
15503 Ventura Blvd.
Encino, CA 91436
(818) 995-3600

Alliance of Practicing CPA's
4401 Atlantic Ave., Suite 239
Long Beach, CA 90807
(310) 984-2040
Job referral service for accountants.

American Academy of Dramatic Arts/West
2550 Paloma St.
Pasadena, CA 91107
(818) 798-0777

American Academy of Sports
Physicians
17113 Gledhill St.
Northridge, CA 91325
(818) 501-4433

American Agents Alliance
260 S. Arroyo Parkway
Pasadena, CA 91105
(213) 684-2560

American Association of Critical Care
Nurses
101 Columbia
Aliso Viejo, CA 92656
(714) 362-2000
(800) 899-ACAN

American Benefit Plan
Administrators
4401 Santa Anita Ave.
El Monte, CA 91731
(818) 442-4500

American Chemical Society
Southern California Chapter
14934 S. Figueroa St.
Gardena, CA 90248
(310) 327-1216
http://www.chem.ucla.edu/~deh/SCALACS

American Cinema Editors
1041 N. Formosa Ave.
West Hollywood, CA 90046
(213) 850-2900

Grocery store networking

One job hunter, fresh out of college and with little work experience, was eager to land a television production job. She knew she'd need to start as a gopher, and was quite willing to do so. Her problem was that she couldn't figure out how to get the job, or even a lead. One day, while shopping at a West Los Angeles grocery store, she overheard the conversation of the patrons in front of her. It was clear that they were in the entertainment business. She politely initiated a conversation and left with the name and phone number of a contact. After making several calls and visits to the set where he worked, she landed exactly what she wanted: a production internship with a network sitcom.

American Constructor Inspectors
Association
P.O. Box 10579
San Bernardino, CA 92423
(909) 594-4914
Publishes *The Inspector* magazine.

American Electronics Association
15300 Ventura Blvd., Suite 226
Sherman Oaks, CA 91403
(818) 986-6944

American Entrepreneurs Association
2939 Morse Ave.
Irvine, CA 92714
(714) 261-2393

American Federation of Musicians
1777 Vine St., Suite 500
Hollywood, CA 90028
(213) 461-3441

American Federation of State, County
and Municipal Employees
234 S. Loma Drive
Los Angeles, CA 90010
(213) 484-8300

American Federation of Television &
Radio Artists
6922 Hollywood Blvd., Suite 800
Los Angeles, CA 90028
(213) 461-8111

American Federation of Television &
Radio Artists
7827 Convoy Court, Suite 400
San Diego, CA 92111
(619) 278-7695

American Film Institute
2021 N. Western Ave.
Los Angeles, CA 90027
(213) 856-7600

American Foreign Language
Newspapers Association
8530 Wilshire Blvd., Suite 404
Beverly Hills, CA 90211
(213) 656-4935

American Institute of Aeronautics
and Astronautics
2221 Rosecrans Ave., Suite 227
El Segundo, CA 90245
(310) 643-7510

American Institute of Architects
Los Angeles Chapter
8687 Melrose Ave., #M-3
Los Angeles, CA 90069
(310) 785-1809

American Institute of Architects
Orange County Chapter
3200 Park Center Drive, #110
Costa Mesa, CA 92626
(714) 557-7796

American Institute of Architects
San Diego Chapter
233 A St., Suite 200
San Diego, CA 92101
(619) 232-0109

American Institute of Graphic Arts
116 the Plaza Pasadena
Pasadena, CA 91101
(818) 952-2442

American Orthopedic Association
501 E. Hardy St., Suite 200
Inglewood, CA 90301
(310) 674-5200

American Philanthropy Association
101 Santa Barbara Plaza
Los Angeles, CA 90008
(213) 295-3707

American Society of
Cinematographers
1782 N. Orange Drive
Hollywood, CA 90028
(213) 876-5080

American Society of Engineers and
Architects
511 Garfield Ave.
South Pasadena, CA 91030
(213) 682-1161

American Society of Music Arrangers
and Composers
P.O. Box 11
Hollywood, CA 90078
(213) 658-5997

American Society of Travel Agents
7060 Hollywood Blvd., Suite 614
Los Angeles, CA 90028
(213) 466-7717

American Sports Medicine
Association
660 W. Duarte Road
Arcadia, CA 91007
(818) 445-1978

American Women in Radio and T.V.
P.O. Box 3615
Los Angeles, CA 90028
(213) 964-2740

Apparel Contractors Alliance of
California
801 Crocker St.
Los Angeles, CA 90021
(213) 623-6991

Asian-American Architects &
Engineers
1200 Wilshire Blvd., Suite 401
Los Angeles, CA 90017
(213) 386-0273

Associated Architects and Planners
15260 Ventura Blvd.
Sherman Oaks, CA 91403
(818) 995-7484

Associated Builders & Contractors of
Southern California
4780 Chino Ave., Suite D
Chino, CA 91710
(909) 627-7880

Associated General Contractors of
California, Los Angeles
1255 Corporate Center Drive,
Suite 100
Monterey Park, CA 91754
(213) 263-1500

Associated General Contractors of
California, San Diego
2231 Hotel Circle South
San Diego, CA 92108
(619) 297-4001

Associated Produce Dealers and
Brokers of Los Angeles
1601 E. Olympic Blvd., Suite 312
Los Angeles, CA 90021
(213) 623-6293

Association of California School
Administrators
4665 Lampson Ave.
Los Alamitos, CA 90720
(310) 493-4431

Association for Women in
Architecture
2550 Beverly Blvd.
Los Angeles, CA 90057
(213) 389-6490

Beverly Hills Bar Association
300 S. Beverly Drive, Suite 201
Beverly Hills, CA 90212
(310) 553-6644

Biomedical Engineering Society
P.O. Box 2399
Culver City, CA 90231
(310) 618-9322

Black Business Association
3550 W. Wilshire Blvd., Suite 816
Los Angeles, CA 90062
(213) 299-9560

Black Women Lawyers Association
3870 Crenshaw Blvd., Suite 818
Los Angeles, CA 90008
(213) 292-6547

Book Publicists of Southern
California
6464 Sunset Blvd., Suite 580
Hollywood, CA 90028
(213) 461-3921

California Association for Counseling and Development
2555 E. Chapman Ave., Suite 201
Fullerton, CA 92631
(714) 871-6460

California Association of Marriage & Family Therapists
8306 Wilshire Blvd., Suite 237
Beverly Hills, CA 90211
(213) 964-3200

California Federation of Teachers
1200 Magnolia Blvd.
Burbank, CA 91506
(818) 843-8226

California Nurses Association
13412 Ventura Blvd., Suite 330
Sherman Oaks, CA 91403
(310) 820-7228

California Organizations of Police and Sheriffs
175 E. Olive Ave., Suite 400
Burbank, CA 91502
(818) 841-2222

California Physical Therapists Association
1350 W. 6th St., Suite 1
San Pedro, CA 90732
(310) 547-3331

California Restaurant Association
3435 Wilshire Blvd., Suite 2606
Los Angeles, CA 90010
(213) 384-1200

California School Employees Association
1100 N. Corporate Center Drive, Suite 207
Monterey Park, CA 91754
(213) 881-9353

California Small Business Association
5300 Beethoven St.
Los Angeles, CA 90066
(310) 306-4540

California Society of Certified Public Accountants
330 N. Brand Ave., Suite 710
Glendale, CA 91203
(818) 246-6000

Chefs de Cuisine Association of Southern California
4580 N. Figueroa St.
Los Angeles, CA 90065
(818) 559-5218

Costume Designers Guild
1349 Ventura Blvd., Suite 309
Sherman Oaks, CA 91423
(818) 905-1557

Directors Guild of America
7920 Sunset Blvd.
Los Angeles, CA 90046
(310) 289-2000

Engineers & Architects Association
350 S. Figueroa, Suite 600
Los Angeles, CA 90071
(213) 620-6920

Financial Women International
c/o Gail M. Harvey
1223 West Blvd.
Los Angeles, CA 90019
(310) 246-3050

Greater Los Angeles Press Club
Hollywood Roosevelt Hotel
700 Hollywood Blvd.
Hollywood, CA 90028
(213) 469-8180

Greater Los Angeles Visitors & Convention Bureau
633 W. 5th St., Suite 6000
Los Angeles, CA 90071
(213) 624-7300

Greater San Diego Sports Association
9449 Friars Road
San Diego, CA 92108
(619) 283-8221

Hispanic Business Association
P.O. Box 2367
Anaheim, CA 92804
(714) 535-5899

Hospital Council of Southern California
201 N. Figueroa St.
Los Angeles, CA 90012
(213) 250-5600

Independent Colleges of Southern California
333 S. Grand Ave., Suite 2660
Los Angeles, CA 90071-1504
(213) 680-1330

Independent Computer Consultants Association
P.O. Box 880038
San Diego, CA 92168
(619) 294-6550

International Animated Film Society
P.O. Box 787
Burbank, CA 91503
(818) 842-8330

International Stunt Association
3518 Cahuenga Blvd. West
Los Angeles, CA 90068
(213) 874-3174

Lawyers Club of Los Angeles County
P.O. Box 71525
Los Angeles, CA 90071
(213) 624-2525

Lawyers Club of San Diego
964 5th Ave., Suite 210
San Diego, CA 92101
(619) 544-1478

League of Women Voters of Los Angeles
6030 Wilshire Blvd., Suite 301
Los Angeles, CA 90036
(213) 939-3535

Los Angeles Advertising Women
P.O. Box 2073
Simi Valley, CA 93062
(818) 712-0802

Los Angeles County Bar Association
617 S. Olive St.
Los Angeles, CA 90014
(213) 627-2727

Los Angeles County Medical Association
1925 Wilshire Blvd.
Los Angeles, CA 90057
(213) 483-1581

Los Angeles Paralegal Association
P.O. Box 241928
Los Angeles, CA 90024
(213) 251-3755

Los Angeles Urban League
5414 Crenshaw Blvd.
Los Angeles, CA 90043
(213) 292-8111

Meeting Planners International
11287 Washington Blvd.
Culver City, CA 90230
(310) 390-6674

Milk Producers Council
13545 Euclid Ave.
Ontario, CA 91761
(909) 628-6018

Motion Pictures Association of America
15503 Ventura Blvd.
Encino, CA 91436
(818) 556-6567

National Academy of Recording Arts
3402 Pico Blvd.
Santa Monica, CA 90405
(310) 392-3777

National Academy of Songwriters
6255 Sunset Blvd., Suite 1023
Hollywood, CA 90028
(213) 463-7178

National Association of Black Accountants
P.O. Box 71175
Los Angeles, CA 90071
(213) 665-2682

National Association of Business Travel Agents
3255 Wilshire Blvd., Suite 1514
Los Angeles, CA 90010-1418
(213) 382-3335

National Association of Composers
P.O. Box 49256
Los Angeles, CA 90049
(310) 541-8213

National Association of Social Workers
6030 Wilshire Blvd., Suite 202
Los Angeles, CA 90036
(213) 935-2050

National Association of Women Business Owners
1804 W. Burbank Blvd.
Burbank, CA 91506-1315
(818) 843-7348

National Association of Women in Construction
P.O. Box 90935
Pasadena, CA 91109
(213) 612-0900

National Health Federation
212 W. Foothill Blvd.
Monrovia, CA 91016

Orange County Bar Association
601 Civic Center Drive West
Santa Ana, CA 92701
(714) 440-6700

Producers Guild of America
453 S. Beverly Drive, Suite 211
Beverly Hills, CA 90212
(310) 557-0807

Professional Insurance Agents Association of California
101 S. 1st St., Suite 304
Burbank, CA 91502
(818) 973-4800

Public Relations Society of America, Los Angeles Chapter
7060 Hollywood Blvd., Suite 614
Los Angeles, CA 90028
(213) 461-4595
http://www.hei.com/~prsa/la.htm

Public Relations Society of America, Orange County Chapter
195 S. C St., Suite 250
Tustin, CA 92680
(714) 669-9341
http://www.hei.com/~prsa/oc.htm

Public Relations Society of America, San Diego Chapter
c/o Peter MacCracken
MacCracken & McGaugh
1701 B St., Suite 2200
San Diego, CA 92101
(619) 696-8282
http://www.hei.com/~prsa.sd.htm

Restaurant Association of Southern California
3435 Wilshire Blvd., Suite 2230
Los Angeles, CA 90010
(213) 384-1200

Sales and Marketing Executives of Los Angeles
900 Wilshire Blvd., Suite 418
Los Angeles, CA 90017
(818) 842-8482

Screen Actors Guild
5757 Wilshire Blvd.
Los Angeles, CA 90036
(213) 954-1600

Society of Children's Book Writers
22736 Van Owens St., Suite 106
West Hills, CA 90035
(818) 888-8760

Society of Motion Picture and
Television Art Directors
11365 Ventura Blvd., Suite 315
Studio City, CA 91604
(818) 762-9995

Society of Women Engineers
9832 Flower St.
Bellflower, CA 90706
(310) 867-6500

Southern California Association of
Philanthropy
315 W. 9th St., Suite 1000
Los Angeles, CA 90015
(213) 489-7307

Southern California Broadcasters
Association
5670 Wilshire Blvd., Suite 910
Los Angeles, CA 90036
(213) 938-3100

Southern California Builders
Association
4552 Lincoln Ave., Suite 207
Cypress, CA 90630
(714) 995-5841

Southern California Contractors
Association
6055 E. Washington Blvd., Suite 200
Los Angeles, CA 90020
(213) 738-7950

Southern California Grocers
Association
100 W. Broadway
Long Beach, CA 90802
(310) 432-8610

Southern California Professional
Engineering Association
14140 Beach Blvd., Suite 114
Westminster, CA 92683
(714) 898-6603

Southern California Restaurant
Association
3435 Wilshire Blvd., Suite 2606
Los Angeles, CA 90010
(213) 384-1200

State Bar of California
1149 S. Hill
Los Angeles, CA 90015
(213) 765-1000

Western States Advertising Agencies
Association
6404 Wilshire Blvd., Suite 111
Los Angeles, CA 90048-5513
(213) 655-1951

Women in Business
7060 Hollywood Blvd., Suite 614
Los Angeles, CA 90028
(213) 461-2936

Women in Communications
P.O. Box 2727
El Segundo, CA 90245
(310) 640-1905

Women in Films
6464 Sunset Blvd., Suite 530
Los Angeles, CA 90028
(213) 463-6040

Another helpful Southern California networking resource is:
Susan Linn's Directory of Orange County Networking Organizations
3334 E. Coast Highway, Suite 291
Corona Del Mar, CA 92625
(714) 768-1320

Includes information on 650+ business and professional organizations, women's groups, and chambers of commerce operating in Orange County.

You've already got lots of contacts

Networking paid off for Liz, a young woman eager to make her way in banking or a related industry. She told us why she's glad she took the time to talk with her friends and neighbors about her job search.

"I was having dinner with close friends and telling them about my job search," says Liz. "During the conversation, they mentioned a banker friend they thought might be hiring. As it turned out, the friend didn't have a job for me. But he suggested I come in, meet with him, and discuss some other possibilities. He put me in touch with an independent marketing firm, servicing the publishing industry. The owner of the firm was looking for someone with my exact qualifications. One thing led to another, and pretty soon I had landed exactly the position I wanted."

six

Developing the Perfect Resume

It seems almost impossible to write the *imperfect* resume, with over 125 books on the market today pertaining solely to resume writing. However, we still anguish over the process, believing it will secure us a job. Keep in mind that no one ever secured a job offer on the basis of a resume alone. The way to land a good position is to succeed in the interview. You have to convince a potential employer that you're the best person for the job. No piece of paper will ever do that for you—but having an excellent resume is a necessary first step.

The resume is an invitation enticing the employer to interview you. With a little success, and some luck, the employer will want to meet you after reading your resume. However, the most effective method of resume delivery is for you to first meet the employer in person; then provide your resume. We understand that this is not always possible.

The French word *résumé* means "a summing up." Thus the purpose of a resume is not to catalogue, in exact detail, your entire biography. You should be concise with your work experience, education, accomplishments, and affiliations. Your goal is to pique the employer's interest. A good rule of thumb is that the resume should be kept to one or at most two pages.

The Basics of a Good Resume

To develop a resume that entices a potential employer to want to meet you, we suggest the following tips:

1. *Tailor your resume to the potential job opening.* The astute job searcher should always research a potential employer and find out as much information as possible on the qualifications needed for a particular job and then tailor his

or her resume to match the qualifications. When listing your experience and education, concentrate on those items that demonstrate your ability to do the job you are applying for. Using a computer will facilitate this process of customizing each resume.

2. *Be concise.* Most employers don't have time to read a two-page resume and usually scan a resume within 10-20 seconds. Thus, you want to capture the reader's attention quickly. Only then will you get a more careful reading. This is not the time to demonstrate your impressive vocabulary. Instead, describe your experience in short, pithy phrases. Give figures and facts when describing your accomplishments. Your resume should read more like a chart than a chapter in a textbook. And it should look more like an ad than a legal document.

3. *Be honest.* Never lie, exaggerate, embellish, or deceive. Be honest about your education, accomplishments, and work experience. A deliberate lie can be grounds for termination and will likely turn up in a background search. If you have gaps between jobs, and gaps are not always as negative as some would have you believe, you may consider listing years worked rather than months.

4. *Have a professional presentation.* Today's high quality computers allow you to prepare your own resume with the same professional results as paid resume preparers. A good rule of thumb: make your resume professional enough to send out on the potential employer's letterhead. If it isn't, it's probably not sharp enough.

Your resume should cover your most current work experiences (three to four jobs), with the name, location, and dates of employment plus a summary of your responsibilities relevant to the qualifications of the job you are seeking. Be sure to state your accomplishments on each job. Present your work history chronologically. Begin with your present position and work backward to your earlier jobs. If you haven't had that many jobs, organize your resume to emphasize the skills you've acquired through experience.

There are no hard and fast rules on what to include in your resume besides work experience, education, and special skills pertinent to the job for which you are applying. Professional affiliations may also be of interest to the employer. Do not list anything personal (such as marital status, date of birth, etc.) that could potentially screen you out. Salary history and references should not be included in your resume; these should be discussed in person during the interview.

Keep in mind that a resume is a sales tool. Make sure that it illustrates your unique strengths in a style and format *you* can be proud of. Be brief, tailor your experiences to the job you are seeking, and provide figures and facts to support your accomplishments.

Elements of a Resume

Here are the five main elements of a resume, with a brief description of each. All need not appear in the same order in every resume, and sometimes one or two are combined or left out, as you'll see in the sample resumes that follow.

NAME
Address
City, State, Zip
Phone
E-Mail Address (optional)

Objective: Employers use this information as a screening device or to assess a job match. It should grab the reader's attention and motivate him or her to read further. Make this relevant to the job for which you are applying!

Experience: The more impressive your work history, the more prominently you should display it. Use facts and figures to support accomplishments and goals reached.

List employment in reverse chronological order, putting the most promotable facts—employer or job title—first.

Give functional description of job if work history is strong and supports job objective.

List dates of employment last. They are the least important of all your information.

Skills: You may want to embed these in the employment section. Or, for career changers, list the skills section first. Highlight skills that are relevant to the potential job opening. Give short, results-oriented statements to support skills. Position your most marketable skills first.

Education: List in reverse chronological order, putting the most salable facts—school or degree—first. Mention honors or achievements, such as a high GPA or Dean's List.

Miscellaneous: Call this section anything applicable: Interests, Activities, Achievements, or Accomplishments.

Give only information that promotes your candidacy for the position for which you are applying.

References: Available upon request. Don't waste space on names and addresses. Have ready on a separate sheet.

Choosing a Resume Format

There are many different but equally acceptable ways to organize your resume. Every resume compiler and career counselor has his or her favorite method and style. The format you use should best present your strongest points and best convey your message to the potential employer. Resume books will use different terms for the various styles, but here are the three most popular types.

1. *The Chronological Resume* is the traditional style, most often used in the workplace and job search. It is also the resume style favored by most employers. That does not mean, however, that it is the most effective. A positive aspect of the chronological resume, aside from it being the traditional approach that employers may expect, is that it emphasizes past jobs that you wish your potential employer to notice. This resume is also very adaptable, with only the reverse chronological order of previous employment an essential ingredient.

2. *The Functional Resume* is most common among those reentering the job market after an absence, career changers, and those wishing to emphasize skills gained through non-work experience. This resume focuses on the many skills gained from employment and the accomplishments one has achieved. It shows a potential employer that you can do and have done a good job. What it doesn't necessarily emphasize is where you have done it and when.

3. *The Combination Resume* merges features of the functional and chronological resumes. This allows job seekers to emphasize accomplishments and skills while still maintaining the traditional format of reverse chronological order of positions held and organizations worked for. This format is perfect if your most current work is not your most impressive.

Sample After-College Chronological Resume

The Chronological Resume format is ideal for someone just graduating with little work experience. Here is a sample:

Ralph Burr
44 Chelsey Drive, Apt. 5
Santa Monica, CA 90405
(310) 555-1002

EDUCATION: University of California, Los Angeles
BA, Political Science, May 1996.
Courses include: Business Law, Applied Probability, Statistics, Calculus, Economics, English, Creative Writing, Spanish.

WORK EXPERIENCE: **Human Resources Intern.** Walt Disney Company, Burbank, CA. Summers 1994-1995.
Coordinated company-wide activities for Disney employees. Planned and publicized events. Organized community service activity involving 100 employees. Used Excel to track employee participation.

Campus Representative. Office of Admissions, University of California, Los Angeles, CA. Academic years 1993-1996.
Organized and implemented recruiting campaign directed at underrepresented high school students. Received a record number of minority student acceptances and matriculates.

ACTIVITIES AND HONORS: President, Black Students' Association
Freshman Advisor, Dean of Students Office
Tutor, high-risk high school students
National Collegiate Minority Leadership Award

COMPUTER SKILLS: Experienced with the World Wide Web, Microsoft Office, Access, and Aldus Pagemaker for PC and Macintosh.

REFERENCES: Available upon request.

Sample Career-Changing Functional Resume

The Functional Resume format is ideal for someone changing careers since it emphasizes skills rather than past employment. Here is a sample:

Michelle Lawrence
876 Brigham Court
San Diego, CA 92121
(619) 555-9987

OBJECTIVE   Position in retail management training program.

AREAS OF EXPERTISE

Administrative

- Managed budget in excess of $50,000 as Treasurer of a non-profit organization.
- Analyzed client accounts for an advertising agency.

Supervision

- Managed 10 employees as Computer Center Coordinator.
- Trained new staff members.

Organizational

- Created weekly work schedules at Computer Center.
- Generated monthly reports and managed data input.

EXPERIENCE   *Computer Analyst*, Techron, San Diego, CA (1994-present)
SUMMARY   *Analyst*, Cargill, Wilson, and Acree, San Diego, CA (1990-93)
Treasurer, Safe for Children, San Diego, CA (1992-3), Volunteer
Computer Center Coordinator, San Diego State University, San Diego, CA (1987-90)

EDUCATION   University of California, San Diego
BA, Mathematics/Computer Science (1987); GPA 3.7/4.0.
Dean's List, three semesters.

REFERENCES   Available upon request.

Sample Combination Resume

The Combination Resume allows you to use aspects of both the chronological and functional formats. This type is good for someone whose present work perhaps does not reflect his or her most impressive skills. Here is a sample:

Paul Wheaton
432 Kingsington Drive
Fullerton, CA 92631
(714) 555-9898

EDUCATION
    University of California, Irvine; GPA 3.7/4.0
    MS, Information and Computer Science, December 1990
    Whittier College; GPA 3.4/4.0
    BA, Mathematics, May 1988

QUALIFICATIONS
    Career-related Projects:
- Designed and implemented multi-tasking operating system for the IBM-PC.
- Implemented compiler for Pascal-like language.
- Designed electronic mail system using PSL/PSA specification.

    Languages and Operating Systems:
- Proficient in Ada, Modula-2, Pascal, C+
- Thorough knowledge of IBM-PC hardware.
- Experienced in UNIX, MS-DOS, CP/M operating systems.

    Hardware:
- IBM-PC (MS-DOS), Pyramid 90x (UNIX), Cyber 990 (NOS)

WORK EXPERIENCE
    Syms Programming Services, Fullerton, CA 3/91-present
    UNIX Programmer
    Responsible for porting MS-DOS database applications to IBM-PC/AT running Xenix System V. System administration.
    Techknowledge, Los Angeles, CA 10/88-12/90
    Computer Programmer
    Performed daily disk backup on Burroughs B-1955 machine. Executed database update programs and checks. Provided user assistance.

REFERENCES
    Available upon request.

Sample Combination Resume for Liberal Arts Major

As mentioned earlier, the Combination Resume allows you to use parts of both the chronological and functional formats. This type is good for liberal arts majors who have several career fields to select among because of their broad educational background. Since Laura (example resume follows) wanted to apply for jobs in broadcasting, magazine publishing, and writing speeches for a member of Congress, she used the combination style.

Laura Kern
6464 Jasmine Street
Arcadia, CA 91007
(818) 555-0011

EDUCATION	B.A., Scripps College, Claremont, CA, May 1996 Major: English literature. Minor: sociology. Overall GPA 3.7/4.0 Study abroad, University of Lancaster, England. Fall 1994
EXPERIENCE	**Public Relations Intern,** spring 1995 to present. Office of Public Relations and Communications, Scripps College, Claremont, CA. Wrote press releases, updated campus activities calendar, proofread copy and checked facts. Reported on campus events. **Marketing Intern,** summer 1994. World Trade Center, Irvine, CA. Prepared marketing materials for conferences and seminars. Researched companies looking to trade overseas. Created database of participating companies using Microsoft Access. **Tourguide,** fall 1993-spring 1994. Office of Admissions, Scripps College, Claremont, CA. Delivered presentations to groups of prospective students and parents. Hosted overnight visits. **Salesperson,** Nordstrom, Santa Anita, CA, summer 1993. Completed nightly closings, and maintained various departments in manager's absence. Rotated throughout store as needed. Highest sales for two months.
LEADERSHIP ACTIVITIES	Team Captain, Women's Cross Country Running Team, 1995. Student Alumnae Council Member, Alumnae Office, fall 1993.
REFERENCES	Available upon request.

Resume Checklist

- Brainstorm a list of the skills and talents you want to convey. These may include character traits such as persistence and assertiveness; work skills such as fluency in languages and computer literacy; and transferable skills such as managing, motivating, and leading people, manipulating data, evaluating and analyzing systems.
- Prepare your resume on a computer and printer that give you the same results as a professionally typeset resume.
- Use heavyweight (at least 20 lb.), high-quality paper and a laser printer if at all possible. White, off-white, or light gray papers (8½ x 11 inches) are usually safe, conservative bets. However, if you are in theater, arts, or advertising, you can be a little more daring. If you have the budget, consider buying 9½ x 12½-inch envelopes so you won't have to fold your resume and cover letter.
- Be concise and brief in your wording.
- Avoid personal pronouns.
- Use active verbs to describe your accomplishments rather than your assigned duties.
- Arrange information in descending order of importance within each section of your resume.
- Be consistent in format and style.
- Tailor your skills and experience as much as possible to each potential job opening.
- Proofread your resume, and then have a few friends proofread it as well.
- Be selective in sending out your resume. Mass mailings usually only result in spending unnecessary time and money.

Using the Computer to Design Your Resume

Welcome to the high-tech world of resume writing. Even if you don't own your own computer, many libraries have them available, and copy stores such as Kinko's rent computer time. So there is no excuse to rule out the computer in designing your resume. There are certain advantages:

- You have the ability to save your resume on a disk, which simplifies editing it for a specific company or position. Revises and updates become simple.
- Computers offer a wide range of type faces, styles (bold, italics, and so on), and sizes. Combined with a laser printout, you can achieve a professional-looking resume at modest expense.

No matter what method you use to prepare your resume, *proofread* it before printing. Misspelled words or typing errors reflect badly on you even if it's not your fault. Recruit a friend to help read your resume, word for word and comma for comma. And don't make last minute changes after everyone has proofed it. Somehow, you *will* end up with an error.

Professional Resume Preparers

It is always better to prepare your own resume, as long as you have reasonable writing skills. However, if you have trouble condensing your writing style and you have no friends who can help, no access to a university career office or books on resumes, then a professional may be able to assist you.

Before choosing a professional resume service, try to get a recommendation from someone whose judgment you trust. Find out the minimum and maximum costs before employing any service. Ask whether the price includes only writing, or typesetting and printing as well. If changes are needed, will it cost extra? Finally, always shop around for the best services available. Don't forget that many career counselors and consultants also provide resume preparation; refer to Chapter 2.

The following are firms that will assist you in preparing your resume. Keep in mind that a listing in this book does not constitute an endorsement.

The laughing stock of the company

Make sure that you don't end up as fodder for employer levity as did the following unfortunates:

One candidate wrote under Job Responsibilities: "Assassinated store manager during busiest retail season." What she meant to write was "assisted."

"Education: College, August 1890–May 1994."

"Here are my qualifications for you to overlook."

"Please call me after 5:30 p.m. because I am self-employed and my employer does not know I am looking for another job."

Reason for leaving last job? The candidate replied: "No special reason." Another replied: "They insisted that all employees get to work by 8:45 every morning. Couldn't work under those conditions."

One applicant submitted a seven-page resume and stated, "This resume is fairly long because I have a lot to offer you."

SELECTED PROFESSIONAL RESUME PREPARERS IN SOUTHERN CALIFORNIA

Below is a list of resume writers certified by the Professional Association of Resume Writers. Remember that working with them is a collaborative effort.

AAA A-1 Certified Resume Writers
23521 Paseo de Valencia, Suite 306
Laguna Hills, CA 92653
(714) 830-1454

Advanced Connection
8707-D Lindley Ave.
Northridge, CA 91325
(818) 772-7643

Affordable Resume Service
5627 Sepulveda Blvd., Suite 207
Van Nuys, CA 91411
(818) 782-8554

AllTypes
4162 Lewis St.
Oceanside, CA 92056
(619) 630-0791

Business Pro Office Services
21755 Ventura Blvd., Suite 453
Woodland Hills, CA 91364
(818) 884-7271

Custom Resumes
14 Fairdawn
Irvine, CA 92714
(714) 551-5004

DCS Resume Specialists
2182 El Camino Real, Suite 112
Oceanside, CA 92056
(619) 721-2728

The Employment Connection
4634 Via Apuesta
Tarzana, CA 91356
(818) 996-1981

First Impressions Resume Service
3444 Seabreeze Walk
Oceanside, CA 92056
(619) 630-8943

Hansen Computer Works
603 E. Verdugo Ave., Suite V
Burbank, CA 91501
(818) 972-9636

Kahl For Secretarial Service
P.O. Box 1923
Monrovia, CA 91016
(818) 358-5119

On Target Resumes
212 S. Glendora Ave.
West Covina, CA 91790
(818) 850-5570

Osborne Career Associates
10721 Treena St., Suite 117
San Diego, CA 92131
(619) 693-0242

Power Resumes
687 Victoria St., #2
Costa Mesa, CA 92627
(714) 558-6133

Professional Services
8181 Clover Way
Buena Park, CA 90620
(714) 994-1284

ProWord Services
9023 Halldale Ave.
Los Angeles, CA 90047
(213) 971-4331

Strategic Edge
8430 P Via Mallorca
La Jolla, CA 92037
(619) 450-1889

West Coast Word Processing
925 Gayley Ave., Suite 1
Los Angeles, CA 90024
(310) 824-2118

WORD-TECH Resumes
121 Linden Ave., Suite A
Long Beach, CA 90802
(310) 432-1515

Preparing Your Resume for Machine Readers

Today's corporations are taking drastic means to accommodate the overwhelming amount of resumes they receive. Microsoft receives thousands of resumes a week. Could you imagine reading 3,000 resumes in one week? Thus, new techniques such as resume-scanning software have been implemented.

Resumix, Inc., in the Silicon Valley, of California, provides software to corporations who have replaced the resume reader with computers capable of scanning resumes and saving corporations valuable time and costs. Therefore, you must not only entice a potential employer with your resume but a computer as well. Your resume is more likely to be scanned by large companies than small, high-tech than non-high-tech.

Here are some hints for preparing the ideal scannable resume:
- Use 8½ x 11-inch paper, light color.
- Avoid dot matrix printouts. Laser prints scan easier.
- If using a computer, use the 12 point font size, and do not condense spacing between letters.
- Avoid using a newspaper-type format, columns, or graphics.
- Be sure to include your name at the top of the second page if your resume is two pages.
- Key words or accomplishments are often scanned; make sure your resume contains words related to the position for which you are applying. Use "hard vocabulary": "computer skills," "software packages," etc. Also avoid flowery language.

Resumix provides a brochure, "Preparing the Ideal Scannable Resume." If you are interested, call Resumix at (408) 988-0444.

The Cover Letter Adds a Custom Touch

Never, never send your resume without a cover letter. Whether you are answering a want ad or following up an inquiry call or interview, you should always include a letter with your resume. Use your researching skills to locate the individual doing the hiring. Using the personal touch of addressing your cover letter to a real person will save you the headache of having your resume sent to H.R.'s stack of resumes, or possibly even being tossed out.

A good cover letter should be brief and interesting enough to grab the reader's attention. If you've spoken with the individual, you may want to remind him or her of the conversation. Or, if you and the person to whom you are writing know someone in common, be sure to mention it.

In the next paragraph or two, specify what you could contribute to the company in terms that indicate you've done your homework on the firm and the industry. Use figures and facts to support your accomplishments that are relevant to the job opening.

Finally, in the last paragraph, either request an interview or tell the reader that you will follow-up with a phone call within a week to arrange a mutually convenient meeting.

Sample Cover Letter

> Marie Baker
> 7645 Harris Drive
> Long Beach, CA 90821

August 12, 1996

Ms. Jacqueline Doheny
Wide World Publishing Company
834 Wilshire Blvd., Suite 2210
Los Angeles, CA 90017

Dear Ms. Doheny:

As an honors graduate of the University of Southern California with two years of copy editing and feature-writing experience with the *Los Angeles Weekly,* I am confident that I would make a successful editorial assistant with Wide World.

Besides my strong editorial background, I offer considerable business experience. I have held summer jobs in an insurance company, a law firm, and a data processing company. My familiarity with on-line research should prove particularly useful to Wide World now that you have become fully automated.

I would like to interview with you as soon as possible and would be happy to check in with your office about an appointment. If you prefer, your office can contact me between the hours of 11 a.m. and 3 p.m. at (310) 555-6886.

Sincerely,

Marie Baker

Sample Cover Letter in Reply to Want Ad

Arthur Barnes
44 Lakeview Ave.
Pasadena, CA 91106

May 15, 1997

Mr. Tom White
Rhone & McMillan
P.O. Box 73
Anaheim, CA 92815

Dear Mr. White:

    My background seems ideal for your advertisement in the May 13 issue of the *Los Angeles Times* for an experienced accountant. My five years of experience in a small accounting firm has prepared me to move on to a more challenging position.

    As you can see from my resume, enclosed, my experience includes not only basic accounting work but also some consulting with a few of our firm's larger clients. This experience combined with an appetite for hard work, an enthusiastic style, and a desire to succeed makes me a strong candidate for your consideration. I assisted the company in expanding its clientele by 30%.

    I would appreciate the opportunity to discuss how my background could meet the needs of Rhone & McMillan. I will call you within a week to arrange a convenient time to meet.

Sincerely,

Arthur Barnes

Sample Networking Cover Letter

Sally Fusaka
7645 Harris Drive
Long Beach, CA 90821

December 2, 1996

Mr. James King
3-Q Inc.
45 Houston St.
Los Angeles, CA 90017

Dear James:

Just when everything seemed to be going smoothly at my job, the company gave us a Christmas present that nobody wanted: management announced that half the department will be laid off before the new year. Nobody knows yet just which heads are going to roll. But whether or not my name is on the list, I am definitely back in the job market.

I have already lined up a few interviews. But knowing how uncertain job hunting can be, I can use all the contacts I can get. You know my record—both from when we worked together at 3-Q and since then. But in case you've forgotten the details, I've enclosed my resume. I know that you often hear of job openings as you wend your way about the area. I'd certainly appreciate your passing along any leads you think might be worthwhile.

My best to you and Susan for the Holidays.

Cordially,

Sally Fusaka

Enclosure

Do's and don'ts for cover letters

Do:

- Send a resume with every cover letter.
- Use high-quality, high-rag-content paper.
- Target an individual person about the job opening.
- Be brief and interesting enough to capture the reader's attention.
- Tailor your experiences to meet the potential job opening.
- Use acceptable business format; letter should be well spaced on the page.
- Have someone check your letter for grammar, spelling, and formatting mistakes.
- Have an agenda in the letter and follow-up in the amount of time you specified.

Don't:

- Send your first draft of a letter just so you can meet the deadline.
- Send your letter to the president of the company simply because you don't know the name of the hiring authority.
- Include information that can be found on your resume.
- Give only one possible time to meet.
- Call the company four times a day after you have sent the letter.

CYBERTIPS FOR RESUME AND COVER LETTER WRITING

Using the Net to find more sample resumes and cover letters is a good place to start. Many of the job-search services or college career center homepages also have tips on resume and cover letter writing. Some on-line services will also post your resume for employer perusal.

Career Channel—The Job Search
http://riceinfo.rice.edu/projects/careers/Channel/seven.html

Catapult Job Search Guides
http://www.wm.edu/catapult/jsguides.html

Cover Letters by the Rensselaer Polytechnic Institute Writing Center
http://www.rpi.edu/dept/llc/writecenter/web/text/coverltr.html

Interactive Employment Network
http://www.espan.com

Resumes from Yahoo
http://www.yahoo.com/Business/Employment/Resumes/Individual_Resumes

Resumes On-Line
http://199.94.216.72:81/online.html

RECOMMENDED BOOKS ON RESUME WRITING

The following books are full of all the how-to information you'll need to prepare an effective resume and most are available from bookstores or your local library.

Corwin, Leonard. *Your Resume: Key to a Better Job.* New York: Arco, 1988.

Fournier, Myra, and Jeffrey Spin. *Encyclopedia of Job-Winning Resumes.* Ridgefield, CT: Round Lake Publishers, 1991.

Hahn, Harley, and Rick Stout. *The Internet Yellow Pages.* Berkeley, CA: Osborne McGraw-Hill, 1994.

Jackson, Tom. *The Perfect Resume.* New York: Anchor/Doubleday, 1990.

Kennedy, Joyce Lain, and Thomas J. Morrow. *Electronic Resume Revolution.* New York: James Wiley & Sons, 1994.

Krannich, Ronald L., and William J. Banis. *High Impact Resumes and Letters.* Career Management Concepts, 1992.

Lewis, Adele. *How to Write a Better Resume.* Woodbury, NY: Barron's, 1993.

Nadler, Burton Jay. *Liberal Arts Power: How to Sell It on Your Resume.* Princeton, NJ: Peterson's Guides, 1989.

Parker, Yana. *Damn Good Resume Guidelines.* Berkeley, CA: Ten Speed Press, 1989.

Smith, Michael H. *The Resume Writer's Handbook.* New York: Harper and Row, 1994.

Weinstein, Bob. *Resumes Don't Get Jobs: The Realities and Myths of Job Hunting.* New York: McGraw-Hill, 1993.

Yate, Marin. *Resumes That Knock 'em Dead.* Holbrook, MA: Bob Adams, 1992.

seven

The Killer Interview

Your networking paid off and your resume was a success. You are now ready to take the next step in your job search. Unfortunately, though, your resume won't automatically grant you a job, and all the contacts in the world won't do you any good if you don't handle yourself well in an interview. All interviews have the same goal: to convince the interviewer that he or she should hire you or recommend that you be hired. That is what counts. Remember, this interview is all that stands between you and the job, so make it a *killer* interview. This chapter will guide you through the steps and give you an idea of what to expect and what to avoid when interviewing.

Dr. Bob's Six Steps to a Killer Interview

STEP 1: Preparing for the Interview

Good preparation shows ambition and zeal and is a key part of interviewing that is often forgotten. The more you prepare, the more you will be relaxed and comfortable with the interview. Additionally, the more you prepare, the greater your chance of impressing someone with your knowledge of the company and the interview process.

Researching the company before the interview is a must in your preparation. You should be familiar with the following company information before your interview begins:

- The interviewer's name.
- General information about the company, such as the location of the home office, number of plants/stores and their locations, names of parent company, subsidiaries, etc.

- Organizational structure, type of supervision, type of training program.
- Philosophy, goals, and image.
- Financial details, including sales volume, stock price, percent of annual growth in earnings per share, recent profits, etc.
- The competition in the industry and the company's place in it.
- The products or services marketed by the company, including recent media coverage of them.
- Career path in your field.
- Recent news items regarding the company or the industry. It is especially important to check the *Wall Street Journal's* business section to see if the company you are interviewing with is mentioned on the morning of the interview. Be prepared to speak on many aspects of the company.

Researching Target Companies via the World Wide Web

One of the easiest ways to research a company or organization is to do so over the Net. While not every organization has a WWW address, more and more companies are beginning to see the benefits of a homepage. This should make your Internet surfing for company information much easier. Library Net addresses, mentioned in Chapter 4, are a good place to check; you can also go directly to company Net addresses.

Many public companies have homepages on the Web. They typically provide information about their products and services, and many provide press releases and other news about themselves that is useful to investors. Increasingly, companies are posting employment opportunities on their Web pages.

Commercial Services on the Net—Open Market
http://www.directory.net
A very large index of commercial Web sites. You should be able to find a company Web page here if it exists.

Computer Related Companies
http://www.xnet.com/~blatura/computer.shtml
An excellent list of U.S. computer-related company Web pages.

Corporate Web Registry—Hoover's Company Profiles
http://www.hoovers.com/bizreg.html
Links to over 1,100 corporate Web sites, combined with extensive information about many corporations, including history, current business, personnel, and office locations. A wonderful resource.

Industrial Companies
http://www.xnet.com/~blatura/industry.shtml
A fine list of U.S. industrial company Web pages.

Hot 1000 List
http://techweb.cmp.com/techweb/ia/hot1000/hot1.html
This list includes any homepages officially established by or for the company among companies comprising the Fortune 1,000.

Public Companies
http://networth.galt.com/www/home/insider/publicco.htm
This list includes any homepages officially established by or for the company. As we go to press, the list contains 688 public companies.

Another part of preparation is constructing a list of questions to ask the interviewer at the end of the meeting. Producing a list of questions and asking intelligent questions about the company indicates that you're prepared and that you did your research. We include a list of possible questions for you to ask later in this chapter.

Practicing Before Your Interview
Another key part of preparation and of conducting the most successful of interviews is to practice the interview as much and in as many ways as possible. This can take many forms. However, the best way is to build a list of the questions you feel will be asked and to make sure that you know how to answer them and have answered them out loud to yourself or to someone helping you with a mock interview. Practice your answers and multiple variations of them and you will be much better prepared for the interview.

STEP 2: Dressing Right: Interviewing Fashion Do's and Don'ts

Never underestimate the power of a sharply dressed man or woman during an interview. Proper attire is a key ingredient to a good first impression with your prospective employer. Hygiene is equally important. Shaving should be done the morning before the interview. Perfume and cologne should be low key. Keep the hair trimmed, fingernails clean, and let your credentials and charm do the rest.

The Career-Dressed Woman
Within reason, a variety of conservative colors are appropriate for most interview situations. Many tasteful suits are available in black, brown, teal, taupe, olive, forest, maroon, burgundy, and plum. When selecting a suit, especially if you are on a limited budget, focus on classic cuts and styles. The proper fit is just as essential as the suit itself. A good suit should last at least five years. Try to select a high-quality fabric such as wool or wool gabardine. These are the coolest fabrics—making them appropriate not only for the stress of interviewing but also for everyday wear year-round.

If the shoe fits wear it! We see countless well-dressed women with shoes with run-down heels and scraped up toes. Don't brainwash yourself by thinking that they are only shoes and nobody looks at your feet anyway. Shoes are one of those make-or-break elements of your wardrobe. Make sure the local shoe repair has done a good job at keeping yours new-looking.

Keep it feminine: a lot of women still hold the idea that professional means masculine. Not true. Women's professional attire has come into its own since the late '80s and early '90s, when stiffly tailored dark suits paired with floppy bows and ties were all the rage. These have been replaced with soft scarves, unique pins, and more attractive colors and styles.

Keep in mind when selecting professional clothing that "feminine" in no way means "sleazy." Tight skirts, too high heels, and low-cut blouses are never appropriate, no matter how conservative their color or casual the office.

The bottom line is that much of business is influenced by image. You may not get that job because you look great, but not looking good may be a reason why you don't get hired.

The Career-Dressed Man
On your big shopping spree for the proper suit, try to be conservative, not flashy. Stick with darker colors like navy blue, dark gray, or black. Single-breasted vs. double-breasted? Whatever you look best in is what you should buy. Usually single-breasted is more conservative and probably best for interviewing.

Shirts and ties are very important in the construction of the perfect suit. Your dress shirts should be comfortable and fit properly around the neck. Tight shirts in the neck area tend to make you resemble Baby Huey or the Pillsbury Doughboy.

The tie can say a lot about the individual, so when choosing your tie be careful and take your time. Try to steer yourself toward the 100% silk ties; they tend to portray a more professional look. Don't allow the tie to overpower your suit with loud colors and crazy patterns. The proper length is also vital in choosing the right tie. Too short a tie makes you look silly. Once knotted, a tie should reach over your belt buckle. Anything higher is not acceptable.

Dress socks are a must. No thick socks and no athletic socks; this is your career, not a gymnasium. Coordinated color socks are essential and they should come over the calf so that when you sit down, you aren't flashing skin between the top of the sock and trouser cuff.

Polished wing-tip shoes are always safe. Make sure that your shoes are as shiny as a new dime. As is the case with women's shoes, your shoes can say a lot about you and should not be in a state of disrepair.

Common Dressing Mistakes Made by Men
Now that you are an expert on career dressing, here are a few mistakes made by men in their quest to dress to impress:

- The belt and suspenders faux pas. You only need one or the other to keep your pants up.
- Make sure that you are not wearing high-water pants. The length of the pant leg should reach the middle of your shoe.
- No knit ties. They went out some years ago with leisure suits.

- Iron your shirt. Wrinkles are not in style.
- No gaudy rings or chains. Save them for bar hopping or the discos. The fact remains that clothes make a difference in our society. One might wish that impressions did not count, but they do!

How to dress

A friend of ours who wanted to break into investment banking finally landed her first big interview with Merrill Lynch. It was fairly easy for her to do her homework on a company of that size. Two days before the interview, however, it suddenly dawned on her that she had no idea how to dress. How did she solve her problem?

"It was pretty easy, actually, and fun, too," says Laura. "All I did was go and hang around outside the office for 15 minutes at lunch time to see what everybody else was wearing."

However, we recommend that even if the office attire is casual, one should still dress professionally. One career counselor recommends that one should "always dress one step above the attire of those in the office where you are interviewing."

STEP 3: The First Impression

The first impression, whether we like it or not, is important in a successful interview. Start off the interview right! Arriving at least ten minutes early helps you relax a little rather than rushing into the meeting all tense and harried. Remember to treat the receptionist, secretary, and anyone else you meet the same way you would treat any potential boss. Be friendly and professional. They often have input into the selection of candidates.

The beginning of the interview is crucial. Many experts feel that the decision to hire you is made during the first four minutes. The rest of the interview is used to justify this earlier decision. Four things are important in creating that first impression. First, a firm handshake, for both men and women, is important. Second, try to make eye contact with the interviewer as much as possible—but don't have a staredown. Third, try to convey a positive attitude with a friendly smile; never underestimate yourself—past jobs and education have equipped you with valuable skills. And finally, say something simple early on to get those first words out of your mouth: "Very nice to meet you" should suffice. It is also important to address your interviewer by last name unless instructed to do otherwise.

STEP 4: Express Yourself

The bulk of the interview is designed for you to answer questions posed by the interviewer. Here are a few tips:

- Be aware of your non-verbal behavior. Wait to sit until you are offered a chair. Look alert, speak in a clear, strong voice, and stay relaxed. Make good eye contact, avoid nervous mannerisms, and try to be a good listener as well as a good talker. Smile.
- Follow the interviewer's lead, but try to get the interviewer to describe the position and duties to you fairly early in the interview so that you can later relate your background and skills in context.
- Be specific, concrete, and detailed in your answers. The more information you volunteer, the better the employer gets to know you and thereby is able to make a wise hiring decision.
- Don't mention salary in a first interview unless the employer does. If asked, give a realistic range and add that the opportunity is the most important factor for you.
- Offer examples of your work and references that will document your best qualities.
- Answer questions as truthfully and as frankly as you can. Never appear to be "glossing over" anything. On the other hand, stick to the point and don't over-answer questions. The interviewer may steer the interview into ticklish political or social questions. If this occurs, answer honestly, trying not to say more than is necessary.
- Never make derogatory remarks about present or former employers or companies.

Questions You May Be Asked During an Interview

Bear in mind that all questions you are asked during an interview serve a specific purpose. Try to put yourself in the interviewer's shoes. Imagine why he or she is asking the questions, and try to provide the answers that, while never dishonest, present you in the most desirable light. Direct your responses toward the particular position for which you are applying. What follows are some questions that employers often ask during interviews. As we mentioned earlier, it is advisable to rehearse answers to these questions prior to your interview so you can appear relaxed and confident.

Ice Breakers

These are designed to put you at ease and to see how well you engage in informal conversation. Be yourself, act natural, and be friendly.

- a. Did you have any trouble finding your way here?
- b. How was your plane flight?

c. Can you believe this weather?
   d. I see you're from Omaha. Why do you want to work in this area?

Work History and Education

These are to assess whether your background and skills are appropriate for the position. Talk about your skills coherently and relate them to the job to be filled. Give specific examples of how you used certain skills in the past. Remember that questions you are asked concerning your past will help the employer determine how you might react and make decisions in the future.

   a. *Tell me about yourself.
   b. Tell me about the most satisfying job/internship you've ever held.
   c. Tell me about the best boss you ever had. The worst.
   d. What have you learned from some of the jobs you've held?
   e. For what achievements were you recognized by your superiors at your last position?
   f. What are you looking for in an employer?
   g. What are you seeking in a position?
   h. Why did you choose to get a degree in the area that you did?
   i. In what activities have you participated outside of work (or class)?
   j. How did you finance your education?
   k. *What do you like/dislike about your current (or last) job?

Ambitions and Plans

These are questions to evaluate your ambition, how clearly you have thought about your future goals, their feasibility, and how actively you seek to meet them.

   a. Are you a joiner or more individually centered? A leader or a group member? A committee member or chairperson? (There isn't necessarily a wrong answer to this type of question. Keep in mind that a ship full of captains will flounder just as badly as a ship with none at all.)
   b. What job in our company would you choose if you were free to do so?
   c. What does success mean to you? How do you judge it?
   d. Assuming you are hired for this job, what do you see as your future?
   e. What personal characteristics do you think are necessary for success in this field?
   f. How far will you go to get ahead in your career?
   g. Are you willing to prove yourself as a staff member of our firm? How do you envision your role?
   h. Are you willing to work overtime?
   i. *Where do you see yourself five years from now?
   j. How much money do you hope to earn in five years? Ten years?

*Note: Questions marked with an asterisk (*) are among the toughest to answer. Further on in this chapter, the "15 Toughest Interview Questions" are treated in some depth so you can "ace" them when the time comes.

Company or Organization

These questions are to determine if you have conscientiously researched the company and if you would be a "match" for them. They also indicate your interest in the company.

a. Do you prefer working for a small or large organization?
b. Do you prefer a private or non-private organization? Why?
c. What do you know about our organization?
d. *Why are you interested in this company?
e. What kind of work are you interested in doing for us?
f. What do you feel our organization has to offer you?
g. *Why do you think you can contribute to our company?

Values and Self-Assessment

These help the interviewer get to know you better and to determine how well you understand yourself. They also help to inform the interviewer of what motivates you.

a. What kinds of personal satisfactions do you hope to gain through work?
b. If you had unlimited funds, what would you do?
c. *If you could live during any time in history, when and where would you live?
d. What motivates you?
e. What are your strengths and weaknesses?
f. How would you describe yourself?
g. What do you do with your free time?
h. What kind of people do you like to work with?
i. How do you adapt to other cultures?
j. *What is your greatest achievement?
k. *How do you manage stress?

How to Handle Objections During the Interview

It is not uncommon to face objections in an interview. It may be that the interviewer believes you lack some skills required. Don't panic! If you keep a level head, you will be able to recover. For example, one woman was applying for an assistant buyer position in the fragrance department of a retail operation although she had never sold perfumes. Her background was in shoes. The interviewer didn't feel she had enough knowledge of perfumes. But by the end of the interview, she had swayed the interviewer with facts of her past achievements as a salesperson, convincing him that skilled people are capable of learning any product line. She even discussed trends in the fragrance industry, which she had researched in a trade magazine—surprising the interviewer, who didn't expect her to know much about the subject.

If an interviewer appears to have an objection to hiring you, ask what it is. With this knowledge, you may be able to change the interviewer's mind or redefine the job description to fit your qualifications.

STEP 5: Questions, You Must Have Questions

A typical interviewer comment toward the close of an interview is to ask if you have any questions. Never just say "no." Keep a list of questions in mind to ask. Sometimes even the worst of interviews can be salvaged by good questions. If you believe that most questions were answered during the interview, try the "not-really-a-question" tactic. This might be a statement such as, "As I mentioned, I believe that my creativity and attention to detail are my strengths. How do you think these would fit into the organization?" Here are a few other questions you might ask.

Questions to Ask Interviewers
- What would a normal working day be like?
- About how many individuals go through your program each year?
- How much contact is there with management?
- During training, are employees transferred among functional fields?
- How soon could I expect to be advanced to the next level in the career path?
- How much travel is normally expected?
- Will I be expected to meet certain deadlines? How frequent are they?
- How often are performance reviews given?
- How much decision-making authority is given after one year?
- Does the company provide any educational benefits?
- How frequently do you relocate professional employees?
- Have any new product lines/services been announced recently?
- What are the essential skills/qualities necessary for an employee to succeed in this position?
- Where are the last two people who held this position (did they leave the company or get promoted)?
- What role would my job play in helping the company achieve its corporate mission and make a profit?
- What are the five most important duties of this job?
- Why did you join the company? What is it about the company that keeps you here?
- What has the company's growth pattern been over the past five years?

At the conclusion of the interview, ask when a hiring decision will be made. This is important not only because it reconfirms your interest in the position but also so you'll know when, realistically, to expect a response. Don't forget, of course, to thank your interviewer for his or her time and to make clear your interest in the position if you feel there may be any doubt about this point.

STEP 6: The Aftermath

As soon as you leave the interview and have a chance, take notes on what you feel you could improve upon for your next interview and on what you feel went particularly well. After all, experience is only valuable to the extent that you're willing to learn from it. It also helps to make a note of something in the interview you might use in your thank-you letter.

The All-Important Thank-You Letter

Always follow up each interview with a prompt thank-you letter—written the same day, if possible. The purpose of the letter is to supplement the presentation you made. Thank the interviewer for his or her hospitality. Express continued interest in the position, and mention up to three additional points to sell yourself further. Highlight how your specific experience or knowledge is directly applicable to the company's immediate needs, and if you forgot to mention something important in the interview, say it now. If possible, try to comment on something the interviewer said. Use that comment to show how your interests and skills perfectly match what they're looking for.

    The thank-you letter should be sent A.S.A.P.! Your name should remain in front of the interviewer as much as possible. Sending the letter immediately will demonstrate how serious you are about the position. It may well be the final factor in helping you land the job.

Get the most from your references

References should remain confidential and never revealed until a company is close to making you an offer and you want to receive one.

    Always brief your references before you supply an interviewer with their names and numbers. Tell the references what company you're interviewing with and what the job is. Give them some background on the company and the responsibilities you'll be asked to handle.

    Your references will then be in a position to help sell your abilities. Finally, don't abuse your references. If you give their names too often, they may lose enthusiasm for your cause.

Waiting

Now the waiting begins. Try not to be too impatient, and remember that for the time being no answer is better than a rejection. There could be many reasons why you haven't heard from the company. It could be that the interview process has not concluded, or that other commitments have kept the company from making a decision. The most important point to remember during this time is that all your hopes shouldn't be pinned on one or two interviews. The job search is continuous and shouldn't stop until you have accepted a job offer. Keeping all your options open is the best possible plan.

However, if much time has passed and you haven't heard anything from a company in which you are particularly interested, a telephone call or letter asking about the status of your application is appropriate. This inquiry should be stated in a manner that is not pushy but shows your continued interest in the firm. Remember that waiting is an integral part of the job hunt, but a demonstration of your continued interest is appropriate.

Many job seekers experience a kind of euphoria after a good interview. Under the impression that a job offer is imminent, a candidate may discontinue the search. This is a serious mistake. The hiring decision may take weeks or may not be made at all. On average, about six weeks elapse between the time a person makes initial contact with a company and receives a final answer. If you let up on your job search, you will prolong it. Maintain a constant sense of urgency. Get on with the next interview. Your search isn't over until an offer is accepted and you actually begin your new job.

15 Toughest Interview Questions—and How To Answer Them

1. Tell me about yourself. This question, in one form or another, is one of the most likely to be asked. It is also one of the most likely questions to be answered poorly. Answer it without going into your personal life or family background. Stick to your professional and educational background and how it applies to the job you are interested in. Focus on your strengths and—especially with this question—remember to keep your response brief.

2. Teach me how to do something. This question is sometimes used in a consulting or sales company interview. One candidate responded by verbally teaching the interviewer how to play tennis. The subject of the lesson isn't what matters but, rather, the teaching presentation. The interviewer is assessing how well you would do in front of a client. Do you have the skills to impress or persuade a person, and are you articulate and sophisticated in your presentation? Most importantly, can you think on your feet?

3. Should city buses be free? You are probably wondering what free buses have to do with you getting the job. Nothing! Instead, the interviewer wants to see how you think the question through. The interviewer doesn't expect you to have expertise in this area and wants dialogue to occur. Don't be afraid to ask questions to determine whether you are heading in the right direction. Always modify your thinking with whatever information the interview may provide to you. Keep in mind that analytical ability is important but so are enthusiasm and creativity.

4. Do you know how to operate a Macintosh computer? On your resume you listed PC knowledge, but you have no experience with the Mac. Then why did the interviewer ask this question? Either the company uses Macs or the interviewer wanted to pull a weakness from your resume. Rather than bluntly saying "no," rephrase your response as: "I have gained a good deal of experience on the PC and with many programs. I feel comfortable with computers, and the transition to the Mac should be fairly easy."

5. Why do you think you can contribute to our company? Most candidates will answer in a typical manner that they are energetic, motivated, and a hard worker. This may or may not be true, but every interviewer has heard this response. What is more effective is to respond with examples or facts from your past experiences that draw the interviewer a picture of how you are a go-getter. This is an excellent question to prepare for, as it gives you an idea of what makes you unique from all other qualified candidates on the market.

6. If you could live during any time in history, when and where would you live? This is an off-the-wall question but it will occur sometimes. The interviewer probably doesn't expect a specific answer. And he may not let you off the hook after you give your answer. Feel free to give yourself time to think before answering; a pensive pause can sometimes even help an interview. Whatever your answer, have a reason for choosing it because almost certainly the interviewer will follow up with, "Why did you choose that?" At work the unexpected happens, and the interviewer wants to see how you deal with it.

7. What is your greatest achievement? This question allows the interviewer to assess both values and skills. What you select as your achievement will express what is important to you. And at the same time your narrative will reveal skills you have acquired. The interviewer will be interested in listening for skills necessary for the job opening.

8. Do you think your grades were a good indication of your academic achievement? If you were an A student, you can respond enthusiastically, "Yes!" However, those of us who had less than fantastic grades will respond differently. There are many reasons you may not have had high grades. For example: you worked full time while attending school or you were involved in many outside organizations. Turn the answer into a positive by explaining the benefits you received from the trade-offs of working and attending school. Emphasize your common sense and creativity rather than your grades. Besides, grades are not everything.

9. Why are you interested in this company? If you've done your homework on the company, you shouldn't sweat over this question. This is your opportunity to show how well your skills and values match that of the company's.

10. What do you like/dislike about your current (or last) job? You need to be alert when answering this question. Criticizing a former employer could send the message that you are a troublemaker or have a negative attitude, which could spell the end to your prospects with this company. Be as positive about your work experience as possible. Emphasize what you contributed and learned from the company. Even a negative experience can be translated into challenges and learning opportunities.

11. Describe how you dealt with a difficult problem. Try to be as positive as you can, and focus on the approach you used rather than any negative outcomes. For example, describe how you examined the problem, developed several alternative solutions, and implemented the solutions. Emphasize any positive outcomes from your solutions.

12. Where do you see yourself five years from now? Be realistic in your answer rather than trying to impress the interviewer. You can reiterate your goals to advance while still being a team player. And you can add that new opportunities are bound to arise within the company, which will also affect what you would like to be doing five years from now. Emphasize how the current job you are interviewing for will prepare you for five-year goals.

13. How do you manage stress? Listen carefully to the question. This isn't asking "can" you manage stress, but rather "how." The basic answer to this question involves giving an example of how you maintained your cool, pulled everyone together, and came up with a positive result, all without becoming overwhelmed.

14. What can you do for our company that someone else cannot? Similar to Question 5, this question usually will come after a description of the job has been provided. You need to reiterate what skills you have that pertain to the position and the company overall. Reemphasize those qualities that you feel are unique and how they might help the organization.

15. Could you explain these gaps in your work history? You may have gaps in your work history for many legitimate reasons. What you want to express is that you enjoy working and that when things aren't going as planned (maybe you were laid off) you are challenged to learn and overcome. Be sure to describe any studying or volunteer work that you may have done while unemployed.

Nine Interview Styles to Watch For

The interviewing process can be tricky at times. Most applicants are clueless as to how the interview will go or what it will entail. Many job seekers and career changers will eventually encounter some of these interview types. Knowing a little about each of them is certainly advantageous. Knowing what to expect will boost your confidence and dry out those nervous, sweaty palms.

Behavioral Interviewing. A new technique for interviewing, behavioral interviewing assumes that past behavior predicts future performance. You can easily recognize when an interviewer is using "behavioral interviewing" because you will be asked questions about how you have worked in the past. For example, "Tell me about a time where you successfully learned a new software package"; or, "Tell me about a conflict you had with a co-worker and how you dealt with it." The employer expects you to tell short stories about yourself to give more insight into how you behave at work.

The best strategy to use when answering behavioral interview questions is the STAR technique. STAR stands for situation, task, action, result. First, describe the situation and task you were assigned in order to set the stage. Next, review the action you took. Plan to spend the most time on this part of the answer because your past performance is what the employer is most interested in. Finally, emphasize the results, the outcome of your actions.

Situation: "I was assigned sales manager for a new product my company was introducing."

Task: "I was to develop a marketing plan to determine best sales techniques."

Action: "I created a market survey instrument and conducted a campaign to assess consumer preference. I also conducted blind taste tests at local supermarkets."

Result: "The result was a successful marketing campaign that saw sales of our product skyrocket by 42%."

With STAR, you are able to convince the employer that you are capable of performing the open job by demonstrating your past success.

The Analytical Interview. The analytical interview is designed to let the interviewer see you think on your feet. The interviewer will ask you challenging questions to see how you analyze and perform under pressure. You may hear some off-the-wall questions like the examples below. In some cases you may be given a pen and paper, but don't be surprised if you're not. Most of the time the interviewer is looking for an answer that is simply in the ball park. If you are totally stumped and caught off guard by the question, think creatively. You also are better off answering humorously than not at all. Remember, the interviewer

is interested in your thinking process, not just in how you derived the answer. Here are some questions that may put you on the spot.
- Why are manhole covers round?
- What are the number of square yards of pizza eaten in the U.S. each year?
- How many gas stations would you estimate there are in the United States?

How much does a 747 weigh?
D. N. Meehan, a senior scientist at Union Pacific Resources Corporation, was interviewing a young man. Meehan asked the candidate to estimate the weight of a fully loaded 747 at takeoff. It's pretty obvious that coming up with the correct answer would be very difficult for almost anyone. Since the applicant was not versed in aviation, he felt he would have to come up with something creative and unique in order to leave a lasting impression on the interviewer. The candidate asked if he could use anything in the room and then proceeded to use Meehan's computer. It was a surprise to Meehan when the candidate turned on the "flight simulator" game and came up with the correct answer.

Tennis, anyone?
Theo Kruijssen, a university student, was asked "How many matches need to be played in a single elimination tennis tournament if there are 256 participants?" Eagerly, Theo began using his math background and developed an equation to solve the problem. Several minutes later, he had his answer. The interviewer, however, was not as impressed as Theo was. The interviewer said that it was quite simple: "There are 255 matches. Each match has one loser and everyone loses once except the winner."

Stress Interviewing. The stress interview is like a horror film. It is more interesting to see than to be in. The intent of the interviewer is to determine how well you can handle pressure or a crisis situation.

Usually, the interviewee doesn't recognize a stress situation. For example, a candidate was taken to lunch by two recruiters. The recruiters informed the candidate that he didn't have the qualifications for the job, and then they began talking among themselves. In reality, they were seeing how he would respond to rejection since the position was in sales, which required dealing with stress and rejection.

Your best strategy for the stress interview is to recognize questions in disguise. Rather than becoming hostile, relax and attempt to present your case to the employer. There are endless cases where the interviewee allows the discussion to get under his skin and make his blood boil. Instead, be humble and try to ignore anything that offends you. Even though questions are designed to insult you, view this as a challenge and answer candidly.

No stress interviewing information would be complete without at least one horror story. A director of a business school placement office told us one that injects new meaning into the word stress. A candidate was interviewing with a Wall Street firm that was known for challenging interviews. He walked into a large boardroom, and at the end of the table, a partner, holding a newspaper in front of his face, said, "Get my attention." Thinking quickly, the candidate took out his lighter and set the newspaper on fire. We're not sure if he got the job, but he did get the partner's attention.

The Manhattan, Kansas, Interview. This type of interview occurs more often than you are aware of since it forms a hidden agenda within the interview itself. We often hear interviewers talk about how they would feel about a candidate if they were stuck with him or her in the airport in Manhattan, Kansas, or anywhere else for that matter, for twenty-four hours. Would you be pals or get on each other's nerves? Many times this assessment is based solely on personality and fit with the interviewer's personality. However, it does serve as a reminder that it is the interviewer who is recommending you for the job, not someone else in the company. You must impress your interviewer while also showing that you're a pretty good person to have around.

Stream of Consciousness Interviewing. This interview goes something like this: "Well let me tell you something about the company, we are located downtown, which is a great place for lunch, as a matter of fact I found a wonderful little restaurant last week that served wonderful pasta, it tasted just like something I had in Italy last year, Italy, now that's a great place to visit, I went there with my sister and we had a blast, Milan, Rome, and Florence, the art is wonderful."

Are you starting to get the picture? Just because you know how to interview doesn't mean your interviewer does. Sometimes you need to learn how to control the interview. For first timers this can be extremely difficult. You also need to be sure that you do not embarrass or insult your interviewer. One way to insert yourself into the stream of consciousness interview is to ask questions about the company and quickly follow up with statements about how your particular strengths would work well in that environment. This type of interview is a real challenge. Make sure that the interviewer leaves with a positive impression of who you are rather than just a feeling of having told a good story.

The Epicurean Interview. If you are in an all-day interview and someone offers to take you to lunch, it may not be as relaxing as it sounds. This is not your moment to put your interviewing skills on the back burner. When going to lunch during the interview process, never let your killer-interview guard down. While conversation may be informal, evaluation is still present. Here are some Epicurean hints for the lunch interview:

- Don't order the most expensive item simply because you are not paying. It is best to order something in the medium price range. Also, don't worry about saving money by ordering the cheapest item; order what you want within reason.
- Stay away from spaghetti, spinach, and shrimp dishes or any other dish that could give you embarrassment. It can be extremely awkward trying to work a piece of food out from between your teeth or slurping up a long pasta noodle.
- If you don't drink alcohol, this is not the time to begin. And if you do drink, we recommend you wait until you have the job. If you must drink, limit yourself to just one. It is best to be as alert as possible during the lunch interview.
- Try to relax. Finding common interests between the interviewer and yourself will help lighten the conversation.

Dear Dr. Bob
How about sharing an interesting Epicurean experience with us.— Sincerely, The Epicurean Club.

Dear Epicurean Club
A student I worked with told me a story about going to a classy restaurant with a potential employer. Having talked a great deal and eaten only a little during the meal, the student decided to order what she thought was a simple dessert. But being a classy restaurant where swank desserts were served, she received a large, flaming dessert. In fact, it was such a large, flaming dessert that the waiter set the plant hanging over the table on fire. Needless to say, the student made a burning impression on the employer. Bon appetit!

The Athletic Interview. From time to time athleticism, or at least some degree of fitness, can help during an interview. I recall one interview where I was told to meet my potential employer on a popular street corner in New York City. We were to meet and then go someplace to talk. As my luck would have it, by the time the interviewer showed up, he was late for a train at Penn Station. However, he was still interested in talking with me, so in business suits and briefcases we jogged to the station. He made his train and I got a second interview. Always be ready for the unexpected, even if it takes a little more out of you than you expected.

The Grunge Interview. We have talked about proper dress during the interview. There are still those, however, who believe that the best way to interview is to feel comfortable with yourself and your dress. In other words, be yourself and the job is bound to come. Wrong! Take this one opportunity to blend in with those that are interviewing you, and do not make an issue or statement with your clothes. Once you get the job and they see what a great employee you are, they will better understand your dressing desires and requirements. No matter how cool it looks to grunge dress and no matter how comfortable you feel, take our advice and hang up the blue jeans for a few hours.

Dr. Bob's Friendly Interview. As I finished up this section on interviewing, a staff member alerted me to the fact that I had not included my own style of interviewing: the "friendly interview," in which the employer is quite pleasant and lulls you into thinking that he likes everyone. The idea is to catch you off guard with a simple question that might reveal more than you planned about who you are. The way to handle this (and every interview) is to understand that your interview face must be on at all times, always presenting your best side. We all know that everyone has weaknesses; the interview, however, is not the time to let people know about them.

A Few Final Tips on Interviewing

In many ways an interview is like a first date. You can't predict how it will turn out. However, like a date, you can prepare yourself to make the best impression possible. You can also assess whether the company is a good match for you. Just as your first date may not be your best, likewise your first interview may not be your best.

However, you can learn from your mistakes and correct them in future interviews. Most importantly, don't forget to follow-up. If you had the dream date, you wouldn't forget to call again—so must you write the "thank-you letter" to the potential employer.

Rejected? How Can It Happen?

Remember that the world is full of rejections and failures. What would motivate us to improve if we didn't have past failures? Everybody flunks at some point in their life; nobody is perfect. To give you a flavor of how to really fail an interview, here are some major employer turn-offs (provided by the Lindquist-Endicott Report, Northwestern University):

Sloppy appearance. Like it or not, people form lasting impressions of you within the first seconds of the interview. When dressing for an interview, pay close attention to details.

Arrogant attitude. If employers had to sum up the qualities they are looking for in candidates in two words, they would likely be "team player." They want people whose first loyalty is to the company and who are willing to work for the good of the group. Arrogant individualists have no place in this environment.

Limited knowledge about the company or the field. No greater turn-off than to expect the employer to tell you about his or her company. One of Procter and Gamble's favorite interview questions is, "Which of the P&G products is your favorite?" Simple question, but it surprises many.

Asking about the salary or benefits too early. Asking about the salary too early in the interview says nothing about what you can do for the company, only what you want from them. You don't want the employer to think that you are selfish with a one-way mind.

Lack of clarity in long-range goals. Employers want to know why you want a particular job and where you want to go with it. Demonstrate that you have some sort of career plan and that that plan fits in with the company's goals.

Failure to ask for the job. Interviewing is like a sales presentation. After you have spent time marketing yourself, don't forget to close the deal. Ask for the job and let them know you are interested.

How to Bounce Back from Rejection

Do these lines sound familiar? "You're really not the right one." "We liked you, but we've decided not to hire right now." "You really don't have the experience we are looking for." "You are overqualified." These phrases occur more often than we would like. It's important to keep your sanity and courage during the interview process.

Anger, stress, guilt, fear, and anxiety are unfortunate companions to any job search. The strategy, therefore, is to learn to deal with rejection in a healthy and constructive manner and not let it distort your judgment. Develop methods to compensate for the beating your ego may take during the job search. Family and friends can be an excellent source for encouragement and positive support. Don't forget to eat well and exercise to relieve the stress involved in the job search. Be persistent and don't give up! Eddie Rickenbacker once said, "Try like hell to win, but don't cry if you lose." This should be one of your mottoes.

What Do Interviewers Really Want To See?

General Personality. Ambition, poise, sincerity, trustworthiness, initiative, and interest in the firm. (General intelligence is assumed.) Different firms look for different kinds of people, personalities, style, appearance, abilities, and technical skills. Always check the job specifications. Don't waste time talking about a job you can't do or for which you don't have the minimum qualifications.

Personal Appearance. A neat, attractive appearance makes a good impression and demonstrates professionalism.

Work Experience. Again, this varies from job to job, so check job specifications. Be able to articulate the importance of what you did in terms of the job for which you are interviewing and in terms of your own growth or learning. Even if the work experience is unrelated to your new field, employers look upon knowledge of the work environment as an asset.

Verbal Communication Skills. The ability to express yourself articulately is very important. This includes the ability to listen effectively, verbalize thoughts clearly, and express yourself confidently.

Skills. The interviewer will evaluate your skills for the job, such as organization, analysis, and research. It is important to emphasize the skills that you feel the employer is seeking and to give specific examples of how you developed them. This is the main reason why it is important to engage in self-assessment prior to the interview.

Goals/Motivation. Employers will assess your ability to articulate your short-term and long-term goals. You should seem ambitious yet realistic about the training and qualifications needed to advance. Demonstrate your interest in the functional area or industry and a desire to succeed and work hard.

Knowledge of the Interviewer's Company and Industry. At a minimum, you are expected to have done some homework on the company. Don't waste interview time asking questions you could have found answers to in printed material. Know the firm's position and character relative to others in the same industry. General awareness of media coverage of a firm and its industry is usually expected.

CYBERTIPS ON INTERVIEWING

As with most aspects of the job search, the Internet is full of sites with tips on interviewing and the latest in interviewing news. We have listed a few below:

Career Channel
http://riceinfo.rice.edu/projects/careers/Channel/seven/Interview/text/The.interview.html

Career Magazine
http://www.careermag.com/careermag/newsarts/interviewing.html

Catapult
http://www.wm.edu/catapult/catapult.html **or**
http://www.wm.edu/catapult/enelow-i.html

BOOKS ON INTERVIEWING

Biegelein, J. I. *Make Your Job Interview a Success.* New York: Arco, 1994.

Danna, Jo. *Winning the Job Interview Game: Tips for the High-Tech Era.* Briarwood, NY: Palamino Press, 1986.

Fear, Richard A. *The Evaluation Interview.* New York: McGraw-Hill, 1990.

King, Julie Adair. *The Smart Woman's Guide to Interviewing and Salary Negotiation.* Hawthorne, NJ: Career Press, 1993.

Krannich, Caryl R. *Interview for Success.* San Luis Obispo, CA: Impact, 1995.

Marcus, John J. *The Complete Job Interview Handbook.* New York: Harper & Row, 1994.

Medley, H. Anthony. *Sweaty Palms: The Neglected Art of Being Interviewed.* Berkeley, CA: Ten Speed Press, 1992.

Pettus, Theodore. *One On One—Win the Interview, Win the Job.* New York: Random House, 1981.

Smart, Bradford D. *The Smart Interviewer.* New York: John Wiley & Sons, 1990.

Stewart, Charles J., and William B. Cash. *Interviewing Principles and Practices.* Dubuque, IA: William C. Brown Publishers, 1994.

Yate, Martin. *Knock 'em Dead.* Holbrook, MA: Adams Publishing, 1995.

Summer, Temporary, and Part-Time Jobs

For some, getting a job is seen as a summer only or as a temporary proposition. If that is the case, this is the chapter for you. First, summer jobs.

Summer Jobs—Findable and Rewarding

Summer provides the unique opportunity for students to brainstorm about careers that strike their interest. This is an experimental time in which the employer takes only a limited risk. But, how does one go about finding a summer job?

Finding a summer job is very similar to finding a permanent job. Persistence and positive attitude are keys for the high school or college job seeker just as they are for the full-time worker. Here are a few simple hints for prospective summer job seekers.

Set realistic expectations. Don't expect to get rich with summer work and, most importantly, realize that you won't get to the top after a week's work. Some progress can be expected, but summer jobbers should realize that they aren't on the same totem pole as permanent workers.

Have the right attitude. Nothing impresses an employer more than the right attitude. What do they want in an employee? Someone who is loyal, respectful, polite, punctual, enthusiastic, and hardworking. Remember that the number of people who really have all these qualities is small. If you can demonstrate your willingness to be the right person, you may get the job.

Dress right. Dress is a real issue with the summer job seeker. The best way to dress for summer jobs is somewhere between a suit and tie, as parents might encourage, and jeans and T-shirt, as friends might suggest. A collared shirt with slacks or khakis for guys, and slacks or skirt for young women are certainly acceptable. Additionally, wear leather shoes, not sneakers.

Be persistent. As a job seeker you can't be persistent enough. A true key to success in a summer job search is to keep trying, often with the same employer. Many summer success stories come from young people who visit their top five summer job sites of choice once a week until they get a job. One common mistake made by summer job seekers is to stop looking once they think they have a job. Even if an interview goes well or an employer says they like you, you must keep going until you have an actual job offer.

Interview well. Hopefully, after all your searching and preparation, your final challenge will be the interview. But don't be too worried; after all, if you get the interview, you do have a good chance of getting the job, or else the company wouldn't be wasting their time with you. For a successful interview, keep in mind these familiar guidelines: (1) Give specific reasons why you are right for the job; (2) Try to relate every question to your strengths of being loyal, enthusiastic, and other desirable qualities; (3) Inject a little humor into your otherwise serious and hardworking nature—but don't overkill on the comedy; and finally (4) Ask lots of questions to demonstrate your interest in the position.

As you go out into the summer job market, there are a few areas that can present stumbling blocks to your search. These include fear of risk; failing to contact the right person within the company; and taking no for an answer. (In other words, not being persistent enough.) If, on the other hand, you avoid these common traps, you will most likely find yourself on your way to a rewarding summer job experience.

If you are hesitant about working during the summer because you would rather be sitting by the pool, consider the many non-indoor summer opportunities. A summer job doesn't have to be inside an office or fast-food restaurant. There are paid internships offered by non-profit organizations that are not the typical office job environment.

As with any summer job, finding a good one requires starting your search as early as possible. The application process alone takes time, not to mention the research portion.

Dr. Bob's Six-Step Summer Job-Hunt System

How do you get a job for the summer? Our tried and true system has worked for students and others for years.

1. **Know what you want to do.** Try to make a decision about what you want to do as early as possible. The sooner you decide, the sooner you can begin your search. Don't forget, the Career Center at your school provides resources and counseling to students. (See Chapter 2 for information on choosing a career.)
2. **Develop a resume.** It is important to accomplish this as early as possible since companies and application deadlines are as early as December for some summer jobs. (See Chapter 6 for details on resume and cover letter writing.)
3. **Write a cover letter.** A good cover letter is essential—it directs attention to your resume. Don't forget to have your resume and cover letter critiqued by a friend and career counselor, if possible.
4. **Do research and make contacts.** This step takes the longest, but hard work here can really pay off. Information interviews (see Chapter 5) with people in your field can help develop contacts. Don't forget your Alumni Office to develop a list of prospective employers. Make as many contacts as possible, and as soon as you have your contact list, begin mailing letters and resumes. A helpful tip is to send your letters in batches so you can track them efficiently and follow up each one with a letter.
5. **Follow-up and persistence.** This is the most important step! Make sure that for every letter you send out, for every person you talk to, and for every potential job site you visit, you continue to call back and let them know you are interested. Failure to follow up is disastrous for many a summer job searcher.
6. **Schedule interviews.** As part of your follow-up, try to schedule interviews. Give your letters time to arrive, then follow up with a phone call. This will keep you a step ahead of most college students, who don't start looking for summer jobs until school is out. Finally, make sure you know how to perform the "killer" interview discussed in Chapter 7.

Summer Job Hunting on the Net

Be sure and use your computer in your summer job search. Below are a few sources to get you started.

Career Mosaic
http://www.careermosaic.com/cm/
Lists job opportunities for cooperative education or internships.

Summer, Temporary, and Part-Time Jobs

CareerNet—Career Resource Center
http://www.careers.org
Be sure to look to CareerNet for links to current jobs, employer sites, newsgroups, and government sites throughout the year.

Cooperative Education/Internships
http://www.jobtrak.com/jobguide/coop.html
Lists cooperative education, internships, and summer work with links to other sources.

JobTrak
http://www.jobtrak.com
An excellent place to look for jobs posted at member colleges and universities. You'll need a password, however. Check with your college placement or career office.

National Internships
http://campus.net/busemp/nintern/
Student internships and part-time jobs in: Southern and Northern CA; Washington, DC; New York City; Seattle; Texas; and many other places. Job opportunities in the private, non-profit, and government sectors.

National Internship Directory
http://www.tripod.com/work/internships

Online Career Center
http://occ.com/occ
Try a keyword search on "internship" to get just a list of these.

Peace Corps
http://www.clark.net/pub/peace/PeaceCorps.html
Those interested can examine frequently asked questions about working for the Peace Corps; timelines for the application process; a list of countries where volunteers are assigned; and a description of the domestic program.

Peterson's Education Center
http://www.petersons.com
Check this new resource for internship opportunities at colleges and universities nationwide. You will also find information on summer job opportunities.

Summer Urban Ministry Opportunities Directory
http://www.fileshop.com/iugm/sumr-dir.html
Lists national and international positions.

Top 11 Summer Internship Programs in Southern California

The following is a list of paid internship programs in Southern California that generally accept applicants from all walks of life—from recent college grads to career changers to people re-entering the workforce. Many of the following internships are available year-round as well.

Academy of Television Arts & Sciences
Internship Program
5220 Lankershim Blvd.
North Hollywood, CA 91601
(818) 754-2830
http://www.emmys.org
Eight-week summer program open to undergraduates and recent graduates. Positions are available within 24 areas ranging from Art Direction and Script Writing to Syndication and Public Relations. Interns receive a stipend, moving allowance for those out of the Southern California area, assistance in finding housing, and special perks such as free screenings and mentoring programs.

Assistant Directors Training Program
15503 Ventura Blvd.
Encino, CA 91436
(818) 386-2545
http://dga.org/trainingprogram/
Elizabeth Stanley, Administrator
During their 400 days of on-the-job training, paid trainees are assigned to work on episodic television, television movies, pilots, and feature films with various studios and production companies. The typical workday is 12-16 hours. Upon completion of the Program, participants are added to the Southern California Area Qualification List, making them available for employment as a Second Assistant Director. Trainees must be at least 21 years of age. The application process includes a written test administered in Los Angeles.

The Coro Foundation
Coro Fellows Program
Southern California Center
811 Wilshire Blvd., Suite 1025
Los Angeles, CA 90017
Open to college graduates of any discipline who are interested in careers in public service. Interns are rotated among five internship sites within Government, Community Organizations, Corporations, Labor Unions, and Political Offices between September and June. Toward the end of the program, each Fellow pursues an individual public service project on a topic of his or her choice.

Disney, Walt, Studios
Internship Program Administration
500 S. Buena Vista St.
Burbank, CA 91521
(818) 560-6335
Offers 20 summer internships in the areas of Production, Finance, or Feature Animation. Disney interns earn a weekly stipend, have access to the Disney lot, and attend seminars with senior-level executives.

Fund for the Feminist Majority
8105 W. 3rd St., Suite 1
Los Angeles, CA 90048
(213) 651-0495
Interns participate in a wide variety of projects from analyzing legislative trends to lobbying and working on current campaigns. The internship is flexible with a rolling admission. College and graduate students are eligible.

Getty Undergraduate Internship in the Arts and Humanities
Department of Education and Academic Affairs
The J. Paul Getty Museum
P.O. Box 2112
Santa Monica, CA 90407
(310) 451-6545
Interns work at full-time summer positions within Southern California museums and galleries and attend special workshops offered by the Getty. Interns work in such varied areas as Administration, Curatorial Research, Education, Computer Technology, and Publications. There is particular emphasis placed on examining the role of cultural diversity within the arts. Interns receive a stipend and assistance with housing.

Interning for the Getty

"I loved my summer there," reports Lynn Charles, who is studying history and economics at Scripps College. Lynn worked as a Getty Intern at the Huntington Museum, Library and Botanical Gardens. As a Manuscript Department Intern, Lynn performed archival research for an upcoming exhibit. Not only did the internship confirm her career interests, Lynn made valuable contacts at the Museum and at the Getty-sponsored seminars. The best part? "They treated me as though I were a staff member."

Los Angeles Times Editorial Internships
Times Mirror Square
Los Angeles, CA 90053
(800) 283-NEWS, ext. 74487
Paid full-time summer programs and part-time spring and fall positions offered to undergraduates and recent grads. Interns work as journalists within daily edition news bureaus. Some opportunities exist to work in photojournalism or copy editing as well.

Mattel
Recruiting Department
333 Continental Blvd.
El Segundo, CA 90245
(310) 524-2000

Twelve-week program places interns in departments such as Marketing, Finance, Design, Chemistry Lab, and Human Resources. Positions are open to high school students, undergraduates, and graduate students. Pay determined according to experience level.

MCA/Universal
Internship Program
100 Universal City Plaza
Universal City, CA 91608
(818) 777-1000
Interns participate in a broad range of duties, usually specializing in Production, Publicity, Casting, Legal, Finance, or Marketing. College juniors, seniors, and grads are eligible to apply. Perks include movie tickets and admission to screenings.

National Aeronautics and Space Administration (NASA)
Jet Propulsion Laboratory(JPL)
Educational Affairs Office
4800 Oak Grove Drive
Pasadena, CA 91109
(818) 354-8251
Known as JPL, the Jet Propulsion Laboratory designs automated spacecraft such as Voyager and Galileo. Summer interns are involved either in business administration or assisting with experiments, designs, and tests. Pay varies with position.

San Diego Zoo
Human Resources
P.O. Box 551
San Diego, CA 92112
(619) 231-1515
Internship programs are established within two departments: the Center for Reproduction of Endangered Animals (CRES) and in Public Relations. The CRES program is a 12-week summer internship during which interns are part of a staff that conducts animal research in behavior, genetics, and physiology. It is open to both college students and recent graduates. Public Relations internships are available throughout the summer, spring, and fall and typically last for 16 weeks. Perks of interning at the San Diego Zoo include free passes to the zoo and "backstage" tours of zoo facilities.

RECOMMENDED SOURCES AND GUIDES FOR INTERNSHIPS

The Academy of Television Arts and Sciences
Student Internship Program, 5220 Lankershim Blvd., North Hollywood, CA 91601, (818) 754-2830 (provides internships in the media field).

The American Institute of Architects
Director, Education Programs, 1735 New York Ave., N.W., Washington, DC 20006 (provides information on architectural internships).

Inroads, Inc.
100 South Broadway, P.O. Box 8766, Suite 700, St. Louis, MO 63102 (African-American, Native American, and Hispanic-American students can intern in the areas of business, engineering, and science).

National Audubon Society
Government Affairs Internship Program, 666 Pennsylvania Ave., S.E., Washington, DC 20003, (202) 547-9009 (provides internships in resource conservation and wildlife management).

National Directory of Internships
National Society for Internships and Experiential Education, 122 St. Mary's St., Raleigh, NC 27605 (provides information on internships in a variety of areas).

National Institutes of Health
Summer Internship Program, Office of Education, Bldg. 10, Room 1C129, 9000 Rockville Pike, Bethesda, MD 20892, (301) 402-2176 (provides internships working alongside influential scientists).

Oldman, Mark, and Samer Hamadeh. *The Princeton Review; America's Top 100 Internships.* New York: Villard Books, 1995.

Temporary/Part-Time Jobs

Locating part-time work in your chosen field is ideal since you can continue to develop your network of contacts. Many professionals can freelance. An administrative assistant, for example, might be able to find part-time work at a law firm. An accountant might be able to do taxes on a part-time basis and still gain access to new referrals.

Another option is independent contracting. For example, if you're a computer programmer and the company you're interviewing with can't justify hiring someone full time because there isn't enough work, suggests that they hire you on a temporary basis for specific projects. Or offer to come in one or two days a week. Or suggest that you work on an as-needed basis. The advantage to the company is that they don't have to pay you benefits (except those you're able to negotiate). The advantage to you is income and experience in your chosen field.

People with technical skills can work themselves into becoming full-time freelancers in precisely this manner. They might even talk an employer OUT of hiring them full time and negotiate contract work in order to maintain the freedom of their self-employed status.

Below are some employment agencies that may assist you in your search for a temporary job.

LOS ANGELES EMPLOYMENT AGENCIES

Accountemps
10877 Wilshire Blvd., Suite 1605
Los Angeles, CA 90024
(310) 286-6800

Career Group
1999 Avenue of the Stars, Suite 1150
Los Angeles, CA 90067
(310) 277-8188
Executive secretaries, administrative assistants, human resources.

Kelly Services
6300 Wilshire Blvd., Suite 1020
Los Angeles, CA 90048
(213) 782-8008

Manpower Inc.
2020 Santa Monica Blvd. Suite 190
Santa Monica, CA 90404
(310) 829-2686

Olsten Staffing Services
5750 Wilshire Blvd., Suite 105
Los Angeles, CA 90036
(213) 930-0530

TAD Resources International
11801 Mississippi Ave.
Los Angeles, CA 90025
(310) 445-8970

Tech Aid
15720 Ventura Blvd., Suite 608
Encino, CA 91436
(818) 995-2910
Engineering, technical personnel.

ORANGE COUNTY EMPLOYMENT AGENCIES

Apple One
1295 N. Euclid St.
Anaheim, CA 92801
(714) 956-5180

Interim Personnel
910 E. Birch St., Suite 200
Brea, CA 92621
(714) 990-2441

Kelly Temporary Services
5 Park Plaza, Suite 1280
Irvine, CA 92714
(714) 252-1755

Olsten Staffing Services
18101 Von Karman Ave., Suite 560
Irvine, CA 92801
(714) 222-0966

TAD Resources International
22600-C Lambert St., Suite 902
Lake Forest, CA 92630
(714) 458-9331

SAN DIEGO EMPLOYMENT AGENCIES

ABCOW Services
2525 Camino del Rio South, Suite 125
San Diego, CA 92108
(619) 291-7000

Accountemps/Office Team
409 Camino del Rio South #305
San Diego, CA 92108
(619) 291-7990
Accounting, clerical, technical personnel.

Adia Personnel Services
8304 Clairmont Mesa Blvd.
San Diego, CA 92111
(619) 549-0616
Light industry, clerical personnel.

Aerotek
5075 Shoreham Place #220
San Diego, CA 92122
(619) 552-9333
Engineering, communications, environmental personnel.

Kelly Services
5030 Camino de la Siesta, Suite 401
San Diego, CA 92108
(619) 298-1631

Legalstaff of San Diego
4250 Executive Square, Suite 520
La Jolla, CA 92037
(619) 597-1170

Manpower Temporary Service
101 W. Broadway, Suite 1400
San Diego, CA 92101
(619) 234-6433

On Call Temporary Mortgage Professionals
12526 High Bluff Drive, Suite 145
San Diego, CA 92130
(619) 794-2870
Mortgage, real estate personnel.

Turning Your Temp Job into Something Permanent

Working as a temporary is a good way to expose yourself to a variety of companies and contacts and to prove your skills to the hiring authority. It can be a foot in the door at a company you are interested in working for, and, at the same time, it allows the company to assess your qualifications rather than depending on a 30-minute interview. So don't take that temporary job too lightly. After all, you never know when it might turn into something permanent.

RECOMMENDED READING ON TEMPORARY/PART-TIME JOBS

Canape, Charlene. *The Part-Time Solution: The New Strategy for Managing Motherhood.* New York: Harper Collins, 1990.

Hawes, Gene R. *College Board Guide to Going to College While Working: Strategies for Success.* New York: College Entrance Examination Board (distributed by College Board Publications), 1985.

Magid, Renee Y. *When Mothers and Fathers Work: Creative Strategies for Balancing Career and Family.* New York: AMACOM, 1987.

Paradis, Adrain A. *Opportunities in Part-Time and Summer Jobs.* Lincolnwood, IL: VGM Career Horizons, 1987.

Rothberg and Cook. *Part-Time Professional.* Washington, DC: Acropolis Books, 1985.

How To Handle a New Job and Workplace

A new job, new colleagues, and a new desk — this is what the job search was all about. How do you handle the new job? Well, let the job experts give you some advice.

Walking into your new everyday life, seeing all those new colleagues, and concentrating on fitting into the atmosphere can be overwhelming. But it is important to keep your cool, stay focused, and be yourself. It is natural to be nervous, but how that nervousness manifests itself is important. Showing too much apprehension or bumbling about a bit too much can give others, and cost you, a bad first impression.

How Significant Is the First Day on the Job?

The first day at work can certainly be one of the most important days during your time at a particular company. This is the day that you begin to establish who you are and what you can contribute to the organization. The first day can show your employer a lot. It will give him or her an idea of what you are like as an employee and how you will fit into the workplace.

In order to ease some of the restraint you may be feeling or cure some of those first-day butterflies, here are some tips that will enable you to feel more comfortable. For starters, promptness is essential and says a lot to the employer. This is important for more than just the first day. If you are constantly late, it reveals a sense of irresponsibility and may cause you some grief down the road.

Once you arrive at work on time, determining your duties and what is expected of you is vital. Take a little time to settle in, but try to get on the job soon, and show enthusiasm and contentment with your new job.

You might want to meet with your boss early in the day. This will show motivation and eagerness and will contribute early on to a good first impression. It will also give you an idea of some of the expectations that the company has for you. This and subsequent meetings should help you determine what drives the company and your superiors.

Learn the chain of command and assess the importance of teamwork. Ask about the long-term goals of the company so you can assess your role in it. Keep in mind on your first day that the old saying is true: you never get a second chance to make a first impression.

First Day Do's and Don'ts

It is important to keep in mind some rudimentary but very significant factors in terms of your on-the-job performance. We have formed a Top Ten list that should guide you through a successful first day on the job.

1. **DON'T** expect the red carpet to roll out for you. Employees may not even be expecting you, and special treatment may not be forthcoming.

2. **DON'T** imagine rewarding accomplishments and important responsibilities to await you on your first day. Be prepared for paperwork and orientations.

3. **DON'T** stress. Just take it one step at a time. The company knows you are new and will help you get acclimated; they want you to perform well.

4. **DON'T** be afraid to ask questions, and make sure you realize that no question is a stupid question.

5. **DON'T** be overwhelmed with all the new information. Concentrate on grasping the major points or the most urgent.

6. **DO** enjoy yourself. Think of your job as a challenge and a way to gain new skills for the future.

7. **DO** be prepared. Show everybody that you have your head on straight, can plan ahead, and know what you are doing.

8. **DO** get involved. Interpersonal communication within a company is very important. Be a part of the team, and show other employees that you have some good ideas.

9. **DO** be confident. You were hired because you are qualified. Don't let anything get in your way and make you think otherwise. If the company believes in you, then by all means you should believe in yourself.

10. **DO** stay focused. Try to maintain a working attitude throughout the day. Daydreaming and other distractions will hinder your professional image. Try not to incorporate your personal life with your professional life for the security of your career.

Adjusting Over the Long Run

A new job can be very intimidating and can fill you with mixed emotions about a career. Here are some helpful hints that will enable you to adjust to the company, fit in, and, most importantly, make an impact as a valuable employee.

Develop good communication skills. Has it come to your attention that most top-notch people in a company seem to know one another? Interpersonal communication is a key ingredient in making your job more productive and pleasant. Listen as well to everybody's input, not just those higher up on the career ladder. Keep in mind that you spend a large portion of your life with your workmates, and most of them have something to offer.

Take risks. Don't be afraid to take risks. A leader will have developed enough self-confidence so that taking a few calculated risks is worth the possible payoff. Overcoming skepticism and taking risks can even be the turning point of a career. Just remember to weigh all the options and be prepared for negative as well as positive results.

Work hard. A hard worker always seems to have a brighter future than someone who settles for being just adequate. Let the company know that you are the "go to" person. If you portray that hard-working image, the next step for most supervisors is to trust you with additional duties.

Honesty is the best policy. Try not to make excuses to bail yourself out of hot water. You are better off apologizing and admitting the fact that you made a mistake. Most importantly, never point your finger at other employees. You will only look foolish and cowardly. You want to set a good example, not be the bad example.

Maintaining a Good Relationship with the Boss

Here are some helpful tips to assist you in maintaining a good relationship with your boss.

- Think of your boss as a customer for the product you are trying to sell: yourself. Keep in mind that there is no such thing as impressing your boss too much.

- Value and respect your boss' time. Managers must handle a number of things all at once. If you see that your boss is busy, try to solve the problem yourself or seek assistance from another employee. Freeing your boss from trivial concerns will make everyone's life easier.
- Be open to advice. Don't be offended when your supervisor tries to steer you in the right direction. Make room for criticism, and view it as information that can make you a more effective employee.
- Never make your boss look foolish. Don't challenge his or her judgment in front of other employees. If you feel that you're right, talk to the boss privately. Involving others will just result in dispute and cause havoc.
- Always make your boss look good. Try to keep him/her informed of new issues and ideas. Remember that the better you do, the better the boss looks; and the better the boss looks, the better your career will be.
- Tell your boss about your career objectives or plans for the future. Inform him/her about your ideas and goals of accomplishment. Be optimistic, not skeptical, when discussing career plans with the head person.
- When confrontation with the boss is necessary, try to find an ice-breaking technique to reduce tension. Try to find a common goal or interest in solving the problem. This brings people together and makes them more open to discussion and less defensive.
- Always listen to your boss, but never let him/her walk all over you. Even though you may not have the final say, your judgments deserve to be heard.

A good professional relationship with the boss is vital in terms of job happiness and success. But don't look for the boss to be either perfect or your good buddy. A boss should be a role model and a leader, the person we answer to and respect.

Dear Dr. Bob
Lately, I've noticed my boss taking all the credit for my hard work. He never mentions my name when receiving glowing remarks about a project. What should I do?—
Unrecognized Employee

Dear Unrecognized Employee
Your situation is an age-old one. We are supposed to make our bosses look good and hope they will return the favor. Unfortunately, that hasn't happened in your case. I am one that believes "what goes around, comes around" and eventually your efforts will be rewarded. You will have other jobs and other bosses, but your ability will stay with

you. In the meantime, use subtle techniques for claiming what is due. Make sure your name appears on written reports. When people praise your boss, mention how hard the whole department has worked as well. In due time, you will receive your just recognition.

Creativity and Innovation in Your Career

Corporations want individuals that can be assets and contribute to the company. New ideas and different approaches are always encouraged. Be creative. Show the company that you have the zeal and ability to bring new concepts to the company. Try not to be a routine employee who comes to work, takes care of her responsibilities, and leaves work exactly on time everyday.

Don't hesitate when you think you have a new idea that might help the company. The reality is that many companies do not recognize the value of the creative process but only the "bottom line" result. Here are a few tips for breaking your own barriers to creativity.

Postpone judgment. Explore an idea before promoting or nixing it. Even patently unrealistic idea may lead to a workable solution to a problem.

Look for the second right answer. Avoid the trap of commiting too soon to single solution to a problem. Always look for the second, less obvious answer.

Take risks. How many models for an airplane did Orville and Wilbur Wright fail with before they found one that worked? Think about that the next time you are hesitant in something.

Look for unlikely connections. Computer guru Steve Jobs once said that when he worked for Atari he applied what he learned about movement from a modern dance class in college to the development of video games. Talk about an unlikely connection!

Allow yourself to be foolish. Kids have a leg up on us when it comes to creativity because they are encouraged to be foolish. Creativity flourishes when you allow your mind to romp. Some experts even suggest keeping toys in your office or home to encourage your playful side.

Creativity is within everyone's grasp. It comes out not when you do something that no one has done before but when you do something that *you* have never done before. Recognizing the barriers you yourself have erected to the creative process is the first step to unleashing your potential. Your career and success can only be enhanced once this is done.

Romance in the Office: A Definite Don't

Many dedicated corporate types have found Cupid's arrow piercing their briefcases and setting their hearts aflutter under their banker pinstripes. What's a person to do when love hits in the workplace? The logical, reasonable answer is, "Don't do it!" But rarely is romance logical or reasonable.

Let's face it. Being in proximity with others for an extended period of time makes the workplace fertile ground for romance to blossom. You share common interests, talk frequently, and may even have similar problems. Next thing you know, you find Mr. or Ms. Right directly under your nose. If you are indeed smitten by a co-worker, we offer a few words of advice about relationships in the workplace.

- Know the company's policy on dating co-workers. Some companies consider it unprofessional or even a conflict of interest. However, it is unlikely that your organization will have a written policy prohibiting such relationships.
- Remember that the workplace is for work. Heated romances should remain outside the workplace.
- Be prepared for people to gossip. Romance is juicy stuff — especially for those who don't have it. There are no easy answers about how to handle gossip. It's best to ignore harmless gossip and to confront people spreading malicious stories (there is harm in a rumor that you or your significant other is pregnant!).
- Think about how to handle the break-up. No one wants to think about the end of a relationship, especially when it is just beginning. However, the number-one workplace hazard is a vindictive ex. Understand that if things don't work out, it is likely that you will still work together. Make sure you are ready for that possibility.
- Finally, never date the boss. Regardless of how professionally you conduct yourself in the office, every action or decision you make will be viewed by others through the lens of your relationship. Additionally, having an ex-significant other for a boss can be terribly awkward.
- If a romance goes sour, there is always the risk of sexual harassment. When one person in a relationship has greater authority over the other, the possibility of sexual harassment exists.

The easiest course is to avoid workplace romances altogether. However, love is capricious, and you may well find that one special person just across the hall. If that's the case, even Cupid understands the importance of separating love and work.

Keeping Your Career on the High Road

Becoming successful and happy is the ultimate dream of those who are trying to get their foot in the door. A true success story involves hard work and a positive professional attitude. Here are some tips that will enable you to take that first step toward a new and fulfilling life.

1. Always maintain a good professional relationship with your co-workers and peers. Knowing a wide array of people is certainly advantageous and can become very helpful when you need a favor or some assistance.
2. Find a mentor, somebody who can develop the best in you and advance your interests in the company.
3. Try to concentrate on small, easy projects at first. Conquering your first assignment will give the company a good initial vision of your work abilities. This will also alleviate the pressures a little and add to your self-esteem and believability.
4. Cater to your clients. Be straightforward and candid with them. Make them see that you are fair and treat them as people not profit figures. Try to value their time by being flexible with your schedule.
5. Never assume that a certain issue is not your job. Try to do whatever you can to make your department and the company work. Even if you are not responsible for certain areas, it won't hinder your career if you attempt to find answers when a problem affects you.
6. Take on as many responsibilities and as much work as you can handle. The operative phrase here, however, is "as much work as you can handle." Willingly accepting additional projects and assignments can ingratiate you with your boss only if you complete them in a timely and professional manner.
7. Accept criticism as a form of information that can make you a better employee. When constructively criticized, determine and take the actions that can correct the problem.
8. Never get stuck in one job. Always look to move forward. If you feel that you don't have a future at a certain company, keep your eyes open for other opportunities. Make sure you gain more and more skills and credibility as you progress.
9. Be a leader. Emphasize your willingness to help others. Gaining leadership status can be challenging, but it will definitely broaden your career in the long run.
10. Stay current on issues in your field. Keeping current enables you to assess the stability of your current job and to predict your next career move.
11. Good people are hard to find. No matter how cliché, it's true. If you excel, you will be in an elite group and in demand by employers.

Keep Your Network Alive

Ideally, this book will help you achieve your dream job. But remember that the average person changes jobs five to eight times in their career. Thus, after you've landed a job, it is important that you notify your network people of your new position and thank them for their assistance. Don't throw away those business cards you worked so hard to accumulate. After all, you never know when you may need to ask them for help again. You've spent months building up a network of professional contacts. Keep your network alive.

Make a "New Year's Resolution" to weigh all aspects of your job annually. Evaluate your current situation and the progress you are making (as measured by increased salary, responsibilities, and skills). Compare the result with what you want from your life's career. Even though you may be completely satisfied in your new job, remember that circumstances can change overnight, and you must always be prepared for the unexpected.

We hope you make good use of the job-search techniques outlined in this book. Perhaps the next time you talk to an unemployed person or someone seeking a new job, you will look at that person with new insight gained from your own job search and career successes. We hope you'll gladly share what you've learned from these pages about how to get a job.

ten

Where Southern California Works

This chapter contains the names, addresses, and phone numbers of Southern California's top 1,500 employers of white-collar workers. The companies are arranged in categories according to the major products they manufacture and the major services they provide. Most categories are broken down into the three major geographical areas: Los Angeles, Orange County, and San Diego. Entries contain the name of the human resources director or other contact, where possible.

This listing is intended to help you survey the major potential employers in fields that interest you. It is selective, not exhaustive. We have not, for example, listed all the advertising agencies in the area as you can find that information in the Yellow Pages. We have simply listed the top twenty-five or so, that is, the largest ones potentially offering the most jobs.

The purpose of this chapter is to get you started, both looking and thinking. This is the kickoff, not the final gun. Browse through the whole chapter, and take some time to check out areas that are unfamiliar to you. Many white-collar skills are transferable. People with marketing, management, data processing, accounting, administrative, secretarial, and other talents are needed in a huge variety of businesses.

Ask yourself in what area your skills could be marketed. Use your imagination, especially if you're in a so-called specialized field. A dietitian, for instance, might look first under Health Care, or maybe Hospitality. But what about financial companies, museums, banks, or the scores of other places that run their own dining rooms for employees or the public? What about food and consumer magazines? Who invents all those recipes and tests those products?

The tips and insider interviews that are scattered throughout this chapter are designed to nudge your creativity and suggest additional ideas for your job search. Much more detailed information on the area's top employers and other, smaller companies can be found in the directories and other resources suggested in Chapter 4. We can't stress strongly enough that you have to do your homework when you're looking for a job, both to unearth places that might need a person with your particular talents and to succeed in the interview once you've lined up a meeting with the hiring authority.

A word about hiring authorities: if you've read Chapter 7, you know that the name of the game is to meet the person with the power to hire you, or get as close to that person as you can. You don't want to go to the chairman or the personnel director if the person who actually makes the decision is the marketing manager or customer service director.

Obviously, we can't list every possible hiring authority in the Southern California's "Top 1,500." If we tried, you'd need a wagon to haul this book around. Besides, directories go out of date—even those that are regularly and conscientiously revised. So always double-check a contact whose name you get from a book or magazine, including this one. If necessary, call the company's switchboard to confirm who heads a particular department or division.

Here, then, are Southern California's 1,500 greatest opportunities, arranged in the following categories:

Accounting/Auditing
Advertising/Market Research
Aircraft/Aerospace
Apparel/Textiles
Architectural Firms
Automotive/Transportation Equipment
Banking
Book Publishers/Literary Agents
Broadcasting
Chemicals
Computers: Consulting/Information Management
Computers: Hardware/Software
Construction
Drugs/Pharmaceuticals/Biotechnology
Educational Institutions
Electronics/Telecommunications
Engineering
Entertainment
Environmental Services
Food/Beverage Producers and Distributors
Foundations/Philanthropies
Government
Health Care
Hospitality: Hotels/Restaurants
Human Services
Insurance
Law Firms

Management Consultants
Media, Print
Museums/Art Galleries
Oil/Gas/Plastics
Paper and Allied Products
Printing/Graphic Arts
Public Relations
Real Estate Developers and Brokers
Retailers/Wholesalers
Sports/Recreation/Fitness
Stock Brokers/Financial Services
Travel/Shipping/Transportation
Utilities

Accounting/Auditing

WEB SITES:

http://www.kentis.com/
is the Accounting Professionals Resource Center site, including links to homepages of CPAs, e-mail discussion groups, and other on-line services.

http://www.rutgers.edu/Accounting/raw/aaa/aaa.htm
is the homepage of the American Accounting Association with areas such as research, teaching, publications, and regional associations

http://howard.hbg.psu.edu/library/acc.html
has links to a large body of on-line accounting resources, an e-mail address directory, CPA exam information, and other relevant sites.

PROFESSIONAL ORGANIZATIONS:

For networking in accounting and related fields, contact the following local professional organizations listed in Chapter 5. Also see **"Banks"** and **"Stockbrokers/Financial Services."**

Alliance of Practicing CPA's
California Society of Certified Public Accountants
National Association of Black Accountants

For additional information, you can contact:

American Institute of CPA's
1211 Avenue of the Americas
New York, NY 10036
(212) 596-6200
Publishes *Journal of Accountancy*

American Society of Women Accountants
1255 Lynnfield Road, Suite 257
Memphis, TN 38119
(901) 680-0470

American Woman's Society of CPA's
401 N. Michigan Avenue
Chicago, IL 60611
(312) 664-6610

California Association of Independent Accountants
17842 Irvine Blvd., Suite 246
Tustin, CA 92680
(714) 838-7134

Institute of Management Accountants
10 Paragon Drive
Montvale, NJ 07645
(201) 573-9000

National Association of Black Accountants
7249-A Hanover Parkway
Greenbelt, MD 20770
(301) 474-6222

National Society of Public Accountants
1010 N. Fairfax Street
Alexandria, VA 22314
(703) 549-6400

Society of California Accountants
2131 Capitol Avenue, Suite 305
Sacramento, CA 95816
(916) 443-2057

PROFESSIONAL PUBLICATIONS:

Accounting Review
California CPA Quarterly
Cash Flow
The CPA Journal
D&B Reports
Journal of Accountancy
Management Accounting
National Public Accountant
The Practical Accountant
The Woman CPA

DIRECTORIES:

Accountants Directory (American Business Directories, Inc., Omaha, NE)

Accounting Firms and Practitioners (American Institute of Certified Public Accountants, New York, NY)
American Woman's Society of Certified Public Accountants Roster (American Woman's Society of Certified Public Accountants, Chicago, IL)
National Directory of Accounting Firms and Accountants (Gale Research, Detroit, MI)
Who Audits America (Data Financial Press, Menlo Park, CA)

Los Angeles Area Employers:

Andersen, Arthur, and Company
633 W. 5th Street
Los Angeles, CA 90071
(213) 614-6500
Job hotline: (213) 614-7579
Human Resources Director: Dana Ellis

BDO Seidman
1900 Avenue of the Stars, 11th Floor
Los Angeles, CA 90067
(310) 557-0300
Managing Partner: Art Nemiroff

Coopers & Lybrand
350 S. Grand Avenue
Los Angeles, CA 90071
(213) 356-6000
Job hotline: (213) 356-6440
Personnel Manager: Harper Bridges

Deloitte & Touche
1000 Wilshire Blvd., Suite 1500
Los Angeles, CA 90017
(213) 688-0800
Job hotline: (213) 688-5222
Managing Partner: John Cardis

Duitch Franklin and Co.
11601 Wilshire Blvd., Suite 2300
Los Angeles, CA 90025
(310) 268-2000
Head of Operations and Administration: Terri Oppelt

Ernst & Young
515 S. Flower Street, Floor 20
Los Angeles, CA 90017
(213) 977-3200
Recruiting Coordinator: Sheryl Mandala

Grant Thorton
1000 Wilshire Blvd., Suite 700
Los Angeles, CA 90017
(213) 627-1717
Managing Partner: Richard Stewart

Grobstein Horwath and Co. LLP
15233 Ventura Blvd., 9th Floor
Sherman Oaks, CA 91403
(818) 501-5200
Office Administrator: Bobbi Goodfried

Kellogg & Andelson Accounting Corporation
14724 Ventura Blvd., 2nd Floor
Sherman Oaks, CA 91403
(818) 971-5100
President: James Walters

KPMG Peat Marwick
725 S. Figueroa
Los Angeles, CA 90017
(213) 972-4000
Job hotline: (213) 955-8880 or
(213) 955-8454
Administrative Recruiter: Karen Black

Leventhal, Kenneth & Company
2049 Century Park East, Suite 1700
Los Angeles, CA 90067
(310) 277-0880
Human Resource Director: Kim Plant

Nigro Karlin and Segal
10100 Santa Monica Blvd., Suite 1300
Los Angeles, CA 90067
(310) 277-4657
Office Manager: Nicole Katz

Miller Kaplan Arase and Co.
10911 Riverside Drive
North Hollywood, CA 91602
(818) 769-2010
Human Resources: Irv Borenweig

Price Waterhouse
400 S. Hope Street, 22nd Floor
Los Angeles, CA 90017
(213) 236-3000
Managing Partner: Greg Garrison

Accounting/Auditing **177**

Orange County Employers:

Andersen, Arthur, and Company
18500 Von Karman Avenue
Irvine, CA 92715
(714)757-3100
Human Resource Director: Vesandra Van Arnem

Conrad and Associates
1100 Main Street
Irvine, CA 92714
(714) 474-2020
Managing Partner: Ronald Conrad

Coopers & Lybrand
4675 MacArthur Court, Suite 1600
Newport Beach, CA 92660
(714) 251-7200
Job hotline: (213) 356-6440
Human Resources: James Keglovitz

Corbin and Wertz
3333 Michelson Drive, Suite 550
Irvine, CA 92715
(714) 756-2120
Tax Partner: Dave Krickl
Audit Partner: Joe Johnson

Deloitte & Touche
695 Town Center Drive, Suite 1200
Costa Mesa, CA 92626-9978
(714) 436-7100
Human Resource Department

E&Y Kenneth Leventhal Group
660 Newport Center Drive, Suite 800
Newport Beach, CA 92660
(714) 640-5000
Human Resources: Kristina Mathosian

Ernst & Young
18400 Von Karman Avenue, Suite 800
Irvine, CA 92715
(714) 252-2300
Recruiting: Sheryl Mandala

Grant Thorton
18300 Van Karman Avenue, Suite 1000
Irvine, CA 92715
(714) 553-1600
Assistant Office Manager: Terry Ellis

KPMG Peat Marwick
650 Town Center Drive, Suite 1000
Costa Mesa, CA 92626
(714) 850-4300
Director of Human Resources: Cindy Patelski

McGladrey & Pullen
222 S. Harbor Blvd., Suite 800
Anaheim, CA 92815
(714) 520-9561
Partner: Mr. Rominger

Price Waterhouse
575 Anton Blvd., Suite 1100
Costa Mesa, CA 92626
(714) 435-8600
Human Resource Director: Nancy Alvarez

San Diego Area Employers:

Anderson, Arthur, and Company
701 B Street, Suite 1600
San Diego, CA 92101
(619) 699-6600
Human Resource Manager: Kim Ototy

Coopers & Lybrand
402 W. Broadway, Suite 1400
San Diego, CA 92101
(619) 525-2300
Personnel Director: Kathy Jennings

Considine & Considine
1501 5th Avenue, Suite 400
San Diego, CA 92101
(619) 231-1977
Managing Partner: Timothy Considine

Deloitte & Touche
701 B Street, Suite 1900
San Diego, CA 92101
(619) 232-6500
Partner: Helen Adams

Ernst & Young
501 W. Broadway, Suite 1100
San Diego, CA 92101
(619) 235-5000
Human Resources: Pat Bedikian

KPMG Peat Marwick
750 B Street, Suite 3000
San Diego, CA 92101
(619) 233-8000
Human Resource Director: Becca Wing

Levitz Zacks and Ciceric
701 B Street, Suite 400
San Diego, CA 92101
(619) 238-1077
Resumes to Office Manager

McGladrey & Pullen
3111 Camino Del Rio N., Suite 1150
San Diego, CA 92108
(619) 280-3022
Director of Finance & Accounting: Gloria Anderson

Peterson & Co.
3655 Nobel Drive, Suite 500
San Diego, CA 92122
(619) 597-4100
Managing Partner: Richard Evans

Price Waterhouse
750 B Street, Suite 2400
San Diego, CA 92101
(619) 231-1200
Human Resources: Roselyn Morgan

West Turnquist and Schmitt
2550 5th Avenue, 10th Floor
San Diego, CA 92103
(619) 234-6775
Human Resources Department: Van Tajxton

Accounting firms big and small

We talked with Richard Craig, a Certified Public Accountant, now a Senior Vice President in finance at a leading data processing firm. We asked how he began his career in accounting and about the advantages and disadvantages associated with the size of the firm you work for.

Said Craig, "I started at Touche Ross (now Deloitte & Touche). Usually, working for a larger firm means learning a specific task. Staffs are larger, so each job is more specialized. You don't usually handle as many components of a job as you would in a smaller firm. You sometimes have more opportunity for hands-on experience in a smaller firm and gain more general management experience," Craig advised.

"But regardless of the size of the firm where you begin your career, if you wish to advance you should remain flexible through the first five years. If your job is not what you expected, be willing to make a change.

"Also, if you want a manager's position, you may have to move around to gain general managerial experience. Sometimes, that will mean a transfer to a department that would not necessarily be your first choice. But if the position rounds out your background, it is usually worth at least a temporary stay."

Advertising/Market Research

WEB SITES:

http://www.commercepark.com/AAAA/
is the homepage of the American Association of Advertising Agencies; includes resource index, publications directory, and applications for membership.

http://www.adage.com/
is the site for *Advertising Age* magazine.

http://www.adweek.com
is the site for *Adweek* magazine. Each Friday, Adweek Online users have early access to help-wanted ads from *Adweek, Brandweek,* and *Mediaweek.*

PROFESSIONAL ORGANIZATIONS:

For networking in advertising/market research, check out the following local professional organizations listed in Chapter 5. Also see **"Public Relations."**
Advertising Club of Los Angeles
Advertising Club of Orange County
Advertising Club of San Diego
Advertising Production Association of Orange County
Los Angeles Advertising Women
Western States Advertising Association

For additional information, you can contact the following:

American Advertising Federation
1101 Vermont Avenue, NW
Suite 500
Washington, DC 20005
(202) 898-0089

American Association of Advertising Agencies
130 Battery Street, Suite 330
San Francisco, CA 94111
(415) 291-4999

American Marketing Association
250 S. Wacker Drive, Suite 200
Chicago, IL 60606
(312) 648-0536

Council of American Survey Research Organizations
170 N. Country Road
Port Jefferson, NY 11777
(516) 928-6954

Marketing Research Association
2189 Silas Deane Highway, Suite 5
P.O. Box 230
Rocky Hill, CT 06067
(203) 257-4008

PROFESSIONAL PUBLICATIONS:

Advertising Age
Adweek
American Demographics
Brandweek
Direct Marketing Magazine
Journal of Marketing Research
Marketing News
Product Marketing

DIRECTORIES:

Advertisers and Their Agencies (Engel Communications, West Trenton, NJ)
American Marketing Association International Membership Directory and Marketing Services Guide (American Marketing Association, Chicago, IL)
Bradford's Directory of Marketing Research Agencies and Management Consultants in the United States and the World (Bradford's Directory of Marketing Research Agencies, Fairfax, VA)
International Directory of Market Research Organizations (MacFarlane & Company, Atlanta, GA)
International Directory of Marketing Research Companies and Services (The Green Book) (American Marketing Association, New York Chapter, New York, NY)

Standard Directory of Advertising Agencies
(National Register Publishing Co., New Providence, NJ)

Los Angeles Area Employers:

Asher/Gould Advertising
5900 Wilshire Blvd., 31st Floor
Los Angeles, CA 90036
(213) 931-4151
Human Resources: Sandi Winston

BBDO
10960 Wilshire Blvd., Suite 1600
Los Angeles, CA 90024
(310) 444-4500
Human Resource Director: Jean Anne Hutchinson

Dailey & Associates
3055 Wilshire Blvd.
Los Angeles, CA 90010
(213) 386-7823
Director, Personnel Administration: Ms. Toby Burke

D'Arcy, Masius, Benton & Bowles
6500 Wilshire Blvd., Suite 1000
Los Angeles, CA 90048
(213) 658-4500
Human Resource Office Administrator: Doug Doty

Davis, Ball & Colombatto Advertising
865 S. Figueroa Street, 12th Floor
Los Angeles, CA 90017
(213) 688-7000
Resumes to Human Resources Department

DDB Needham Worldwide
11601 Wilshire Blvd., 8th Floor
Los Angeles, CA 90025
(310) 996-5700
Human Resource Manager: Andre DeChannes

Grey Advertising
6100 Wilshire Blvd.
Los Angeles, CA 90048
(213) 936-6060
Human Resource Manager: Joy Wilden

Ketchum Los Angeles
11755 Wilshire Blvd., Suite 1900
Los Angeles, CA 90025
(310) 444-5000
Job hotline: (800) 894-0611
http://www.ketchum.com
Vice President: Elizabeth Gaudio

Kresser Stein Robaire
2501 Colorado Avenue, 2nd Floor
Santa Monica, CA 90404
(310) 315-3000
Human Resources: Denise Hebert

Lintas Campbell-Ewald
11100 Santa Monica Blvd., Suite 600
Los Angeles, CA 90025
(310) 914-2200
Executive Vice President: Iam McGregor

Lord Dentsu & Partners
4751 Wilshire Blvd., 3rd Floor
Los Angeles, CA 90010
(213) 930-5000
Executive Vice President: Pat Rogge

McCann-Erickson Los Angeles
6300 Wilshire Blvd., Suite 2100
Los Angeles, CA 90048
(213) 655-9420
Human Resource Director: Linda Friedman

Ogilvy & Mather
11766 Wilshire Blvd., Suite 900
Los Angeles, CA 90025
(310) 996-0400
Director of Human Resources: Annabella Bechtel

Rubin Postaer & Associates
1333 Second Street
Santa Monica, CA 90401
(310) 394-4000
Vice President: Lark Baskerville

Saatchi & Saatchi DFS/Pacific
3501 Sepulveda Blvd.
Torrance, CA 90505
(310) 214-6000
Human Resource Manager: Karen Hill

Advertising/Market Research

Seiniger Advertising
9320 Wilshire Blvd.
Beverly Hills, CA 90212
(310) 777-6800
Hiring: Steven Hayman

TBWA/Chiat Day
340 Main Street
Venice, CA 90291
(310) 314-5000
Human Resources: Amy Norton
You can learn more about TBWA/Chiat Day in the "10 Best Places to Work in Southern California" section of Chapter 1.

Team One Advertising
1960 E. Grand Avenue
El Segundo, CA 90245
(310) 615-2000
Human Resource Director: Lisa Edmonson

Orange County Employers:

Auto Pacific
12812 Panorama View
Santa Ana, CA 92705
(715) 838-4234
Executive Vice President: Mr. Lynn Imus
Market research firm.

Bates USA West
2010 Main Street, Suite 700
Irvine CA 92714
(714) 261-0330
Vice President: Susan Bock

Bozell/Salvati Montgomery Sakoda
535 Anton Blvd., Suite 700
Costa Mesa, CA 92626
(714) 966-0200
Human Resources: Jim Bogart

Casanova Pendrill Publicidad
3333 Michelson Drive, Suite 300
Irvine CA 92715
(714) 474-5001
Treasurer: Barbara Casanova

dGWB Advertising
20 Executive Park, Suite 200
Irvine, CA 92714
(714) 863-0404
Office Manager: Teena Schmidt

Foote, Cone & Belding
4 Hutton Center Drive
Santa Anna, CA 92707
(714)662-6500
Hiring: A. Cristine Springston

Forsythe Marcelli Johnson
610 Newport Center Drive, Suite 500
Newport Beach, CA 92660
(714) 759-9500
Office Manager: Ann Forsythe

Gallup Organization
18200 Von Karman Avenue, Suite 110
Irvine, CA 92715
(714) 474-7900
Senior Vice President: Kelly Aylward

G2 Advertising
7711 Center Avenue, Suite 400
Huntington Beach, CA 92647
(714) 372-6600
Office Administrator: Evie Jenner

Heil Brice Retail Advertising
4 Corporate Park, Suite 100
Newport Beach, CA 92660
(714) 644-7477
Director of Operations: Robert Guevarra

Mendoza Dillon & Associates
4100 Newport Place, Suite 600
Newport Beach, CA 92660
(714) 851-1811
Office Manager: Carla Ondatjes

Nielsen, A.C.
6 Hutton Centre Drive, Suite 1100
Santa Ana, CA 92707
(714) 549-9500
Human Resources: Vivian Espinoza
Market research firm.

Peryam & Kroll
4175 E. La Palma Avenue, Suite 205
Anaheim, CA 92807
(714) 572-6888
Human Resources: Steve Cini
Market research firm.

Roper Starch Worldwide
4299 Mac Arthur Blvd., Suite 105

Newport Beach, CA 92660
(714) 756-2600
Market research firm.

Shafer Advertising
18300 Von Karmen Avenue, Suite 800
Irvine CA 92715
(714) 553-1177
Human Resource Director: Marie Smythe

San Diego Area Employers:

Capener Matthews & Walcher
620 C Street Suite 600
San Diego, CA 92101
(619) 238-8500
Office Manager: Diane Scott

Di Zinno Thompson Integrated Marketing Solutions
715 J Street, Suite 100
San Diego, CA 92101
(619) 237-5011
Operations Manager: Leslie Sphire

Franklin Stoorza
225 Broadway, Suite 1600
San Diego, CA 92101
(619) 236-9061
Manager of Administrative Services: Joni Solan

Lambesis
100 Via de la Valle
Del Mar, CA 92014
(619) 794-6444
Principal: Vicki Hoekstra

McCann-Erickson
6863 Friars Road
San Diego, CA 92108
(619) 574-0808
Human Resource Director: Ann Collins

McQuerter Group
5752 Oberlin Drive, Suite 106
San Diego, CA 92121
(619) 450-0030
Human Resources Manager: Janie Vlessinger

Think Tank Inc.
4225 Executive Square, Suite 1160
La Jolla, CA 92037
(619) 452-3020
CEO: Ron Detrick

Warner Design Associates
3920 Conde Street
San Diego, CA 92110
(619) 297-4455
http://home.earthlink.net/~warnerdesign/
President: Richard Warner

Aircraft/Aerospace

WEB SITES:

http://www.aiaa.org/
is the homepage for the American Institute of Aeronautics and Astronautics; links to information on conferences, membership, and publications.

http://www.galcit.caltech.edu/~aure/htmls/aerolinks.html
links to aeronautics resources.

http://www.nasa.gov/NASA_homepage.html/
is NASA's official homepage with topics including Aeronautics, Space Science, and Technology Development.

PROFESSIONAL ORGANIZATIONS:

For networking in aerospace, check out the following local organization listed in Chapter 5:

American Institute of Aeronautics and Astronautics

For additional information, you can contact the following:

Aerospace Education Foundation
1501 Lee Highway
Arlington, VA 22209
(703)247-5839

Aerospace Industries Association of America
1250 I Street, NW
Washington, DC 20005
(202) 371-8400

American Institute of Aeronautics and Astronautics
370 L'Enfant Promendade, SW
Washington, DC 20024
(202) 646-7400

International Association of Machinists & Aerospace Workers
9000 Machinists Place
Upper Marlboro, MD 20772
(301) 967-4500

Women in Aerospace
P.O. Box 44492
Washington, DC 20026
(202) 547-9451

PROFESSIONAL PUBLICATIONS:

Aerospace America
Aerospace Daily
Aerospace Engineering
AIAA Journal
Air Jobs Digest
Aviation Week & Space Technology
Business and Commercial Aviation
Space Commerce Week

DIRECTORIES:

Aerospace Technology Centers (Gale Research, Detroit, MI)
American Institute of Aeronautics and Astronautics Roster (American Institute of Aeronautics and Astronautics)
Aviation Week & Space Technology, Marketing Directory Issue (McGraw-Hill Publishing Company, New York, NY)
Space Industry International (Gale Research, Detroit, MI)

Los Angeles Area Employers:

Allied Signal Aerospace Co.
2525 W. 190th Street
Torrance, CA 90504
(310) 323-9500
Job hotline: (310) 512-2012
Hiring: Jeff Shulman

Arral Industries
2101 Carillo Road
Ontario, CA 91761
(909) 947-6585
Employment: Sharon Moore

C&D Aerospace Group
5412 Argosy Drive
Huntington Beach, CA 92649
(714) 891-1906

Ducommun Incorporated
23301 S. Wilmington Avenue
Carson, CA 90745
(310) 513-7200
Human Resources: Ken Pearson

Hughes Aircraft Company
P.O. Box 80028
Los Angeles, CA 90080
(310) 568-7100
Resume to Human Resource Center

Infotec Development
3611 S. Harbor Blvd.
Santa Ana, CA 92704
(714) 549-2182

Kaiser Marquardt
16555 Saticoy Street
Van Nuys, CA 91406
(818) 989-6400
Human Resource Director: Robert Bonney

Litton Industries
21240 Burbank Blvd.
Woodland Hills, CA 91367
(818) 598-5000
Human Resources Director: Nancy Gayman

Murdock Inc.
15800 S. Avalon Blvd.
Compton, CA 90220
(213) 770-0220
Director of Personnel: Ron Williams

Northrop Grumman Corp.
1840 Century Park East
Los Angeles, CA 90067
(310) 553-6262
Job hotline: (310) 942-5001
http://www.northgrum.com
Corporate Staffing Director: Robert Navarro
Employment Manager: Ms. Mickey Leong

Whittaker Corp.
1955 N. Surveyor Avenue
Simi Valley, CA 93063
(805) 526-5700
Personnel: Sue Thomas

Orange County Employers:

Aerodynamic Engineering
15495 Graham Street
Huntington Beach, CA 92649
(714) 891-2651

C&D Aerospace Group
5412 Argosy Drive
Huntington Beach, CA 92641
(714) 891-1906
Personnel: Dawn Woodruff-Greene

Datum Inc.
9975 Toledo Way
Irvine, CA 92618
(714) 380-8880
Human Resource Manager: Judy McBride

Irvine Sensors Corp.
3001 Redhill Avenue
Costa Mesa, CA 92626
(714) 549-8211
Human Resources Director: David Greenhut

Lockheed Martin
29947 Avenida de las Banderas
Rancho Santo Margarita, CA 92688
(714) 459-3000

McDonald Douglas
5301 Bolsa Avenue
Huntington Beach, CA 92647
(714) 896-3311

San Diego Area Employers:

Computer Sciences Corporation
P.O. Box 929011
San Diego, CA 92193
(619) 573-8000

Cubic Corp.
9333 Balboa Avenue
San Diego, CA 92123

(619) 277-6780
Job hotline: (619) 505-1540
www.ds.cubic.com
Hiring: Bob Stamp

GDE Systems
P.O. Box 509009
San Diego, CA 92150
(619) 573-8000

General Dynamics
P.O. Box 85377
San Diego, CA 92186
(619) 694-7339

Lockheed Martin
P.O. Box 80667
San Diego, CA 92138
(619) 573-8000

Rohr, Inc.
850 Lagoon Drive
Chula Vista, CA 91910
(619) 691-4111
Human Resources: Judy Herbert

Apparel/Textiles

WEB SITE:

http://www.apparelex.com/
is the homepage of the Apparel Exchange with links to over 26,000 apparel and textile companies.

http://www.texi.org/library.htm/
links to The Textile Institute Virtual Library, a resource directory with trade associations, educational information, and other Internet resources.

http://www.ita.doc.gov/industry/textiles/
is the US Department of Commerce's Office of Textiles and Apparel (OTEXA) with information on related government publications.

PROFESSIONAL ORGANIZATIONS:

For networking in the apparel and textile industries and related fields, contact the following professional organization listed in Chapter 5:

Apparel Contractors Alliance of California

For additional information, you can contact the following:

American Apparel Manufacturers Association
2500 Wilson Blvd., Suite 301
Arlington, VA 22201
(703) 524-1864

Council of Fashion Designers of America
1412 Broadway, Suite 2206
New York, NY 10018
(212) 302-1821

International Association of Clothing Designers
475 Park Avenue S.
New York, NY 10016
(212) 685-6602

Textile Distributors Association
45 W. 36th Street, 3rd Floor
New York, NY 10018
(212) 563-0400

Textile Research Institute
P.O. Box 625
Princeton, NJ 08540
(609) 924-3150

United Textile Workers of America
2 Echelon Plaza, Suite 200
Voorhees, NJ 08043
(609) 772-9699

PROFESSIONAL PUBLICATIONS:

Apparel Industry Magazine
California Apparel News
Fashion Newsletter
Home Textiles Today

Textile Chemist and Colorist
Textile World
Women's Wear Daily

DIRECTORIES:

American Apparel Manufacturers Association Membership Directory (American Apparel Manufacturers Association, Arlington, VA)
Apparel Industry Sourcebook (Denyse & Co., Inc., North Hollywood, CA)
Garment Manufacturer's Index (Klevens Publications, Littlerock, CA)
Textile Blue Book (Davison Publishing Co., Ridgewood, NJ)

Los Angeles Area Employers:

Authentic Fitness Corporation
6040 Bandini Blvd.
Commerce, CA 90040
(213) 726-1262

Bugle Boy Industries
2900 Madera Road
Simi Valley, CA 93065
(805) 582-1010

Carol Little, Inc.
3434 S. Grande Avenue
Los Angeles, CA 90007
(213) 743-9000
Human Resource Director: Mary Ciarabino

Cherokee Group
6835 Valjean Avenue
Van Nuys, CA 91406
(818) 908-9868
Assistant Vice President: Sherida Kasteler

Chorus Line Corp.
4505 Bandini Blvd.
Vernon, CA 90040
(213) 881-3200

Classic Clothing
1450 Santa Fe Avenue
Long Beach, CA 90813
(310) 432-5627

Guess?
1444 S. Alameda Street
Los Angeles, CA 90021
(213) 765-3100

Jalate Ltd.
1675 South Alameda Street
Los Angeles, CA 90021
(213) 765-5000

Joni Blair of California
P.O. Box 9267
South El Monte, 91733
(818) 579-5151

K-Swiss Inc.
20664 Bahama Street
Chatsworth, CA 91311
(818) 998-3388
Personnel: Lorena Agraz

L&L Manufacturing
2250 S. Maple
Los Angeles, CA 90011
(213) 747-6164

Patagonia
259 W. Santa Clara Street
Ventura, CA 93001
(805) 643-8616
Job hotline: (805) 667-4614
http://www.patagonia.com

Rampage Clothing Corp.
2825 S. Santa Fe Avenue
Vernon, CA 90058
(213) 584-1300

Tarrant Apparel Group
3151 E. Washington Blvd.
Los Angeles, CA 90023
(213) 780-8250

Yes Clothing Company
1380 W. Washington Blvd.
Los Angeles, CA 90007
(213) 765-7800
Human Resources: Tessie Garcia

Apparel/Textiles

Orange County Employers:

Catalina Swimwear
131 N. Gilbert Street
Fullerton, CA 92633
(714) 871-7310

Mossimo Inc.
15320 Barranca Parkway
Irvine, CA 92618
(714) 453-1300

Quicksilver Inc.
1740 Monrovia Avenue
Costa Mesa, CA 92627
(714) 645-1395

St. John's Knits
2722 Michaelson
Irvine, CA 92713
(714) 863-1171
Human Resources: Najla Debow

Vans Inc.
2095 N. Batavia Street
Orange, CA 92865
(714) 974-7414

San Diego Area Employers:

American Fashion
642 Arizona Street
Chula Vista, CA 91911
(619) 426-1212

Ashworth
2791 Loker Avenue West
Carlsbad, CA 92008
(619) 438-6610

F Fashion
1414 S. Tremont Street
Oceanside, CA 92054
(619) 722-4241

Weekend Exercise Company
8960 Carroll Way
San Diego, CA 92121
(619) 295-4124

Architectural Firms

WEB SITES:

http://arch.buffalo.edu/pairc/
is a resource directory listing over 2,300 links to architectural sites.

http://www.aia.org/
links to the homepage of the American Institute of Architects with information on trends, schools, career development, and on-line resources.

http://www.aecinfo.com/arch/assoc.html/
is a listing of links to architectural associations and institutes.

PROFESSIONAL ORGANIZATIONS:

To network in architecture and related fields, contact the following professional organizations listed in Chapter 5. Also see "Construction" and "Engineering."

American Institute of Architects, Los Angeles
American Institute of Architects, Orange County
American Institute of Architects, San Diego
American Society of Engineers and Architects
Asian-American Architects & Engineers
Associated Architects and Planners
Association for Women in Architecture
Engineers & Architects Association

For additional information, you can contact the following:

American Institute of Architects
1735 New York Avenue, NW
Washington, DC 20006
(202) 626-7300

American Society of Landscape Architects
4401 Connecticut Avenue, NW
Washington, DC 20008
(202) 686-2752

National Organization of Minority Architects
P.O. Box 535
Bellwood, IL 60104
(708) 544-3333

PROFESSIONAL PUBLICATIONS:

AIA Journal
Architectural Record
Architecture
Interiors
Landscape Architecture
Progressive Architecture

DIRECTORIES:

Architects Directory (American Business Information, Inc., Omaha, NE)
Directory of Minority and Women-Owned Engineering and Architectural Firms (American Consulting Engineers Council, Washington DC)
Penguin Directory of Architecture (Viking Penguin, New York, NY)
ProFile/The Official Directory of the AIA (American Institute of Architects, Washington, DC)
Society of American Registered Architects National Membership Directory (Society of American Registered Architects, Lombard, IL)

Los Angeles Area Employers:

Altoon & Porter
5700 Wilshire Blvd., Suite 100
Los Angeles, CA 90036
(310) 939-1900

Anshen & Allen
5055 Wilshire Blvd.
Los Angeles, CA 90036
(213) 525-0500

Architectural Firms

Daniel Mann Johnson & Mendenhall
3250 Wilshire Blvd.
Los Angeles, CA 90010
(213) 381-3663
Recruiting Officer: John Dyer

Dworsky Associates
3530 Wilshire Blvd., Suite 1000
Los Angeles, CA 90010
(213) 380-9100
President: Robert Nasraway

Gensler & Associates
2500 Broadway, Suite 300
Santa Monica, CA 90404
(310) 449-5600
Human Resource Director: Sue Andrews

Gruen Associates
6330 San Vicente Blvd.
Los Angeles, CA 90048
(213) 937-4270
Managing Partner: Ki Suh Park

Hellmuth Obata & Kassabaum
1655 26th Street, Suite 200
Santa Monica, CA 90404
(310) 453-0100
Human Resource Director: Jan Harmon

HNTB Corp.
665 S. Oxford Avenue
Los Angeles, CA 90005
(213) 386-7070
Vice President: Edward McSpedon

Jerde Partnership, The
913 Ocean Front Walk
Venice, CA 90291
(310) 399-1558
President: John Jerde

Lee Burkhart Liu
2890 Colorado Avenue
Santa Monica, CA 90404
(310) 829-2249
Office Manager: Georgia Ford
Levin, Brenda

Martin, Albert C., & Associates
811W. 7th Street
Los Angeles, CA 90017
(213) 683-1900
Managing Partner: Christopher Martin

McClellan Cruz/Gaylord & Associates
200 S. Los Robles Avenue, Suite 300
Pasadena, CA 91101
(213) 681-8461
Production Director: Randy Werner

Musil Perkowitz Ruth
911 Studebaker Road
Long Beach, CA 90815
(310) 594-9333
Office Manager: Sandra Brooks

Nadel Partnership, The
1990 Bundy Drive
Los Angeles, CA 90025
(310) 826-2100
CEO/President: Harbert Nadel

Rochlin Baran & Balbona
10980 Wilshire Blvd.
Los Angeles, CA 90024
(310) 473-3555
Vice President: Art Border

RTKL Associates
818 W. 7th Street, Suite 300
Los Angeles, CA 90017
(213) 627-7373
Vice Chairman: David Brotman

Orange County Employers:

Coleman/Caskey Architects
100 Pacifica, Suite 300
Irvine, CA 92618
(714) 727-4400
President: Richard Coleman

Danielian Associates
60 Corporate Park
Irvine, CA 92714
(714) 474-6030
President: Arthur Danielian

HNTB Corp.
36 Executive Park, Suite 200
Irvine, CA 92614
(714) 752-6940
Executive Vice President: Ronald L. Harjte

Holmes & Narver
999 Town & Country Road
Orange, CA 92668
(714) 567-2400
Human Resources: Marlis Ayer

Klages, Carter, Vail & Partners
200 Baker Street, Suite 201
Costa Mesa, CA 92626
(714) 641-0191

Leesak Architects
16842 Von Karman Avenue, Suite 300
Irvine, CA 92606
(714) 261-1100

LPA Inc.
17848 Sky Park Circle
Irvine, CA 92714
(714) 753-1001
Hiring: Jim Kelly

McLarand, Vasquez & Partners
695 Town Center Drive, Suite 300
Costa Mesa, CA 92626
(714) 549-2207

TBP/Blurock Partnership
2300 Newport Blvd.
Newport Beach, CA 92663
(714) 673-0300
President: Alan Smith

Wimberly Allison Tong & Goo
2260 University Drive
Newport Beach, CA 92660
(714) 574-8500
Administrator: Dee Bartlett

San Diego Area Employers:

Carrier Johnson Wu
919 4th Avenue, Suite 200
San Diego, CA 92101
(619) 239-2353
Project Architect: Ann Whitman

City Design
308 G Street
San Diego, CA 92101
(619) 232-1736

Delawie Wilkes Rodrigues Barker & Bretton
2827 Presidio Drive
San Diego, CA 92110
(619) 299-6690

KMA Architecture & Engineering
1515 Morena Blvd.
San Diego, CA 92110
(619) 276-7710

LPA Inc.
4350 LaJolla Village Drive, Suite 130
San Diego, CA 92122
(619) 587-6665

McGraw/Baldwin Architects
701 B. Street, Suite 200
San Diego, CA 92101
(619) 231-0751
Principals: James McGraw, Kennon Baldwin

Neptune Thomas Davis
4719 Viewridge Avenue, Suite 200
San Diego, CA 92123
(619) 277-5115

Salerno/Livingston Architects
363 5th Avenue, 3rd Floor
San Diego, CA 92101
(619) 234-7471
Office Manager: Harry Stephens

SGPA Architecture & Planning
1545 Hotel Circle South, Suite 200
San Diego, CA 92108
(619) 297-0131
President: Art Allard

Stichler Design Group
9655 Granite Ridge Drive, Suite 400
San Diego, CA 92123
(619) 565-4440
Principal: Tom Todd

Tucker Sadler & Associates
2411 2nd Avenue
San Diego, CA 92101
(619) 236-1662
Vice President: Art Castro

Wong, Joseph, Design Associates
2359 4th Avenue, Suite 300
San Diego, CA 92101
(619) 233-6777
Principal: Joseph Wong

Automotive/Transportation Equipment

WEB SITES:

http://autocenter.com
is a directory of automotive manufacturers.

http://cyberlot.net/dealonly/assc.htm/
is a link to the Auto Industry Association's homepage.

PROFESSIONAL ORGANIZATIONS:

For industry information, you can contact the following:

American International Automobile Dealers Association
99 Canal Center Plaza, Suite 500
Alexandria, VA 22314
(703) 519-7800

American Trucking Association
2200 Mill Road
Alexandria, VA 22314
(703) 838-1700

Automotive Service Industry Association
25 Northwest Point Blvd.
Elk Grove Village, IL 60067
(847) 228-1310

Society of Automotive Engineers
400 Commonwealth Drive
Warrendale, PA 15096
(412) 776-4841

PROFESSIONAL PUBLICATIONS:

Automotive Engineering Magazine
Automotive Industries Insider
Automotive News
Motor Age
Motor Trend
Trux

DIRECTORIES:

Automotive News, Market Data Book
  (Crain Communications, Detroit, MI)

Automotive Service Industry Association Manufacturers' Representatives Directory
  (Automotive Service Industry Association, Elk Grove Village, IL)
Ward's Automotive Yearbook (Ward's Communications, Detroit, MI)

Los Angeles Area Employers:

Air Sensors
16804 Gridley Place
Cerritos, CA 90703
(310) 860-6666
Hiring and Recruiting: Lisa Kitching

American Racings
19067 Reyes
Rancho Dominguez, CA 90221
(310) 635-7806
Human Resources: Mary Dollberg

Amerigon Inc.
404 E. Huntington Drive
Monrovia, CA 91016
(8181) 932-1200
Human Resource Manager: Carol Caraway

Clifford Electronics
20750 Lassen Street
Chatsworth, CA 91311
(818) 709-7551
Manufactures automotive security systems.

Edelbrock Corp.
2700 California Street
Torrance, CA 90503
(310) 781-2222

Eldorado National Corporation
13900 Sycamore Way
Chino, CA 91710
(909) 591-9557
Bus manufacturer.

Hooker Industries
1024 W. Brook Street
Ontario, CA 91762
(909) 983-5871
Motor vehicle accessories.

Kexhall Industries
25655 Springbrook Avenue
Santa Clarita, CA 91380
(805) 253-1295

Kraco Enterprises
505 E. Euclid Avenue
Compton, CA 90222
(310) 639-0666
Hiring: Andy Hernandez

Motorcar Parts & Accessories
2727 Maricopa Street
Torrance, CA 90503
(310) 212-7910

Oliver & Winston
900 W. Alameda Street
Burbank, CA 91506
(818) 972-1200
Human Resources: Lauren Smith

Superior Industries
7800 Woodley Avenue
Van Nuys, CA 91406
(818) 781-4973

Thompson PBE
4553 Glencoe Avenue, Suite 200
Marina del Rey, CA 90292
(310) 306-7112

TRW Technar
6010 Irwindale Avenue
Irwindale, CA 91706
(818) 334-0250
Auto components.

Orange County Employers:

Armor All Products Corp.
6 Liberty
Aliso Viejo, CA 92656
(714) 362-0600
Human Resource Manager: Charlene Jurak

Boyds Wheels
8380 Cerritos Avenue
Stanton, CA 90680
(714) 952-4038

Friction
17152 Daimler Street
Irvine, CA 92714
(714) 474-8990
Rebuilds brakes and related items.

Safety Components International
3190 Pullman Street
Costa Mesa, CA 92626
(714) 662-7756

Wynns International
500 N. State College Blvd., Suite 700
Orange, CA 92868
(714) 938-3700

San Diego Area Employers:

Auto Parts Club, LLC
5825 Oberlin Drive, Suite 100
San Diego, CA 92121
(619) 622-5050
Human Resource Director: Jerry Gow

Genvine Parts
7440 Convoy Ct.
San Diego, CA 92111
(619) 279-6900

H&L Products
P.O. Box 1445
National City, CA 91951
(619) 477-2738
Auto accessories.

Nissan Design International
9800 Campus Pt. Drive
San Diego, CA 92121
(619) 457-4400

Banking

WEB SITES:

http://www.cybercash.com/cybercash/banks/directory.html
is a directory of consumer banks.

http://www.bai.org/
links to the Bank Administrative Institute with a listing of on-line publications, mailing lists, and other Internet resources.

PROFESSIONAL ORGANIZATIONS:

To network within the banking industry, contact the following professional organization listed in Chapter 5. Also see "Stockbrokers/Financial Services."

Financial Women International, Los Angeles

For additional information, you can contact the following:

American Bankers Association
1120 Connecticut Avenue, NW
Washington, DC 20036
(202) 663-5000
Publishes ABA *Banking Journal*.

America's Community Bankers
900 19th Street, NW
Washington, DC 20006
(202) 857-3100

Mortgage Bankers Association of America
1125 15th Street, NW
Washington, DC 20005
(202) 861-6500

National Bankers Association
1802 T Street, NW
Washington, DC 20009
(202) 588-5432
Minority bankers.

PROFESSIONAL PUBLICATIONS:

ABA Banking Journal
American Banker
Financial Management
Financial World
Journal of Finance
Mortgage Banking

DIRECTORIES:

American Bank Directory (McFadden Business Publications, Norcross, GA)
American Banker, 500 Largest World Banks Issue (International Thomson Publishing Corp., New York, NY)
American Banker, 300 Largest U.S. Commercial Banks Issue (International Thomson Publishing Corp. New York, NY)
American Bankers Association Directory (American Bankers Association, Washington, DC)
The Bankers' Almanac and Yearbook (International Publications Service, New York, NY)
Moody's Bank and Finance Manual (Moody's Investors Service, Inc., New York, NY)
National Council of Savings Institutions Directory (National Council of Savings Institutions, Washington, DC)
Polk's Bank Directory (R.L. Polk & Company, Nashville, TN)
Rand McNally Bankers Directory (Rand McNally & Company, Chicago, IL)
Who's Who in International Banking (Reed Reference Publishing, New Providence, NJ)

Los Angeles Area Employers:

California Federal Bank
8700 Wilshire Blvd.
Los Angeles, CA 90036
(213) 932-6712
Job hotline: (213) 930-6712

California State Bank
100 N. Barranca Street
West Covina, CA 91791
(818) 915-4424
Chairman: Thomas Bishop

Cathay Bancorp
777 North Broadway
Los Angeles, CA 90012
(213) 625-4700
President: Dunson Cheng

City National Corp.
400 N. Roxbury Drive
Beverly Hills, CA 90210
(310) 888-6000
Chairman: Bram Goldsmith

Coast Savings Financial
1000 Wilshire Blvd.
Los Angeles, CA 90017
(213) 362-2000
Job hotline: (818) 316-8730
Employment Manager: Connie Ogas

Farmers & Merchants Bank of Long Beach
302 Pine Avenue
Long Beach, CA 90802
(310) 437-0011
President: Kenneth Walker

FirstFed Financial Corp.
401 Wilshire Blvd.
Santa Monica, CA 90401
(310) 319-6000
Hiring: Jackie Kittaka

Glendale Federal Bank
414 N. Central Avenue
Glendale, CA 91203
(818) 500-2000
Chairman: Stephen Trafton

Great Western Financial Corp.
9200 Oakdale Avenue
Chatsworth, CA 91311
(818) 775-3411
Job Hotline: 1-800-367-3411

Home Savings of America
4900 Rivergrade Road
Irwindale, CA 91706
(818) 960-6311
Chairman: Charles Rinehart

Imperial Bancorp
9920 S. La Cienega
Inglewood, CA 90301
(310) 417-5600
Job hotline: (310) 417-5433
Corporate Staffing Office: Terry Stidd

Manufacturers Bank
515 S. Figueroa Street
Los Angeles, CA 90071
(213) 489-6200
Chairman: Masato Keneko

Metrobank
10900 Wilshire Blvd.
Los Angeles, CA 90024
(310) 824-5700

Sanwa Bank California
601 S. Figueroa Street
Los Angeles, CA 90017
(213) 896-7000
Job hotline: 213-896-7214
Human Resource Specialist: Marilyn Perry

Southern Pacific Thrift & Loan Association
12300 Wilshire Blvd., Suite 200
Los Angeles, CA 90025
(310) 442-3300
President: Stephen Shugerman

Tokai Bank of California
300 S. Grand Avenue
Los Angeles, CA 90071
(213) 972-0200

Orange County Employers:

Bank of America
300 S. Harbor Blvd.
Anaheim, CA 92805
(714) 778-7299
Job hotline: (714) 254-6071
Vice President, Human Resources: Cathy Carpenter

California Federal Bank
4050 Metropolitan Drive
Orange, CA 92668
(714) 634-8391

Downey Financial Corporation
3501 Jamboree Road
Newport Beach, CA 92660
(714) 854-3100
Job hotline: 714-509-4310

Eldorado Bank
19100 Von Karman Avenue, Suite 550
Irvine, CA 92612
(714) 798-1100
Chairman: J.B. Crowell

Great Western Bank
3200 Park Center Drive, Suite 200
Costa Mesa, CA 92626
(714) 433-3625
Recruiter: Diana Baduria

Home Savings of America
3600 S. Bristol Street
Santa Ana, CA 92704
(714) 437-7550
All hiring through Irwindale Office: (818) 960-6311.

National Bank of Southern California
4100 Newport Place, Suite 100
Newport Beach, CA 92660
(714) 863-2300
Vice President, Human Resources: Sharon Dresser

Southern California Bank
3800 E. La Palma Avenue
Anaheim, CA 92807
(714) 238-3110

Wells Fargo Bank
100 N. Harbor Blvd.
Anaheim, CA 92805
(714) 491-3118
Retail Banking Manager: Pam Conboy

Western Financial Savings Bank
23 Pasteur
Irvine, CA 92618
(714) 727-1000
President: Ernest Rady

World Savings & Loan
1901 N. Euclid Street
Fullerton, CA 92635
(714) 879-4601
Human Resource Manager: Tonya Martin

San Diego Area Employers:

Bank of America
450 B Street, 5th Floor
San Diego, CA 92101
(619) 515-7575
Executive Vice President: Douglas Sawyer

Bank of Commerce
600 W. Broadway, Suite 100
San Diego, CA 92101
(619) 232-2096

Bank of Southern California
1620 5th Avenue, Suite 725
San Diego, CA 92101
(619) 338-1400
Human Resource Director: Nancy MacKinnon

First National Bank
401 W. A Street
San Diego, CA 92101
(619) 233-5588

First Pacific National Bank
613 W. Valley Parkway
Escondido, CA 92025
(619) 741-3312

Grossmont Bank
4230 La Jolla Village Drive, Suite 250
San Diego, CA 92122
(619) 623-3190
Hiring: Karen Filimon

Imperial Bank
701 B Street
San Diego, CA 92101

Manufacturers Bank
320 B Street
San Diego, CA 92101
(619) 544-3030

Metrobank
3131 Camino del Rio North
San Diego, CA 92108
(619) 563-9400

North County Bank
444 S. Escondido Blvd.
Escondido, CA 92025
(619) 743-2200

Peninsula Bank of San Diego
1331 Rosecrans Street
San Diego, CA 92106
(619) 226-5401
President: John Rebelo

San Diego National Bank
1420 Kettner Blvd.
San Diego, CA 92101
(619) 233-1234
Hiring: Connie Reckling

Sanwa Bank California
1280 4th Avenue
San Diego, CA 92101
(619) 234-3511

Scripps Bank
7817 Ivanhoe Avenue
La Jolla, CA 92037
(619) 456-2265
President: Ronald Carlson

Sumitomo Bank of California
410 A Street
San Diego, CA 92101
(619) 557-4900

Union Bank
530 B Street, Suite 1200
San Diego, CA 92101
(619) 230-4195
Executive Vice President: Ronald Kendrick

Wells Fargo Bank
1350 Fashion Valley Road
San Diego, CA 92108
(619) 688-3400

Banking on success

We talked with Stephen M. Hanzo, Branch Manager for a Los Angeles bank, about what it takes to do well in the banking industry. "A good banker needs to be a self-starter and goal oriented. Good communication skills are a must, as is the ability to get along well with many different types of people." Steve adds, "There is no specific career path in banking." He recommends experiencing different parts of banking, from international to domestic, consumer to business, operations to sales.

Steve's own career began with an international banking internship that led to a position in a management training program. He's also worked as a Financial Services Manager and Business Development Officer.

According to Steve, the banking industry is going through a wave of tremendous change which may impact the number of banks and employees in the banking industry. He advises, "Given all of the changes in banking, my philosophy is that if you perform extremely well in your job, you will probably survive merger-related layoffs. Otherwise, local competitors will gladly hire someone who has been successful in their market."

Book Publishers/Literary Agents

WEB SITES:

http://www.morganprice.com/contents.htm/
links to the *Publisher's Yellow Pages,* including company listings, products, services, and conferences.

http://www.scescape.com/worldlibrary/business/companies/publish.html/
links to book publishers.

http://www.bocklabs.wisc.edu/ims/agents.html/
is a directory of literary agents.

PROFESSIONAL ORGANIZATIONS:

To network in the publishing field, contact the following local professional organizations listed in Chapter 5. Also see **"Media, Print."**

Book Publicists of Southern California
Society of Children's Book Writers

For additional information, you can contact the following:

American Booksellers Association
828 S. Broadway
Tarrytown, NY 10591
(914) 591-2665

Association of American Publishers
71 5th Avenue
New York, NY 10003
(212) 255-0200

Association of Authors' Representatives
10 Astor Place, 3rd Floor
New York, NY 10003
(212) 353-3709

Western Publications Association
2401 Pacific Coast Highway, #102
Hermosa Beach, CA 90254
(310) 318-9697

Women's National Book Association
160 5th Avenue, Room 625
New York, NY 10010
(212) 675-7805

PROFESSIONAL PUBLICATIONS:

Editor and Publisher
Publishers' Auxiliary
Publishers Weekly
Small Press
Western Publisher

DIRECTORIES:

Editor & Publisher International Year Book (Editor & Publisher Company, Inc., New York, NY)
International Directory of Children's Literature (George Kurlan Reference Books, Baldwin Place, NY)
Literary Marketplace (R.R. Bowker Company, New Providence, NJ)
Publishers Directory (Gale Research, Detroit, MI)
Publishers, Distributors and Wholesalers of the United States (R.R. Bowker Company, New Providence, NJ)

Los Angeles Area Employers:

Amster, Betsy, Literary Enterprises
2151 Kenilworth Avenue
Los Angeles, CA 90039
(213) 662-1987

Donnelley, R.R., & Sons
19681 Pacific Gateway Drive
Torrance, CA 90502
(310) 516-3100

Gem Guides Book Company
315 Cloverleaf Drive, Suite F
Baldwin Park, CA 91706
(818) 855-1611

Glencoe/McGraw Hill Education Division
P.O. Box 9606

Mission Hills, CA 91346
(818) 898-1391

Intervisual Books
2850 Ocean Park Blvd., Suite 225
Santa Monica, CA 90405
(310) 396-8708

J2 Communications
10850 Wilshire Blvd., Suite 1000
Los Angeles, CA 90024
(310) 474-5252

Los Angeles Literary Associates
6324 Tahoe Drive
Los Angeles, CA 90068
(213) 464-6444

Petersen Publishing Company
6420 Wilshire Blvd., 2nd Floor
Los Angeles, CA 90048
(213) 782-2000

Practice Management Information Corporation
4717 Wilshire Blvd.
Los Angeles, CA 90010
(213) 954-0224
Administrative Manager: Tony Franco

Price Stern Sloan
11835 Olympic Blvd., Suite 500
Los Angeles, CA 90064
(310) 477-6100

United Publishers Corporation
100 N. Sepulveda, Suite 200
El Segundo, CA 90245
(310) 647-1500

Orange County Employers:

Books on Tape
729 Farad Street
Costa Mesa, CA 92627
(714) 548-5525
Human Resources: Ms. Jo Bradley

Creative Teaching Press
P.O. Box 6017
Cypress, CA 90630
(714) 995-7888
Specializes in elementary school teaching materials.

Donnelley Information Publishing
681 S. Parker Street
Orange, CA 92668
(714) 564-2800

Thomas Brothers Maps
17731 Cowan
Irvine, CA 92714
(714) 863-1985

San Diego Area Employers:

Academic Press
1250 6th Avenue
San Diego, CA 92101
(619) 699-6345

Advanced Marketing Services
5880 Oberlin Drive
San Diego, CA 92121
(619) 457-2500

Harcourt Brace & Company
525 B Street, Suite 1900
San Diego, CA 92101
(619) 231-6616

Lucent Books
P.O. Box 289011
San Diego, CA 92128
(619) 485-7424

Parker Publications
5900 La Place Court, Suite 107
Carlsbad, CA 92008
(619) 931-5979
Specializes in law books.

Trans Western Publishing
8328 Clairmont Mesa Blvd.
San Diego, CA 92111
(619) 292-8302

Broadcasting

WEB SITES:

http://www.hollywood-vine.com/1110_9_2.htm/
links to the television database list.

http://omnibus-eye.rtvf.nwu.edu/broadcasting.html/
is a resource listing for television and radio broadcasters, including links to newsgroups, Nielsen ratings, FCC, and broadcast stations.

http://www.broadcast.net/
is the Broadcast Net homepage with links to equipment, services, and broadcast information.

PROFESSIONAL ORGANIZATIONS:

To network within the field of broadcasting, contact these local professional organizations listed in Chapter 5:

American Federation of Television & Radio Artists, Los Angeles
American Federation of Television & Radio Artists, San Diego
American Women in Radio and Television
Southern California Broadcasters Association
Women in Communications

For additional information, you can contact the following:

American Radio Association
17 Battery Place, Room 1443
New York, NY 10004
(212) 809-0600

American Sportscasters Association
5 Beekman Street, Suite 814
New York, NY 10038
(212) 227-8080

California Cable TV Association
1121 L Street, Suite 400
Sacramento, CA 95814
(916) 446-7732

Corporation for Public Broadcasting
901 E Street, NW
Washington, DC. 20004
(202) 879-9600

National Academy of Television Arts & Sciences
111 W. 57th Street, Room 1020
New York, NY 10019
(212) 586-8424

National Association of Black Owned Broadcasters
1730 M Street, NW, Room 412
Washington, DC 20036
(202) 463-8970

National Association of Broadcasters
1771 N Street, NW
Washington, DC. 20036
(202) 429-5300
Operates employment clearinghouse.

National Cable Television Association
1724 Massachusetts Avenue, NW
Washington, DC. 20036
(202) 775-3550

National Radio Broadcasters Association
1771 N Street, NW
Washington, DC 20036
(202) 429-5420

Society of Motion Picture and Television Engineers
595 W. Hartsdale Avenue
New York, NY 10607
(914) 761-1100

PROFESSIONAL PUBLICATIONS:

Billboard
Broadcasting Magazine
Cable World

200 How To Get a Job

Electronic Media
Hollywood Reporter
Television Broadcast
Television/Radio Age
Variety

DIRECTORIES:

Broadcasting/Cable Yearbook (R.R. Bowker, New Providence, NJ)
Gale Directory of Publications and Broadcast Media (Gale Research, Detroit, MI)
International Television and Video Almanac (Quigley Publishing Company, New York, NY)
News Media Yellow Book (Leadership Directories, Inc., New York, NY)
Television and Cable Factbook (Television Digest, Inc., Washington, DC.)
Who's Who in the Television Industry (Packard Publishing, Beverly Hills, CA)

Los Angeles Area Radio Employers:

KBIG-FM (104.3)
7755 Sunset Blvd.
Los Angeles, CA 90046
(213) 874-7700
Resumes to Human Resources.

KFI-AM (640)
610 S. Ardmore Avenue
Los Angeles, CA 90005
(213) 385-0101
General Manager: Howard Neal

KIIS-FM (103.7)
3400 Riverside Drive, Suite 800
Burbank, CA 91505
(818) 845-1027
Human Resource Director: Bridget Agullera

KKBT-FM (92.3)
6735 Yucca Street
Los Angeles, CA 90028
(213) 466-9566
General Manager: Craig Wilbraham

KLAX-FM (97.9)
5700 Sunset Blvd.
Hollywood, CA 90028
(213) 466-3001
Spanish language format.

KLVE-FM (107.5)
1645 N. Vine Street, Suite 200
Hollywood, CA 90028
(213) 456-3171
President: Richard Heffel

KOST-FM (103.5)
610 S. Ardmore Avenue
Los Angeles, CA 90005
(213) 427-1035
Program Director: Johnie Kaye

KPWR-FM (105.9)
2600 W. Olive Avenue
Suite 850, 8th Floor
Burbank, CA 91505
(818) 953-4200
President: Doyle Rose

KROQ-FM (106.7)
3500 W. Olive Avenue, Suite 900
Burbank, CA 91505
(818) 567-1067
General Manager: Trip Reeb

KRTH-FM (101.1)
5901 Venice Blvd.
Los Angeles, CA 90034
(213) 937-5230

San Diego Area Radio Employers:

KFMB-AM/FM
7677 Engineer Road
San Diego, CA 92111
(619) 292-7600
Job hotline: (619) 495-8640

KMKX/KYXY-FM
8033 Linda Vista Road
San Diego, CA 92111
(619) 571-7600
General Manager: Jim Donahoe

KOGO-AM/KKLQ-FM/K102 FM
5745 Kearney Villa Road
San Diego, CA 92123
(619) 565-6006
Human Resource Director: Fran Jue

KPOP-AM/KGB-FM
7150 Engineer Road
San Diego, CA 92111
(619) 292-1360
General Manager: Tom Baker

KSDO-AM/KKBH-FM
5050 Murphy Canyon Road
San Diego, CA 92123
(619) 278-1130
General Manager: Susan Hoffman

XHTZ-FM/SLTN-FM/XHKY-FM
1229 3rd Avenue, Suite C
Chula Vista, CA 91911
(619) 585-9090
Business Manager: Nancy Miller

XTRA-AM/91X -FM
4891 Pacific Highway
San Diego, CA 92110
(619) 291-9191
General Manager: Mike Glickenhaus

Los Angeles Area Television Employers:

CBS-TV Channel 2
7800 Beverly Blvd.
Los Angeles, CA 90036
(213) 852-2345

KABC Channel 7
4151 Prospect Avenue
Los Angeles, CA 90027
(310) 557-7777
Job hotline: (310) 557-4222
Human Resource Manager: Dean Feruce

KCAL Channel 9
5515 Melrose Avenue
Los Angeles, CA 90038
(213) 467-5459
Job hotline: (213) 960-3770
Resumes to Human Resources.

KCET Channel 28
4401 Sunset Boulevard
Los Angeles, CA 90027
(213) 666-6500
Job hotline: (619) 953-5236
Human Resource Director: Ms. Lou Nunez-Burgess

KCOP Channel 13
915 N. La Brea Avenue
Los Angeles, CA 90038
(213) 851-1000
Job hotline: through operator switchboard
Personnel Manager: Vivian Rodriguez

KMEX Channel 34
6701 Center Drive West, 15th Floor
Los Angeles, CA 90045
(310) 216-3434
Spanish language programming.

KNBC Channel 4
3000 W. Alameda Avenue
Burbank, CA 91523
(818) 840-4444

KTLA Channel 5
5100 W. Sunset Blvd.
Los Angeles, CA 90028
(213) 460-5500

KTTV Channel 11
1999 S. Bundy Drive
Los Angeles, CA 90025
(310) 584-2000
Resumes to Recruitment.

San Diego Area Television Employers:

KFMB Channel 8
7677 Engineer Road
San Diego, CA 92111
(619) 571-8888
General Manager: Arnold Kleiner

KGTV Channel 10
P.O. Box 85347
San Diego, CA 92186
(619) 237-1010
Job hotline: (619) 237-6250

KNSD Channel 39
8330 Engineer Road
San Diego, CA 92111
(619) 279-3939
Job hotline: (619) 467-7605
Office Manager: Darcey Gulen

KPBS-TV Channel 15
5200 Campanile Drive

San Diego, CA 92182
(619) 594-1515
Job hotline: (619) 594-5703

KUSI-TV Channel 51
P.O. Box 719051
San Diego, CA 92171
(619) 571-5151
General Manger: Michael McKinnon

XETV-Fox Channel 6
8253 Ronson Road
San Diego, CA 92111
(619) 279-6666
Business Manager: Bob Taylor

Chemicals

WEB SITES:

http://www.acs.org/
is the homepage of the American Chemical Society with links to publications, career services, education, events, and membership.

http://www.cas.or/
links to the Chemistry Abstracts Service, providing information from print publications and on-line resources.

PROFESSIONAL ORGANIZATIONS:

For networking in the chemical industry and related fields, check out the following local professional organization listed in Chapter 5. Also see **"Drugs/Pharmaceuticals/Biotechnology."**

American Chemical Society, Southern California Chapter

For additional information, you can contact the following:

American Chemical Society
1155 16th Street, NW.
Washington, DC. 20036
(202) 872-4600

American Institute of Chemists
501 Wythe Street
Alexandria, VA 22314
(703) 836-2090

Chemical Manufacturers Association
1300 Wilson
Arlington, VA 22209
(703) 741-5000

PROFESSIONAL PUBLICATIONS:

Chemical & Engineering News
Chemical Week
The Chemist

DIRECTORIES:

American Institute of Chemists Professional Directory (Bethesda, MD)
Chemclopedia (American Chemical Society, Washington, DC.)
Chemicals Directory (Cahners Publishing Company, Netwon, MA)
Chemical Week, Financial Survey of the 300 Largest Companies (McGraw-Hill, New York, NY)
Directory of Chemical Producers USA (SRI International, Menlo Park, CA)
Guide to Products and Services of Small Chemical Businesses (American Chemical Society Division of Small Chemical Businesses, Columbus, OH)

Los Angeles Area Employers:

Advanced Materials Group
20211 S. Susana Road
Rancho Dominguez, CA 90221
(310) 537-5444

American Vanguard Corporation
4100 E. Washington Blvd.
Los Angeles, CA 90023
(213) 264-3910

Ashland Chemical Company
6608 E. 26th Street
Los Angeles, CA 90040
(213) 724-2440

Brogdex Company
1441 W. 2nd Street
Pomona, CA 91766
(909) 622-1021

Ecolab Inc.
15736 Valley Blvd.
City of Industry, CA 91744
(818) 855-2835

Flamemaster Corp.
11120 Sherman Way
Sun Valley, CA 91352
(818) 982-1650

Los Angeles Chemical Corp.
4545 Ardine Street
P.O. Box 1987
South Gate, CA 90280
(213) 583-4761

Pacer Technology
9420 San Anita Avenue
Rancho Cucamonga, CA 91730
(909) 987-0550
Administrative Assistant: Helen Komorek

PMC Inc.
12243 Branford Street
Sun Valley, CA 91352
(818) 896-1101
Personnel: Karen Ferguson

Thompson PBE
4553 Glencoe Avenue
Marina del Rey, CA 90292
(310) 306-7112

United States Borax & Chemical Corp.
26877 Tourney Road
Valencia, CA 91355
(805) 287-5400

Whittaker Corp.
1955 N. Surveyor Avenue
Simi Valley, CA 93063
(818) 526-5700

Orange County Employers:

Dow Corning USA
5 Corporate Park #280
Irvine, CA 92714
(714) 757-5000

Hill Brothers Chemical
1675 N. Main Street
Orange, CA 92867
(714) 998-8800
Hiring: Ms. Gudrun Wolf

Morton Electronic Materials
2631 Michelle Drive
Tustin, CA 92681
(714) 730-4200

Rohm & Haas
14445 Alondra Blvd.
La Mirada, CA 90638
(714) 228-4700
Hiring: Kathy Huerta

Union Carbide Corp.
P.O. Box 5068
Costa Mesa, CA 92628
(714) 662-4300
Hiring: Winnie Zardeneta

Urethane Technologies
1202 E. Wakeham Avenue
Santa Ana, CA 92705
(714) 973-0800
Human Resources: Kimberly Akers

San Diego Area Employers:

Hills Brothers Chemical
1680 Logan Avenue
San Diego, CA 92113
(619) 233-7171

Kelco
8355 Aero Drive
San Diego, CA 92123
(619) 292-4900
Division of Merck & Co.

Schumacher, J.C., Company
1969 Palomar Oaks Way
Carlsbad, CA 92009
(619) 931-9555

WD-40 Company
1061 Cudahy Place
San Diego, CA 92110
(619) 275-1400
Vice President, Administration: Dawn Martin

Chemical careers

Virgil Lee is a Research Scientist working for a Los Angeles area company. We asked him about job opportunities within Southern California. "The primary chemical opportunities in Southern California are in the oil and biotech industries. The Los Angeles area is also rich with quality control chemical positions which employ mainly B.S. level chemists. For these positions, familiarity with instrumentation is a great benefit." Virgil also recommends obtaining research experience to best position oneself for such positions. Virgil's own background includes two years experience in an academic laboratory and another year as a Synthetic Chemist for a start-up company in Pasadena.

While Virgil expects that job prospects for the near future will be good, he cautioned that chemistry positions are affected by shifts in specialized fields such as the petroleum industry. He adds that, "Chemistry, in general, is a stable field with a low unemployment rate."

Computers: Consulting/Information Management

WEB SITES:

http://www.cais.com/ntsa/
links to the National Technical Services Association with information on jobs, events, membership, and professional chat rooms.

http://www.usenix.org/
is a resource guide for computing professionals including links to publications, events, and directories.

PROFESSIONAL ORGANIZATIONS:

For networking in the computer consulting/information management field, check out the following local professional organization listed in Chapter 5. Also see "Computers: Hardware/Software."

Independent Computer Consultant Association

For additional information, you can contact the following:

American Society for Information Science
8720 Georgia Avenue, Suite 501
Silver Spring, MD 20910
(301)495-0900

Information Technology Association of America
1616 N. Ft. Myer Drive, Suite 1300
Arlington, VA 22209
(703) 522-5055

Society for Information Management
401 N. Michigan Avenue
Chicago, IL 60611
(312) 644-6610

PROFESSIONAL PUBLICATIONS:

Computer Communications Review
Computerworld
CTI for Management
Information Week
Journal of Systems Management
Network World

DIRECTORIES:

Computer and Computing Information Resources Directory (Gale Research, Detroit, MI)
Data Sources (Ziff-Davis Publishing, New York, NY)
Information Industry Directory (Gale Research, Detroit, MI)
Information Sources (Information Industry Association, Washington, D.C.)

Employers:

American Management Systems
201 S. Figueroa Street, Suite 300
Los Angeles, CA 90012
(213) 613-5400
Recruiting Manager: Carol Bates

Andersen Consulting
2101 Rosecrans Avenue, Suite 3300
El Segundo, CA 90245
(310) 726-2700
Personnel Specialist: Kathleen Atkinson

Coopers & Lybrand Consulting
4675 MacArthur Court, Suite 1500
Newport Beach, CA 92660
(714) 251-7340

EarthLink Network
3100 New York Drive, Suite 201
Pasadena, CA 91107
(818) 296-2400
Internet access provider.

Nettleship Group
2665 Main Street, Suite 220
Santa Monica, CA 90405
(310) 392-8585

SHL Systemhouse
12750 Center Court Drive
Cerritos, CA 90701
(310) 860-3635

Source Consulting
1025 W. 190th Street, Suite 165
Gardena, CA 90248
(310) 323-9337

Technical Directions
8880 Rio San Diego Drive
San Diego, CA 92108
(619) 297-5611

Warner Group, The
5950 Canoga Avenue, Suite 600
Woodland Hills, CA 91367
(818) 380-1177

Booting up big $$$ in computer sales

Philip Daniels competes in the fast lane as a computer sales engineer. His clients are Fortune 500 companies, and his products are communications boards, controllers, and disk and tape subsystems manufactured by a relatively new specialty company. "It's an emotionally and physically stressful environment where I constantly have to prove myself," says Philip.

We asked how he got there and what keeps him successful.

"I use every skill and all the experience I've ever had," said the former teacher and editorial assistant for a steel company's community relations department. "When I decided to go back to school for an associate's degree in computers, I needed a job as well. So I sold cars, and that provided invaluable marketing and people experience, plus communications skills that are absolutely essential in my present business.

"Once I got into computer courses, I realized I couldn't settle for a $25,000 programming job and began laying more plans. And, incidentally, you must prepare yourself for the entry positions in this field. My first job-strictly commission-was with a small systems house, and within a year I was director of marketing with a sales staff of six. I got a total overview of the business so that I could talk from that perspective on my next round of interviews.

"I used an employment agent who specializes in computer sales to get this position and was very specific with him about my requirements."

Asked to explain his current success, Philip responds: "I'd have to say the number one factor is technical expertise-with sales ability second. I read, listen, and pick brains to stay on top of the products and a changing market place so that my company provides a service to the client by sending me. By the way, with little more education than a $25,000 programmer, I'll make at least three times that this year. And the perks are great, too."

Computers: Hardware/Software

WEB SITES:

http://www.acm.org/
links to the Association for Computing Machinery with links to publications, conferences, and career opportunities.

http://www.spa.org/
is the homepage of the Software Publishers Association, with information on conferences, job search, education, research, and conferences.

PROFESSIONAL ORGANIZATIONS:

For networking in the computer industry, contact the following organizations. See also "**Computers: Consulting/Information Management**" and "**Electronics/Telecomunications.**"

American Electronics Association
5201 Great America Parkway, Suite 520
Santa Clara, CA 95054
(408) 987-4200

Computer and Communications Industry Association
666 11th Street, NW
Washington, DC. 20001
(202) 783-0070

IEEE Computer Society
1730 Massachusetts Ave., NW
Washington, DC 20036
(202) 371-0101

Semiconductor Industry Association
4300 Stevens Creek Blvd.
San Jose, CA 95129
(408) 246-2711

Software Publishers Association
1730 M Street, NW, Suite 700
Washington, DC 20036
(202) 452-1600

PROFESSIONAL PUBLICATIONS:

Byte
Computer Industry Report
Computer World
Info World
PC Magazine
PC Week
PC World

DIRECTORIES:

Computer Industry Almanac (Simon & Schuster, New York, NY)
Data Sources: Hardware-Data Communications Directory (Ziff-Davis, New York, NY)
Data Sources: Software Directory (Ziff-Davis, New York, NY)
Datapro Directory of Microcomputer Software (Datapro Information Services Group, Delran, NJ)
Guide to High Technology Companies (Corp. Technology Information Services, Woburn, MA)
ICP Software Directory (International Computer Programs, Indianapolis, IN)
Membership Directory (Information Technology Assoc. of America, Arlington, VA)
Software Publishers' Catalog Annual (Meckler Corp., Westport, CT)

Los Angeles Area Employers:

Activision
11601 Wilshire Blvd., Suite 300
Los Angeles, CA 90025
(310) 473-9200

Candle Corp.
2425 Olympic Blvd.
Santa Monica, CA 90404
(310) 829-5800

Davidson & Associates
19840 Pioneer Avenue

Torrance, CA 90503
(310) 793-0600
Job hotline: (310) 793-0599
Human Resources: Melanie Doell

Internal & External Communications
4215 Glencoe Avenue, Suite 100
Marina del Rey, CA 90292
(310) 827-4464

Knowledge Adventure
1311 Grand Central Avenue
Glendale, CA 91201
(818) 246-4400
Job hotline: (818) 246-7330
Human Resources: Sandy Lopez

Locus Computing Corp.
9800 La Cienega Blvd.
Inglewood, CA 90301
(310) 670-6500

Logicon Inc.
3701 Skypark Drive
Torrance, CA 90505
(310) 373-0220

MacNeal-Schwendler Corp.
815 Colorado Blvd.
Los Angeles, CA 90041
(213) 258-9111

Merisel Inc.
200 Continental Blvd.
El Segundo, CA 90245
(310) 615-3080

PCC Group
163 University Parkway
Pomona, CA 91768
(909) 869-6133

Quarterdeck Corporation
13160 Mindanao Way, 3rd Floor
Marina del Rey, CA 90292
(310) 309-3700
http://quarterdeck.com

Software Dynamics
9400 Topanga Canyon Blvd.
Chatsworth, CA 91311
(818) 773-0330

Orange County Employers:

Advanced Logic Research
9401 Jeronimo Road
Irvine, CA 92618
(714) 581-6770
CEO: Gene Lu

Alpha Microsystems
2722 S. Fairview Street
Santa Ana, CA 92704
(714) 957-8500
Hiring: Peggy Denson

AST Computer
16215 Alton Parkway
Irvine, CA 92618
(714) 727-4141
Chairman: Safi Qureshey

FileNet Corp.
3565 Harbor Blvd.
Costa Mesa, CA 92626
(714) 966-3400
CEO: Ted Smith

Interplay Productions
17922 Fitch Avenue
Irvine, CA 92714
(714) 553-6655
http://www.interplay.com
CEO: Brian Fargo

Platinum Software Corporation
195 Technology Drive
Irvine, CA 92718
(714) 453-4000
Senior Human Resource Representative: Carrie Masotto

Rainbow Technologies
50 Technology Drive West
Irvine, CA 92718
(714) 450-7300
Hiring: Kay Skinner

Simulation Sciences
601 S. Valencia Avenue
Brea, CA 92621
(714) 579-0412
Human Resource Manager: Kathy Murphy

Computers: Hardware/Software

Smith Micro Software
51 Columbia
Aliso Viejo, CA 92656
(714) 362-5800

State of the Art
56 Technology West
Irvine, CA 92718
(714) 753-1222
Job hotline: (714) 753-4080
http://www.state of the art.com
Human Resource Director: Kelly Henry

Toshiba America Information Systems
9740 Irvine Blvd.   461-4949 JOBLINE
Irvine, CA 92718
(714) 583-3000
FAX 587-6436

Unisys Corp.
30200 Avenida del Las Banderas
Rancho Santa Margarita, CA 92688
(714) 858-2000
Vice President: Ben Swenson

Virgin Interactive Entertainment
18061 Fitch Avenue
Irvine, CA 92714   FAX 833-8717
(714) 833-8710
http://www.vie.com
President: Martin Alper

Western Digital Corp.
8105 Irvine Center Drive   CB
Irvine, CA 92718
(714) 932-5000
http://www.wdc.com
CEO: Chuck Haggerty

Wonderware
100 Technology Drive
Irvine, CA 92718
(714) 727-3200   CB
Job hotline: 1-800-541-6930
http://www.wonderware.com
Human Resource Director: Ernie Bloch

San Diego Area Employers:

Biosym Technologies
9685 Scranton Road
San Diego, CA 92121
(619) 458-9990

http://www.msi.com
Human Resource Director: Judy Ohrn

DataWorks
5910 Pacific Center Blvd.
San Diego, CA 92121
(619) 546-9600
http://www.dataworks.com
President: Stuart Clifton

Excalibur Technologies Corporation
1959 Palomar Oaks Way
Carlsbad, CA 92009
(619) 438-7900
President/CEO: J. Michael Kennedy

Executive Business Services
5473 Kearney Villa Road, Suite 210
San Diego, CA 92123
(619) 279-6005

GERS Retail Systems
9725-C Scranton Road
San Diego, CA 92121
(619) 457-3888
http://www.GERS.com

Horizons Technology
3990 Ruffin Road
San Diego, CA 92123
(619) 292-8331
Job hotline: (619) 292-8860 x855
http://www.horizons.com
Human Resource Manager: Marianna Koehmskedt

Interactive Group
5095 Murphy Canyon Road
San Diego, CA 92123
(619) 560-8525
http://www.infoflo.com
Human Resource Manager: Collette Shea

Peregrine Systems
1260 High Bluff Drive
San Diego, CA 92130
(619) 481-5000
Human Resource Manager: Diane Olivo

Stac Electronics
12636 High Bluff Drive
San Diego, CA 92130

(619) 794-4300
Job hotline: (619) 794-4739
http://www.stac.com
Employment Consultant: Simon Meth

VisiCom Laboratories
10052 Mesa Ridge Court
San Diego, CA 92121
(619) 457-2111
Recruiter: Wilson Gilinsky

Construction

WEB SITES:

http://www.abc.org/
is the homepage of the Associated Builders and Contractors organization; includes information on education, legal assistance, and government affairs.

http://www.building.org/
links to Building Industry Exchange page with a directory and search engine for the construction industry.

http://scescape.com/worldlibrary/business/companies/construct/html/
links to construction companies.

PROFESSIONAL ORGANIZATIONS:

To network within the construction industry, contact the following local professional organizations listed in Chapter 5. Also see "**Engineering.**"

Air Conditioning and Refrigeration Contractors Association
American Constructor Inspectors Association
Associated Builders & Contractors of Southern California
Associated General Contractors of California, Los Angeles Chapter
Associated General Contractors of California, San Diego Chapter
National Association of Women in Construction, Los Angeles
Southern California Builders Association
Southern California Contractors Association

For additional information, you can contact the following:

Associated General Contractors of America
1957 E Street, NW
Washington, DC 20006
(202) 393-2040

Building Industry Association of Southern CA
1330 S. Valley Vista Drive
Diamond Bar, CA 91765
(909)396-9993

Building Industry Association of San Diego
6336 Greenwich Drive, Suite A
San Diego, CA 92122
(619) 450-1221

Building Service Contractors Association International
10201 Lee Highway, Suite 225
Fairfax, VA 22030
(703) 359-7090

National Association of Home Builders of the U.S.
1201 15th Street, NW
Washington, DC 20005
(202) 822-0200

National Association of Minority Contractors
1333 F Street, NW, Suite 500
Washington, DC 20004
(202) 347-8259

National Association of Women in Construction
327 S. Adams Street
Fort Worth, TX 76104
(817) 877-5551

Construction

PROFESSIONAL PUBLICATIONS:

Builder
Builder and Contractor
Construction Review
Constructor
Pit & Quarry
Professional Builder

DIRECTORIES:

Associated Builders and Contractors Membership Directory Issue (Associated Builders and Contractors, Washington, DC)
Blue Book of Major Homebuilders (LSI Systems, Inc., Crofton, MD)
Building Contractors Directory (American Business Directories, Omaha, NE)
Constructor, Directory Issue (Associated General Contractors of America, Washington, DC)
Southern California Building Industry Directory (Building Industry Association, Diamond Bar, CA)

Los Angeles Area Employers:

Dinwiddie Construction Company
1145 Wilshire Blvd. Suite 200
Los Angeles, CA 90017
(213) 482-1900
Vice President: Bill Vanleven

Jacobs Engineering Group
251 S. Lake Avenue
Pasadena, CA 91101
(818) 449-2171
CEO: N. Watson

Kajima Engineering & Construction
200 S. Los Robles, Suite 400
Pasadena, CA 91101
(818) 440-0033
Human Resource Manager: Nancy Osa

Keller Construction Company LTD
9950 E. Baldwin Place
El Monte, CA 91734
(818) 443-6633
Vice President: Tom Keeton

Morley Group
2901 28th Street
Santa Monica, CA 90405
(310) 399-1600
CEO: Mark Benjamin

Pankow, Charles, Builders LTD
2476 N. Lake Avenue
Altadena, CA 91001
(213) 684-2320
Chairman: Charles Pankow

Peck/Jones Construction
10866 Wilshire Blvd., Suite 700
Los Angeles, CA 90024
(310) 470-1885
Vice President, Administration: Susan Schmidt

Shapell Industries
8383 Wilshire Blvd., Suite 700
Beverly Hills, CA 90211
(213) 655-7330

Swinerton & Walberg
865 S. Figueroa, Suite 3000
Los Angeles, CA 90017
(213) 896-3400
Office Manager: Colleen Edwards

Turner Construction Company
555 W. 5th Street
Los Angeles, CA 90013
(213) 891-3000
Personnel Manager: Tom Turner

Tutor-Saliba Corp
15901 Olden Street
Sylmar, CA 91342
(818) 362-8391
Controller: Bob Husted

Orange County Employers:

Baldwin Company
500 Newport Center Drive, Suite 700
Newport beach, CA 92660
(714) 640-0540

California Pacific Homes
1 Civic Plaza, Suite 275
Newport Beach, CA 92660
(714) 719-3000
Human Resource Director: Vivien Wrapp

Fieldstone Company
14 Corporate Plaza
Newport Beach, CA 92660
(714) 851-8313
Human Resources: Don Hendricks

Fluor Corp.
3333 Michelson Drive
Irvine, CA 92730
(714) 975-2000
Job hotline: (714) 975-5253

Greystone Homes
7 Upper Newport Plaza Drive
Newport Beach, CA 92660
(714) 852-9411
President: Larry Webb

Hensel Phelps Construction
2415 Campus Drive, Suite 100
Irvine, CA 92715
(714) 852-0111
Vice President: Wayne Lindholm

Honvian, K., Companies
3991 MacArthur Blvd., Suite 300
Newport Beach, CA 92660
(714) 660-1130

Kaufman & Broad Homes
100 Bayview Circle, South Tower, Suite 100
Newport Beach, CA 92626
(714) 509-2400
President: Ronald Osgood

McCarthy Brothers Company
100 Bay View Circle, Suite 3000
Newport Beach, CA 92660
(714) 854-8383
Division President; Michael Bolen

Standard Pacific Corp.
1565 W. MacArthur Blvd.
Costa Mesa, CA 92626
(714) 546-1161

San Diego Area Employers:

FCI Constructors
12707 High Bluff Drive
San Diego, CA 92130
(619) 481-6900
Office Manager: Karen Kaminar

Filanc, J.R., Construction Company
4616 North Avenue
Oceanside, CA 92056
(619) 941-7130

Harris, Sim J., Company
9229 Harris Plant Road
San Diego, CA 92145
(619) 277-5481

Koll Construction
7330 Engineer Road
San Diego, CA 92111
(619) 292-5550

Lusardi Construction Company
1570 Linda Vista Drive
San Marcos, CA 92069
(619) 744-3133

Nielsen Construction Company
3127 Jefferson Street
San Diego, CA 92110
(619) 291-6330

XXSYS Technologies
4619 Viewridge Avenue
San Diego, CA 92123
(619) 974-8200

Drugs/Pharmaceuticals/Biotechnology

WEB SITES:

http://pharminfo.com/pharmmall/pm_hp.html
is the homepage of the Pharmaceutical Information Network; includes jobs and publications.

http://www.biospace.com/
is an educational forum for the biotechnology industry with a career center, resource directory, and news updates.

http://www.bio.com/
links to Bio On-line, providing company profiles, job postings, and industry news.

PROFESSIONAL ORGANIZATIONS:

To network within the pharmaceutical and biotechnology industries, contact the following local professional organization listed in Chapter 5:

Biomedical Engineering Society

For additional information, you can contact the following:

American Association of Pharmaceutical Scientists
1650 King Street
Alexandria VA 22314
(703) 548-3000

American Pharmaceutical Association
2215 Constitution Avenue, NW
Washington, DC 20037
(202) 628-4410

Biotechnology Industry Organization
1625 K Street, NW
Washington, DC 20006
(202) 857-0244

Industrial Biotechnology Association
1625 K Street, NW., Suite 1100
Washington, DC. 20006
(202) 857-0244

National Association of Pharmaceutical Manufacturers
320 Old Country Road
Garden City, NY 11530
(516) 741-3699

Pharmaceutical Manufacturers Association
1100 15th Street, NW
Washington, DC. 20005
(202) 835-3400

PROFESSIONAL PUBLICATIONS:

American Druggist
Biotechnology Advances
Cosmetics and Toiletries
Drug and Cosmetic Industry
Pharmaceutical Executive
Pharmaceutical Technology

DIRECTORIES:

Biotechnology Directory (Stockton Press, New York, NY)
Biotechnology Industry Guide (Institute for Biotechnology Information, Triangle Park NC)
Cosmetics & Toiletries: Who's Who in R&D (Allured Publishing Corporation, Carol Stream, IL)
Directory of Custom Pharmaceutical Manufacturers (Delphi Marketing Services, Inc., New York, NY)
Drug Topics Red Book (Litton Publications, Oradell, NJ)
Genetic Engineering & Biotechnology Worldwide Directory (Mega-Type Publishing, Princeton Junction, NJ)
Medical and Health Information Directory (Gale Research, Detroit, MI)
NWDA-Membership & Executive Directory (National Wholesale Druggists Association, Reston, VA)
Pharmaceutical Industry Guide (Institute for Biotechnology Information, Triangle Park, NC)
Pharmaceutical Manufacturers of the U.S. (Noyes Data Corp., Park Ridge, NJ)

Los Angeles Area Employers:

Alpha Therapeutic Corporation
5555 Valley Blvd.
Los Angeles, CA 90032
(213) 225-2221

Amgen, Inc.
1840 Dehavilland Drive
Thousand Oaks, CA 91320
(805) 447-1000
Job hotline: (800) 446-4007
See the "Best Employers in Southern California" section of Chapter 1 for additional information.

Chantal Pharmaceutical Corp.
12121 Wilshire Blvd., Suite 1120
Los Angeles, CA 90025
(310) 207-1950

Dep Corporation
2101 E. Vida Arado
Rancho Dominguez, CA 90220
(310) 604-0777

Lee Pharmaceuticals
1444 Santa Anita Avenue
El Monte, CA 91733
(818) 442-3141

PDT, Inc.
7408 Hollister Avenue
Santa Barbara, CA 93117
(805) 685-9880
Resumes to Director of Human Resources

St. Ives Laboratories
9201 Oakdale Avenue
Chatsworth, CA 91311
(818) 709-5500

Syncor International Corp.
20001 Prairie Street
Chatsworth, CA 91311
(818) 886-7400
Manager of Human Resource Operations: Deborah Hildebrand

Watson Pharmaceuticals
P.O. Box 1900
311 Bonnie Circle
Corona, CA 91718

(909) 270-1400
Vice President: George Leischer
See the "Fastest Growing Southern California Companies" section of Chapter 1 for additional information.

Orange County Employers:

Allergan
2525 Dupont Drive
Irvine, CA 92715
(714) 752-4500
Human Resources

Bergen Brunswig Corp.
4000 Metropolitan Drive
Orange, CA 92668-3510
(714) 385-4000
Human Resource Manager: Sherie Mullins

Cortex Pharmaceuticals
15241 Barrance Parkway
Irvine, CA 92718
(714) 727-3157

Hycor Biomedical
18800 Von Karman Avenue
Irvine, CA 92715
(714) 440-2000

ICN Pharmaceuticals
3300 Hyland Avenue
Costa Mesa, CA 92626
(714) 545-0100

Interpore International
181 Technology Drive
Irvine, CA 92718
(714) 453-3200
Human Resources

Nucleic Acid Research Institute
3300 Hyland Avenue
Costa Mesa, CA 92626
(714) 641-7201

San Diego Area Employers:

Advanced Tissue Sciences
10933 N. Torrey Pines Road
La Jolla, CA 92037-1005
Job hotline: (619) 450-5854
Recruiting Manager: Tom Murphy

Drugs/Pharmaceuticals/Biotechnology

Agouron Pharmaceuticals
10350 N. Torrey Pines Road
La Jolla, CA 92037
(619) 622-3000
Managing Principal: Peter Johnson

Alliance Pharmaceutical Corp.
3040 Science Park Road
San Diego, CA 92121
(619) 558-4300
Human Resources: Susan Nixon

Amylin Pharmaceuticals
9373 Town Center Drive
San Diego, CA 92121
(619) 552-2200
Principal: Howard Greene

Corvas International
3030 Science Park Road
San Diego, CA 92121
(619) 455-9800
Human Resource Assistant: Linda Knight

Cytel Corp.
3525 John Hopkins Court
San Diego, CA 92121
(619) 552-3000
Job hotline: (619) 552-2733
Director of Human Resources: Sherlyn Leyton

Dura Pharmaceuticals
5880 Pacific Center Blvd.
San Diego, CA 92121
(619) 457-2553

Gen-Probe
9880 Campus Point Drive
San Diego, CA 92121
(619) 546-8000
Job hotline: (619) 625-8666

Gensia
9360 Towne Center Drive
San Diego, CA 92121
(619) 546-8300
Job hotline: (619) 622-3821

Hybritech
P.O. Box 269006
San Diego, CA 92196
(619) 455-6700

IDEC Pharmaceutical Corp
11011 N. Torreyana Road
San Diego, CA 92121
(619) 550-8500

Immune Response Corp.
5935 Darwin Court
Carlsbad, CA 92008
(619) 431-7080
Job hotline: through main switchboard
Human Resources Coordinator: Lisa Gonzales

Isis Pharmaceuticals
2292 Faraday Avenue
Carlsbad, CA 92008
(619) 931-9200

Johnson, R.W., Pharmaceutical Research Institute
3535 General Atomic Court, #100
San Diego, CA 92121
(619) 450-2000

La Jolla Pharmaceutical
6455 Nancy Ridge Drive
San Diego, CA 92121
(619) 452-6600
Job hotline: through main switchboard
Director of Human Resources: Kimberly Ellstrom

Ligand Pharmaceuticals
9393 Towne Centre Drive, Suite 100
San Diego, CA 92121
(619) 535-3900

Molecular Biosystems
10030 Barnes Canyon Road
San Diego, CA 92121
(619) 452-0681
Job hotline: (619) 824-2290
Resumes to Human Resources Department

Mycogen Corp.
5501 Oberlin Drive
San Diego, CA 92121-1764
(619) 453-8030
Job hotline: (619) 453-7812
Human Resources Specialist: Susanne Rinehart

PharMingen
10975 Torreyana Road
San Diego, CA 92121-1111
(619) 677-7737
Job hotline: through main switchboard
Human Resources Supervisor: Diana Shatz

Quidel Corp.
10165 McKellar Court
San Diego, CA 92121
(619) 552-1100
Senior Human Resource Director: Kellie Potter

Viagene
11055 Roselle Street
San Diego, CA 92121
(619) 452-1288

Vical Inc.
9373 Towne Centre Drive, Suite 100
San Diego, CA 92121-3027
(619) 453-9900
Job hotline: (619) 646-1143

Getting through the "glass ceiling"

We asked Ellen King, a Projects Manager for a Southern California pharmaceutical company, for her advice on breaking into the pharmaceutical industry in Southern California. "If it is a first job which is being sought, I recommend taking almost any lab-related position. Once an individual is working with a particular company, work hard at learning more than is required for the specific job."

She adds that within the pharmaceutical industry there is a very real "glass ceiling." "If an individual wishes to make a career in a laboratory, an advanced degree is almost a must. However, more mobility may be found in the administrative functions within the industry without an advanced degree."

Ellen adds, "Irrespective of level of education, there are several skills which are extremely valuable. First and foremost is the ability to write. Technical writing is a skill that can be utilized in almost any job in industry. Secondly, do your best to have a "can-do" attitude. Lastly, I recommend that people do their best to be good listeners. Especially early in your career, there is so much to learn from so many coworkers that the ability to listen and learn cannot be overstated."

When asked about employment prospects within the pharmaceutical industry, Ellen is realistic. "In the pharmaceutical industry, one should constantly expect corporate changes such as mergers, buyouts, and acquisitions, all of which can affect one's position at a company."

Educational Institutions

WEB SITES:

http://www.petersons.com
links to public and private schools, colleges, and universities, arranged by geography.

http://www.mit.edu8001/people/cdmello/univ.html
links to over 3,000 college and university homepages.

http://chronicle.com/
is the homepage of *ACADEME This Week*; lists job opportunities.

http://volvo.glis.utexas.edu/~acadres/geographic.html
links to college and university homepages.

http://www.calstate.edu
is the California State University System homepage.

http://pages.prodigy.com/luca52a/edet.htm
K-12 job listings within five Southern California counties.

http://www.usjobnet.com/jobs.html
K-12 teaching opportunities mostly within California.

http://www.naspa.org
has job listings within higher education administration.

PROFESSIONAL ORGANIZATIONS:

To network within the field of education, contact the following local professional organizations listed in Chapter 5:

Association of California School Administrators
California Federation of Teachers
California School Employees Association
Independent Colleges of Southern California

For additional information, you can contact the following:

American Association of School Administrators
1801 N. Moore Street
Arlington, VA 22209
(703) 528-0700

American Association of University Women
1111 16th Street, NW
Washington, DC 20036
(202) 785-7700

American Montessori Society
281 Park Avenue South, 6th Floor
New York, NY 10010
(212) 358-1250

California Teachers Association
5757 W. Century Blvd., Suite 508
Los Angeles, CA 90045
(310) 642-6622

California Teachers Association
10393 San Diego Mission Road, Suite 110A
San Diego, CA 92108
(619) 280-6252

National Art Education Association
1916 Association Drive
Reston, VA 20191
(703) 860-8000

National Association for the Education of Young Children
1509 16th Street, NW
Washington, DC 20036
(202) 232-8777
(800) 424-2460

National Education Association
1201 16th Street, NW
Washington, DC 20036
(202) 833-4000

Teachers of English to Speakers of Other Languages
1600 Cameron Street, Suite 300
Alexandria, VA 22314
(703) 836-0774

PROFESSIONAL PUBLICATIONS:

California Teacher
Chronicle of Higher Education
Education Week
Instructor
School Administrator
Teaching K-8
Technology and Learning
Today's Catholic Teacher

DIRECTORIES:

Boarding Schools Directory (National Association of Independent Schools, Boston MA)
Directory of Public School Systems in the U.S. (Association for School, College and University Staffing, Evanston, IL)
National Directory of Alternative Schools (National Coalition of Alternative Community Schools, Summertown, TN)
Nursery Schools & Kindergartens (American Business Directories, Omaha, NE)
Peterson's Guide to Four Year Colleges (Peterson's Guides, Princeton, NJ)
Peterson's Guide to Independent Secondary Schools (Peterson's Guides, Princeton, NJ)

Los Angeles Area College Employers:

California Institute of the Arts
24700 McBean Parkway
Valencia, CA 91355
(805) 255-1050
http://www.calarts.edu

California Institute of Technology
Human Resources
Mail Stop 101-06
Pasadena, CA 91125
(818) 395-4661
Job hotline: 818-395-4660
http://www.caltech.edu
See the "Top Ten Employers" section of Chapter 1 for additional information.

California Polytechnic University-Pomona
3801 W. Temple Avenue
Pomona, CA 91768
(909) 869-2000
hppt://www.cuspomona.edu/employment/welcome.htm

California State University, Dominguez Hills
Human Resource Office, ERC B518
1000 E. Victoria Street
Carson, CA 90747
(310) 516-3600
http://www.csudh.edu/

California State University, Long Beach
Staff Personnel Services
1250 Bellflower Blvd.
Long Beach, CA 90840
(310) 985-5471
http://www.csulb.edu/

California State University, Los Angeles
Human Resource Management
5151 State University Drive, ADM 605
Los Angeles, CA 90032
(213) 343-3901
http://www.calstatela.edu/

California State University, Northridge
18111 Nordhoff Street
Northridge, CA 91330
(818) 885-1200
http://www.hrs.csun.edu/

Claremont Colleges, The
(Claremont Graduate School, Claremont McKenna, Harvey Mudd, Pomona, Pitzer, and Scripps Colleges)
Personnel Office
150 E. 8th Street
Claremont, CA 91711
(909) 621-8048
Job hotline: (909) 607-7373
http://www.claremont.edu/

Mount St. Mary's College
Chalon Campus
12001 Chalon Road
Los Angeles, CA 90049
(310) 476-2237

Educational Institutions

Occidental College
1600 Campus Road
Los Angeles, CA 90041
(213) 259-2500
http://www.oxy.edu

Otis College of Art & Design
2401 Wilshire Blvd.
Los Angeles, CA 90057
(213) 251-0500

Pepperdine University
24255 Pacific Coast Highway
Malibu, CA 90263
(310) 456-4000
http://www.pepperdine.edu/

University of California, Los Angeles (UCLA)
Staff Employment
10920 Wilshire Blvd., Suite 205
Los Angeles, CA 90024
(310) 825-4321
Job hotline: (310) 794-0890
http://www.ucla.edu

University of Southern California (USC)
Personnel Services
3535 S. Figueroa Street, Room 100
Los Angeles, CA 90089
(213) 740-7252
http://cwis.usc.edu

Whittier College
13406 E. Philadelphia Street
Whittier, CA 90608
(310) 907-4200
http://www.whittier.edu

Orange County College Employers:

California State University, Fullerton
P.O. Box 34080 Building (T-14-P)
Fullerton, CA 92634
(714) 773-2425
Job hotline: (714) 773-3385
http://www.fullerton.edu/joblist/joblist.html

University of California, Irvine
501 Administration
Irvine, CA 92717
(714) 856-5011
http://www.uci.edu/depts/humrs

San Diego Area College Employers:

San Diego State University
5500 Campanile Drive
San Diego, CA 92182
http://www.sdsu.edu/

University of California, San Diego
Human Resources
9500 Gilman Drive
La Jolla, CA 92093
(619) 534-2812
http://www-hr.ucsd.edu/

University of San Diego
5998 Alcala Park
San Diego, CA 92110
(619) 260-4600
http://www.acusd.edu/

K-12 Employers:

Alemany High School
15241 Rinaldi Street
Mission Hills, CA 91345
(818) 361-9714

Anaheim City School District
890 S. Olive
Anaheim, CA 92805
(714) 535-6001

Brentwood School
100 S. Barrington Place
Los Angeles, CA 90049
(310) 476-9633

Buckley School, The
P.O. Box 5949
Sherman Oaks, CA 91423
(818) 783-1610

Campbell Hall
4533 Laurel Canyon Blvd.
North Hollywood, CA 91607
(818) 980-7280

Chadwick School
26800 S. Academy Drive
Palos Verdes, CA 90274

Chamindale College Preparatory
7500 Chamindale Avenue
West Hills, CA 91304
(818) 347-8300

Crossroads School for Arts & Sciences
1714 21st Street
Santa Monica, CA 90404
(310) 829-7391

Flintridge Preparatory School
4543 Crown Avenue
La Canada Flintridge, CA 91011
(818) 790-1178

Francis Parker School
6501 Linda Vista Road
San Diego, CA 92111
(619) 569-7900

Harvard-Westlake School
3700 Coldwater Canyon
North Hollywood, CA 91604
(310) 274-7281

Immaculate Heart High School
5515 Franklin Avenue
Los Angeles, CA 90028
(213) 461-3651

La Jolla Country Day School
9490 Genessee Avenue
La Jolla, CA 92037
(619) 453-3440

Le Lycee Francais de Los Angeles
3261 Overland Avenue
Los Angeles, CA 90034
(310) 836-5557

Long Beach Unified School District
701 Locust Avenue
Long Beach, CA 90813
(310) 436-9931

Los Angeles Baptist High School
9825 Woodley Avenue
North Hills, CA 91343
(818) 894-5742

Los Angeles Unified School District
District Headquarters
450 N. Grand Avenue, Building A
Los Angeles, CA 90012
(213) 625-6000

Loyola High School
1901 Venice Blvd.
Los Angeles, CA 90006
(213) 381-5121

Marlborough School
250 S. Rossmore Avenue
Los Angeles, CA 90004
(213) 935-1147

Marymount High School
10643 Sunset Blvd.
Los Angeles, CA 90077
(310) 472-1205

Montclair College Preparatory School
8071 Sepulveda Blvd.
Van Nuys, CA 91402
(818) 787-5290

Oakwood School
11600 Magnolia Blvd.
North Hollywood, CA 91601
(818) 752-4400

Orange County Department of Education
200 Kalmus Drive
Costa Mesa, CA 92828
(714) 966-4000

Polytechnic School
1030 E. California Blvd.
Pasadena, CA 91106
(818) 792-2147

San Diego Unified School District
4100 Normal Street
San Diego, CA 92103
(619) 293-8418

St. Augustine High School
3266 Nutmeg Street
San Diego, CA 92104
(619) 282-2184

St. Margaret's
31641 LaNovia Avenue
San Juan Capistrano, CA 92675
(714) 661-0108

University of San Diego High School
5961 Linda Vista Road
San Diego, CA 92110
(619) 298-8277

Web School of California
1175 W. Baseline Road
Claremont, CA 91711
(909) 626-3587

Westridge School
324 Madeline Drive
Pasadena, CA 91105
(818) 799-1153

Whittier Christian High School
P.O. Box 1307
Whittier, CA 90609
(310) 694-3803

Uncertified? Teach anyhow

Are you thinking about a teaching job but aren't certified within California? Certification is not required to teach in private schools within the state. Typically, schools look for candidates with a Bachelor's degree, an interest in teaching and the educational process, ability to coach and advise school activities, and experience working with students. Bilingual (English/Spanish) teachers and those within math and science fields are especially in demand.

Electronics/Telecommunications

WEB SITES:

http://arioch.gsfc.nasa.gov/wwwvl/ee.html
is the Web's virtual electrical engineering library.

http://www.wiltel.com/library/library.html
is a telecommunications library.

http://www.utsi.com/telecomm.html
links to telecom companies.

http://www.spp.umich.edu/telecom/online-pubs.html
links to telecom companies and on-line publications.

http://www.ee.uts.edu.au/~dinh/sites/telecoms/mobile.htm
links to telecommunications sites.

http://www.sddt.com/jobsource
lists high-tech job openings in San Diego.

PROFESSIONAL ORGANIZATIONS:

To network within the electronics and telecommunications industries, contact the following local professional organization listed in Chapter 5. Also see both sections on **"Computers."**

American Electronics Association, Southern California Chapter

For additional information, you can contact the following:

American Electronics Association
5201 Great America Parkway, Suite 520
Santa Clara, CA 95054
(408) 987-4200

Electronics Industry Association
2500 Wilson Blvd.
Arlington, VA 22201
(703) 907-7500

Institute of Electrical & Electronics Engineers (IEEE)
345 E. 47th Street
New York, NY 10017
(212) 705-7900

Multimedia Telecommunications Association
1820 Jefferson Place, NW
Washington, DC 20036
(202) 296-9800

North American Telecommunications Association
2000 M Street, NW
Washington, DC 20036
(202) 296-9800

Telecommunications Industry Association
2500 Wilson Blvd.
Arlington, VA 22201
(703) 907-7700

PROFESSIONAL PUBLICATIONS:

Cellular Business
Communications News
Electronic Business
Electronics News
Tele.com
Telecommunications Magazine
Wireless

DIRECTORIES:

American Electronics Association Directory (American Electronics Association, Santa Clara, CA)
Electronics Industry Association Trade Directory & Membership List (Electronics Industry Association, Washington, DC)
North American Telecommunications Association Telecom Source (North American Telecommunications Association, Washington, DC)

Electronics/Telecommunications

Los Angeles Area Employers:

Bell Industries
11812 San Vicente Blvd.
Los Angeles, CA 90049
(310) 826-2355
Director of Recruiting: Steve Orzeck

California Amplifier
460 Calle San Pablo
Camarillo, CA 93012
(815) 987-9000
http://www.caytv.com/calAmp
Human Resource Manager: Jackie Sheehan

Diodes Inc.
3050 E. Hillcrest Drive, Suite 200
Westlake Village, CA 91362
(805) 446-4800
http://www.diodes.com

GTE
1 GTE Place
Thousand Oaks, CA 91362
(805) 372-6000
Telecommunications.

Incomnet
21031 Ventura Blvd., #1100
Woodland Hills, CA 91364
(818) 887-3400

Los Angeles Cellular Telephone Company
17785 Center Court Drive North
Cerritos, CA 90703
(310) 924-000
Job hotline: (310) 403-8519
Telecommunications.

Marshall Industries
9320 Telstar Avenue
El Monte, CA 91731
(818) 307-6000

MCI Communications Corporation
700 S. Flower Street, Suite 1600
Los Angeles, CA 90017
(213) 239-2300

MICOM Communications Corp.
4100 Los Angeles Avenue
Simi Valley, CA 93063
(805) 583-8600
http://www.MICOM.com
Human Resource Supervisor: Ms. Jessie Williams

MVR Communications
8917 Fullbright Avenue
Chatsworth, CA 91311
(818) 773-9044
Personnel: Shelley Diaz

Ortel Corp.
2015 W. Chestnut Street
Alhambra, CA 91803
(818) 281-3636
Human Resources: Harvey Nafius

Osicom Technologies
2800 28th Street, Suite 100
Santa Monica, CA 90405
(310) 828-7496

Pico Products
12500 Foothill Blvd.
Lakeview Terrace, CA 91342
(818) 897-0028
Human Resource Manager: Molly Coutler

Special Devices
16830 W. Placentia Canyon Road
Newhall, CA 91321
(805) 259-0753
Human Resources: Sabra Bennett

Trio Tech International
355 Parkside Drive
San Fernando, CA 92626
(818) 365-9200
Personnel Director: Maria Chittim

US Sprint
1025 W. 190th Street, Suite 400
Gardena, CA 90248
(310) 515-5353
Hiring: Randy Grofik

Zero Corp.
444 S. Flower Street, Suite 2100
Los Angeles, CA 90071
(213) 629-7000
Human Resource Director: Javene Black

County Employers:

Cellular Telephone Company
Irvine, CA 92714
(714) 223-1500
Job hotline: (714) 222-8888
General Manager: Brian Jones

AT&T
8001 Irvine Center Drive
Irvine CA 92718
(714) 727-5550

Aurora Electronics
2030 Main Street, Suite 1120
Irvine, CA 92714
(714) 660-1232
Human Resource Director: Peggy Edgingston

Elexysys International
18522 Von Karman Avenue
Irvine, CA 92715
(714) 833-0870

Irvine Sensors Corp.
3001 Redhill Avenue, Building 3
Costa Mesa, CA 92626
(714) 549-8211
Human Resource Manager: Gail Lafferty

MicroSemi Corp.
2830 S. Fairview Street
Santa Ana, CA 92704
(714) 979-8220
Personnel Assistant: Maritza Casas

Pacific Scientific Co.
620 Newport Center Drive
Newport Beach, CA 92660
(714) 720-1714
Director of Human Resources: Tom Griffith

Pairgain Technologies
14402 Franklin Avenue
Tustin, CA 92680
(714) 832-9922
Resumes to Recruiting Department

Smartflex Systems
14312 Franklin Avenue
Tustin, CA 92780
(714) 838-8737

STM Wireless
1 Mauchly
Irvine, CA 92718
(714) 753-7864
Human Resources Manager: Valeria Rhodes

Vista-United Telecommunications
2400 E. Cerritos Avenue
Anaheim, CA 92806
(714) 938-3700

Closing the deal on sales

Jerry Packer put in a long and successful stint in sales at Xerox, then got an MBA and went to work as district manager for a comparatively risky, aggressive new electronics manufacturing company. We asked him about the differences between selling for a giant and taking a risk with a relatively unknown firm.

"Xerox is probably typical of any large corporation," says Jerry, "in that they are very structured. It was a good place to work, but it didn't provide much opportunity for individual decision making. A new company offers a fantastic chance to exercise some entrepreneurial skills. The corporation sets general goals, but it's up to me how I meet them. I can try out different marketing techniques, divide up the territory in new ways, create teams, whatever. It's neat to be able to exercise that kind of flexibility."

We asked Jerry what it takes to be a good salesperson. "A lot of folks think that salespeople are forever buying lunches for clients and playing golf," says Jerry. "But in order to be really successful, you have to work hard. I don't necessarily mean 80 hours a week. But you need to put in sufficient time to do the things that are necessary. A second important requirement is an absolutely thorough understanding of the products you're selling. Not only your own products but also your competitors'.

"In high-level selling, sales people have to be especially sharp in terms of interpersonal skills. There's an old saying, and it's true: people don't buy from companies, they buy from people. When you're selling systems that range upward of $5 million, you're also selling yourself. It's important that your clients feel you'll be around after the sale to handle any problems that might come up. To establish that kind of rapport, you have to act responsibly and be very articulate. It also helps if you have good written communication skills."

San Diego Area Employers:

Applied Digital Access
9855 Scranton Road
San Diego, CA 92121
(619) 623-2200
CEO: Peter Savage

Cohu, Inc.
5755 Kearney Villa Road
San Diego, CA 92123
(619) 277-6700
Resumes to Human Resources

ComStream Corp.
10180 Barnes Canyon Road
San Diego, CA 92121
(619) 458-1800
Job hotline: (619) 657-5085
http://www.comstream.com

Datron Systems
304 Enterprise Street
Escondido, CA 92029
(619) 747-1079
President: David Derby

DH Technology
15070 Avenue of Science
San Diego, CA 92128
(619) 451-3485
Resumes to Human Resources

GDE Systems
16550 W. Bernardo Drive
San Diego, CA 92127
(619) 675-2600
Job hotline: 1-800-545-0506
http://www.GDESystems.com

General Instruments Corp.
Communications Division
6262 Lusk Blvd.
San Diego, CA 92121
(619) 455-1500

GTI Corporation
9715 Business Park Avenue
San Diego, CA 92131
(619) 537-2500
Job hotline: ext. 424
Applications Engineer: William Malherbe

Hewlett-Packard Company
16399 W. Bernardo Drive
San Diego, CA 92127
(619) 655-4100

Osicom Technologies
9990 Mesa Rim Road
San Diego, CA 92121
(619) 597-9595
Human Resource Manager: Velinda White

Pacific Bell
525 B Street, Room 1780
San Diego, CA 92101
(619) 237-3707

Proxima Corporation
9440 Carroll Park Drive
San Diego, CA 92121
(619) 457-5500
Resumes to Human Resources

Qualcomm Incorporated
6455 Lusk Blvd.
San Diego, CA 92121
(619) 587-1121
Job hotline: (619) 658-JOBS
http://www.qualcomm.com
Human Resource Staffing
See the "Fastest Growing Companies in Southern California" section of Chapter 1 for additional information.

Sony Electronics
San Diego Manufacturing Center
16450 W. Bernardo Drive
San Diego, CA 92127
(619) 487-8500
Job hotline: (619) 673-2600

TV/COM International
16516 Via Esprillo
San Diego, CA 92127
(619) 451-1500
http://www.TV.com
President: Hank Hanselaar

Engineering

WEB SITES:

http://www.webcreations.com/bolton/ is a job-search page for engineers.

PROFESSIONAL ORGANIZATIONS:

To network within the field of engineering, contact the following local professional organizations listed in Chapter 5. Also see "Architecture" and "Construction."

American Society of Engineers and Architects
Asian-American Architects and Engineers
Engineers & Architects Association
Society of Women Engineers
Southern California Professional Engineering Association

For additional information, you can contact the following:

American Association of Engineering Societies
1111 19th Street, NW, Suite 608
Washington, DC 20036
(202) 296-2237

American Society of Engineers and Architects
511 Garfield Avenue
South Pasadena, CA 91030
(213) 682-1161

California Society of Professional Engineers
910 Florin Road
Sacramento, CA 95831
(916) 422-7788

National Society of Professional Engineers
1420 King Street
Alexandria, VA 22314
(703) 684-2800

Society of Women Engineers
120 Wall Street
New York, NY 10005
(212) 509-9577

United Engineering Center
345 E. 47th Street
New York, NY 10017
(212) 509-9577

PROFESSIONAL PUBLICATIONS:

California Engineer
Civil Engineering
Mechanical Engineering
Minority Engineer
US Women Engineers

DIRECTORIES:

Directory of Engineers in Private Practice (National Society of Professional Engineers, Alexandria, VA)
Directory of Minority and Women-Owned Engineering and Architectural Firms (American Consulting Engineers Council, Washington, DC.)
Professional Engineering Directory (National Society of Professional Engineers, Alexandria, VA)
Who's Who in Engineering (American Association of Engineering Societies, Washington, DC.)

Los Angeles Area Employers:

Aerospace Corporation
2350 E. El Segundo Blvd.
El Segundo, CA 90245
(310) 336-1614
http://www.aero.org
Staffing Resource Manager: Walter Caldwell

ASL Consulting Engineers
3280 E. Foothill Blvd., Suite 350
Pasadena, CA 91107
(818) 683-0066

Aura Systems
2335 Alaska Avenue
El Segundo, CA 90245
(310) 643-5300
Human Resource Director: Rachel Choppin

Brown & Caldwell
150 S. Arroyo Parkway
Pasadena, CA 91105
(818) 577-1020

Brown & Root
1000 S. Fremont Avenue
Alhambra, CA 91803
(818) 300-1000

Converse Consultants West
3393 E. Foothill Blvd.
Pasadena, CA 91107
(818) 440-0800

Dames & Moore
911 Wilshire Blvd., Suite 700
Los Angeles, CA 90017
(213) 683-1560

Engineering Technology
14148 Magnolia Blvd.
Sherman Oaks, CA 91423
(818) 905-2800

Englekirk, Robert, Consulting Structural Engineers
2116 Arlington Avenue
Los Angeles, CA 90018
(213) 733-6673

FSEC
100 Corson Street
Pasadena, CA 91103
(818) 568-2290

General Devices
11964 Aviation Blvd.
Inglewood, CA 90304
(310) 643-7621

Geodynamics Corporation
21171 S. Western Avenue
Torrance, CA 90501
(310) 781-3616

Hood Corporation
8201 S. Sorensen Avenue
Whittier, CA 90607
(213) 685-5640

International Technology Corporation
23456 Hawthorne Blvd., Suite 300
Torrance, CA 90505
(310) 378-9933

Lee & Ro Consulting Engineers
1199 Fullerton Road
City of Industry, CA 91748
(818) 912-3391

Montgomery Watson
300 N. Lake Avenue, Suite 1200
Pasadena, CA 91101
(818) 796-9141
Human Resource Manager: Garey Melillo

National Technical Systems
240007 Ventura Blvd.
Calabasas, CA 91302
(818) 591-0776
Human Resources; Linda Freeman

Parsons Corporation, The
100 W. Walnut Street
Pasadena, Ca 91124
(818) 440-2000

RAND
P.O. Box 2138
Santa Monica, CA 90407
(310) 393-0411

Skyska & Hennessy
11500 W. Olympic Blvd.
Los Angeles, CA 90064
(310) 312-0200

VTN West
8540 Balboa Blvd., Suite 200
Northridge, CA 91325
(181) 894-8261

Orange County Employers:

Austin Company, The
3 Imperial Promenade
Santa Ana, CA 92707
(714) 434-8900

Engineering 229

Bein, Robert/William Frost
14725 Alton Parkway
Irvine, CA 92718
(714) 472-3505
Personnel Manager: Chris Connolly

CH2M Hill
2510 Red Hill Avenue
Santa Ana, CA 92705
(714) 250-1900
Human Resources: Mindy Spiro

Fluor Daniel
3333 Michelson Drive
Irvine, CA 92730
(714) 975-2000
Job hotline: (714) 975-5253

HNTB Corp.
36 Executive Park, Suite 200
Irvine, CA 92714
(714) 752-6940
Executive Vice President: Ronald Hartje

Holmes & Narver
999 Town & Country Road
P.O. Box 624
Orange, CA 92613
(714) 567-2400
Human Resources: Pam Cooper

Hunsaker & Associates
3 Hughes
Irvine, CA 92718
(714) 583-1010
Employment: Renee Jara

Keith Companies
2955 Red Hill Avenue
Costa Mesa, CA 92626
(714) 540-0800
Personnel: Chris Bryant

Mclaren Hart
16755 Von Karman Avenue
Irvine, CA 92714
(714) 756-2667

MK Centennial
17300 Red Hill Avenue, Suite 150
Irvine, CA 92718

(714) 756-6006
Executive Vice President: Robert D. Stevens

Sverdrup Corp.
600 Anton Blvd., Suite 400
Costa Mesa, CA 92626
(714) 549-5050
Human Resource Assistant: Cindy Lovett

Tait & Associates
1100 Town & Country Road, Suite 1200
Orange, CA 92668
(714) 560-8200

San Diego Area Employers:

Avacon Corporation
1455 Frazee Road, Suite 400
San Diego, CA 92108
(619) 296-5727

Barrett Consulting Group
9675 Business Park Avenue
San Diego, CA 92131
(619) 536-5610

Boyle Engineering Corporation
7807 Convoy Court, Suite 200
San Diego, CA 92111
(619) 268-8080
General Manager: Don MacFarlane

BSI/Berryman & Henigar
11590 W. Bernardo Court, Suite 100
San Diego, CA 92127
(619) 451-6100
Human Resource Director: Dan Saletta

Burkett & Wong
3434 4th Avenue
San Diego, CA 92103
(619) 299-5550

CH&A Corporation
3467 Kurtz Street
San Diego, CA 92110
(619) 225-9641

Dames & Moore
9665 Chesapeake Drive, Suite 201
San Diego, CA 92123
(619) 541-0833

Dudek & Associates
605 3rd Street
Encinitas, CA 92024
(619) 942-5147
Controller: Lucy Myers

Geocon
6960 Flanders Drive
San Diego, CA 92121
(619) 558-6900

Hunsaker & Associates
10179 Huennekens Street
San Diego, CA 92121
(619) 558-4500

Kercheval Engineers
4740 Murphy Canyon Road, #310
San Diego, CA 92123
(619) 571-0520

Kleinfelder
9555 Chesapeake Drive, Suite 101
San Diego, CA 92123
(619) 541-1145

Law/Crandall
9177 Sky Park Court
San Diego, CA 92123
(619) 278-3600
Human Resources: Kittie Zeleniak

Leighton & Associates
3934 Murphy Canyon Road, Suite B205
San Diego, CA 92123
(619) 723-3049

Montgomery Watson
750 B Street, Suite 1610
San Diego, CA 92101
(619) 239-3888
Hiring: Bill Scarborough

Muller, J., International
9444 Balboa Avenue, Suite 200
San Diego, CA 92123
(619) 974-5005
Managing Partner: Antonio Dinis
Bridge design and technology.

Nasland Engineering
4740 Ruffner Street
San Diego, CA 92111
(619) 292-7770

Nolte & Associates
5469 Kearny Villa Road, Suite 305
San Diego, CA 92123
(619) 278-9392

P&D Consultants
401 W. A Street, Suite 2500
San Diego, CA 92101
(619) 232-4466
Human Resources: Grace Alexander

Parsons Brinckerhoff
1230 Columbia Street, Suite 640
San Diego, CA 92101
(619) 338-9376
Area Manager: Ann Koby

Parsons Engineering Science
9404 Genesee Avenue, Suite 140
La Jolla, CA 92037
(619) 453-9650
Managing Partner: Greg McBain

Project Design Consultants
701 B Street, Suite 800
San Diego, CA 92101
(619) 235-6471

Woodward-Clyde Consultants
1615 Murray Canyon Road, Suite 1000
San Diego, CA 92108
(619) 294-9400
Partner: Scott Moorhouse

Entertainment

WEB SITES:

http://www.mandy.com/index.html
Mandy's International Film & TV Production Directory.

http://wwww.auditions.com
has casting/audition notices for the Los Angeles area.

http://www.ern.com/ern.htm
has links to companies and individuals in the entertainment industry.

http://www.ose.com/ose/
links to the entertainment and music industries.

http://www.hollywoodreporter.com/
links to entertainment companies and acting resources in the Los Angeles area.

http://www.ircam.fr/divers/theatre-e.html
is a guide to theater resources.

http://www.showbizjobs.com
entertainment recruiting network.

PROFESSIONAL ORGANIZATIONS:

To network within the entertainment industry, contact the following Southern California professional organizations listed in Chapter 5:

Academy of Country Music
Academy of Motion Picture Arts and Sciences
Academy of Motion Picture and Television Producers
Academy of Television Arts and Sciences
Actors Fund of America
American Academy of Dramatic Arts/West
American Cinema Editors
American Federation of Musicians
American Film Institute
American Society of Cinematographers
American Society of Music Arrangers and Composers
Costume Designers Guild
Directors Guild of America
International Animated Film Society
International Stunt Association
Motion Picture Association of America
National Academy of Recording Arts
National Academy of Songwriters
National Association of Composers
Producers Guild of America
Screen Actors Guild
Society of Motion Picture and Television Art Directors
Women in Film

For more information you can contact:

Academy of Motion Picture Arts and Sciences
8949 Wilshire Blvd.
Beverly Hills, CA 90211
(310) 247-3000

American Film Institute
Kennedy Center for the Performing Arts
Washington, DC 20566
(202) 828-4000

Film Arts Foundation
346 9th Street, 2nd Floor
San Francisco, CA 94103
(415) 552-8760

Recording Industry Association of America
1020 19th Street, NW, Suite 200
Washington, DC 20036
(202) 775-0101

PROFESSIONAL PUBLICATIONS:

American Cinematographer
Animation Magazine
Backstage West
Billboard
Cable World

Daily Variety
Electronic Media
Film & Video
Hollywood Reporter
Radio & Records
Variety

DIRECTORIES:

Blue Book (Hollywood Reporter, Hollywood, CA)
Film Producers, Studios and Agents Guide (Lone Eagle Publishing, Los Angeles, CA)
Pacific Coast Studio Directory (Pacific Coast Studio Directory, Pine Mountain, CA)
Recording Industry Sourcebook (Ascona Communications, Los Angeles, CA)
U.S. Directory of Entertainment Employers (Monumental Communications, Van Nuys, CA)
Who's Who in the Motion Picture Industry (Packard House, Beverly Hills, CA)
Who's Who in Television (Packard House, Beverly Hills, CA)

Theaters:

AMC Theaters
2049 Century Park E, Suite 1020
Los Angeles, CA 90067
(310) 553-0515

Edward's Theaters
300 Newport Center Drive
Newport Beach, CA 92660
(714) 640-4603

Music Center of Los Angeles County
(Mark Taper Forum, Ahmanson Theatre, Los Angeles Opera)
135 N. Grand Avenue
Los Angeles, CA 90012
(213) 972-7211

Old Globe Theatre
P.O. Box 2171
San Diego, CA 92112
(619) 231-1941

Orange County Performing Arts Center
600 Town Center Drive
Costa Mesa, CA 92626
(714) 556-2121
Hiring: Peggy Armstrong

South Coast Repertory
P.O. Box 2197
Costa Mesa, CA 92628
(714) 957-2602

Breaking into film production

Tracey Barnett was working in public relations when she decided to break into film production. Although she didn't know anyone in the industry when she began, today she is a successful freelance production manager. We asked her how she did it.

"Most important was my desire to do it," says Tracey, "and I didn't get discouraged. I began by making a few contacts in the industry through people I knew in related fields. Then I set up interviews with these contacts. At the end of each interview, I asked for the names of three to five other contacts. This strategy opened a lot of doors for me. I followed up each interview with a phone call. I also kept in touch with my contacts on a monthly basis."

We asked Tracey what jobs are available for beginners in the film business and what qualifications are needed for those jobs.

"Entry-level positions include production assistant, stylist, assistant wardrobe manager, and grip," says Tracey. "There are no special requirements for these jobs. You don't need a degree in film to work in the business. In fact, people with film degrees begin at the same level as everybody else. What does count is intelligence and the ability to get things done quickly and efficiently. You need to think on your feet and be able to anticipate what needs to be done."

According to Tracey, freelance production assistants begin at about $75-$100 per day. More experienced production assistants can make as much as $175 per day. "But keep in mind that as a freelancer, you don't have the security of a regular paycheck," says Tracey. "You may not work every day." She advises those who need a more reliable income to look for a staff position in the industry.

Tracey advises those who want to break into the film business to keep at it: "Don't count your inexperience as a negative. Tenacity and enthusiasm will get you the first job. Approach your contacts and keep approaching them-over and over and over again."

Production & Distribution Companies:

ABC Productions
2020 Avenue of the Stars
Los Angeles, CA 90067
(310) 557-6860
Job hotline: (310) 557-4222

AIMS Media
9710 de Soto Avenue
Chatsworth, CA 91311
(818) 773-4300
Hiring: Adele Brant

Educational films.
All American Communications
808 Wilshire Blvd.
Santa Monica, CA 90405
(310) 656-1100
See Chapter 1 for additional information.

CBS Entertainment Productions
7800 Beverly Blvd.
Los Angeles, CA 90036
(213) 852-2345
Job hotline: (213) 852-2008

Cinema Products Corp.
3211 S. La Cienega Blvd.
Los Angeles, CA 90016
(310) 836-7991

Clark, Dick, Productions
3003 W. Olive Avenue
Burbank, CA 91510
(818) 841-3003
Human Resources: Andrea Hicks
Assistant to Vice President, Production: Gary Kay

Disney, The Walt, Company
500 S. Buena Vista Street

Burbank, CA 91521
(818) 560-1000
Job hotline: 818-558-2222
http://www.disney.com/
Home to Walt Disney and Touchstone Pictures, Buena Vista Productions, Television and Home Video. For more information, see "Southern California's Largest Employers" in Chapter 1.

Dreamworks SKG
100 Universal Plaza
Bungalow 477
Universal City, CA 91608
(818) 733-7000

E! Entertainment Television
5670 Wilshire Blvd.
Los Angeles, CA 90036
(213) 954-2400
Job hotline: (213) 954-2666

Four Media Company
2813 W. Alameda Avenue
Burbank, CA 91505
(818) 840-7000
Post-production company.

Goldwyn, Samuel, Company
10203 Santa Monica Blvd.
Los Angeles, CA 90067
(310) 552-2255
Job hotline: 310-284-9229

Hanna-Barbera Productions
3400 W. Cahuenga Blvd. West
Los Angeles, CA 90068
(213) 851-5000

Henson, Jim, Productions
5358 Melrose Avenue, Suite 300 West
Hollywood, CA 90038
(213) 960-4096
Human Resource Manager: DeeDee Degelia

Kushner-Locke Company
11601 Wilshire Blvd., 21st Floor
Los Angeles, CA 90025
(310) 445-1111
Office Manager: Sherry Mills

Metro Goldwyn Mayer
2500 Broadway Street
Santa Monica, CA 90404
(310) 449-3000
Job hotline: (310) 449-3569
Resumes to Human Resource Departme

NBC Studios
330 Bob Hope Drive
Burbank, CA 91523
(818) 840-7500
Job hotline: (818) 840-4397

Netter Digital Entertainment
5200 Lankersheim Blvd., Suite 280
North Hollywood, CA 91610
(818) 753-1990
Digital film production.

NTN Communications,
The Campus, 5966 La Place Court
Carlsbad, CA 92008
(619) 438-7400
Human Resource Manager: Genice Eichert
Interactive media.

Orion Pictures Corporation
1888 Century Park E
Los Angeles, CA 90067
(310) 282-0550
Job hotline: (310) 282-2811

Paramount Pictures
5555 Melrose Avenue
Los Angeles, CA 90038
(213) 956-5000
Includes Paramount Pictures, Viacom Entertainment Groups.

PSI
18019 Sky Park Circle #A
Irvine, CA 92614
(714) 261-6119

Rank Video Services
12691 Pala Drive
Garden Grove, CA 92841
(714) 891-7306

Sony Pictures Entertainment
10202 Washington Blvd.

Culver City, CA 90232
(310) 280-8000
Job hotline: (310) 280-4436
Includes Columbia and Tri Star Pictures.

Spelling Entertainment Group
5700 Wilshire Blvd.
Los Angeles, CA 90036
(213) 965-5700
Job hotline: (213) 634-3700

Turner Home Entertainment
1888 Century Park East, Suite 1200
Los Angeles, CA 90067
(310) 551-6300

Twentieth Century Fox
10201 W. Pico Blvd.
Los Angeles, CA 90035
(310) 277-2211
Job hotline: (310) 369-2804

Universal City Studios
100 Universal City Plaza
Universal City, CA 91608
(818) 777-1000
Job hotline: (818) 777-5627

MCA, Inc. and Universal Pictures.
Warner Brothers
4000 Warner Blvd.
Burbank, CA 91522
(818) 954-6000
Job hotline: (818) 954-5400

Television Syndication:

Carsey-Warner Distribution
4024 Radford Avenue
Los Angeles, CA 91604
(818) 760-5598

King World Productions
12400 Wilshire Blvd., Suite 1200
Los Angeles, CA 90025
(310) 826-1108

Casting Companies:

Central Casting
1700 W. Burbank Blvd.
Burbank, CA 91506
(818) 562-2700
Extra casting.

Creative Image Management
721 N. La Brea Avenue, Suite 106
Los Angeles, CA 90038
(213) 935-7655

Twentieth Century Fox Casting
10201 W. Pico Blvd.
Los Angeles, CA 90035
(310) 3 69-1824

Talent Agents:

Artists Agency
10000 Santa Monica Blvd., Suite 305
Los Angeles, CA 90067
(310) 277-7779

Creative Artists Agency
9830 Wilshire Blvd.
Beverly Hills, CA 90212
(310) 288-4545

International Creative Management
8942 Wilshire Blvd.
Los Angeles, CA 90211
(310) 550-4000

Morris, William, Agency
151 El Camino Drive
Beverly Hills, CA 90212
(310) 274-7451

Recording Companies:

Atlantic Records
9229 Sunset Blvd., 9th Floor
Los Angeles, CA 90069
(310) 205-7450
Job hotline: (310) 205-7450, ext. 8
Resumes to Human Resources

Capitol Records
1750 N. Vine Street
Hollywood, CA 90028
(213) 462-6252
Job hotline: (213) 871-5763
Resumes to Human Resources

Elecktra Records
345 N. Maple Drive, Suite 123
Beverly Hills, CA 90210
(310) 288-3800

Geffen Records
9130 Sunset Blvd.
Los Angeles, CA 90069
(310) 278-9010
Job hotline: (310) 278-9010, ext. 2
Resumes to Human Resources.

Harmony Holdings
6806 Lexington Avenue
Hollywood, CA 90038
(213) 960-1400
Human Resources: Carol Swan

Hollywood Records
500 S. Buena Vista Street
Burbank, CA 90028
(818) 560-5670
Hiring: Debbie Taylor

MCA Records
70 Universal Plaza
Universal City, CA 91608
(818) 777-4000
Job hotline: (818) 777-5627

Rhino Records
10635 Santa Monica Blvd., Suite 200
Los Angeles, CA 90025
(310) 474-4778

Virgin Records
338 N. Foothill Drive
Beverly Hills, CA 90210
(310) 278-1181
Vice President, Administration: Kelly Darr

Warner Brothers Records
3300 Warner Blvd.
Burbank, CA 91510
(818) 846-9090
Resumes to Human Resources

Animation/Special Effects Companies:

Amblin Imaging
100 Universal City Plaza, #447
Universal City, CA 91608
(818) 777-4600

Disney Feature Animation
500 S. Buena Vista Street
Burbank, CA 91521
(818) 560-8000

Sony Pictures Imageworks
Tristar Building, #206
Culver City, CA 90232
(310) 280-7600
Job hotline: (310) 280-4436

Special Effects Unlimited
1005 Lillian Way
Los Angeles, CA 90038
(213) 466-3361

Warner Brothers Animation
15303 Ventura Blvd., Suite 800
Sherman Oaks, CA 91403
(818) 379-9401
Job hotline: (818) 954-5400

Entertaining idea

Are you looking for a way to network within the entertainment industry? The Academy of Television Arts & Sciences offers student memberships. As a student affiliate, you receive invitations for free screenings, retrospectives, seminars, and other events where you can meet industry professionals. Full-time students studying film, television, journalism, or communications are eligible; you can extend your student membership one year after graduation. For more information, contact the Television Academy at (818) 754-2880, ext. 6.

Environmental Services

WEB SITES:

http://www.webdirectory.com/
environmental organization Web directory.

http://envirolink.org/envirowebs.html
links to publications, organizations, government, and industry sites.

http://www.econet.apc.org/econet/
links to industry news and organizations.

PROFESSIONAL ORGANIZATIONS:

For additional information, you can contact the following:

Air & Waste Management Association
2500 Wilson Blvd.
Arlington, VA 22201
(703) 907-7500

Center for Marine Conservation
1725 DeSales Street, NW
Washington, DC 20036
(202) 429-5609

Defenders of Wildlife
1101 14th Street, NW, Suite 1400
Washington, DC 20005
(202) 789-2844

Environmental Business Association
1150 Connecticut Avenue, NW
Washington, DC 20036
(201) 862-4363

Environmental Careers Organization
Southwest Office
381 Bush Street, Suite 700
San Francisco, CA 94101
(415) 362-5552

National Association of Environmental Professionals
5165 MacArthur Blvd., NW
Washington, DC 20016
(202) 966-1500

Solid Waste Association of North America
P.O. Box 7219
Silver Spring, MD 20907
(301) 585-2898

Water Environment Foundation
601 Wythe Street
Alexandria, VA 22314
(703) 684-2400

PROFESSIONAL PUBLICATIONS:

E, The Environmental Magazine
Earthwatch
Environmental Times
Recycling Today
Pollution Engineering
Solid Waste News
Water and Wastes Digest

DIRECTORIES:

California Environmental Directory
   (California Institute of Public Affairs, Sacramento, CA)
Conservation Directory (National Wildlife Federation, Washington, DC)
Directory of National Environmental Organizations (US Environmental Directories, St. Paul, MN)
Environmental Information Directory (Gale Research, Detroit, MI)
Environmental Services Directory (Environmental Information, Minneapolis, MN)
Solid Waste & Power's Industry Directory (HCI Publications, Kansas City, MO)

Los Angeles Area Employers:

AEC Environmental
201 S. Figueroa, Suite 230
Los Angeles, CA 90012
(213) 312-9023
President: Diana Lickar

AeroVironment
222 E. Huntington Drive

Monrovia, CA 91016
(818) 357-9983
Technical Recruiter: Ron Farnham

Baker Pacific Corp.
3220 E. 29th Street
Long Beach, CA 90806
(310) 426-0755
Resumes to Human Resources

Brown and Caldwell
150 S. Arroyo Parkway
Pasadena, CA 91109
(818) 577-1020
Regional Vice President: Pervaiz Anwar

Dames and Moore
911 Wilshire Blvd., Suite 700
Los Angeles, CA 90017
(213) 683-1560
Resumes to Human Resources

Impco Technologies/AirSensors
16804 Gridley Place
Cerritos, CA 90701
(310) 860-6666
Human Resources; Lisa Kitching

International Technology Corp.
23456 Hawthorne Blvd.
Torrance, CA 90505
(310) 378-9933
CEO: Robert Sheh

Jacobs Engineering Group
251 S. Lake Avenue
Pasadena, CA 91101
(818) 449-2171
CEO: Noel Watson

Kinetics Technology International
650 Cienega Avenue
San Dimas, CA 91772
(909) 592-4455
Personnel Director: Kathy Barrett

LVI Environmental Services
13025 Meyer Road
Whittier, CA 90605
(310) 944-8971
Resumes to Human Resources

Marcor of California
12940 Sunnyside Place
Santa Fe Springs, CA 90670
(310) 906-2628
Vice President: Mathew Westrup

Montgomery Watson
300 N. Lake Avenue
Pasadena, CA 91109
(818) 796-9141
Human Resource Manager: Gary Mellillo

Parsons Corporation
100 W. Walnut Street
Pasadena, CA 91124
(818) 440-6000
Human Resources: Phil Williams

Stephens, P.W., Contractors
727 S. 9th Avenue
City of Industry, CA 91745
(818) 330-7221
Resumes to Personnel

TEG-The Environmental Group
4710 S. Eastern Avenue
Commerce, CA 90040
(213) 726-9696

Orange County Employers:

Dames & Moore
6 Hutton Center Drive, Suite 700
Santa Ana, CA 92707
(714) 433-2000
Regional Manager: Bill Webb
Energy and Environmental Research

18 Mason
Irvine, CA 92718
(714) 859-8851

Environmental Science & Engineering
17390 Brookhurst Street, Suite 110
Fountain Valley, CA 92708
(714) 964-8722

IT Corp.
2355 Main Street, Suite 100
Irvine, CA 92714
(714)) 261-6441
Job hotline: (714) 660-5434

Environmental Services

Leighton and Associates
17781 Cowan
Irvine, CA 92714-6009
(714) 250-1421
Human Resources

P&D Environmental Services
1100 Town and Country Road, Suite 300
Orange, CA 92668
(714) 835-4447
Human Resources

Radian Corporation
16845 Von Karman Avenue
Irvine, CA 92714
(714) 261-8611
Vice President: Jim Dickerman

Woodward-Clyde Consultants
2020 E. 1st Street, Suite 400
Santa Ana, CA 92705
(714) 835-6886
Vice President: Steve Pearson

San Diego Area Employers:

Brown & Caldwell
9040 Friars Road, Suite 220
San Diego, CA 92108
(619) 528-9090

Dudek & Associates
605 3rd Street
Encinitas, CA 92024
(619) 942-5147
Controller: Lucy Myers

Greenfield Environmental
750 Design Court, Suite 105
Chula Vista, CA 91911
(619) 421-1175

Hargis & Associates
2223 Avenida de la Playa, Suite 300
La Jolla, CA 92037
(619) 454-0165
Human Resource Coordinator: Jennifer Hurlbert

Kleinfelder Inc.
9555 Chesapeake Drive, Suite 101
San Diego, CA 92123
(619) 541-1145
Administrative Manager: Michele Casey

Law/Crandall, Inc.
9177 Sky Park Court
San Diego, CA 92123
(619) 278-3600
Human Resources: Kittie Zeleniak

Maxwell Laboratories, S-Cubed Division
8888 Balboa Avenue
San Diego, CA 92123
(619) 279-5100
Resumes to Human Resources

MEC Analytical Systems
2433 Impala Drive
Carlsbad, CA 92008
(619) 931-8081
Human Relations: Michelle Hinojosa

Metcalf & Eddy
701 B Street, Suite 1100
San Diego, CA 92101
(619) 233-7855

Ogden Environmental and Energy Services Company
5510 Morehouse Drive
San Diego, CA 92121
(619) 458-9044
Human Resources: Mary Bibbi

P&D Consultants
401 W. A Street, Suite 2500
San Diego, CA 92101
(619) 232-4466
Vice President: Chuck Moore

Woodward-Clyde Consultants
1615 Murray Canyon Road, Suite 1000
San Diego, CA 92108
(619) 294-9400

Food/Beverage Producers and Distributors

WEB SITES:

http://www.pvo.com/~pvo-plus/ provides a directory of food and beverage businesses, industry professionals, events, and an interactive bulletin board.

PROFESSIONAL ORGANIZATIONS:

To network within the food/beverage industry, contact the following local professional organizations listed in Chapter 5. Also see "Hospitality" and, for grocery chains, "Retailers."

Associated Produce Dealers and Brokers of Los Angeles
Milk Producers Council
Southern California Grocers Association

For additional information, you can contact the following:

Food Marketing Institute
800 Connecticut Avenue, NW, Suite 400
Washington, DC 20006
(202) 452-8444

Grocer Manufacturers of America
1010 Wisconsin Avenue, NW, Suite 800
Washington, DC 20007
(202) 337-9200

National Frozen Food Association
4755 Linglestown Road, Suite 300
Harrisburg, PA 17112
(717) 657-8601

National Soft Drink Association
1101 16th Street, NW
Washington, DC 20036
(202) 463-6732

Southern CA Grocers Association
100 W. Broadway
Long Beach, CA 90802
(310) 432-8610

PROFESSIONAL PUBLICATIONS:

Beverage World
Fancy Food
Food Industry News
Food Management
Food Technology
Health Foods Business
Journal of Food Products Marketing
Supermarket News
Wines and Vines
The Wine Spectator

DIRECTORIES:

American Frozen Food Industry Directory (American Frozen Food Institute, McLean, VA)
Bakery Red Book (Gorman Publishing, Chicago, IL)
Food Marketing Institute Membership Directory (Food Marketing Institute, Washington, DC)
Hereld's 5000: The Directory of Leading US Food, Confectionery and Beverage Manufacturers (SIC Publishing Co., Hamden, CT)
National Food Brokers Association Directory of Members (National Food Brokers Association, Washington, DC)
Prepared Foods Industry Sourcebook (Gorman Publishing, Chicago, IL)
Wines & Vines-Directory of the Wine Industry in North America (Hiaring Co., San Rafael, CA)

Los Angeles Area Employers:

Altadena Dairy
17637 E. Valley Blvd.
City of Industry, CA 91744
(818) 964-6401
Job hotline: through main switchboard

California Milk Producers
11709 E. Artesia Blvd.
Artesia, CA 90701
(310) 865-1291

Food/Beverage Producers and Distributors

Certified Grocers of California Ltd.
2601 S. Eastern Avenue
Los Angeles, CA 90040
(213) 723-7476
Job hotline: through main switchboard

Coca-Cola Bottling Co. of Los Angeles
1334 S. Central Avenue
Los Angeles, CA 90021
(213) 746-5555
Job hotline: through main switchboard

Dole Food Company
5795 Lindero Canyon Road
Westlake Village, CA 91361
(818) 879-6600
Job hotline: (818) 874-4999
http://www.dole5aday.com/dole.html
One of Southern California's largest employers. See Chapter 1 for more information.

Fishking Processors
P.O. Box 21385
Los Angeles, CA 90021
(213) 746-1307

Good Stuff Food Co.
1771 W. Blake Avenue
Los Angeles, CA 90031
(213) 913-7200
Human Resources: Carol Begley

La Reina, Inc.
316 N. Ford Blvd.
Los Angeles, CA 90022
(213) 268-2791
New Hiring: Luz Salazar

Mission Foods Corp.
5750 Grace Place
Los Angeles, CA 90022
(213) 722-8790

Nakano Foods
10037 8th Street
Rancho Cucamonga, CA 91730
(909) 989-4211

Pepsi-Cola West
19700 S. Figueroa Street
Carson, CA 90745
(310) 327-4222
Job hotline: (310) 527-3333

Presto Foods Products
18275 Arenth Avenue
City of Industry, CA 91748
(818) 810-1775
Job Hotline: ext. 5912

Randall Foods
4901 S. Boyle Avenue
Vernon, CA 90058
(213) 587-2383

Rykoff-Sexton
761 Terminal Street
Los Angeles, CA 90021
(213) 622-4131

Vestro Natural Foods
1065 E. Walnut Street
Carson, CA 90174
(310) 886-8200

Vitex Foods
1821 E. 48th Place
Los Angeles, CA 90058
(213) 234-4400

Westco Products
7351 Cirder Avenue
Pico Rivera, CA 90660
(310) 949-1054

Orange County Employers:

Adohr Farms
4002 Westminster Avenue
Santa Ana, CA 92703
(714) 775-5000
Human Resources: Debbie Procincio

Bridgford Food Corp.
1308 N. Patt Street
Anaheim, CA 92801
(714) 526-5533

Golden State Foods Corp.
18301 Von Karman Avenue, Suite 1100
Irvine, CA 92715
(714) 252-2000

Hansen Natural Corp.
2401 E. Katella Avenue, Suite 650
Anaheim, CA 92806
(714) 634-4200

President Global Corp.
6965 Aragon Circle
Buena Park, CA 90620
(714) 994-2990

Seven-Up/ Royal Crown Bottling Co.
7225 Orangethorpe Avenue
Buena Park, CA 90621
(714) 522-2877
Job hotline: (213)267-6405

Shasco, Inc.
14405 Artesia Blvd.
La Mirada, CA 90638
(714) 523-2280

Young's Market Company
2164 N. Batavia Street
Orange, CA 92665
(714) 283-4933
Employee Relations: Sherry Merrifield

San Diego Area Employers:

Coast Citrus Distributors
7597 Bristow Court
San Diego, CA 92173
(619) 661-7950
Human Resources: Jorge Gutierrez

Cohn Wholesale Fruit & Grain
P.O. Box 900169
San Diego, CA 92190
(619) 528-1113
Resumes to Aaron Cohn

Coca-Cola Bottling of San Diego
1348 47th Street
San Diego, CA 92102
(619) 266-3300
Job hotline: through switchboard

Lenore, John, and Co.
1250 Delevan Drive
San Diego, CA 92102
(619) 232-6136
Administrative Supervisor: Roger Carey

Liquid Investments
9970 Liquid Court
San Diego, CA 92121
(619) 452-2300
Job hotline: through switchboard

Seven-Up/ Royal Crown Bottling Co.
5770 Morehouse Drive
San Diego, CA 92121
(619)457-3177

Mouth-watering opportunities in food service management

Kate Williams, manager of the dietary department of a suburban hospital, sees the food service industry as a growing field with tremendous potential. Hospitals offer varied opportunities in food services. Some of the jobs, such as clinical or administrative dietitian, require a college degree in nutrition. But many do not.

"Some employees have experience working at a fast-food restaurant," says Kate. "Others just learn on the job. Still others have completed one- or two-year programs in food service offered by various colleges."

Besides registered dietitians, Kate's staff includes food service supervisors, who manage the personnel who prepare food; diet technicians, who prepare and implement menus based on information about the patient; diet aides, who perform such tasks as delivering meals to patients; a chef and cooking staff; and a food purchasing agent.

Kate is optimistic about employment prospects in the food service industry as a whole. "There are tremendous opportunities for those with culinary arts skills, as well as for hotel or restaurant food service managers. Opportunities exist in food equipment companies, public and private schools, contract food companies, and food service consulting firms. Right now the possibilities in food marketing are phenomenal.

"The nutritional needs of the growing elderly population," Kate adds, "will also create many new jobs in the food service business as hospitals and other organizations become involved in long-term care."

Foundations/Philanthropies

WEB SITES:

http://www.philanthropy-journal.org/ provides links to philanthropies, non-profits, foundations, charities, and organizations.

http://www.mtn.org/nonprofit.html lists non-profit sites, funders on the Internet.

http://fdncenter.org provides information on how to research foundations.

PROFESSIONAL ORGANIZATIONS:

To network within the field of foundations/philanthropy, contact the following local professional organizations listed in Chapter 5:

American Philanthropy Association
Southern California Association of Philanthropy

For additional information, you can contact:

Council on Foundations
1828 L Street, NW, Suite 300
Washington, DC 20036
(202) 466-6512

The Foundation Center
79 5th Avenue
New York, NY 10003
(212) 620-4230

PROFESSIONAL PUBLICATIONS:

Chronicle of Philanthropy
Foundation Giving Watch
Foundation News
Philanthropy Journal

DIRECTORIES:

Annual Register of Grant Support: A Directory of Funding Sources (National Register Publishing Company, Willamette, IL)

Corporate Giving Yellow Pages (Taft Group, Rockville, MD)
The Foundation Directory (The Foundation Center, New York, NY)
International Foundation Directory (Gale Research, Detroit, MI)

Employers:

Ahmanson Foundation
9215 Wilshire Blvd.
Beverly Hills, CA 90210
(310) 278-0770
Vice President & Managing Director: Lee E. Walcott

Autry Foundation
4383 Colfax Avenue
Studio City, CA 91604
(818) 752-7770
Secretary: Karla Buhlman

Beckman, Arnold & Mabel, Foundation
Grants Advisory Council
100 Academy Drive
Irvine, CA 92715
(714) 721-2222
Administrator: Ron Henderson

Bettingen, Burton G., Corporation
9777 Wilshire Blvd., Suite 615
Beverly Hills, CA 90212
(310) 276-4115
Executive Director: Patricia A. Brown

Burns, Fritz B., Foundation
4001 W. Alameda Avenue, Suite 201
Burbank, CA 91505
(818) 840-8802
President: Joseph E. Rawlinson

California Community Foundation
606 S. Olive Street, Suite 2400
Los Angeles, CA 90014
(213) 413-4042

California Wellness Foundation
6320 Canoga Avenue, Suite 1700
Woodland Hills, CA 91367
(818) 593-6600
Program Assistant: Joan Hurley

Doheny, Carrie Estelle, Foundation
911 Wilshire Blvd., Suite 1750
Los Angeles, CA 90017
(213) 488-1122
President: Robert A. Smith III

Foundations of the Milken Families
1250 4th Street, 6th Floor
Santa Monica, CA 90401
(310) 998-2800
Executive Director: Dr. Julius Lesner

Geffen, David, Foundation
9130 Sunset Blvd.
Los Angeles, CA 90067
(310) 285-7969
President: Andy Spahn

Goldwyn, Samuel, Foundation
10203 Santa Monica Blvd., Suite 500
Los Angeles, CA 90067
(213) 552-2255

Jones, Fletcher, Foundation
624 S. Grand Avenue
1 Wilshire Building, Suite 1210
Los Angeles, CA 90017
(213) 689-9292
Executive Director: John W. Smythe

Keck, W. M., Foundation
555 S. Flower Street, Suite 3230
Los Angeles, CA 90071
(213) 680-3833

Kest, Sol and Clara, Family Fund
5150 Overland Avenue
Culver City, CA 90230
(213) 204-2050

Leavey, Thomas and Dorothy, Foundation
4680 Wilshire Blvd.
Los Angeles, CA 90010
(213) 930-4252
Chair: J. Thomas McCarthy

Murphy, Dan, Foundation
P.O. Box 711267
Los Angeles, CA 90071
(213) 623-3120
President: Daniel J. Donohue

**Norris, Kenneth T. & Eileen L.,
Foundation**
11 Golden Shore, Suite 450
Long Beach, CA 90802
(310) 435-8444
Executive Director: Ronald R. Barnes

Parsons, Ralph M., Foundation
1055 Wilshire Blvd., Suite 1701
Los Angeles, CA 90017
(213) 482-3185
Executive Director: Christine Sisley

Powell, Charles Lee, Foundation
7742 Herschel Avenue, Suite A
La Jolla, CA 92037
(619) 459-3699
Executive Director: Herbert Kunzel

San Diego Community Foundation
Wells Fargo Bank Building
101 W. Broadway, Suite 1120
San Diego, CA 92101
(619) 239-8815
CEO: Robert A. Kelly

Steele, Harry and Grace, Foundation
441 Old Newport Blvd., Suite 301
Newport Beach, CA 92663
(714) 631-9158
Assistant Secretary: Marie F. Kowert

Stein, Jules and Doris, Foundation
P.O. Box 30
Beverly Hills, CA 90213
(310) 276-2101
Program Officer: Linda L. Valliant

Times Mirror Fund
Times Mirror Square
Los Angeles, CA 90053
(213) 237-3945
Treasurer: Cassandra Malry

Weingart Foundation
1055 W. 7th Street, Suite 3050
Los Angeles, CA 90017
(213) 688-7799
President: John G. Ovellet

Government

WEB SITES:

http://www.jobweb.org/fedjobsr.htm
lets you search federal jobs by state.

http://www.law.vill.edu/Fed-Agency/fedwebloc.html
lists over 200 federal government Web servers.

http://www.jobtrak/com/jobguide/gov.html
lists government job openings.

http://www.fedworld.gov/jobs/jobsearch.html
U.S. government bulletin board searchable by state.

ftp://ftp.fedworld.gov/pub/jobs/ca.txt
federal government jobs in California.

PROFESSIONAL ORGANIZATIONS:

To network within the field of government, contact the following local professional organizations listed in Chapter 5:

American Federation of State, County, and Municipal Employees
California Organizations of Police and Sheriffs

For additional information, you can contact:

American Federation of Government Employees
80 F Street, NW
Washington, DC 20001
(202) 737-8700

American Society for Public Administration
1120 G Street, NW, Suite 700
Washington, DC 20005
(202) 393-7878

Federal Job Information Center
9650 Flair Drive, Suite 100A
El Monte, CA 91731
(818) 575-6510

International City Management Association
777 N. Capitol Street, NE, Suite 500
Washington, DC 20002
(202) 289-4262

PROFESSIONAL PUBLICATIONS:

California Journal
City and State
Federal Times
Public Employee
Public Management

DIRECTORIES:

California Handbook (California Institut of Public Affairs, Sacramento, CA)
Braddock's Federal-State-Local Governme Directory (Braddock Communications Inc., Alexandria, VA)
California Roster (Office of the Secretary of State, Sacramento, CA)
Federal Yellow Book (Leadership Directories, Inc., New York, NY)
Government Affairs Yellow Book (Leadership Directories, Inc., New York, NY)
National Directory of State Agencies (Carroll Publishing Company, Washing ton, DC)
State Yellow Book (Monitor Publishing Company, Washington, DC)
U.S. Government Offices in California (California Institute of Public Affairs, Claremont, CA)
Who's Who in Local Government Management (International City Management Association , Washington, DC)

State/Local Government Employers:

California Film Commission
6922 Hollywood Blvd., #600
Hollywood, CA 90028
(213) 736-2465

Government 247

California Highway Patrol
4016 Rosewood Avenue
Los Angeles, CA 90004
(213) 736-4400

California Trade & Commerce Agency
200 E. Del Mar Avenue, #302
Pasadena, CA 91105
(818) 683-2619

City of Los Angeles Employment Opportunities
700 E. Temple Street, Room 100
Los Angeles, CA
(213) 847-9424
Job hotline: (213) 847-9424
http://www.ci.la.ca.us/dept/PER/index.htm

City of San Diego
Employment Information Office
202 C St.
San Diego, CA 92101
(619) 236-6467

County of San Diego
Department of Human Resources
1600 Pacific Hwy., Room 207
San Diego, CA 92101
(619) 531-5764

Department of Consumer Affairs
107 S. Broadway
Los Angeles, CA 90012
(800) 344-9940

Department of Parks & Recreation
433 S. Vermont Avenue
Los Angeles, CA 90012
(213) 738-2991

Department of Rehabilitation
Central Los Angeles District
3251 W. 6th Street
Los Angeles, CA 90020
(213) 736-3904

Orange County Transportation Authority
550 S. Main Street
Orange, CA 92613
(714) 560-6282

State Employment Office
P.O. Box 944210
Sacramento, CA 94244
Job Information Line: (619) 237-6163

Federal Government Employers:

All federal civil service job openings are listed with the government's Office of Personnel Management (OPM). The office serving all of California is in San Francisco:

Office of Personnel Management
120 Howard St., Room 735
San Francisco, CA 94105
(415) 744-5627

We have listed below a few of the major U.S. agencies in Southern California, where you might make informational inquiries.

Department of Housing and Urban Development
1615 W. Olympic Blvd.
Los Angeles, CA 90015
(213) 251-7001

Department of Labor
300 N. Los Angeles Street, Room 8126
Los Angeles, CA 90053
(213) 894-4980

Federal Bureau of Investigation
11000 Wilshire Blvd.
Los Angeles, CA 90024
(310) 477-6565

Federal Trade Commission
11000 Wilshire Blvd., # 13209
Los Angeles, CA 90056
(310) 235-4000
http://www.ftc.gov

Food and Drug Administration
1521 W. Pico Blvd.
Los Angeles, CA 90015
(310) 831-6123

Small Business Administration
880 Front Street, Suite 4237
San Diego, CA 92101
(619) 557-5440

U.S. Department of Agriculture, Office of Food and Nutrition
417 S. Hill Street
Los Angeles, CA 90013
(213) 894-3178

U.S. Forest Service
Angeles National Forest
701 N. Santa Anita Avenue
Arcadia, CA 91006
(818) 574-1613

U.S. Immigration and Naturalization Service
Federal Building
880 Front Street
San Diego, CA 92188
(619) 557-5570

U.S. Maritime Administration
11th District
400 Oceangate, Suite 606
Long Beach, CA 90822
(310) 514-6370

U.S. Peace Corps
11000 Wilshire Blvd., Suite 8104
West Los Angeles, CA 90024
(310) 235-7444
(800) 424-8580, ext. 1

Veterans Administration
11000 Wilshire Blvd.
Los Angeles, CA 90024
(310) 478-3711

Health Care

WEB SITES:

http://debra.dgbt.doc.ca/~mike/healthnet/key.html
links to health care resources.

http://medsearch.com/
medical jobs searchable by state.

PROFESSIONAL ORGANIZATIONS:

To network within the field of health care, contact the following local professional organizations listed in Chapter 5:

American Academy of Sports Physicians
American Association of Critical Care Nurses
American Orthopedic Association
American Sports Medicine Association
California Nurses Association
California Physical Therapists Association
Hospital Council of Southern California
Los Angeles County Medical Association
National Health Federation

For additional information, you can contact:

American Academy of Physician Assistants
950 N. Washington Street
Alexandria, VA 22314
(703) 836-2272

American Dental Association
211 E. Chicago Avenue
Chicago, IL 60611
312-440-2500

American Health Care Association
1201 L Street, NW
Washington, DC 20005
(202) 842-4444

American Hospital Association
1 N. Franklin
Chicago, IL 60606
(312) 422-3000

American Medical Association
515 N. State Street
Chicago, IL 60610
(312) 644-5000

Health Care

American Physical Therapy Association
111 N. Fairfax Street
Alexandria, VA 22314
(703) 684-2782

American Public Health Association
1015 15th Street, NW, Suite 300
Washington, DC 20005
(202) 789-5600

PROFESSIONAL PUBLICATIONS:

American Dental Association News
American Journal of Nursing
American Journal of Public Health
American Hospital Association Guide
HMO Magazine
Journal of the American Medical Association
Journal of Practical Nursing
Modern Healthcare
The Nation's Health
The New England Journal of Medicine
Nursing Outlook
Pediatrics
Physical Therapy
Physicians Assistant

DIRECTORIES:

Alternative Medicine Yellow Pages (Future Medicine Publishing, Puyallup, WA)
American Hospital Association Guide to the Health Care Field (American Hospital Association, Chicago, IL)
American Journal of Nursing, Directory of Nursing Organizations Issue (American Journal of Nursing Company, New York, NY)
California Association of Hospitals Membership Directory (California Association of Hospitals, Sacramento, CA)
HMO/PPO Directory (Medical Economics Data, Montvale, NJ)
Hospitals Directory (American Business Directories, Inc., Omaha, NE)
Medical and Health Information Directory (Gale Research, Detroit MI)
Physical Therapists Directory (American Business Directories, Inc., Omaha, NE)

Who's Who in American Nursing (Society of Nursing Professionals, Owings Mills, MD)

Los Angeles Area Employers:

Blue Cross/California Care
21555 Oxnard Street
Woodland Hills, CA 91367
(818) 703-2345

Blue Shield Preferred Plan
6701 Center Drive West, Suite 800
Los Angeles, CA 90045
(310) 670-4040

BPS Healthcare
888 S. Figueroa Street, Suite 1400
Los Angeles, CA 90017
(213) 489-2694

Brotman Medical Center
3828 Delmas Terrace
Culver City, CA 90231
(310) 836-7000

Cedars-Sinai Medical Center
8700 Beverly Blvd.
Los Angeles, CA 90048
(310) 855-5000
Job hotline: (310) 967-8230

Children's Hospital of Los Angeles
Employment Office
4601 Sunset Blvd.
Los Angeles, CA 90027
(213) 660-2450

CIGNA HealthCare of California
505 N. Brand Blvd., Suite 500
Glendale, CA 91203
(818) 500-6262

Community Health Plan
313 N. Figueroa Street, 6th Floor
Los Angeles, CA 90012
(213) 240-7783

Foundation Health
333 S. Arroyo Parkway
Pasadena, CA 91108
(310) 989-5610

Good Samaritan Hospital
1225 Wilshire Blvd.
Los Angeles, CA 90017
(213) 977-2121

Harbor-UCLA Medical Center
1000 W. Carson Street
Torrance, CA 90509
(310) 222-3231
Job hotline: (310) 222-3241
Human Resource Director: Judy Hardy

Health Net
21600 Oxnard Street, 10th Floor
Woodland Hills, CA 91367
(818) 719-6775
Job hotline: (818) 593-7236

Huntington Memorial Hospital
100 W. California Blvd.
Pasadena, CA 91109
(818) 397-5000
Job hotline: (818) 397-8504

Kaiser Permanente
393 E. Walnut Street
Pasadena, CA 91188
(818) 405-5000
Job hotline: (818)405-3280
Personnel Director: Andrew Carota

Kaiser Permanente Medical Center
4867 Sunset Blvd.
Los Angeles, CA 90027
(213) 667-4011
Job hotline: (213) 857-2615

Loma Linda University Medical Center
11234 Anderson Street
Loma Linda, CA 92354
(909) 824-0800

Long Beach Memorial Medical Center
2801 Atlantic Avenue
Long Beach, CA 90801
(310) 933-2000
Job hotline: (310) 933-3399

Los Angeles County/USC Medical Center
1200 N. State Street, Suite 1112
Los Angeles, CA 90033
(213) 226-2622

Metlife Health Care Network
4500 E. Pacific Coast Highway, Suite 120
Long Beach, CA 90804
(310) 498-5200

Pomona Valley Hospital Medical Center
1798 N. Garey Avenue
Pomona, CA 91767
(909) 865-9500

Preferred Health Network
301 E. Ocean Blvd., Suite 900
Long Beach, CA 90802
(310) 983-1616
Human Resource Director: Edna Roesler

PruCare of California
5800 Canoga Avenue
Woodland Hills, CA 91367
(818) 992-2093

St. John's Hospital & Health Center
1328 22nd Street
Santa Monica, CA 90404
(310) 829-5511

St. Joseph Medical Center
501 S. Buena Vista Street
Burbank, CA 91505
(818) 843-5111
Hiring Manager: Julia McQuillan

Tenet Healthcare Corporation
3820 State Street
Santa Barbara, CA 93105
(805) 563-7000
Human Resource Director: Jim Ferrier

UCLA Medical Center
10833 Le Conte Avenue
Los Angeles, CA 90095
(310) 825-9111

United Health Plan
3405 W. Imperial Highway, Suite 304
Inglewood, CA 90303
(310) 671-3465

Universal Care Health Plan
1600 E. Hill Street
Signal Hill, CA 90806
(310) 424-6200

Health Care

VA Medical Center
11301 Wilshire Blvd.
Los Angeles, CA 90073
(310) 268-3132
Human Resource Director: Elaine Marshall

Orange County Employers:

Admar Corp.
1551 N. Tustin Avenue, Suite 300
Santa Ana, CA 92705
(714) 953-9600
Hiring: Carolyn Sheilds

Aetna Health Plans
2677 N. Main Street
Santa Ana, CA 92701
(714) 648-3894

AllNet Preferred Providers
18300 Von Karman Avenue, Suite 620
Irvine, CA 92612
(714) 553-1717
Network Manager: Gillian Simpkin

Anaheim General Hospital
3350 W. Ball Road
Anaheim, CA 92804
(714) 827-6700

Anaheim Memorial Medical Center
1111 W. La Palma Avenue
Anaheim, CA 92801
(714) 774-1450

Beech Street of California
173 Technology
Irvine, CA 92718
(714) 727-9300
Vice President, Human Resources: Martin Torrez

Blue Cross of California
2201 Dupont Drive, Suite 600
Irvine, CA 92715
(714) 641-1201

Blue Shield of California
625 The City Drive South, Suite 400
Orange, CA 92668
(714) 663-4200

Brea Community Hospital
380 W. Central Avenue
Brea, CA 92621
(714) 529-0211

California Care Health Plans
2201 Dupont Drive, Suite 600
Irvine, CA 92715
(714) 622-7900

Capp Care
4000 Mac Arthur Blvd., Suite 10000
Newport Beach, CA 92658
(714) 251-2200
Hiring: Pat Szatkowski

CareAmnerica Health Plans
1800 E. Lambert Road, Suite 150
Brea, CA 92621
(714) 256-4180

Chapman Medical Center
2601 E. Chapman Avenue
Orange, CA 92669
(714) 633-0011

Children's Hospital of Orange County
455 S. Main Street
Orange, CA 92668
(714) 997-3000

Cigna Healthcare of California
2400 E. Katella Avenue, Suite 250-A
Anaheim, CA 92806
(714) 939-5858

Community Care Network
5251 Viewridge Court
San Diego, CA 92123
(619) 278-2273

FHP
9900 Talbert Avenue
Fountain Valley, CA 92708
(714) 963-7233

Fountain Valley Regional Hospital
17100 Euclid Avenue
Fountain Valley, CA 92708
(714) 979-1211
Job hotline: (714) 979-8108

252 How To Get a Job

Friendly Hills Regional Medical Center
1251 W. Lambert Road
La Habra, CA 90631
(310) 905-5266

Garden Grove Hospital & Medial Center
12601 Garden Grove Blvd.
Garden Grove, CA 92643
(714) 537-5160

Health Net
3187 Red Hill Avenue, Suite 200
Costa Mesa, CA 92626
(714) 253-6100

Hoag Memorial Hospital
1 Hoag Drive
Newport Beach, CA 92663
(714) 645-8600
Job hotline: (714) 760-5826

Huntington Beach Hospital and Medical Center
17772 Beach Blvd.
Huntington Beach, CA 92647
(714) 842-1473

Irvine Medical Center
16200 Sand Canyon Avenue
Irvine, CA 92618
(714) 753-2000

Kaiser Permanente Medical Care Program
441 N. Lakeview Avenue
Anaheim, CA 92807
(714) 978-4000

Mission Hospital Regional Medical Center
27700 Medical Center Road
Mission Viejo, CA 92691
(714) 582-2300

Orange County Community Hospital
4015 Tustin Avenue
Orange, CA 92666
(714) 771-9971

Orange Foundation for Medical Care
300 S. Flower Street
Orange, CA 92668
(714) 978-5048

Pacifica Hospital
18800 Delaware Street
Huntington Beach, CA 92648
(714) 842-0611

PacifiCare of California
5701 Katella Avenue
Cypress, CA 90630
(714) 952-1121
Human Resources: Barbara Effler

Private Healthcare Systems
3345 Michelson Avenue, Suite 200
Irvine, CA 92715
(714) 476-9816

PruCare of California
15635 Alton Parkway, Suite 100
Irvine, CA 92718
(714) 727-0749

Saddleback Memorial Medical Center
24451 Health Center Drive
Laguna Hills, CA 92653
(714) 837-4500

Santa Ana Hospital Medical Center
1901 N. Fairview Street
Santa Ana, CA 92706
(714) 554-1653

South Coast Medical Center
31872 Coast Highway
South Laguna, CA 92677
(714) 499-1311

St. Joseph Hospital
1100 W. Stewart Drive
Orange, CA 92868
(714) 633-9111
Job hotline: (714) 744-8557

St. Jude Medical Center
101 E. Valencia Mesa Drive
Fullerton, CA 92835
(714) 992-3000
Job hotline: (714) 992-3925

University of California Irvine Medical Center
101 The City Drive
Orange, CA 92868

Health Care   **253**

(714) 456-6011
Job hotline: (714) 456-5744

West Anaheim Mecial Center
3033 W. Orange Avenue
Anaheim, CA 92804
(714) 827-3000

Western Medical Center
1001 N. Tustin Avenue
Santa Ana, CA 92705
(714) 835-3555
Job hotline: (714) 480-5234

San Diego Area Employers:

Aetna Health Plans of San Diego
7676 Hazard Center Drive, Suite 1100
San Diego, CA 92108
(619) 497-0046
Hiring: Roberta Michaels

Alvarado Hospital Medical Center
6655 Alvarado Rd.
San Diego, CA 92120
(619) 287-3270

Blue Cross of California
3655 Nobel Drive, Suite 250
San Diego, CA 92122
(619) 450-9800
Regional Sales Director: Ed Johnson

Blue Shield of California
2525 Camino del Rio S., Suite 220
San Diego, CA 92108
(619) 296-1551
Hiring: Sharon Miller

Children's Hospital & Health Center
3020 Children's Way
San Diego, CA 92123
(619) 576-1700
Job hotline: (619) 576-5880

CIGNA Preferred Provider Program
9808 Scranton Road, Suite 400
San Diego, CA 92121
(619) 457-5402
Hiring: Kristin Graham

Community Care Network
5251 Viewridge Court
San Diego, CA 92123
(619) 278-2273

Community Health Group
740 Bay Blvd.
Chula Vista, CA 91910
(619) 422-0422

Grossmont Hospital
5555 Grossmont Center Drive
La Mesa, CA 91944
(619) 644-4210

Harbor View Medical Center
120 Elm Street
San Diego, CA 92101
(619) 232-4331

Health Net
3131 Camino del Rio N., Suite 1100
San Diego, CA 92108
(619) 521-4900

Kaiser Permanente
4647 Zion Avenue
San Diego, CA 92120
(619) 528-5000
Job hotline: (619) 528-3071

Mercy Hospital and Medical Center
4077 5th Avenue
San Diego, CA 92103
(619) 294-8111

Mesa Vista Hospital
7850 Vista Hill Avenue
San Diego, CA 92123
(619) 694-8300

Mission Bay Memorial Hospital
3030 Bunker Hill Street
San Diego, CA 92109
(619) 274-7721

PacifiCare of California
2878 Camino del Rio S., Suite 510
San Diego, CA 92108
(619) 297-4646
Area Sales Manager: Diane Gaswirth

Palomar Medical Center
555 E. Valley Parkway
Escondido, CA 92025
(619) 739-3000
Job hotline: (619) 739-3950

Paradise Valley Hospital
2400 E. 4th Street
National City, CA 91950
(619) 470-4321

Prudential Healthcare Plan of California
9171 Town Centre Drive, Suite 38
San Diego, CA 92122
(619) 457-4354

Scripps Clinic
10666 N. Torrey Pines Road
La Jolla, CA 92037
(619) 455-9100
Job hotline: (619) 554-8400

Scripps Community Health Network
10666 N. Torrey Pines Road
La Jolla, CA 92037
(619) 554-9700

Scripps Memorial Hospital
9888 Genesee Avenue
La Jolla, CA 92037
(619) 457-4123
Job hotline: 619-554-8400

Sharp Cabrillo Hospital
3475 Kenyon Street
San Diego, CA 92110
(619) 221-3400

Sharp Chula Vista Medical Center
751 Medical Center Court
Chula Vista, CA 91911
(619) 482-5800

Sharp Health Plan
9325 Sky Park Court, Suite 300
San Diego, CA 92123
(619) 637-6530

Sharp Memorial Hospital
7901 Frost Street
San Diego, CA 92123
(619) 541-3400

Tri-City Medical Center
4002 Vista Way
Oceanside, CA 92056
(619) 742-8411

University of California San Diego Medical Center
200 W. Arbor Drive
San Diego, CA 92103
(619) 543-6222
Job hotline: (619) 682-1001

Vista Health Plans
2355 Northside Drive, 3rd Floor
San Diego, CA 92108
(619) 521-4400

Nursing specialties set you apart

We asked Kathleen Kawakami, Head Nurse for General and Vascular Surgery at UCLA Medical Center, about career prospects in her field. She addressed some myths within the nursing field. "It has been said that a nurse can always find a job. This is true only if you have experience in nursing. It is important to work in the clinic setting while attending school. For an experienced nurse there are many opportunities for positions." Her own background includes a 6-month post graduate program focusing on perioperative nursing. She highly recommends that beginning nurses seek out specialized post-graduate programs.

Kathleen added that "Present employment opportunities are in a constant state of change. The future is not necessarily one of downsizing but one of changing roles. Nurses today often act as coordinators of patient care activities. In the future the nurse's role will continue to change as a result of economic conditions and technological advances."

Hospitality: Hotels/Restaurants

WEB SITES:

http://www.hospitalitynet.nl/
is a central source for the hospitality industry; includes a "virtual job exchange."

http://www.vnr.com/vnr/arch_ch.html
is the culinary and hospitality on-line newsletter.

PROFESSIONAL ORGANIZATIONS:

To network within the hospitality, convention services, and restaurant fields, contact the following local professional organizations listed in Chapter 5:

California Restaurant Association
Chefs de Cuisine Association of Southern California
Meeting Planners International
Restaurant Association of Southern California
Southern California Restaurant Association

For more information, you can contact:

American Hotel and Motel Association
1201 New York Avenue, NW, Suite 600
Washington, DC 20005
(202) 289-3100

California Hotel & Motel Association
P.O. Box 16405
414 29th Street
Sacramento, CA 95816
(916) 444-5780

Los Angeles Convention Center & Visitors Bureau
633 W. 5th Street, Suite 6000
Los Angeles, CA 90071
(213) 624-7300

Meeting Planners International
4455 LBJ Freeway, Suite 1200
Dallas, TX 75244
(214) 702-3000

National Restaurant Association
1200 17th Street, NW
Washington, DC 20036
(202) 331-5900

San Diego Convention and Visitor's Bureau
401 B Street, Suite 1400
San Diego, CA 92101
(619) 232-3101

PROFESSIONAL PUBLICATIONS:

Business Travel News
Food Management
Food and Wine
Hotel and Motel Management
Lodging Magazine
Meeting Manager
Meetings and Conventions
Restaurants and Institutions
Restaurant Business
Successful Meetings

DIRECTORIES:

Directory of Hotel and Motel Companies (American Hotel Association Directory Corp., New York, NY)
High Volume Independent Restaurants (Chain Store Guide Information Services, New York, NY)
Hotel and Motel Redbook (American Hotel Association Directory Corporation, New York, NY)
Meeting News Directory (Miller Freeman, New York, NY)
National Restaurant Association Directory (National Restaurant Association, Washington, DC)
Official Hotel and Resort Guide (Murdoch Magazines Division, Secaucus, NJ)
Resorts Directory (American Business Directories, Inc., Omaha, NE)
Restaurants Directory (American Business Directories, Omaha, NE)
Who's Who in the Lodging Industry (American Hotel and Motel Association, Washington, DC)

Los Angeles Area Employers:

Airport Marina Resort Hotel & Towers
8601 Lincoln Blvd.
Los Angeles, CA 90045
(310) 670-8111
Human Resource Director: Otho Boggs

Bel Air, Hotel
701 Stone Canyon Road
Los Angeles, CA 90077
(310) 472-1211
Hiring: Cynthia Blankenship

Biltmore Hotel
506 S. Grand Avenue
Los Angeles, CA 90071
(213) 624-1011
Hiring: Selene Rubio

Burbank Airport Hilton & Convention Center
2500 N. Hollywood Way
Burbank, CA 91505
(818) 843-6000

California Pizza Kitchen
6053 W. Century Blvd.
Los Angeles, CA 90045
(310) 342-5000

Century Plaza Hotel & Tower
2025 Avenue of the Stars
Los Angeles, CA 90067
(310) 277-2000

Cheescake Factory
26950 Agoura Road
Calabasas Hills, CA 91301
(818) 880-9323
Human Resource Director: Jennifer Jackson

Doubletree Hotel Los Angeles Airport
5400 W. Century Blvd.
Los Angeles, CA 90045
(310)216-5858
Hiring: Fernanda Aguirre

Four Seasons Los Angeles
300 S. Doheny Drive
Los Angeles, CA 90048
(310) 273-2222

Grill Concepts
11661 San Vicente Blvd., Suite 404
Los Angeles, CA 90049
(310) 820-5559
Human Resources: Margie Bayard

Guest Quarters Suite Hotel
1707 4th Street
Santa Monica, CA 90401
(310) 395-3332

Hamburger Hamlet Restaurants
14156 Magnolia Blvd.
Sherman Oaks, CA 91423
(818) 995-7333
Human Resources: Tom Whaley

Hilton Hotels Corp.
9336 Civic Center Drive
Beverly Hills, CA 90210
(310) 278-4321
Job hotline: (310) 205-7692
Hiring: Christine Koslowski
One of the "10 Largest Employers in Southern California." See Chapter 1 for additional information.

Holiday Inn Burbank
150 E. Angeleno Avenue
Burbank, CA 91502
(818) 843-6000

Holiday Inn Crowne Plaza
5985 W. Century Blvd.
Los Angeles, CA 90045
(310) 642-7500

Hyatt Hotel at Los Angeles International Airport
6225 W. Century Blvd.
Los Angeles, CA 90045
(310) 337-1234

Hyatt Regency Los Angeles
711 S. Hope Street
Los Angeles, CA 90017
(213) 683-1234
Human Resource Director: Anita Goldin

IHOP Corp.
525 N. Brand Blvd.
Glendale, CA 91203

Hospitality: Hotels/Restaurants

(818) 240-6055
Vice President: Naomi Shively

Loews Santa Monica Beach Hotel
1700 Ocean Avenue
Santa Monica, CA 90401
(310) 458-6700
Human Resources: Trudy Warm

Omni Los Angeles Hotel and Centre
930 Wilshire Blvd.
Los Angeles, CA 90017
(213) 688-7777
Employment Manager: Janice Kim

Panda Management Company
899 El Centro Street
S. Pasadena, CA 91030
(818) 799-9898
Hiring: Patty Brown

Red Lion Hotel
100 W. Glenoaks Blvd.
Glendale, CA 91202
(818) 956-5466

Ritz-Carlton Huntington Hotel
1401 S. Oak Knoll Avenue
Pasadena, CA 91106
(818) 568-3900

Sizzler International
12655 W. Jefferson Blvd.
Los Angeles, CA 90066
(310) 827-2300
Hiring: Lori Linogon

Sheraton Grande Hotel
333 S. Figueroa Street
Los Angeles, CA 90071
(213) 617-1133

United Restaurants
1990 Westwood Blvd., Penthouse
Los Angeles, CA 90025
(310) 475-5600
Hiring: Steve Ousdahl

Westin Bonaventure Hotel and Suites
404 S. Figueroa Street
Los Angeles, CA 90071
(213) 624-1000
Human Resources: Linda Michaels

Orange County Employers:

American Restaurant Group
450 Newport Center Drive, Suite 600
Newport Beach, CA 92660
(714) 721-8000

Callender, Marie, Pie Shops
1100 Town & Country Road, Suite 1300
Orange, CA 92868
(714) 542-3355
Hiring: Cathryn O'Brian

CKE Restaurants
P.O. Box 4349
1200 North Harbor Blvd.
Anaheim, CA 92803
(714) 774-5796

Days Inn Anaheim-Fullerton
1500 S. Raymond Avenue
Fullerton, CA 92631
(714) 635-9000

Disneyland Hotel
1150 W. Cerritos Avenue
Anaheim, CA 92802
(714) 778-6600
Casting Office: (714) 781-1600 (Coordinates hiring for the Hotel/Park)
Job hotline: (714) 781-4407

Doubletree Hotel
100 The City Drive
Orange, CA 92668
(714) 634-4500

Family Restaurants
18831 Von Karman Avenue
Irvine, CA 92715
(714) 757-7900
Hiring: Beth Libhart

Hilton & Towers, Anaheim
777 Convention Way
Anaheim, CA 92802
(714) 750-4321
Hiring: Valerie Becker

Howard Johnson Hotel
1380 S. Harbor Blvd.
Anaheim, CA 92802
(714) 776-6120

Hyatt Regency, Irvine
17900 Jamboree Road
Irvine, CA 92714
(714) 975-1234

Marriott, Anaheim
700 W. Convention Way
Anaheim, CA 92802
(714) 750-8000
Human Resources: Sharon Lockwood

Marriott, Newport Beach
900 Newport Center Drive
Newport Beach, CA 92660
(714) 640-4000
Hiring: Tony Hughes

Ritz Carlton
33533 Ritz-Carlton Drive
Laguna Niguel, CA 92629
(714) 240-2000
Hiring: Steve Hoftetter

Specialty Restaurants Corp.
4155 E. La Palma Avenue, Suite 250
Anaheim, CA 92807
(714) 579-3900
Hiring: David Faulds

San Diego Area Employers:

Atlas Hotels
500 Hotel Circle North
San Diego, CA 92108
(619) 291-7131
Human Resource Director: Alma Gonzalez

Best Western Seven Seas
411 Hotel Circle South
San Diego, CA 92108
(619) 291-1300

Chart House Enterprises
115 S. Acacia Avenue
Solana Beach, CA 92075
(619) 755-8281

Doubletree Hotel at Horton Plaza
910 Broadway Circle
San Diego, CA 92101
(619) 239-2200
Hiring: Liz Pula

Embassy Suites La Jolla
4550 La Jolla Village Drive
San Diego, CA 92122
(619) 453-0400

Foodmaker, Inc.
9330 Balboa Avenue
San Diego, CA 92123
(619) 571-2121
Hiring: Judy Fein

Garden Fresh Restaurant Corp.
17180 Bernardo Center Drive
San Diego, CA 92128
(619) 675-1600
Hiring: Kristin Carpenter

Holiday Inn on the Bay
1355 N. Harbor Drive
San Diego, CA 92101
(619) 232-3861

HomeTown Buffet
9171 Town Center Drive, Suite 575
San Diego, CA 92122
(619) 546-9096
http://www.buffet.com/
Hiring: Cindy Bezella
See Chapter 1, "10 Fastest Growing Employers in Southern California."

Hotel del Coronado
1500 Orange Avenue
Coronado, CA 92118
(619) 435-6611
Employment Manager: Mary Peters

Hyatt Regency San Diego
1 Market Place
San Diego, CA 92101
(619) 232-1234
Hiring: Enrique Guajardo

La Costa Resort and Spa
Costa del Mar Road
Carlsbad, CA 92009
(619) 438-9111
Hiring: Kristie Whitman

Marriott Mission Valley, San Diego
8757 Rio San Diego Drive
San Diego, CA 92108
(619) 692-3800
Hiring: Mary Staples

Hospitality: Hotels/Restaurants **259**

Premier Food Services
7966 Arjons Drive
San Diego, CA 92126
(619) 621-5151

San Diego Princess Resort
1404 W. Vacation Road
San Diego, CA 92109
(619) 274-4630
Hiring: Cheri Abbott

Sheraton Harbor Island Resort
1380 Harbor Island Drive
San Diego, CA 92101
(619) 291-2900
Hiring: Sandy Grove

Travelodge Hotel on Harbor Island
1960 Harbor Island Drive
San Diego, CA 92101
(619) 291-6700

Hotel management: more than puttin' on the Ritz
With a little more than two years' experience in the hotel business, our friend Kirk landed a job as hotel sales manager. We asked him for an overview of the hospitality industry.

"If you want to move up quickly," says Kirk, "this industry is the place to be. It's anything but a dead-end business. Some people stay with the same organization for most of their careers. But I'd say the average is probably around five years with any given company. People are constantly calling and making job offers.

"I studied hotel management and general business. But you can't just walk out of college and into a middle-management position. I started as a receptionist. Then I became a secretary. I don't know anyone who hasn't paid dues for a year or two. If you're interested in food or beverages, you might start out as a dining room assistant. Essentially, you'd be doing the same thing as a secretary—typing up contracts or menus, that sort of thing. You really have to learn the business from the bottom up.

"In sales you move from secretarial work to a full-fledged sales position. I was a sales representative, then was promoted to sales manager. The next step might logically be director of sales or marketing, where I'd be responsible for advertising and marketing strategies, developing budgets, and so on. An equivalent position would be director of food and beverages, the person who's responsible for all the food and drink served in the hotel, room service, all the dining rooms, special banquets, everything. After director of sales or food and beverages, you go on to general manager.

"I'd say the competition is about average-not nearly as fierce as the advertising industry, for example. Earning potential is pretty good, too, depending, of course, on the size of the hotel and the city you're in and what kind of company you're working for. You start out pretty low, maybe around $20,000 or $21,000 a year. But each time you move up, you get a hefty raise, or ought to."

Human Services

WEB SITES:

http://lib4.fisher.su.oz.au/Social_Work/socwkls.html
links to journals, newsgroups, and listserves.

http://naswca.org/
jobs bulletin from California chapter of National Association of Social Workers.

http://http.bsd.uchicago.edu/~r-tell/socwork.html
provides comprehensive links to social work sites.

http://www.philanthropy.journal.org/
meta-index of non-profit organizations.

http://www.essential.org/goodworks/
non-profit jobs searchable by state.

PROFESSIONAL ORGANIZATIONS:

For networking in human services and related fields, check out the following local and professional organizations listed in Chapter 5. Also see **"Foundations"** and **"Health Care."**

California Association for Counseling & Development
California Association of Marriage & Family Therapists
National Association of Social Workers, California Chapter

For more information, you can contact:

ACCESS/Networking in the Public Interest
1001 Connecticut Avenue, NW, Suite 838
Washington, DC 20036
(202) 785-4233

American Counseling Association
5999 Stevenson Avenue
Alexandria, VA 22304
(703) 823-9800

California Department of Social Services
744 P Street
Sacramento, CA 95814
(916) 657-3661

Center for Human Services
7200 Wisconsin Avenue, Suite 600
Chevy Chase, MD 20814
(301) 654-8338

National Association of Social Workers
750 1st Street, NE, Suite 700
Washington, DC 20002
(202) 408-8600

PROFESSIONAL PUBLICATIONS:

Child Welfare
Community Jobs
The NonProfit Times
Society

DIRECTORIES:

Human Services Organizations Directory
 (American Business Directories, Omaha, NE)

Los Angeles County Social Service Resource Directory (Glenda Riddick-Norton, Orange, CA)
National Directory of Children, Youth and Family Services (Marion L. Peterson, Publisher, Longmont, CO)
Orange County Social Service Resource Directory (Glenda Riddick-Norton, Orange, CA)
San Bernardino County Social Service Resource Directory (Glenda Riddick-Norton, Orange, CA)
Social Service Organizations and Agencies Directory (Gale Research, Detroit, MI)
Who's Who Among Human Service Professionals (National Reference Institute, Owings Mills, MD)

Los Angeles Area Employers:

American Cancer Society
3255 Wilshire Blvd., Suite 701
Los Angeles, CA 90010
(213) 386-6102
Locations throughout Los Angeles County.

American Heart Association
1055 Wilshire Blvd., Suite 900
Los Angeles, CA 385-4231
Human Resources: Venus Taylor

American Lung Association
5858 Wilshire Blvd., Suite 300
Los Angeles, CA 90036
(213) 935-5864

American Red Cross
P.O. Box 57930
Los Angeles, CA 90057
(213) 739-5200
Human Resource Director: Jennie Braun

Arthritis Foundation, The
4311 Wilshire Blvd., Suite 530
Los Angeles, CA 90010
(213) 954-5750
Personnel Administrator: Rica Angelo

Assistance League of Southern California
1370 N. St. Andrews Place
Los Angeles, CA 90028

(213) 469-1973
Human Resource Director: Gloria Arnett

Big Brothers of Greater Los Angeles
1486 Colorado Blvd.
Los Angeles, CA 90011
(213) 258-3333
Social Services: Mark Wild

Braille Institute
3450 Cahuenga Blvd.
Los Angeles, CA 90068
(213) 851-5695
Hiring: Elva Tamashiro

Childhelp USA
1345 N. El Centro Avenue
Hollywood, CA 90028
(213) 465-1345
Administrative Assistant: Annette Miller

Children's Institute International
711 S. New Hampshire Avenue
Los Angeles, CA 90005
(213) 385-5100
Personnel Director: Daphne Howell

Goodwill Industries
8120 Palm Lane
San Bernardino, CA 92402-0760
(909) 885-3831
Supervisor of Personnel: Diane Strong

Greater Los Angeles Council on Deafness
2222 Laverna Avenue
Los Angeles, CA 90041
(213) 478-8000
Executive Assistant: Linda Noblejas

International Institute of Los Angeles
4520 S. Huntington Drive
Los Angeles, CA 90032
(213) 227-5544

Lanterman, Frank D., Regional Center
3440 Wilshire Blvd., Suite 400
Los Angeles, CA 90010
(213) 383-1300
Human Resource Assistant: Schella Radford

Los Angeles Regional Family Planning Council
3600 Wilshire Blvd., Suite 600
Los Angeles, CA 90010
(213) 386-5614
Human Resource Manager: Pat Few

Muscular Dystrophy Association
3450 Wilshire Blvd., Suite 507
Los Angeles, CA 90010
District Director: Susan DeLatte

Permanent Charities Committee of Entertainment
11132 Ventura Blvd., Suite 401
Studio City, CA 91604
(818) 760-7722

Salvation Army, The
P.O. Box 15899 Del Valle Station
Los Angeles, CA 90015
(213) 627-5571
Hiring: Laura Youhanna

United Way
523 W. 6th Street
Los Angeles, CA 90014
(213) 630-2388
Director of Employment and Employee Relations: Keith Green

YMCA of Metropolitan Los Angeles
625 S. New Hampshire Avenue
Los Angeles, CA 90005
(213) 380-6448

YWCA of Los Angeles
3345 Wilshire Blvd., Suite 3300
Los Angeles, CA 90010
(213) 365- 2991

Orange County Employers:

American Red Cross
601 N. Golden Circle Drive
Santa Ana, CA 92705
(714) 835-5381
Job hotline: (213) 739-5582

Children's Home Society of California
300 S. Sycamore Street
Santa Ana, CA 92701
(714) 542-1147

National Council on Alcoholism
22471 Aspan Street, Suite 103
Lake Forest, CA 92630
(714) 770-2189
Program Director: Sharon Herbert

Project Independence
300 S. Harbor Blvd., Suite 816
Anaheim, CA 92805
(714) 772-5061

San Diego Area Employers:

American Cancer Society
8880 Rio San Diego Drive, Suite 100
San Diego, CA 92108
(619) 299-4200
Hiring: Samantha Andrews

American Heart Association
3640 5th Avenue
San Diego, CA 92103
(619) 291-7454
Executive Director: Cathy Shafer

American Red Cross
3650 5th Avenue
San Diego, CA 92103
(619) 291-2620

Arthritis Foundation, The
9089 Clairmont Mesa Blvd. #300
San Diego, CA 92123
(619) 492-1090
President: Delores Gieseke

Association for Retarded Citizens
1550 Hotel Circle North, Suite 400
San Diego, CA 92108
(619) 574-7575
Hiring: Catherine Talley

Catholic Charities
349 Cedar Street
San Diego, CA 92101
(619) 231-2828

Chicano Federation of San Diego County
610 22nd Street
San Diego, CA 92102
(619) 236-1228

Crime Victims Fund, The
P.O. Box 86318
San Diego, CA 92138
(619) 238-1988

Social Advocates for Youth
3615 Kearney Villa Road, Suite 101
San Diego, CA 92123
(619) 565-4148

Insurance

WEB SITES:

http://insurancenet.com/index.html
links to a directory of insurance resources on the Net.

http://www.connectyou.com/talent/
insurance career center.

PROFESSIONAL ORGANIZATIONS:

To network within the insurance industry, contact the following local professional organizations listed in Chapter 5:

American Benefit Plan Administrators
Professional Insurance Agents Association of California

For more information, you can also contact:

American Academy of Actuaries
1100 17th Street, NW, 7th Floor
Washington, DC 20036
(202) 223-8196

American Council of Life Insurance
1001 Pennsylvania Avenue, NW, Suite 500-S
Washington, DC. 20004
(202) 624-2000

American Insurance Association
1130 Connecticut Avenue, NW, Suite 1000
Washington, DC 20036
(202) 828-7100

National Association of Insurance Women International
1847 E. 15th Street
P.O. Box 4410
Tulsa, OK 74159
(918) 744-5195

National Association of Professional Insurance Agents
400 N. Washington Street
Alexandria, VA 22314
(703)836-9340

Society of Actuaries
P.O. Box 95668
Chicago, IL 60694
(847) 706-3500

PROFESSIONAL PUBLICATIONS:

Best's Review
Independent Agent
Insurance Journal
Insurance Week
National Underwriter

DIRECTORIES:

American Academy of Actuaries Yearbook (American Academy of Actuaries, Washington, DC)
American Council of Life Insurance Directory (American Council of Life Insurance, Washington, DC)
Best's Agents Guide to Life Insurance Companies (A.M. Best Company, Oldwick NJ)
Best's Insurance Reports, Property/Casualty Edition (A.M. Best Company, Oldwick NJ)
Best's Insurance Reports, Life/Health Edition (A.M. Best Company, Oldwick NJ)
Insurance Almanac (Underwriter Printing and Publishing Company, Englewood, NJ)
Society of Actuaries Yearbook (Society of Actuaries, Chicago, IL)

Southern California Insurance Directory (Underwriters Report, San Francisco, CA)

S&P's Insurance Book (Standard and Poor's Rating Group, New York, NY)

Who's Who in Insurance (Underwriter Printing and Publishing Company, Englewood, NJ)

Los Angeles Area Employers:

Access Insurance Services
303 Live Oak Avenue
Arcadia, Ca 91006
(818) 445-5428
Underwriting Assistant: Jennifer Han

Alexander & Alexander of California
801 S. Figueroa, Suite 700
Los Angeles, CA 90017
(213) 599-4000

Amwest Insurance Group
6320 Canoga Avenue
Woodland Hills, CA 91367
(818) 704-1111
Human Resources: Audra Townsend

Andreine and Co.
1401 Ocean Avenue, Suite 310
Santa Monica, CA 90401
(310) 260-6161
Resumes to Office Manager

Bolton/RGV Insurance Brokers
1100 El Centro Street
South Pasadena, CA 91030
(818)799-7000
Human Resource Director: Donna Bobi

Fremont General Corp.
2020 Santa Monica Blvd.
Santa Monica, CA 90404
(310) 315-5500
Personnel and Employment: Melody Bellmar

Golden Pacific Insurance Service
3280 E. Foothill Blvd., Suite 100
Pasadena, CA 91107
(818) 583-1900
Office Manager: Shirley Gorby

ISU Insurance Group
3750 E. Foothill Blvd.
Pasadena, CA 91107
(818) 440-0262
President: Kenneth Anderson

Johnson & Higgins
2029 Century Park East
Los Angeles, CA 90067
(310) 552-8700
Vice President, Human Resources: Caroline Galgraith

Keenan & Associates
2355 Crenshaw Blvd., Suite 200
Torrance, CA 90501
(310) 212-3344
CEO: John Keenan

Kessler, Sander A., and Associates
9570 W. Pico Blvd.
Los Angeles, CA 90035
(310) 247-3200
Human Resources Representative: Kathleen Heath

Marsh & McLennan
777 S. Figueroa Street
Los Angeles, CA 90017
(213) 624-5555
Human Resource Manager: Janine Hettem

Maxicare Health Plans
1149 S. Broadway Street, Suite 826
Los Angeles, CA 90015
(213) 765-2000
Employee Services

Mercury General Corp.
4484 Wilshire Blvd.
Los Angeles, CA 90010
(213) 937-1060
Human Resources

Peterson International Insurance Brokers
23929 Valencia Blvd., Suite 215
Valencia, CA 91355
(805) 254-0006

Randall, E. Broox, and Son
4751 Wilshire Blvd., Suite 204

Los Angeles, CA 90010
(213) 936-1010
Office Manager: Patricia Sullivan

Sedgwick Group, PLC
3435 Wilshire Blvd., Suite 500
Los Angeles, CA 90010
(213) 385-0545
Human Resources: Andrea Chasse

TriWest Insurance Services
14140 Ventura Blvd., 3rd Floor
Sherman Oaks, CA 91423
(818) 906-3350
CEO: Paul Bronow

Twentieth Century Industries
6301 Owensmouth Avenue
Woodland Hills, CA 91367
(818) 704-3700
Resumes to Employment Department

Willis Corroon Corporation of Los Angeles
801 N. Brand Blvd., Suite 400
Glendale, CA 91203
(818) 548-7500
Human Resource Manager: Annette Zeidman

Orange County Employers:

Akasaka Ortiz Varela Insurance
333 City Blvd. West, Suite 200
Orange, CA 92668
(714) 937-1800
President: Richard Akasaka

Anderson & Anderson
2495 Campus Drive
Irvine, CA 92715
(714) 476-4300
CEO: Robert Anderson

Armstrong Robitaille Welsh Insurance Services
17501 E. 17th Street
Tustin, CA 92680
(714) 832-5500

Brakke-Schafnitz Insurance Brokers
28202 Cabot Road, Suite 500
Laguna Niguel, CA 92677-1251
(714) 365-5100
CEO: Matthew Schafnitz

Cal-Surance Company
333 City Blvd West, Suite 900
Orange, CA 92668
(800) 762-7800

Fidelity National Financial
17911 Von Karman Avenue
Irvine, CA 92714
(714) 622-5000
Human Resource Manager: Patti Moore

First American Financial
114 E. 5th Street
Santa Ana, CA 92701
(714) 558-3211
Human Resources Director: Lane Heslington

Johnson & Higgins
695 Town Center Drive, Suite 700
Costa Mesa, CA 92626
(714) 641-8899

Marsh and McLennan
4695 MacArthur Court, Suite 550
Newport Beach, CA 92660
(714) 253-5800
Human Resources: Sondra McCullough

PacifiCare Health Systems
5995 Plaza Drive
Cypress, CA 90630
(714) 952-1121
Human Resources

Sullivan & Curtis Insurance Brokers
2100 Main Street, Suite 350
Ivrine, CA 92714
(714) 250-7172
Human Resource Manager: Catheryn Contreras

Sedgwick James
18201 Von Karman Avenue, Suite 800
Irvine, CA 92612
(714) 553-1760
Human Resources Director: Claudia Walker

Willis Corroon Corporation of Orange County
1551 N. Tustin Avenue
Santa Ana, CA 92701-3085
(714) 953-9521
Human Resources: Erica Nicholson

San Diego Area Employers:

Barney & Barney
9171 Towne Center Drive
San Diego, CA 92122
(619) 457-3414
Operations Manager: Dennis Pearce

Burnham, John, & Co.
610 W. Ash Street
San Diego, CA 92101
(619) 231-1010
Human Resource Director: Denise Hujung

Driver, Robert F., Co.
1620 5th Avenue
San Diego, CA 92101
(619) 238-1828
Human Resource Director: Barbara Weiland

Grant Nelson Group
3131 Camino del Rio North, #350
San Diego, CA 92108
(619) 521-5710
Regional Manager: Ms. Ronnie Adair

Insurance Services Network
7801 Mission Center Court, Suite 303
San Diego, CA 92108
(619) 298-1165
Senior Vice President: Kathleen Serrano

JMC Group
9710 Scranton Road
San Diego, CA 92121
(619) 450-0055
Human Resource Manager

Mills, Timothy S., Insurance Services
4265 Executive Drive, Suite 1400
San Diego, CA 92121
(619) 535-1800
President: Timothy S. Mills

Murria and Frick Insurance Agency
380 Stevens Avenue, Suite 115
Solana Beach, CA 92075
(619) 259-5800
Office Manager: Deborah Grady

Nico Insurance Services
7290 Navajo Road, Suite 111
San Diego, CA 92119
(619) 667-2111
President: Phil Nico

Phelps, E.J., & Co.
2250 4th Avenue, Suite 200
San Diego, CA 92101
(619) 231-1643
Vice President, Administration: Kim Webster

Wateridge Insurance Services
10525 Vista Sorrento Parkway, Suite 300
San Diego, CA 92121
(619) 452-2200
Owner: John Clanton

Law Firms

WEB SITES:

http://www.law.indiana.edu/law/lawindex.html
is a virtual law library; also connects to all law firms on the Net.

http://www.abanet.org/
is the homepage of the American Bar Association.

http://holmes.law.cwru.edu/cwrulaw/career/jobs.html
links to career opportunities in the field.

http://www.lawjobs.com/
allows you to search law jobs by state.

PROFESSIONAL ORGANIZATIONS:

To network within the field of law, contact the following local professional organizations listed in Chapter 5:

Association of California State Attorneys
Beverly Hills Bar Association
Black Women's Lawyer's Association
Lawyers Club of Los Angeles County
Lawyers Club of San Diego
Los Angeles County Bar Association
Los Angeles Paralegal Association
Orange County Bar Association
State Bar of California

For additional information, you can contact:

American Bar Association
750 N. Lake Shore Drive
Chicago, IL 60611
(312) 988-5000

National Association for Law Placement
1666 Connecticut Avenue, Suite 325
Washington, DC 20009
(202) 667-1666

National Association of Legal Assistants
1516 S. Boston Avenue, Suite 200
Tulsa, OK 74119
(918) 587-6828

National Conference of Black Lawyers
2 W. 125th Street
New York, NY 10027
(212) 864-4000

National Paralegal Association
P. O. Box 406
Solebury, PA 18963
(215) 297-8333

PROFESSIONAL PUBLICATIONS:

American Bar Association Journal
American Lawyer
California Lawyer
The Lawyer's Weekly
Legal Times
National Law Journal
The Paralegal

DIRECTORIES:

ABA Directory (American Bar Association, Chicago, IL)
Directory of Legal Employers (National Association for Law Placement, Washington, DC)
Directory of Local Paralegal Clubs (National Paralegal Association, Solebury, PA)
Ford's National Referral Directory of Law Firms by Specialties (Austin System, Inc., Verdugo City, CA)
Law Firms Yellow Book (Leadership Directories, Inc., New York, NY)
Law and Legal Information Directory (Gale Research, Detroit, MI)
Martindale-Hubbell Law Directory (Martindale-Hubbell, Summit, NJ)

Los Angeles Area Employers:

Buchalter Nemer Fields & Younger
601 S. Figueroa Street, Suite 2400
Los Angeles, CA 90017
(213) 891-5600

Christensen White Miller Fink & Jacobs
2121 Avenue of the Stars, 18th Floor
Los Angeles, CA 90067
(310) 553-3000

Gibson Dunn & Crutcher
333 S. Grand Avenue
Los Angeles, CA 90071
(213) 229-7000
Assistant Office Manager: Jennifer Lomeli

Graham and James
801 S. Figueroa Street, 14th Floor
Los Angeles, CA 90017
(213) 624-2500
Human Resource Manager: Gloria McCullen

Greenberg Flusker Fields Claman & Machtinger
1900 Avenue of the Stars, Suite 2000
Los Angeles, CA 90067
(310) 553-3610

Haight Brown & Bonesteel
1620 26th Street, Suite 4000 North
Santa Monica, CA 90404
(310) 449-6000
Managing Partner: Michael McCarthy

Hill Wynne Troop and Meisinger
10940 Wilshire Blvd.
Los Angeles, CA 90024
(310) 824-7000
Recruiting Administrator: Dottie Miller

Irell & Manella
1800 Avenue of the Stars, Suite 900
Los Angeles, CA 90067
(310) 277-1010
Human Resources: Laura Henry

Jeffer Mangels Butler & Marmaro
2121 Avenue of the Stars, 10th Floor
Los Angeles, CA 90067
(310) 203-8080

Jones Day Reavis & Pogue
555 W. 5th Street, Suite 4600
Los Angeles, CA 90013
(213) 489-3939

Latham & Watkins
633 W. 5th Street
Los Angeles, CA 90071
(213) 485-1234
Managing Partner: Robert Dell

Lewis D'Amato Brisbois & Bisgaard
221 N. Figueroa Street, Suite 1200
Los Angeles, CA 90012
(213) 250-1800

Loeb & Loeb
1000 Wilshire Blvd., Suite 1800
Los Angeles, CA 90017
(213) 688-3400

Manatt Phelps and Phillips
11355 W. Olympic Blvd.
Los Angeles, CA 90064
(310) 312-4000
Recruiting Coordinator: Jennifer Malis

Mitchell Silberberg & Knupp
11377 W. Olympic Blvd.
Los Angeles, CA 90064
(310) 312-2000
Human Resources: Cathy Letizia

Morgan Lewis & Bocklus
801 S. Grand Avenue, 22nd Floor
Los Angeles, CA 90017
(213) 612-2500

Morrison & Foerster
555 W. 5th Street, Suite 3500
Los Angeles, CA 90013
(213) 892-5200

Munger Tolles & Olson
355 S. Grand Avenue, 35th Floor
Los Angeles, CA 90071
(213) 683-9100

Musick Peeler & Garrett
624 S. Grand Avenue, Suite 2000
Los Angeles, CA 90017
(213) 629-7600

O'Melveny & Myers
400 S. Hope Street
Los Angeles, CA 90071
(213) 669-6000
Job hotline: (213) 669-6662

Paul Hastings Janofsky & Walker
555 S. Flower Street, 23rd Floor
Los Angeles, CA 90071
(213) 683-6000
Job hotline: (213) 683-5015

Pillsbury Madison & Sutro
725 S. Figueroa Street, Suite 1200
Los Angeles, CA 90017
(213) 488-7100
Human Resource Director: Mary Ellen Hatch

Sheppard Mullin Richter & Hampton
333 S. Hope Street, 48th Floor
Los Angeles, CA 90071
(213) 620-1780
Managing Partner: Carlton Varner

Sidley & Austin
555 W. 5th Street, Suite 4000
Los Angeles, CA 90013
(213) 896-6000

Skadden Arps Slate Meagher & Flom
300 S. Grand Avenue, Suite 3400
Los Angeles, CA 90071
(213) 687-5000

Orange County Employers:

Allen Matkins Leck Gamble & Mallory
18400 Von Karman Avenue, 4th Floor
Irvine, CA 92715
(714) 553-1313

Berger Kahn Shafton Moss Figler Simon & Gladstone
2 Park Plaza, Suite 650
Irvine, CA 92714
(714) 474-1880

Brobeck Phleger and Harrison
4675 MacArthur Court, Suite 1000
Newport Beach, CA 92660-1836
(714) 752-7535
Office Administrator: Gail Ballinger

Callahan McCune & Willis
111 Fashion Lane
Tustin, CA 92680
(714) 730-5700

Cooksey Howard Martin & Toolen
535 Anton Blvd., 10th Floor
Costa Mesa, CA 92626
(714) 431-1100

DiCarlo Highman D'Antony Dillard Fuller and Gregor
100 Pacifica, Suite 200
Irvine, CA 92718
(714) 727-7077
Office Manager: J.J. Tucker

Gibson Dunn & Crutcher
4 Park Plaza
Irvine, CA 92714
(714) 451-3800
Office Manager: Bryna Bock

Irell & Manella
840 Newport Center Drive, Suite 500
Newport Beach, CA 92660
(714) 760-0991

Knobble Martens Olson & Bear
620 Newport Center Drive, 16th Floor
Newport Beach, CA 92660
(714) 760-0404
Job hotline: (714) 721-2929
Administrator: Alice Hwa

Latham & Watkins
650 Town Centre Drive, 20th Floor
Costa Mesa, CA 92626
(714) 540-1235

Lewis D'Amato Brisbois & Bisgaard
650 Town Centre Drive
Costa Mesa, CA 92626
(714) 545-9200

Morrison and Foerster
19900 MacArthur Blvd., 12th Floor
Irvine, CA 92715-2443
(714) 251-7500
Managing Partner: Ronald DeFelice

Murtaugh Miller Meyer & Nelson
3200 Park Center Drive, 9th Floor
Costa Mesa, CA 92628
(714) 513-6800

O'Melveny & Meyers
610 Newport Center Drive, 17th Floor
Newport Beach, CA 92660
(714) 760-9600
Job hotline: (213) 669-6662
Administrator: Carolyn Berger

Palmieri Tyler Winer Wilhelm & Waldron
2603 Main Street, Suite 1300
Irvine, CA 92714
(714) 851-9400
Office Manager: Judy Goodlin

Paul Hastings Janofsky & Walker
695 Town Centre Drive, 77th Floor
Costa Mesa, CA 92626
(714) 668-6200

Pillsbury Madison & Sutro
600 Anton Blvd., Suite 1100
Costa Mesa, CA 92626
(714) 436-6800

Rutan & Tucker
611 Anton Blvd, Suite 1400
Costa Mesa, CA 92626
(714) 641-5100
Human Resources: Denise Pritchett

Snell and Wilmer
1920 Main Street, Suite 1200
Irvine, CA 92714
(714) 253-2700
Administrator: Barron Harley

Stradling Yocca Carlson & Rauth
660 Newport Center Drive, Suite 1600
Newport Beach, CA 92660
(714) 725-4000
Office Manager: Judy Gonzalez

San Diego Area Employers:

Ault Deuprey Jones & Gorman
402 W. Broadway, 16th Floor
San Diego, CA 92101
(619) 544-8300
Administrator: Douglas Hiatt

Baker & McKenzie
101 W. Broadway, 12th Floor
San Diego, CA 92101
(619) 236-1441

Brobeck Phleger and Harrison
550 W. C Street, Suite 1200
San Diego, CA 92101
(619) 234-1966
Hiring: Andrea Uy

Chapin Fleming & Winet
1320 Columbia Street
San Diego, CA 92101
(619) 232-4261

Edward White & Sooy
101 W. Broadway, 9th Floor
San Diego, CA 92101
(619) 231-1500

Gray Cary Ware & Freidenrich
401 B Street, Suite 1700
San Diego, CA 92101
(619) 699-2700
Personnel Director: Andrea Klein

Higgs Fletcher & Mack
401 W. A Street, Suite 2000
San Diego, CA 92101
(619) 236-1551
Executive Director: Mary Wright

Hillyer and Irwin
550 W. C Street, 16th Floor
San Diego, CA 92101
(619) 234-6121
Managing Partner: James Ehlers

Hinchy Witte Wood Anderson & Hodges
1901 1st Avenue
San Diego, CA 92101
(619) 239-1901

Latham & Watkins
701 B Street, Suite 2100
San Diego, CA 92101
(619) 236-1234
Managing Partner: Donald Newell

Lewis D'Amato Brisbois & Bisgaard
550 W. C Street, Suite 800
San Diego, CA 92101
(619) 233-1006

Littler Mendelson Fastiff Ticky & Mathiason
701 B Street, Suite 300
San Diego, CA 92101
(619) 232-0441

Lorenz Alhadeff Cannon & Rose
550 W. C Street, 19th Floor
San Diego, CA 92101
(619) 231-8700

Luce Forward Hamilton & Scripps
600 W. Broadway, Suite 2600
San Diego, CA 92101
(619) 236-1414
Human Resource Director: Ray Berry

McInnis Fitzgerald Rees & Sharkey
1230 Columbia Street, Suite 800
San Diego, CA 92101
(619) 236-1711
Operations Director: Kathy Barrett

Milberg Weis Bershad Hynes & Lerach
600 W. Broadway, Suite 1800
San Diego, CA 92101
(619) 231-1058
Office Manager: Kathi Strozza

Mulvaney Kahan & Barry
401 W. A Street, 17th Floor
San Diego, CA 92101
(619) 238-1010

Neil Dymott Perkins Brown & Frank
1010 2nd Avenue, Suite 2500
San Diego, CA 92101
(619) 238-1712

Pillsbury Madison & Sutro
101 W. Broadway, Suite 1800
San Diego, CA 92101
(619) 234-5000

Post Kirby Naonan & Sweat
600 W. Broadway, Suite 1100
San Diego, CA 92101
(619) 231-8666

Procopio Cory Hargreaves and Savitch
530 B Street, Suite 2100
San Diego, CA 92101
(619) 238-1900
Human Resource Manager: John Ehrmantraut

Seltzer Caplan Wilkins & McMahon
750 B Street, Suite 2100
San Diego, CA 92101
(619) 685-3003
Job hotline: (619) 685-3127
Recruitment Coordinator: Lucy Fredrick

Sheppard Mullin Richter and Hampton
501 W. Broadway, 19th Floor
San Diego, CA 92101
(619) 338-6500
Administrative Personnel: Cindy Ward

Shifflet Walters Kane & Konoske
750 B Street, 26th Floor
San Diego, CA 92101
(619) 239-0871

Management Consultants

WEB SITES:

http://www.scescape.com/worldlibrary/business/companies/consult.html
links to consulting companies.

http://www.cob.ohio-state.edu/~fin/jobs/consult.htm
company descriptions and links.

PROFESSIONAL ORGANIZATIONS:

For information about management consulting and related fields, you can contact:

Institute of Management Consultants
521 5th Avenue, 35th Floor
New York NY 100175
(212) 697-8262

National Bureau of Professional Management Consultants
2728 5th Avenue
San Diego, CA 92103
(619) 297-2207

World Association of Management Consulting Firms(ACME)
591 5th Avenue, 35th Floor
New York, NY 10175
(212) 697-9693

PROFESSIONAL PUBLICATIONS:

Academy of Management Journal
Association of Management Consultants Newsletter
Consultants Bulletin
Harvard Business Review

DIRECTORIES:

Consultants and Consulting Organizations Directory (Gale Research, Detroit, MI)
Dun's Consultants Directory (Dun & Bradstreet Corporation, Parsippany, NJ)
Management Consulting (Harvard Business School Press, Boston, MA)

Who's Who in Consulting (American Association of Professional Consultants, Kansas City, MO)

Employers:

Alexander & Alexander Consulting
801 S. Figueroa, Suite 700
Los Angeles, CA 90017
(213) 599-4000
Human Resource Manager: Barbara Errigan

American Management Systems
201 S. Figueroa Street, Suite 300
Los Angeles, CA 90012
(213) 613-5400 x 5410
Recruiting Manager: Carol Bates
TARA GRIMES   FAX: 613-5430

Andersen Consulting
2101 Rosecrans Avenue, Suite 3300
El Segundo, CA 90245
(310) 726-2700
Personnel Specialist: Kathleen Atkinson

AT Kearney [KIMBERLY YOUNG RC]
600 Anton Blvd., Suite 1000
Costa Mesa, CA 92626
(714) 445-6800 x 6880 FAX 445-6999
CHUCK GRISMER

Barry, Theodore, & Associates
1520 Wilshire Blvd.
Los Angeles, CA 90017
(213) 413-6080

Booz Allen & Hamilton
523 W. 6th Street, Suite 650
Los Angeles, CA 90014
(213) 620-1900
Office Manager: Ruby Sakai
http://www.bah.com
703-902-5000

Boston Consulting Group
333 S. Grand Avenue, Suite 4262
Los Angeles, CA 90071
(213) 621-2772
http://www.bcg.com

pwcglobal.com

Management Consultants

Coopers & Lybrand Consulting
350 S. Grand Avenue
Los Angeles, CA 90071
(213) 356-6000
Hiring: Robert Cassidy

Deloitte & Touche
1000 Wilshire Blvd., Suite 1500
Los Angeles, CA 90017 *CHARLIE STACY*
(213) 688-0800
(213) 694-5758 GANNON

DMR Group
550 N. Brand Blvd., Suite 1060
Glendale, CA 91203
(818) 249-0613

Economic Research Associates
10990 Wilshire Blvd., Suite 1600
Los Angeles, CA 90024
(310) 477-9585

Ernst & Young
515 S. Flower Street, Suite 2500
Los Angeles, CA 90071
(213) 977-3200 *(213) 977-3419 FAX*
Human Resource Director: Kevin Kelly

Grant Thorton
1000 Wilshire Blvd., Suite 700
Los Angeles, CA 90017
(213) 627-1717
Management Consulting Manager:
Michael Brigs

Hay Group
700 S. Flower Street, Suite 1500
Los Angeles, CA 90017
(213) 629-3921
General Manager: Laurence Karsh

Hewitt Associates
100 Bayview Circle
Newport Beach, CA 92660
(714) 725-4500
Recruiter: Marcina Simons

Higgins, A. Foster, & Co.
2029 Century Park East, Suite 1400
Los Angeles, CA 90067
(310) 551-4600
Hiring: Marie Cardenas

Korn Ferry International
1800 Century Park East, Suite 9(
Los Angeles, CA 90067
(310) 552-1834
FAX: 310 553-6452

KPMG Peat Marwick LLP
725 S. Figueroa Street
Los Angeles, CA 90017
(213) 972-4000

LEK/Alcar Consulting Group, The
12100 Wilshire Blvd., Suite 1700
Los Angeles, CA 90025
(310) 442-6500
Recruiting Coordinator: Jill Beliveau

Leventhal, Kenneth, & Co.
2049 Century Park East, 17th Floor
Los Angeles, CA 90067
(310) 277-0880

McKinsey & Company
400 S. Hope Street, Suite 700
Los Angeles, CA 90071
(213) 624-1414 *(213) 622-9399 MATT*
Recruiting Administrator: Tricia Cook

Mercer, William M.
777 S. Figueroa Street, Suite 2000
Los Angeles, CA 90017
(213) 346-2200
Personnel Manager: Juana Lara

Murphy, P., & Associates
4405 Riverside Drive, Suite 105
Burbank, CA 91505
(818) 841-2002

Price Waterhouse LLP
400 S. Hope Street
Los Angeles, CA 90071
(213) 326-3000
Hiring: Kathy Fink

Right Associates
2 N. Lake Avenue, Suite 1030
Pasadena, CA 91101
(818) 577-4448
Pasadena Hiring: Amy Halvorson

Regional Hiring: Karen Milliken
Source Consulting

879 W. 190th Street, Suite 250
Gardena, CA 90248
(310) 323-9337

Towers Perrin
1925 Century Park East, Suite 1500
Los Angeles, CA 90067
(310) 551-5600
Human Resource Coordinator: Lorraine Wood

Warner Group, The
5950 Canoga Avenue, Suite 600
Woodland Hills, CA 91367
(818) 710-8855

Watson Wyatt Worldwide
15303 Venutra Blvd., Suite 700
Sherman Oaks, CA 91403
(818) 906-2631
Hiring: Rose Menza

Media, Print

WEB SITES:

http://www.enews.com/
is the homepage of the Web's electronic newsstand.

http://www.mediainfo.com/
links to newspapers on the Net.

http://ww.yahoo.com/News/Newspapers/Regional/
is Yahoo's listing of newspapers on-line.

PROFESSIONAL ORGANIZATIONS:

To network within print media, contact the following local professional organizations listed in Chapter 5. Also see **"Broadcasting"** and **"Book Publishers."**

American Foreign Language Newspapers Association
Greater Los Angeles Press Club
Women in Communications

For additional information, you can contact:

American Society of Journalists and Authors
1501 Broadway, Suite 302
New York, NY 10036
(212) 997-0947

California Newspaper Publishers Association
1225 8th Street, Suite 260
Sacramento, CA 95814
(916) 443-5991

Magazine Publishers of America
919 3rd Avenue, 22nd Floor
New York, NY 10022
(212) 752-0055

National Newspaper Association
1525 Wilson Blvd.
Arlington, VA 22209
(703) 907-7900

Newspaper Association of America
11600 Sunrise Valley Drive
Reston, VA 22091
(703) 648-1000

PROFESSIONAL PUBLICATIONS:

Editor and Publisher
Electronic Publishing
Folio
Magazine Design and Production
The Writer
Writer's Digest

DIRECTORIES:

Directory of Leading Magazines and Newspapers (Publishers Media, El Cajon, CA)
Editor and Publisher International Year Book (Editor and Publisher Company, New York NY)
International Directory of Little Magazines and Small Presses (Dustbooks, Paradise, CA)
International Media Guide: Newspapers Worldwide (Directories International, Inc. South Nowalk, CT)

Media, Print

National Directory of Magazines (Oxbridge Communications, New York NY)
Publishers Directory (Gale Research, Detroit, MI)

Employers:

Adweek Magazine
5055 Wilshire Blvd.
Los Angeles, CA 90036
(213) 525-2270
Architectural Digest

Knapp Communications Corporation
6300 Wilshire Blvd.
Los Angeles, CA 90048
(213) 965-3700

Back Stage West
5055 Wilshire Blvd., 6th Floor
Los Angeles, CA 90036
(213) 525-2356

Billboard (BPI)
5055 Wilshire Blvd.
Los Angeles, CA 90036
(213) 525-2270

California Apparel News
110 E. 9th Street, Suite A-777
Los Angeles, CA 90079
(213) 627-3737

Canon Communications
3340 Ocean Park Blvd., Suite 1000
Santa Monica, CA 90405
(310) 392-5509

Copley Los Angeles Newspapers
5215 Torrance Blvd.
Torrance, CA 90509
(310) 540-5511
Human Resources: Lisa Henry

Daily Variety
5700 Wilshire Blvd., Suite 120
Los Angeles, CA 90036
(213) 857-6600

Fancy Publications
2401 Beverly Blvd.
Los Angeles, CA 90057
(213) 385-2222

Hachette-Filipacci Magazines
1499 Monvoriva Avenue
Newport Beach, CA 92663
(714) 720-5300
Publishes *Road & Track, Cycle World.*

Hollywood Reporter
5055 Wilshire Blvd., Suite 600
Los Angeles, CA 90036
(213) 876-1000

Inland Valley Daily Bulletin
2041 E. 4th Street
Ontario, CA 91764
(909) 987-6397
Hiring: Elliott Andorko

Investor's Business Daily
12655 Beatrice Street
Los Angeles, CA 90066
(310) 448-6000

La Opinion
411 W. 5th Street
Los Angeles, CA 90013
(213) 622-8332
Human Resources: Brian Lee
Spanish-language newspaper.

Long Beach Press-Telegram
604 Pine Avenue
P.O. Box 230
Long Beach, CA 90844
(310) 435-1161
Vice President, Human Resources: Jack Wilson

Los Angeles Daily Journal
915 E. 1st Street
Los Angeles, CA 90012
(213) 229-5300
Hiring: Dorothy Salzman

Los Angeles Daily News
Tower Media Group
21221 Oxnard Street
Woodland Hills, CA 91365
(818) 713-3000
Hiring: Erma Moore

Los Angeles Magazine
11100 Santa Monica Blvd., 7th Floor
Los Angeles, CA 90025
(310) 477-1181

Los Angeles New Times
2342 Sawtelle Blvd..
Los Angeles, CA 900064
(310) 477-0403
Executive Managing Editor: Christine Fleming

Los Angeles Times
Times Mirror Square
Los Angeles, CA 90053
(213) 237-3000
http://www.latimes.com/HOME/

Los Angeles Weekly
6715 Sunset Blvd.
Los Angeles, CA 90028
(213) 465-9909

North County Times
207 E. Pennsylvania Avenue
Escondido, CA 92025
(619) 745-6611

Orange Coast Magazine
245-D Fischer #8
Costa Mesa, CA 92626
(714) 545-1900

Orange County Register
625 N. Grand Avenue
Santa Ana, CA 92701
(714) 835-1234
Employment Supervisor: Lisa Hughes

Pasadena Star-News
San Gabriel Valley Newspapers
525 E. Colorado Blvd.
Pasadena, CA 91109
(800) 788-1200

San Diego Magazine
4206 Westpoint Loma Blvd.
San Diego, CA 92110
(619) 225-8953

San Diego Union-Tribune
350 Camino de la Reina
San Diego, CA 92108
(619) 299-3131
http://www.uniontrib.com/aboutut/
Human Resources: Bobbie Espinosa

Time
11766 Wilshire Blvd., 17th Floor
Los Angeles, CA 90025
(310) 268-7200

TV Guide
5750 Wilshire Blvd., Suite 375
Los Angeles, CA 90036
(213) 549-2300
Human Resources: Sally Preston

Variety/Daily Variety
5700 Wilshire Blvd., Suite 120
Los Angeles, CA 90036
(213) 857-6600

Weider Health & Fitness
21100 Erwin Street
Woodland Hills, CA 91367
(818) 884-6800

Western Outdoors Publications
3197-E Airport Loop Drive
Costa Mesa, CA 92626
(714) 546-4370

Networking for culture vultures
One of the least expensive "clubs" you can join, if you want to network with Southern California's cultural and business elite, is a gallery or museum. You'll be invited to "openings" and members' nights where you can network to your heart's content in stimulating surroundings.

Museums/Art Galleries

WEB SITES:

http://www.comlab.ox.ac.uk/archive/other/museums.html
searches for museums on the Web.

http://artscenecal.com/
guide to art galleries and museums in Southern California.

PROFESSIONAL ORGANIZATIONS:

To learn more about museum/gallery employment, you can contact:

American Association of Museums
1225 I Street, NW, Suite 200
Washington, DC 20036
(202) 289-6578

National Antique and Art Dealers Association of America
12 E. 56th Street
New York, NY 10022
(212) 826-9707

Western States Art Federation
236 Montezuma Avenue
Santa Fe, NM 87501
(505) 471-4148

PROFESSIONAL PUBLICATIONS:

Art in America
Art Business News
Artweek
ArtWorld
Museum News

DIRECTORIES:

American Art Directory (Reed Reference Publishing, New Providence, NJ)
Art & Auction International Directory (Des Moines, IA)
California Museum Directory (California Institute of Public Affairs, Sacramento, CA)
International Directory of Art (Gale Research, Detroit, MI)
International Directory of Corporate Art Collections (ARTnews, New York, NY)
National Directory of Arts Internships (National Network for Artist Placement, Los Angeles, CA)
Official Museum Directory (American Association of Museums, Washington, DC.)
Who's Who in Art (Gale Research, Detroit, MI)

Los Angeles Area Employers:

California Museum of Science & Industry
700 State Drive
Exposition Park
Los Angeles, CA 90037
(213) 744-7400

Craft & Folk Art Museum
5800 Wilshire Blvd.
Los Angeles, CA 90036
(213) 937-5544
Acting Director: Nancy Fister

Getty, J. Paul, Trust
401 Wilshire Blvd., Suite 900
Santa Monica, CA 90401
(310) 458-2003
Job hotline: (310) 451-6556

Griffith Observatory
2800 E. Observatory Road
Los Angeles, CA 90027
(213) 664-1181

Huntington Library, Art Collections and Botanical Gardens
1151 Oxford Road
San Marino, CA 91108
(818) 405-2100
Hiring: Carl Foote

Kidspace Museum
390 S. El Molino
Pasadena, CA 91101
(818) 449-9144

Los Angeles Children's Museum
310 N. Main Street
Los Angeles, CA 90012
(213) 687-8801

Los Angeles County Museum of Art
5905 Wilshire Blvd.
Los Angeles, CA 90036
(213) 857-6111
Hiring: Beth Barriger
http://ww.lacma.org/

Museum of African American Art
4005 Crenshaw Blvd.
Los Angeles, CA 9008
(213) 294-7071

Museum of Contemporary Art
250 S. Grand
Los Angeles, CA 90012
(213) 621-2766
Hiring: Kim Franklin

Museum of Tolerance
9786 W. Pico Blvd.
Los Angeles, CA 90035
(310) 553-8403
Hiring: Theresa Sage

Norton Simon Museum
411 West Colorado Blvd.
Pasadena, CA 91105
(818) 449-6840

Pacific Asia Museum
46 N. Los Robles Avenue
Pasadena, CA 91101
(818) 449-2742
Hiring: Edward Prohaska

Santa Monica Museum of Art
2437 Main Street
Santa Monica, CA 90405
(310) 399-0433
Director: Thomas Rhoades

Sotheby's
308 N. Rodeo Drive
Beverly Hills, CA 90210
(310) 274-0340
Hiring: Christa Gruener

Southwest Museum
234 Museum Drive
Los Angeles, CA 90065
(213) 221-2164
Director: Duane H. King

UCLA/Armand Hammer Museum of Art and Cultural Center
10899 Wilshire Blvd.
Los Angeles, CA 90024
(310) 208-3915
Director: Henry Hopkins

Orange County Employers:

Laguna Art Museum
307 Cliff Drive
Laguna Beach, 92651
(714) 494-6531
Acting Director: Susan Anderson

Newport Harbor Art Museum
850 San Clemente Drive
Newport Beach, CA 92660
(714) 759-1122
Director: Michael Botwinick

San Diego Area Employers:

Fleet, Reuben H., Space Theater and Science Center
1875 El Prado, Balboa Park
San Diego, CA 92101
(619) 238-1233

Natural History Museum, Balboa Park
San Diego, CA 92112
(619) 232-3821

San Diego Museum of Art
1450 El Prado, Balboa Park
San Diego, CA 92101
(619) 232-7931
http://www.sddt.com/sdma.html/

San Diego Museum of Contemporary Art
700 Prospect Street
La Jolla, CA 92037
(619) 454-3541
Human Resources: DeAnn Long

Oil/Gas/Plastics

WEB SITES:

http://www.pennwell.com/ogj.html is the homepage of *Oil and Gas Journal*.

http://www.utsi.com/oil_gas.html links to oil and gas industry sites.

http://www.echi.com/live/visit/visit.html is The Plastics Network; connects to companies and directories.

PROFESSIONAL ORGANIZATIONS:

For information about oil, gas, plastics, and related fields, you can contact the following organizations. Also see **"Chemicals"** and **"Engineering."**

American Gas Association
1515 Wilson Blvd.
Arlington, VA 22209
(703) 841-8400

American Petroleum Institute
1220 L Street, NW
Washington, DC 20005
(202) 682-8000

Petroleum Industry Research Foundation
122 E. 42nd Street
New York, NY 10168
(212) 867-0052

Society of Plastics Engineers
14 Fairfield Drive
Brookfield, CT 06804
(203) 775-0471

Society of the Plastics Industry
1275 K Street, NW
Washington, DC 20005
(202) 371-5200

PROFESSIONAL PUBLICATIONS:

Drilling Contractor
Gas Industries Magazine
Lundberg Letter
Modern Plastics
National Petroleum News
Oil Daily
Oil and Gas Journal
Plastics World
World Oil

DIRECTORIES:

Energy Job Finder (Mainstream Access, New York, NY)
Gas Industry Training Directory (American Gas Association, Arlington, VA)
International Petroleum Encyclopedia (PennWell Publishing Co., Tulsa, OK)
Modern Plastics, Encyclopedia Issue (McGraw-Hill, New York, NY)
National Petroleum News-Market Facts (Hunter Publishing Co., Des Plaines, IL)
Oil and Gas Directory (Geophysical Directory, Inc., Houston, TX)
Plastics World, Directory Issue (Cahners, Newton, MA)
US Oil Industry Directory (Penwell Publishing, Tulsa, OK)

Employers:

ARCO
515 S. Flower Street
Los Angeles, CA 90071
(213) 486-3511
Job hotline: (213) 486-3345
Vice President, Human Resources: John Kelly

Benton Oil and Gas Co.
1145 Eugenia Place, Suite 200
Carpinteria, CA 93013
(805) 566-5600

Calnetics Corp.
P.O. Box 2378
Chatsworth, CA 91311
(818) 886-9819
Comptroller: Barbara Guyer

Chevron USA Production Company
646 County Square Drive
Ventura, CA 93003
(805) 658-4300
Resume to Human Resources

Daleco Resources Corp.
10350 Santa Monica Blvd., Suite 250
Los Angeles, CA 90025
(310) 282-9999
Office Manager: Jody Spencer

Exxon Company USA
225 W. Hillcrest Drive
Thousand Oaks, CA 91360
(805) 494-2000

Furon Company
29982 Ivy Glenn Drive
Laguna Niguel, CA 92677
(714) 831-5350

Kleer-Vu Industries
921 W. Artesia Blvd.
Compton, CA 90220
(310) 603-9330
Resume to Human Resources

McFarland Energy
10425 S. Painter Avenue
Santa Fe Springs, CA 90670
(310) 944-0181

Occidental Petroleum
10889 Wilshire Blvd.
Los Angeles, CA 90024
(213) 879-1700

Pacific Enterprises
633 W. 5th Street, Suite 5400
Los Angeles, CA 90017
(213) 895-5000

Rotonics Manufacturing
17022 S. Figueroa Street
Gardena, CA 90248
(310) 538-4932

SEDA Specialty Packaging Corp.
2501 W. Rosecrans Avenue
Los Angeles, CA 90059
(310) 635-4444

Texaco
9966 San Diego Mission Road
San Diego, CA 92108
(619) 283-7376

UNOCAL
2141 Rosecrans Avenue
El Segundo, CA 90245
(310) 726-7600

Varco International
743 N. Eckhoff Street
Orange, CA 92668
(714) 978-1900

Western Atlas
360 N. Crescent Drive
Beverly Hills, CA 90210
(310) 888-2500

World Oil Company
9302 S. Garfield Avenue
South Gate, CA 90208
(310) 928-0100

Paper and Allied Products

WEB SITES:

http://www.tappi.org/
is the homepage of the Technical Association of the Paper and Pulp Industry.

http://www.curbet.com/print/merch.html
links to paper merchants.

PROFESSIONAL ORGANIZATIONS

For more information about the paper industry, you can contact:

American Forest and Paper Association
1111 19th Street, NW
Washington, DC 20036
(212) 463-2700

Paper Industry Management Association
1699 Wall Street, Suite 212
Mount Prospect, IL 60056
(847) 956-0250

Sales Association of the Paper Industry
P.O. Box 21926
Columbus, OH 43221
(614) 326-3911

Technical Association of the Paper and Pulp Industry
Technology Park, Box 105113
Atlanta, GA 30348
(404) 446-1400

PROFESSIONAL PUBLICATIONS:

Good Packaging Magazine
Packaging
Paper Age
Paper Sales
Pulp and Paper
Pulp and Paper Week

DIRECTORIES:

American Papermaker, Mill and Personnel Issue (ASM Communications, Inc., Atlanta, GA)
Lockwood-Post's Directory of the Paper and Allied Trades (Miller Freeman, New York, NY)
Paper Yearbook (Harcourt Brace Jovanovich, New York, NY)
Pulp and Paper, Buyer's Guide Issue (Miller Freeman, San Francisco, CA)
TAPPI Membership Directory (Technical Association of the Paper and Pulp Industry, Atlanta, GA)
Walden's ABC Guide and Paper Production Yearbook (Walden-Mott Corp., Ramsey, NJ)

Los Angeles Area Employers:

Gleason Industries
5033 W. 147th Street
Hawthorne, CA 90250
(213) 772-3471

Ingram Paper Company
17411 Valley Blvd.
City of Industry, CA 91744
(818) 854-5400
Hiring: Nancy Boehm

Ivy Hill Packaging
4800 S. Santa Fe Avenue
Los Angeles, CA 90058
213-587-3131

Keldon Paper Company
4510 Loma Vista Road
Los Angeles, CA 90058
(213) 584-7788

Kelly Paper Company
1441 E. 16th Street
Los Angeles, CA 90021
(213) 749-1311

Kirk Paper Company
7500 Amigos Avenue
Downey, CA 90242
(310) 803-0550

Los Angeles Paper Box and Board Mills
P.O. Box 60830
Los Angeles, CA 90060
(213) 685-8900
Hiring: Linda Jackson

Nationwide Papers
3100 E. 44th Street
Los Angeles, CA 90058
(213) 581-1441

Packaging Advantage Corporation
4633 Downey Road
Los Angeles, CA 90058
(213) 589-8181

Sealright Company
4209 E. Noakes Street
Los Angeles, CA 90023
(213) 269-0151

SEDA Specialty Packaging Corp.
2501 W. Rosecrans Avenue
Los Angeles, CA 90059
(310) 635-4444

Specialty Paper Mills
8834 Millergrove Drive
Santa Fe Springs, CA 90670
(310) 692-8737
Hiring: Lorenzo Apostol

Unisource Corporation
2600 S. Commerce Way
City of Commerce, CA 90040
(213) 725-3700

Vernon Sanitation Supply Co.
4622 Alcoa Avenue
Los Angeles, CA 90058
(213) 583-3191

Zellerbach Paper
4000 E. Union Pacific Avenue
Los Angeles, CA 90023
(800) 372-6666

Orange County Employers:

Kimberly Clark
2001 E. Orangethrope Avenue
Fullerton, CA 92631
(714) 773-7500

Sunclipse Inc.
6600 Valley View
Buena Park, CA 90620
(714) 562-6000
Hiring: Charlie Mason

San Diego Area Employers:

H&L Enterprises
1844 Friendship Drive
El Cajon, CA 92020
(619) 448-0883

San Diego Paper Box
10605 Jamacha Blvd.
Spring Valley, CA 91978
(619) 660-9566

Southland Envelope Company
8616 Cuyamaca Street
Santee, CA 92071
(619) 449-3553
Hiring: Diane Gonzalez

Unisource Corporation
6650 Top Gun Street
San Diego, CA 92121
(619) 452-0880
Hiring: Judy Graham

Temple Inland Food Service
1160 Vernon Way
El Cajon, CA 92020
(619) 448-0333

Printing/Graphic Arts

WEB SITES:

http://www.curbet.com/print/plink.html
links to commercial printers, paper merchants, and printing associations.

http://www.commarts.com/
job listings updated daily.

http://www.gag.org/
graphic artists guild homepage.

PROFESSIONAL ORGANIZATIONS:

To network within the printing/graphic design fields, contact the following local organization listed in Chapter 5:
American Institute of Graphic Arts

For more information, you can contact:

National Association of Printers and Lithographers
780 Palisade Ave.
Teaneck, NJ 07666
(201) 342-0700

National Computer Graphics Association
2722 Merrilee Drive
Fairfax, VA 22031
(703) 698-9600

Printing Industries of America
100 Daingerfield Road
Alexandria, VA 22314
(703) 519-8100

Technical Association of the Graphic Arts
68 Lomb Memorial Drive
Rochester, NY 14623
(716) 475-7470

PROFESSIONAL PUBLICATIONS:

American Printer
Communication Arts
Graphic Arts Monthly
Printing Impressions
Printing News
Who's Printing What

DIRECTORIES:

Design Firms Directory (Welfer and Associates, Evanston, IL)
Directory of Typographic Services (National Composition Association, Arlington, VA)
Graphic Arts Blue Book (A.F. Lewis & Co., New York, NY)
Graphic Arts Monthly, Printing Industry Sourcebook (Cahners Magazines, New York, NY)
National Computer Graphics Association Membership Directory (National Computer Graphics Association, Fairfax, VA)
Printers Directory (American Business Directories, Omaha, NE)

Los Angeles Area Employers:

Alan Lithograph
550 N. Oak Street
Inglewood, CA 90302
(310) 330-3800
President: Jerry Waxman

Anderson Lithograph Company
3217 S. Garfield Avenue
Los Angeles, CA 90040
(213) 727-7767
Hiring: Betty Miyahira

Apperson Business Forms
6855 E. Gage Avenue
Commerce, CA 90040
(310) 927-4718

Bert Co. Industries
1855 Glendale Blvd.
Los Angeles, CA 90026
(213) 669-5700
Hiring: RuthAnn Tubbs

Brubaker Group, The
10560 Dolcedo Way
Los Angeles, CA 90077
(310) 472-4766

California Offset Printers
620 W. Elk Avenue
Glendale, CA 91204
(213) 245-6446
Hiring: Jessica Anderson

Cliff & Associates
715 Fremont Avenue
South Pasadena, CA 91030
(818) 799-5906

ColorGraphics
150 N. Myers Street
Los Angeles, CA 90033
(213) 261-7171
Hiring: Cindy Brooks

Delta Lithograph Company
28210 N. Avenue Stanford
Valencia, CA 91355
(805) 257-0584
President: Rals Bierfischer

Denton Design Associates
491 Arbor Street
Pasadena, CA 91105
(818) 792-7141

Erwin Advertising & Design
829 Ocean Avenue
Seal Beach, CA 90740
(310) 598-3345

Evanson Design Group
4445 Overland Avenue
Culver City, CA 90230
(310) 204-1995

Gore Graphics
340 N. Madison Avenue
Los Angeles, CA 90004
(213) 668-2111

Graphic Design Concepts
4123 Wade Street
Los Angeles, CA 90066
(310) 306-8143
Human Resource Director: Greta Craddolph

Lithographix Inc.
13500 S. Figueroa Street
Los Angeles, CA 90061
(213) 770-1000
Hiring: Karen Milke

O'Neil Data Systems
12655 Beatrice Street
Los Angeles, CA 90066
(310) 448-6400
Hiring: Mary Maynard

Pacific Printing Industries
707 E. 62nd Street
Los Angeles, CA 90001
(213) 235-4011
President: Tom Wood

Penn Lithographics
16221 Arthur Street
Cerritos, CA 90703
(310) 926-0455
Employment: Jan Miller

Riccobon Business Forms
13827 Carmenita Road
Santa Fe Springs, CA 90670
(310) 921-7719
Hiring: Sue Simon

Rice, George, & Sons
2001 N. Soto Street
Los Angeles, CA 90032
(213) 223-2020
President: Gary Minnig

Sinclair Printing Company
4005 Whiteside Street
Los Angeles, CA 90063
(213) 264-4000
President: Robert Sinclair

Southern California Graphic Corporation
8432 Steller Drive
Culver City, CA 90230
(310) 559-3600

Superior Lithographics
3059 Bandini Blvd.
Los Angeles, CA 90023
(213) 263-8400
Hiring: Stephen Lau

Printing/Graphic Arts **285**

Orange County Employers:

Carson & Company
4701 Teller Avenue
Newport Beach, CA 92660
(714) 833-8435

Dot Printers
2424 McGaw Avenue
Irvine, CA 92714
(714) 474-1100
Hiring: Jim Voss

FEC
P.O. Box 3217
Cerritos, CA 90703
(714) 994-4961
Hiring: Janet Black

Frye & Smith
150 E. Baker Street
Costa Mesa, CA 92626
(714) 540-7005
Hiring: Lisa Holmes

San Diego Area Employers:

Advanced Web Offset
1211 Liberty Way
Vista, CA 92083
(619) 727-1700

A&L Lithographers
1910 Diamond
Escondido, CA 92029
(800) 321-5794

Commercial Press
955 Gateway Center Way
San Diego, CA 92120
(619) 527-4600

Graphic Data
5111 Mission Blvd.
San Diego, CA 92169
(619) 274-4511

Mitchell Web Press
11620 Sorrento Valley Road
San Diego, CA 92102
(619) 755-6500

Neyenesch Printers
P.O. Box 81184
San Diego, CA 92138
(619) 297-2281

Precision Lithographers
1185 Joshua Way
Vista, CA 92083
(619) 727-9400

San Dieguito Publishers
1910 Diamond Street
San Marcos, CA 92069
(619) 744-0910

Spectrum Printing
4395 El Cajon Blvd.
San Diego, CA 92105
(619) 283-7205
Administrative Hiring: Linda Taylor

Vanard Lithographers
3220 Kurtz Street
San Diego, CA 92110
(619) 291-5571

Webtrend Graphics
1311 Specialty Drive
Vista, CA 92083
(619) 598-4800
Resumes to Human Resource Manager.

Public Relations

WEB SITES:

http://www.prsa.org/
is the homepage of the Public Relations Society of America.

http://www.prcentral.com/
links to major agencies.

PROFESSIONAL ORGANIZATIONS:

To network within the field of public relations, contact the following local professional organizations listed in Chapter 5. Also see "**Advertising/Market Research.**"

Public Relations Society of America, Los Angeles Chapter
Public Relations Society of America, Orange County Chapter
Public Relations Society of America, San Diego Chapter
Women in Communications

For additional information, you can contact:

Public Relations Society of America
33 Irving Place
New York, NY 10003
(212) 995-2230

Women in Communications
2101 Wilson Blvd., Suite 417
Arlington, VA 22201
(703) 528-4200

PROFESSIONAL PUBLICATIONS:

Communication World
Inside PR
O'Dwyer's Newsletter
PR News
Public Relations Journal

DIRECTORIES:

Beacon's Publicity Checker (Beacon's Publishing Company, Chicago, IL)
O'Dwyer's Directory of Public Relations Firms (O'Dwyer Company, New York, NY)
Who's Who in PR (PR Publishing Company, Exeter, NH)

Los Angeles Area Employers:

Bender Goldman and Helper
11500 W. Olympic Blvd., Suite 655
Los Angeles, CA 90064
(310) 473-4147
V.P. of Administration & Operations: Donald Draper

Bohie Co.
1999 Avenue of the Stars, Suite 550
Los Angeles, CA 90067
(310) 785-0515
Office Manager: Dana Baldwin

Braun Ketchum Public Relations
11755 Wilshire Blvd., Suite 1900
Los Angeles, CA 90025
(310) 444-5000
Resumes to Director of Human Resources

Burson-Marsteller
1800 Century Park East, Suite 200
Los Angeles, CA 90067
(310) 226-3000
Office Administrator: Judy Young

Davidson, Dennis, Associates
5670 Wilshire Blvd., Suite 700
Los Angeles, CA 90036
(213) 954-5858
Controller: Susan Raines

Edelman Public Relations Worldwide
5670 Wilshire Blvd., Suite 1500
Los Angeles, CA 90036
(213) 857-9100
Office Manager: Sonia Conway

GCI Spindler
6100 Wilshire Blvd., Suite 840
Los Angeles, CA 90048
(213) 930-0811
Resumes to Human Resources

Golin/Harris Communications
601 W. 5th Street, Suite 400
Los Angeles, CA 90071
(213) 623-4200
General Manager: Fred Cook

Public Relations

Lippin Group
6100 Wilshire Blvd., Suite 400
Los Angeles, CA 90048
(213) 965-1990
Senior Vice President: Jan Fisher

Pacific West Communications Group
3435 Wilshire Blvd., Suite 2850
Los Angeles, CA 90010
(213) 487-0830
Human Resources: Maggie Wilson

Orange County Employers:

Amies Communications
18552 MacArthur Blvd., Suite 390
Irvine, CA 92715
(714) 863-1910
Vice President: Rick Miltonberger

Fisher Business Communications
5 Hutton Centre Drive, Suite 120
Santa Ana, CA 92707
(714) 556-1010
Vice President: Bill Pritchard

Gladstone International
18101 Von Karman Avenue, Suite 1280
Irvine, CA 92715
(714) 955-5252
President: Joan Gladstone

Maples & Associates
2201 Dupont Drive, Suite 740
Irvine, CA 92715
(714) 253-8737
Principal: Robert Maples

Shafer Public Relations
18200 Von Karman Avenue, Suite 800
Irvine, CA 92715
(714) 553-1177
Human Resource Director: Marie Smythe

South Coast Communications Group
2010 Main Street, Suite 220
Irvine, CA 92714
(714) 252-8440
Executive Vice Preisdent: Rene Karen

San Diego Area Employers:

Beck-Ellman Agency
4700 Spring Street, Suite 304
La Mesa, CA 91941
(619) 469-3500

Carpenter Matthews & Walcher
620 C Street, 6th Floor
San Diego, CA 92101
(619) 238-8500
Office Manager: Diane Scott

Cooper Iverson Marketing
8334 Clairemont Mesa Blvd.
San Diego, CA 92111
(619) 292-7400
President: Doug Cooper

Creative Communications Services
2385 Camino Vide Roble, Suite 205
Carlsbad, CA 92009
(619) 438-5250
General Manager: Gayle Mestel

Flannery Group
402 W. Broadway, Suite 1150
San Diego, CA 92101
(619) 239-5558
Administrator: K.C. Davis

Gable Group
701 B Street, Suite 1400
San Diego, CA 92101
(619) 234-1300
President: Joe Charest

Hicks, Roni, & Associates
1875 3rd Avenue
San Diego, CA 92101
(619) 238-8787
Principal: Roni Hicks Clemens

Nuffer Smith Tucker
3170 4th Avenue, Suite 300
San Diego, CA 92103
(619) 296-0605
Vice President: Larry Nuffer

Stock Alper & Associates
241 Ivy Street
San Diego, CA 92101
(619) 696-0832

Stoorza Ziegaus & Metzger
225 Broadway, Suite 1600
San Diego, CA 92101
(619) 236-1332
Administrative Manager: Joni Solan

Real Estate Developers and Brokers

WEB SITES:

http://www.ired.com
is an international real estate directory.

http://www.infowest.com/realnet/links/
links you to real estate links, searchable by state.

PROFESSIONAL ORGANIZATIONS:

To learn more about the real estate field, contact the following organizations.

American Society of Appraisers
535 Herndon Parkway
Herndon, VA 22070
(202) 478-2228

National Association of Real Estate Companies
P.O. Box 958
Columbia, MD 21044
(410) 821-1614

National Association of Realtors
430 N. Michigan Avenue
Chicago, IL 60611
(312) 329-8200

National Network of Commercial Real Estate Women
3115 W. 6th Street, Suite C-122
Lawrence, KS 66049
(913) 832-1808

PROFESSIONAL PUBLICATIONS:

Appraiser News
National Real Estate Investor
Real Estate Issues
Real Estate News
Real Estate Review

DIRECTORIES:

Directory of Certified Residential Brokers
 (Retail National Marketing Institute, Chicago, IL)

National Association of Realtors Roster of Realtors (National Association of Realtors, Chicago, IL)
National Real Estate Investor Directory
 (Real Estate Publications, Tampa, FL)
Southern California Building Industry Guide (Building Industry of California, Diamond Bar, CA)

Los Angeles Area Employers:

Beitler Commercial Realty Services
825 S. Barrington Avenue
Los Angeles, CA 90049
(310) 820-2955
Hiring: Carla Victor

CB Commercial Real Estate Group
533 S. Fremont Avenue
Los Angeles, CA 90071
(213) 613-3700
Hiring: Nancy Morris

Coldwell Banker Los Angeles
15280 Antioch Street
Pacific Palisades, CA 90272
(310) 459-0480

Cushman Realty Corp.
601 S. Figueroa Street, 47th Floor
Los Angeles, CA 90017
(213) 627-4700

Haagan, Alexander, Properties
3500 Sepulveda Blvd.
Manhattan Beach, CA 90266
(310) 546-4520
Human Resource Director: Lorie Schkud

Lee & Associates
13181 Crossroads Parkway North,
Suite 300
City of Industry, CA 91746
(310) 699-7500
Hiring: Linda Rubio

Maguire Thomas Partners
355 S. Grand Avenue, Suite 4500
Los Angeles, CA 90071

Real Estate Developers and Brokers

(213) 626-3300
Development company.

Majestic Realty Company
13191 Crossroads Parkway North, 6th Floor
City of Industry, CA 91746
(310) 692-9581

Metrospace Corporation
11726 San Vicente Blvd., Suite 500
Los Angeles, CA 90049
(310) 207-1700
Hiring: Daphne Duncan

RE/MAX Beach Cities Realty
225 S. Sepulveda Blvd., Suite 250
Manhattan Beach, CA 90266
(310) 376-2225
Hiring: Lori Robinson

Seeley Company
911 Wilshire Blvd., Suite 800
Los Angeles, CA 90017
(213) 627-1214
Hiring: Tracy Thomas

Shea Homes
655 Brea Canyon Road
Walnut, CA 91789
(909) 598-1841
Hiring: Georgia Volmer

Shorewood Realtors
1050 Duncan Avenue, Suite D
Manhattan Beach, CA 90266
(310) 376-8021
Hiring: Adrienne Sanders

Tishman West Companies
10900 Wilshire Blvd., Suite 510
Los Angeles, CA 90024
(310) 477-1919

Trammel Crow Company
5801 S. Eastern Avenue, Suite 100
Los Angeles, CA 90040
(213) 724-2246
Hiring: Susan Bergmann

Wilson, William, Company
146 S. Lake Avenue, Suite 103
Pasadena, CA 91101
(818) 793-8111

Zugsmith-Thind
16000 Ventura Blvd., Suite 900
Encino, CA 91436
(818) 906-1211

Orange County Employers:

California Pacific Homes
5 Civic Plaza, Suite 275
Newport Beach, CA 92660
(714) 719-3000
Hiring: Vivien Rapp

CB Commercial Real Estate
2400 E. Katella Avenue, 7th Floor
Anaheim, CA 92806
(714) 939-2100
Hiring: Sandy Herring

Collins Fuller
5000 Birch Street, Suite 1400
Newport Beach, CA 92660
(714) 851-2300
Hiring: Jim Collins

Insignia Commercial Group
1 Technology Drive, Building G
Irvine, CA 92618
(714) 788-3000
Developer.

Kaufman & Broad Homes
100 Bayview Circle
South Tower, Suite 100
Newport Beach, CA 92660
(714) 509-2400
Hiring: Suzette Morley

Koll Real Estate Group
4343 Von Karman Avenue
Newport Beach, CA 92660
(714) 833-3030
Human Resource Representative: Lisa Klarin
Developer.

Lee & Associates
3991 MacArthur Blvd., Suite 100
Newport Beach, CA 92660
(714) 724-1000

Sperry Van Ness
1301 Dove Street, Suite 101

Newport Beach, CA 92660
(714) 250-4100
Hiring: Yolanda Love

TD Service Financial Corporation
601 S. Lewis Street
Orange, CA 92668
(714) 385-4700

Voit Commercial Brokerage
18500 Von Karman Avenue, Suite 150
Irvine, CA 92715
(714) 851-5110

San Diego Area Employers:

ACI Commercial
2635 Camino del Rio S., Suite 200
San Diego, CA 92108
(619) 299-3000
Administrative hiring: Karen Buteyn
Broker representative: Charles Hoffman

Allen, Willis M., Company
1131 Wall Street
La Jolla, CA 92037
(619) 459-4033

Burnham, John, & Company
610 W. Ash Street
San Diego, CA 92112
(619) 236-1555
Hiring: Denise Hujing

Business Real Estate Brokerage Company
4380 La Jolla Village Drive, Suite 200
San Diego, CA 92122
(619) 546-5400

CB Commercial Real Estate Group
1365 4th Avenue
San Diego, CA 92101

(619) 236-1231
Hiring: Cindee Hodge

Century 21 Klowden-Forness
7439 Jackson Drive
San Diego, CA 92119
(619) 462-4300
Hiring: Eileen Parsley

Coldwell Banker Residential Brokerage Company
1660 Hotel Circle N., Suite 109
San Diego, CA 92108
(619) 574-5100

Excel Realty Trust
16955 Via Del Campo, Suite 120
San Diego, CA 92127
(619) 485-9400

Flocke & Avoyer Commercial Real Estate
3131 Camino del Rio N., Suite 190
San Diego, CA 92108
(619) 280-2600
Hiring: Gale Courtney

Irving Group, The
501 W. Broadway, Suite 2020
San Diego, CA 92101
(619) 238-4393
Hiring: Sherry Burton

Pacific Southwest Realty Services
P.O. Box 85012
San Diego, CA 92186
(619) 298-9222
Hiring: Nancy Meyer

Prudential California Realty
7780 Girard Avenue
La Jolla, CA 92037
(619) 454-0755
Hiring: Neta Tays

Location, location, location

Jane Billingsley is a partner in a firm that leases office space. We talked with her recently about getting started in commercial real estate. "Leasing commercial real estate is a very tough business," says Billingsley. "You don't make any money during your first year or two in the business. There's a very high attrition rate.

"But if you stick with it, you can make more money than your peers in other fields ever dreamed of. Six-figure incomes are not uncommon among people who have been in the business only five years.

"At our firm, we don't hire people right out of school; we look for people with some experience in the business world and in real estate. But many of the larger firms will hire recent grads and train them. In fact, some large firms have formal training programs.

"If you're a young person just starting out, I'd suggest getting a job with a bigger firm. Then be like a blotter-soak up everything they can teach you. After a few years, reevaluate your position with the company. The problem with the bigger firms is that they sometimes tend to ignore you once they've trained you. In a smaller firm, the senior people see more of a relationship between your success and the overall success of the company. Also, there's a lot of competition within a large firm. It's easy to get lost in the shuffle."

We asked Billingsley what qualifications are needed to succeed in commercial real estate. "You have to be tough because you'll face a certain amount of rejection. You have to be hungry because this is an extremely competitive business. A college degree is helpful, but it isn't required. This business is basically sales-getting out and seeing people, convincing them that your skills and knowledge are up to snuff. When you're just starting out, it's also very important to have a mentor in the company-someone to help you and look out for you."

Retailers/Wholesalers

WEB SITES:

http://hitech.retailer.com/vl/vretail.html is the WWW virtual library homepage for retailing.

http://www.inetbiz.com/market/ is a worldwide marketplace of wholesalers.

PROFESSIONAL ORGANIZATIONS:

For information about the retail and wholesale industries, contact the following national organizations:

Manufacturers' Agents National Association
23016 Mill Creek Road
Laguna Hills, CA 92654
(714) 859-4040

National Association of Convenience Stores
1605 King Street
Alexandria, VA 22314
(703) 684-3600

National Association of Wholesale Distributors
1725 K Street, NW
Washington, DC 20006
(202) 872-0883

National Retail Federation
325 7th Street, NW, Suite 1000
Washington, DC 20004
(202) 783-7971

PROFESSIONAL PUBLICATIONS:

Convenience Store News
Discount Store News
Health Foods Retailing
Merchandising
Monitor: The Magazine of Shopping Center Retailing Stores
Stores
Women's Wear Daily

DIRECTORIES:

Associate Directory (National Retail Federation, New York, NY)
Department Stores (Chain Store Guide Information Services, New York, NY)
Directory of General Merchandise, Variety/Specialty Chains and Specialty Stores (Chain Store Guide Information Services, New York, NY)
Discount Department Stores (Chain Store Guide Information Services, New York, NY)
National Association of Convenience Stores Membership Directory (National Association of Convenience Stores, Alexandria, VA)
Sheldon's Major Stores and Chains (Phelon, Sheldon & Marsar, Fairview, NJ)
Stores, Top 100 Issue (National Retail Merchants Association, New York, NY)

Employers:

Aaron Brothers
1270 Goodrich Blvd.
Commerce, CA 90022
(213) 725-6226

✓**Albertson's**
200 N. Puente Street
Brea, CA 92821
(714) 990-8200
Hiring: Sue Caro

Arden Group
2020 South Central Avenue
Compton, CA 90220
(310) 638-2842
Hiring: Wayne Brennan

Big 5 Sporting Goods Corp.
2525 E. El Segundo Blvd.
El Segundo, CA 90245
(310) 536-0611

Herbalife International
9800 La Cienega Blvd.
Inglewood, CA 90301
(310) 410-9600

Retailers/Wholesalers   293

House of Fabrics
13400 Riverside Drive
Sherman Oaks, CA 91423
(818) 995-7000
Hiring: Joy Dacumos

Hughes Markets
14005 Live Oak Avenue
Irwindale, CA 91706
(818) 856-6580
Hiring: Dave McMahon

Krause's Sofa Factory
200 N. Berry Street
Brea, CA 92621
(714) 990-3100

Levitz Furniture Company
7441 Edinger Avenue
Huntington Beach, CA 92647
(714) 898-3300

Montgomery Ward & Company
1288 Camino Real North
San Diego, CA 92108
(619) 692-5400

Neiman-Marcus
280 Fashion Valley Road
San Diego, CA 92108
(619) 692-9100
Hiring: Sandy Freese

Penny, J.C.
6131 Orangethrope Avenue
Buena Park, CA 90620
(714) 523-5900
Hiring: Henry Burt

Petco Animal Supplies
9125 Rehco Road
San Diego, CA 92121
(619) 453-7845
Hiring: Tom Roh

Price Club
3560 W. Century Blvd.
Inglewood, CA 90303
(310) 672-1251

Robinsons-May Company
6160 Laurel Canyon Blvd.
North Hollywood, CA 91606

(818) 508-5226
Hiring: Jim Lynch

Saks Fifth Avenue
333 Bristol Street
Costa Mesa, CA 92626
(714) 540-3233
Hiring: Jeri Galasso

Sav On Drugs
1500 S. Anaheim Blvd.
Anaheim, CA 92805
(714) 778-2300 → 774-3381

Stater Brothers Holdings
21700 Barton Road
Colton, CA 92324
(909) 783-5000
Hiring: Don Baker

Strouds Inc.
780 S. Nogales Street
City of Industry, CA 91748
(818) 912-2866
Recruiting Manager: Sue Stenbo

✓**Target Stores**
14750 Miller Avenue, Suite 5045
Fontana, CA 92336
(909) 355-6000
Hiring: Carol Walker

Three D Departments
535 Hyland Avenue, Suite 200
Costa Mesa, CA 92626
(714) 662-0818
Hiring: Kathi Alverado

Thrifty Corporation
3424 Wilshire Blvd.
Los Angeles, CA 90010
(213) 251-6000

Trader Joe's Company
538 Mission Street
South Pasadena, CA 91031
626 (818) 441-1177
Hiring: Rosella Moore

Viking Office Products
P.O. Box 61144
Los Angeles, CA 90061
(310) 225-4500
Hiring: Irene Gonzales

Vons Companies
618 Michillinda Avenue
Arcadia, CA 91007
(818) 821-7000

Wherehouse Entertainment
19701 Hamilton Avenue
Torrance, CA 90502
(310) 538-2314
Hiring: Stacey Lewis

Sports/Recreation/Fitness

WEB SITES:

http://www.sportsite.com/
is the SportsLink page, listing companies, publications, industry news, and jobs.

http://www.onlinesports.com/pages/CareerCenter.html
is the on-line Sports Career Center, with career opportunities and a resume bank.

http://www.fitnessworld.com/
links to fitness Web sites.

http://agency.resource.ca.gov/parks/dpr.html
homepage of California State Parks & Recreation.

http://www.yahoo.com/Entertainment/Amusment_Theme_Parks/
theme park links.

PROFESSIONAL ORGANIZATIONS:

To network within the sports and recreation fields, contact the following local organization listed in Chapter 5:

Greater San Diego Sports Association

For more information, you can contact:

Aerobics & Fitness Association of America
15250 Ventura Blvd., Suite 200
Sherman Oaks, CA 91403
(818) 905-0040

American Association for Leisure and Recreation
1900 Association Drive
Reston, VA 22091
(703) 476-3400

California Recreation & Parks Association
P.O. Box 161118
Sacramento, CA 95816
(916) 446-2777

National Recreation & Parks Association
2775 S. Quincy Street
Alexandria, VA 22302
(703) 820-4940

National Sporting Goods Association
1699 Wall Street
Mt. Prospect, IL 60056
(847) 439-4000

PROFESSIONAL PUBLICATIONS:

American Fitness
Amusement Business
Athletic Business
Parks and Recreation
Sporting Goods Dealer
Sporting Goods Market
Sporting Goods Retailers
Team Lineup

DIRECTORIES:

Athletic Business, Buyers Guide issue (Athletic Business Publications, Madison, WI)
Health Clubs Directory (American Business Directories, Omaha, NE)
Parks and Recreation Buyers Guide (National Recreation and Parks Association, Arlington, VA)
Sporting Goods Retailers Directory (American Business Directories, Omaha, NE)
Sports Market Place (Sports Guide, Phoenix, AZ)

Sports/Recreation/Fitness

Los Angeles Area Employers:

Cinema Ride
12001 Ventura Place, Suite 600
Studio City, CA 91604
(818) 761-1002

Bally's Nautilus Aerobics Plus
11500 W. Olympic Blvd.
Los Angeles, CA 90064
(310) 479-6310

Bally's Sports Connection
8612 Santa Monica Blvd.
Los Angeles, CA 90069
(310) 652-7440

Bodies In Motion
10542 W. Pico Blvd.
Los Angeles, CA 90064
(310) 836-8000

Family Fitness Centers
9911 W. Pico Blvd.
Los Angeles, CA 90035
(310) 553-7600

Family Fitness Centers
5711 W. Century Blvd.
Los Angeles, CA 90045
(310) 479-9909

Great Western Forum
3900 W. Manchester Blvd.
Inglewood, CA 90305
(310) 419-3100
Human Resource Director: Joan McLaughlin
Home to the Los Angeles Lakers and Kings.

Hollywood Park Race Track & Casino
1050 S. Prairie
Inglewood, CA 90306
(310) 419-1500

Los Angeles Athletic Club
431 W. 7th Street
Los Angeles, CA 90014
(213) 625-2211

Los Angeles Clippers
3939 S. Figueroa Street
Los Angeles, CA 90037
(213) 748-8000

Los Angeles Dodgers
1000 Elysian Park Avenue
Los Angeles, CA 90012
(213) 224-1500

Santa Anita Racetrack
285 W. Huntington Drive
Arcadia, CA 91007
(818) 574-7223

Six Flags Magic Mountain
26101 Magic Mountain Parkway
Valencia, CA 91385
(805) 255-4100
Job hotline: (805) 255-4800
Staffing Coordinator: Kim Hagel

Sports Club Company, The
11100 Santa Monica Blvd., Suite 300
Los Angeles, CA 90025
(310) 479-5200

Ticketmaster Corp.
3701 Wilshire Blvd.
Los Angeles, CA 90010
(213) 381-2000

Universal Studios Hollywood Theme Park
100 Universal City Plaza
Universal City, CA 91608
(818) 508-9600

Orange County Employers:

Anaheim Mighty Ducks
2695 Katella Avenue
Anaheim, CA 92806
(714) 704-2700

Bally's Nautilus Aerobics Plus
2301 Campus Drive
Irvine, CA 92715
(714) 752-7084

Disneyland
1313 S. Harbor Blvd.
Anaheim, CA 92802
(714) 939-5155
Casting Office: (714) 781-1600 (Coordinates hiring for the Park/Hotel)
Job hotline: (714) 781-4407

Golden West Baseball Company (Angels)
2000 Gene Autry Way
Anaheim, CA 92806
(714) 937-7200

Knott's Berry Farm
8039 Beach Blvd.
Buena Park, CA 90620
(714) 827-1776
Job hotline: (714) 995-6688

LA Fitness Sports Clubs
17850 Sky Park Circle
Irvine, CA 92714
(714) 261-7500

San Diego Area Employers:

Callaway Golf Company
2285 Rutherford Road
Carlsbad, CA 92008
(619) 931-1771

Del Mar Race Track
Jimmy Durante Blvd. at Fairgrounds
Del Mar, CA 92014
(619) 755-1141

Family Fitness Centers
17170 Bernardo Center Drive
San Diego, CA 92128
(619) 485-7177

Family Fitness Centers
7620 Balboa Avenue
San Diego, CA 92111
(619) 292-7079

Gold's Gym San Diego
2949 Garnet Avenue
San Diego, CA 92109
(619) 272-3400

Health Fitness Corporation
1201 Camino del Mar, Suite 206
Del Mar, CA 92014
(619) 481-9445

International Lottery & Totalizer Systems
2131 Faraday Avenue
Carlsbad, CA 92008
(619) 931-4000

Jazzercise International Headquarters
9235 Activity Road
San Diego, CA 92126
(619) 695-1503

Lottery Enterprises
9190 Activity Road
San Diego, CA 92126
(619) 621-5050

San Diego Chargers Football Company
9449 Friars Road
Jack Murphy Stadium
San Diego, CA 92108
(619) 280-2111

San Diego Padres Baseball Club
P.O. Box 2000
San Diego, CA 92108
(619) 283-4494

San Diego Zoo/Wild Animal Park
2920 Zoo Drive
San Diego, CA 92103
(619) 231-1515
Job hotline, Zoo: (619) 557-3968 Zoo
Job hotline, Wild Animal Park: (619) 738-5006

Sea World
1720 S. Shore Drive
San Diego, CA 92109
(619) 222-6363

Stock Brokers/Financial Services

WEB SITES:

http://bank.net/home.rich.html
links to investment industry sites and directories.

http://www.io.org/~invest/places.htm
links to finance-related groups, newsletters, and corporate information.

http://www.cob.ohio-state.edu/~fin/osujobs/htm
links to finance employers.

PROFESSIONAL ORGANIZATIONS:

For information about securities trading, finance, and related fields, contact the following organizations. Also see "Banking."

Association for Investment Management and Research
5 Boar's Head Lane
Charlottesville, VA 22903
(804) 977-660

Financial Executives Institute
10 Madison Ave.
Morristown, NJ 07962
(201) 898-4600

National Association of Personal Financial Advisors
1130 Lake Cook Road, Suite. 105
Buffalo Grove, IL 60089
(847) 537-7722

National Association of Securities Dealers
1735 K Street, NW
Washington, DC 20006
(202) 728-8000

National Venture Capital Association
1655 N. Fort Meyer Drive, Suite 700
Arlington, VA 22209
(703) 351-5269

Securities Industry Association
635 Slaters Lane, Suite 110
Alexandria, VA 22314
(703) 683-2075

PROFESSIONAL PUBLICATIONS:

Barron's National Business and Financial Weekly
CFO
D & B Reports
Commodity Journal
Corporate Finance Letter
Corporate Financing Week
Credit and Financial Management
Dun's Business Month
Financial Executive
Financial World
Institutional Investor
Investment Dealer's Digest
Journal of Finance
Securities Week
Stock Market Magazine
Traders Magazine
Wall Street Letter

DIRECTORIES:

Corporate Finance Sourcebook (National Register Publishing, New Providence, NJ)
CUSIP Master Directory (Standard & Poor's, New York, NY)
Directory of Registered Investment Advisors (Money Market Directories, Charlottesville, VA)
Financial Yellow Book (Monitor Publishing Co., New York, NY)
Handbook of Financial Markets and Institutions (John Wiley and Sons, New York, NY)
Investment & Securities Directory (American Business Directories, Omaha, NE)
Money Market Directory (Money Market Directories, Inc., Charlottesville, VA)
Nelson's Directory of Investment Research (W.R. Nelson, Port Chester, NY)

Securities Industry Yearbook (Securities Industry Association, New York, NY)
Security Dealers of North America (Standard and Poor's, New York, NY)
STA Traders Annual (Security Traders Association, New York, NY)
Who's Who in Finance and Industry (Reed Reference Publishing, New Providence, NJ)

Los Angeles Area Employers:

Aames Financial Corporation
3731 Wilshire Blvd., 10th Floor
Los Angeles, CA 90010
(213) 351-6100
Employment Coordinator: Meredith Hauger
Human Resource Director: Nanette Duff Sullivan

Bear Stearns & Co.
1999 Avenue of the Stars
Los Angeles, CA 90067
(310) 201-2600

Crowell Weedon & Co.
624 S. Grand Avenue, Suite 2600
Los Angeles, CA 90017
(213) 620-1850
Hiring: Dom Bonet

Dean Witter Reynolds
601 S. Figueroa Street, 29th Floor
Los Angeles, CA 90017
(213) 362-4500
Regional Director: Raymond Anderson

EVEREN Securities
355 S. Grand Avenue, Suite 3000
Los Angeles, CA 90071
(213) 356-5600
Executive Vice President: Terry Chase

Financial Network Investment Corp.
2780 Skypark Drive, Suite 300
Torrance, CA 90505
(310) 326-3100
Hiring: Nancy Bauman

JB Oxford Holdings
9665 Wilshire Blvd., Suite 300
Beverly Hills, CA 90212
(310) 777-8888
Hiring: Neilja Harewood

Jefferies Group
11100 Santa Monica Blvd., 10th Floor
Los Angeles, CA 90025
(310) 445-1199
Human Resources: Mel Locke

Kennedy Cabot & Co.
9470 Wilshire Blvd.
Beverly Hills, CA 90212
(310) 550-0711

Merrill Lynch Pierce Fenner & Smith
350 S. Grand Avenue, Suite 2700
Los Angeles, CA 90071
(213) 627-7900
Hiring: Jeanne Smith

Paine Webber
725 S. Figueroa Street, Suite 4100
Los Angeles, CA 90017
(213) 972-1511
Hiring: Cynthia Walker

Smith Barney
15260 Ventura Blvd., Suite 1900
Sherman Oaks, CA 91403
(818) 907-3700
Assistant to the Manager: Kathy Barnes

Sutro & Company
11150 Santa Monica Blvd., Suite 1500
Los Angeles, CA 90025
(310) 914-0718

Orange County Employers:

Cruttenden Roth
18301 Von Karman Avenue, Suite 100
Irvine, CA 92612
(714) 757-5700
Human Resources: Joyce Hooley

Dean Witter Reynolds
2677 N. Main Street, Suite 1000
Santa Ana, CA 92705
(714) 836-5181
Administrative hiring: Diane Burke

Stock Brokers/Financial Services 299

Edwards, A.G., & Sons
18881 Von Karman Avenue, Suite 150
Irvine, CA 92715
(714) 756-0353
Hiring: Terry Overturf

Fidelity National Financial
17911 Von Karmen Avenue
Irvine, CA 92614
(714) 852-9770

First American Financial Corp.
114 E. 5th Street
Santa Ana, CA 92701
(714) 558-3211

Gilford Securities
550 C Newport Center Drive
Newport Beach, CA 92660
(714) 852-7000
Managing Director: Doyle Holmes

Kemper Securities
620 Newport Center Drive, Suite 1300
Newport Beach, CA 92658
(714) 476-5100
Hiring: Jeff Johnson

Merrill Lynch Pierce Fenner & Smith
19200 Von Karman Avenue, Suite 1000
Irvine, CA 92715
(714) 752-7900
Hiring: Melinda Taylor

Paine Webber
4675 MacArthur Court, Suite 100
Newport Beach, CA 92660
(714) 253-6300
Division Manager: Michael Davis

PIMCO
700 Newport Center Drive
Newport Beach, CA 92660
(714) 640-3011
Assistant Vice President: Peggy Schmidt

Prudential Securities
4695 MacArthur Court, Suite 900
Newport Beach, CA 92660
(714) 752-2180
Hiring: Sharon Paturzo

San Diego Area Employers:

American Express Financial Advisors
8910 University Center Lane, Suite 200
San Diego, CA 92122
(619) 535-1331
Operations Manager: Debra Dumont

Dean Witter Reynolds
5464 Grossmont Center Drive
La Mesa, CA 91942
(619) 668-4300
Office Manager: Jeanette Cameron

Edwards, A.G., & Sons
8880 Rio San Diego Drive, Suite 1150
San Diego, CA 92108
(619) 298-9700
Manager: Timothy Cronin

Equitable, The
701 B Street, Suite 1500
San Diego, CA 92101
(619) 239-0018
Hiring: Carol Fracasso

JMC Group
9710 Scranton Road, Suite 100
San Diego, CA 92121
(619) 450-0055

Merrill Lynch Pierce Fenner & Smith
701 B Street, Suite 2400
San Diego, CA 92101
(619) 699-3700
Hiring: Randy Avey

Prudential Securities
701 B Street, Suite 1700
San Diego, CA 92101
(619) 236-1173
Branch Administrator: Patricia Lindroth

Sentra Securities/Spelman & Co.
2355 Northside Drive, Suite 200
San Diego, CA 92108
(619) 584-7000

White, Jack, & Co.
9191 Towne Center Drive, Suite 220
San Diego, CA 92122
(619) 587-2000

Travel/Shipping/Transportation

WEB SITES:

http://www.earthlink.net/~hotelanywhere/
links to travel-related industry sites.

http://www.sirius.com/~one/ta/tawww.html
is a site for professional travel agents.

http://www.yahoo.com/Business_and_Economy/Companies/Shipping
lists shipping companies on the Net.

http://iti.acns.nwu.edu/tran_res.html
links to transportation sites and news groups.

http://www.itsonline.com/
is the Independent Forum for Intelligent Transportation Systems.

PROFESSIONAL ORGANIZATIONS:

To network within the travel, shipping, or transportation industries, contact the following local professional organizations listed in Chapter 5:

Air Transport Association of America
American Society of Travel Agents
National Association of Business Travel Agents

For more information, you can contact:

Airline Pilots Association
1625 Massachusetts Avenue, NW
Washington, DC 20036
(703) 689-2270

American Public Transit Association
1201 New York Avenue, NW, Suite 400
Washington, DC 20005
(202) 898-4000

American Society of Travel Agents
1101 King Street
Alexandria, VA 22314
(703) 739-2782

American Trucking Association
2200 Mill Road
Alexandria, VA 22314
(703) 838-1700

Institute of Transportation Engineers
525 School Street, SW, Suite 410
Washington, DC 20024
(202) 554-8050

National Air Transportation Association
4226 King Street
Alexandria, VA 22302
(703) 845-9000

Travel Industry Association of America
1133 21st Street, NW
Washington, DC 20036
(202) 293-1433

United States Tour Operators Association (USTA)
211 E. 51st Street, Suite 12B
New York, NY 10022
(212) 750-7371

PROFESSIONAL PUBLICATIONS:

Air Travel Journal
ASTA Travel News
Aviation Week and Space Technology
Business and Commercial Aviation
Daily Traffic World
Mass Transit
Passenger Transport
Tours and Resorts
Tour and Travel News
Traffic Management Daily
Travel Agent
Travel Trade: The Business Paper of the Travel Industry
Travel Weekly
Trux
Urban Transport News

DIRECTORIES:

American Society of Travel Agents, Membership Directory (ASTA, Alexandria, VA)

Aviation Directory (E.A. Brennan Co., Garden Grove, CA)
Mass Transit: Consultants (PTN Publishing Corp., Melville, NY)
Moody's Transportation Manual (Moody's Travel Service, New York, NY)
Official Directory of Industrial and Commercial Traffic Executives (K-III Information Co., New York, NY)
Travel Agencies Directory (American Business Directories, Omaha, NE)
Travel Weekly's World Travel Directory (Reed Travel Group, Secaucus, NJ)
Worldwide Travel Information Contact Book (Gale Research, Detroit, MI)

Los Angeles Area Employers:

Airborne Express
4895 W. 147th Street
Hawthorne, CA 90250
(310) 331-4595

Alaska Airlines
6033 W. Century Blvd., Suite 560
Los Angeles, CA 90045
(310) 337-9512

American Airlines
5908 Avion Drive
Los Angeles, CA 90045
(310) 646-5563

American Tours
6053 Century Blvd.
Los Angeles, CA 90045
(310) 641-9953

Crystal Cruise Line
2121 Avenue of the Stars, Suite 200
Los Angeles, CA 90067
(310) 785-9300

Delta Airlines
6150 W. Century Blvd.
Los Angeles, CA 90045
(310) 216-2200

DHL Worldwide Express
4950 W. 145th Street
Hawthorne, CA 90250
(310) 973-7300

Emery Worldwide
3600 W. Century Blvd.
Inglewood, CA 90303
(310) 672-8964

Federal Express
333 S. Grand Avenue
Los Angeles, CA 90007
(213) 687-9767

Greyhound Venture
1716 E. 7th Street
Los Angeles, CA 90021
(213) 629-8487

Japan Travel Bureau International
707 Wilshire Blvd., Suite 3800
Los Angeles, CA 90017
(213) 687-9881

Korean Air
6101 W. Imperial Highway
Los Angeles, CA 90045
(213) 417-5200

Los Angeles County Metropolitan Transportation Authority
425 S. Main Street
Los Angeles, CA 90013
(213) 972-6000

Lykes Brothers Steamship Company
P.O. Box 910
Long Beach, CA 90801
(310) 435-7979
Ocean cargo transportation.

Mercury Air Group
5456 McConnell Avenue
Los Angeles, CA 90066
(310) 827-2737

Midnite Express International Couriers
925 W. Hyde Park Blvd.
Inglewood, CA 90302
(310) 672-1100

Northwest Airlines
11101 Aviation Blvd.
Los Angeles, CA 90045
(310) 646-7700

Norton Lilly International
606 S. Olive Street, Suite 2100
Los Angeles, CA 90014
(213) 689-9100
Foreign freight shipping.

Pleasant Hawaiian Holidays
2404 Townsgate Road
Westlake Village, CA 91361
(818) 991-3390

Princess Cruises
10100 Santa Monica Blvd., Suite 1800
Los Angeles, CA 90067
(310) 553-1770

Revel Travel Service
449 S. Beverly Drive
Beverly Hills, CA 92715
(714) 752-5456

Royal Caribbean
310 E. B Street
Wilmington, CA 90744
(310) 952-1147

Southwest Airlines
5777 W. Century Blvd., Suite 1190
Los Angeles, CA 90045
(310) 670-3565

Target Airfreight
3460 Wilshire Blvd., Suite 700
Los Angeles, CA 90010
(213) 387-6666

TWA
1545 Wilshire Blvd., Suite 411
Los Angeles, CA 90017
(213) 413-7286

United Airlines
1955 E. Grand
El Segundo, CA 90245
(213) 772-2121

Yellow Freight Systems
1955 E. Washington Blvd.
Los Angeles, CA 90021
(213) 742-0511

Orange County Employers:

American Express Travel
18301 Von Karman Avenue, Suite 490
Irvine, CA 92715
(714) 852-5001 (714) 975-1211

America West Airlines
4440 Von Karman Avenue
Newport Beach, CA 92660
(800) 548-8969

Associated Travel Management
1241 E. Dyer Road, Suite 110
Santa Ana, CA 92705
(714) 549-2552

Burlington Air Express
18200 Von Karman Avenue
Irvine, CA 92715
(714) 752-1212

DHL Worldwide Express
17102 Newhope Street
Fountain Valley, CA 927008
(714) 241-7421

First Class Travel Management
4100 Newport Place, Suite 850
Newport Beach, CA 92660
(714) 222-0800

Hickory/Cal-Mart Travel Service
17890 Sky Park Circle
Irvine, CA 92714
(714) 660-9200

Hobbs Trucking
501 E. Juliana Street
Anaheim, CA 92801
(714) 776-2520

John Wayne Airport
3151 Airway Avenue, Building K-101
Costa Mesa, CA 92626
(714) 252-5171

Orange County Transportation Authority
550 S. Main Street
Orange, CA 92613
(714) 560-6282

Travel/Shipping/Transportation **303**

Service Craft Distribution Systems
5650 Dolly Avenue
Buena Park, CA 90621
(714) 994-0821

Sundance Travel
19800 MacArthur Blvd., Suite 100
Irvine, CA 92715
(714) 752-5456

Trans-Box Courier Systems
7050 Village Drive, Suite B
Buena Park, CA 90621
(714) 739-4885

Tri Modal Distribution Service
505 S. Anaheim Blvd.
Anaheim, CA 92805
(714) 535-2863

United Parcel Service
1331 Vernon Avenue
Anaheim, CA 92805
(714) 491-7000

World Travel Bureau
620 N. Main Street
Santa Ana, CA 92701
(714) 835-0591

San Diego Area Employers:

Airborne Express
3602 Kurtz Street
San Diego, CA 92110
(619) 293-7570

Balboa Travel
909 W. Laurel Street
San Diego, CA 92101
(619) 234-8700

Carlson Travel
5405 Morehouse Drive, Suite 120
San Diego, CA 92121
(619) 458-2900

Federal Express
9192 Kearny Villa
San Diego, CA 92123
(619) 295-5545

San Diego Harbor Excursions
P.O. Box 751
San Diego, CA 92112
(619) 234-4111

San Diego Transit Corporation
100 16th Street
San Diego, CA 92101
(619) 238-0100

United Airlines
2375 Air Lane
San Diego, CA 92101
(619) 231-5638

Utilities

WEB SITES:

http://www.energy.ca.gov/energy/ is the California energy commission homepage.

http://www.energynet.com/ is a homepage for the public utilities sector.

http://www.aga.com/ homepage for the American Gas Association.

PROFESSIONAL ORGANIZATIONS:

For information about the utilities industry, contact the following organizations. See also **"Electronics/Telecommunications"** for major phone and cellular companies and **"Oil/Gas/Plastics."**

American Gas Association
1515 Wilson Blvd.
Arlington, VA 22209
(703) 841-8400

American Public Gas Association
11094 "D" Lee Highway
Fairfax, VA 22030
(703) 352-3890

American Public Power Association
2301 M Street, NW
Washington, DC 20037
(202) 467-2900

California Public Utilities Commission
505 Van Ness Avenue
San Francisco, CA 94102
(800) 848-5580

United States Telephone Association
1401 H Street, NW, Suite 600
Washington, DC 20005
(202) 326-7300

PROFESSIONAL PUBLICATIONS:

Electric Light and Power
Electrical World
Public Power
Public Utilities
Public Utility Fortnightly
Telephone Engineering and Management
Telephony

DIRECTORIES:

APGA Directory of Municipal Gas Systems (American Public Gas Assoc., Fairfax, VA)
Brown's Directories of North American Gas Companies (Edgel Communications, Cleveland, OH)
Electrical World Directory of Electrical Utilities (McGraw-Hill, New York, NY)
Moody's Public Utility Manual (Moody's Investors Service, New York, NY)

Employers:

Dominguez Water Corp.
21718 S. Alameda Street
Long Beach, CA 90810
(310) 834-2625
Human Resources: Jan Amaral

Edison International
2244 Walnut Grove Avenue
Rosemead, CA 91770
(818) 302-2222
Electric utilities.

Pacific Enterprises
555 W. 5th Street
Los Angeles, CA 90013
(213) 895-5000
Natural gas.

PacTel Meridian Systems
5785 Corporate Avenue, 2nd Floor
Cypress, CA 90630
(310) 493-7555

San Diego Gas & Electric Company
101 Ash Street
San Diego, CA 92101
(619) 696-2000
Resumes to Employee Services Department

Southern California Gas Company
555 W. 5th Street
Los Angeles, CA 90013
(213) 244-1200
Job hotline: (213) 244-1234
Personnel Manager: Craig Wert

Southern California Water Company
630 E. Foothill Blvd
San Dimas, CA 91773
(909) 394-3600

Southwest Water Company
225 N. Barranca Avenue
West Covina, CA 91791
(818) 915-1551

Employers Index

A

A&L Lithographers, 285
Aames Financial Corporation, 298
Aaron Brothers, 292
ABC Productions, 233
Academic Press, 198
Access Insurance Services, 264
ACI Commercial, 290
Activision, 207
Admar Corp., 251
Adohr Farms, 241
Advanced Logic Research, 208
Advanced Marketing Services, 198
Advanced Materials Group, 202
Advanced Tissue Sciences, 214
Advanced Web Offset, 285
Adweek Magazine, 275
AEC Environmental, 237
Aerodynamic Engineering, 184
Aerospace Corporation, 227
AeroVironment, 237
Aetna Health Plans, 251
Aetna Health Plans of San Diego, 253
Agouron Pharmaceuticals, 215
Ahmanson Foundation, 244
AIMS Media, 233
Air Sensors, 191
Airborne Express, 301, 303
Airport Marina Resort Hotel & Towers, 256
AirTouch Cellular Telephone Company, 224
Akasaka Ortiz Varela Insurance, 265
Alan Lithograph, 283
Alaska Airlines, 301
Albertson's, 292
Alemany High School, 219
Alexander & Alexander Consulting, 272
Alexander & Alexander of California, 264
Allen Matkins Leck Gamble & Mallory, 269
Allen, Willis M., Company, 290
Allergan, 214
Alliance Pharmaceutical Corp., 215
Allied Signal Aerospace Co., 183
AllNet Preferred Providers, 251
Alpha Microsystems, 208
Alpha Therapeutic Corporation, 214
Altadena Dairy, 240
Altoon & Porter, 188
Alvarado Hospital Medical Center, 253
Amblin Imaging, 236
AMC Theaters, 232
America West Airlines, 302
American Airlines, 301
American Cancer Society, 261, 262
American Express Financial Advisors, 299
American Express Travel, 302
American Fashion, 187
American Heart Association, 261, 262
American Lung Association, 261

Employers Index **307**

American Management Systems, 205, 272
American Racings, 191
American Red Cross, 261, 262
American Restaurant Group, 257
American Tours, 301
American Vanguard Corporation, 203
Amerigon Inc., 191
Amgen, Inc., 214
Amies Communications, 287
Amster, Betsy, Literary Enterprises, 197
Amwest Insurance Group, 264
Amylin Pharmaceuticals, 215
Anaheim City School District, 219
Anaheim General Hospital, 251
Anaheim Memorial Medical Center, 251
Anaheim Mighty Ducks, 295
Andersen, Arthur, and Company, 176, 177
Andersen Consulting, 205, 272
Anderson & Anderson, 265
Anderson Lithograph Company, 283
Andreine and Co., 264
Anshen & Allen, 188
Apperson Business Forms, 283
Applied Digital Access, 225
ARCO, 279
Arden Group, 292
Armor All Products Corp., 192
Armstrong Robitaille Welsh Insurance Services, 265
Arral Industries, 183
Arthritis Foundation, The, 261, 262
Artists Agency, 235
Asher/Gould Advertising, 180
Ashland Chemical Company, 203
Ashworth, 187
ASL Consulting Engineers, 227
Assistance League of Southern California, 261
Associated Travel Management, 302
Association for Retarded Citizens, 262
AST Computer, 208
AT Kearney, 272
AT&T, 224
Atlantic Records, 235
Atlas Hotels, 258
Ault Deuprey Jones & Gorman, 270
Aura Systems, 228

Aurora Electronics, 224
Austin Company, The, 228
Authentic Fitness Corporation, 186
Auto Pacific, 181
Auto Parts Club, LLC, 192
Autry Foundation, 244
Avacon Corporation, 229

B

Back Stage West, 275
Baker & McKenzie, 270
Baker Pacific Corp., 238
Balboa Travel, 303
Baldwin Company, 211
Bally's Nautilus Aerobics Plus, 295
Bally's Sports Connection, 295
Bank of America, 194, 195
Bank of Commerce, 195
Bank of Southern California, 195
Barney & Barney, 266
Barrett Consulting Group, 229
Barry, Theodore, & Associates, 272
Bates USA West, 181
BBDO, 180
BDO Seidman, 176
Bear Stearns & Co., 298
Beck-Ellman Agency, 287
Beckman, Arnold & Mabel, Foundation, 244
Beech Street of California, 251
Bein, Robert/William Frost, 229
Beitler Commercial Realty Services, 288
Bel Air, Hotel,, 256
Bell Industries, 223
Bender Goldman and Helper, 286
Benton Oil and Gas Co., 279
Bergen Brunswig Corp., 214
Berger Kahn Shafton Moss Figler Simon & Gladstone, 269
Bert Co. Industries, 283
Best Western Seven Seas, 258
Bettingen, Burton G., Corporation, 244
Big 5 Sporting Goods Corp., 292
Big Brothers of Greater Los Angeles, 261
Billboard (BPI), 275
Biltmore Hotel, 256
Biosym Technologies, 209

Blue Cross of California, 251, 253
Blue Cross/California Care, 249
Blue Shield of California, 251, 253
Blue Shield Preferred Plan, 249
Bodies In Motion, 295
Bohie Co., 286
Bolton/RGV Insurance Brokers, 264
Books on Tape, 198
Booz Allen & Hamilton, 272
Boston Consulting Group, 272
Boyds Wheels, 192
Boyle Engineering Corporation, 229
Bozell/Salvati Montgomery Sakoda, 181
BPS Healthcare, 249
Braille Institute, 261
Brakke-Schafnitz Insurance Brokers, 265
Braun Ketchum Public Relations, 286
Brea Community Hospital, 251
Brentwood School, 219
Bridge design and technology., 230
Bridgford Food Corp., 241
Brobeck Phleger and Harrison, 269, 270
Brogdex Company, 203
Brotman Medical Center, 249
Brown & Caldwell, 228, 239
Brown & Root, 228
Brown and Caldwell, 238
Brubaker Group, The, 284
BSI/Berryman & Henigar, 229
Buchalter Nemer Fields & Younger, 267
Buckley School, The, 219
Bugle Boy Industries, 186
Burbank Airport Hilton & Convention Center, 256
Burkett & Wong, 229
Burlington Air Express, 302
Burnham, John, & Co., 266
Burnham, John, & Company, 290
Burns, Fritz B., Foundation, 244
Business Real Estate Brokerage Company, 290

C

C&D Aerospace Group, 184
Cal-Surance Company, 265
California Amplifier, 223
California Apparel News, 275
California Care Health Plans, 251
California Community Foundation, 244
California Federal Bank, 193, 195
California Film Commission, 246
California Highway Patrol, 247
California Institute of Technology, 218
California Institute of the Arts, 218
California Milk Producers, 240
California Museum of Science & Industry, 277
California Offset Printers, 284
California Pacific Homes, 211, 289
California Pizza Kitchen, 256
California Polytechnic, 218
California State Bank, 194
California State University,, 218
California State University, Fullerton, 219
California State University, Long Beach, 218
California State University, Los Angeles, 218
California State University, Northridge, 218
California Trade & Commerce Agency, 247
California Wellness Foundation, 244
Callahan McCune & Willis, 269
Callaway Golf Company, 296
Callender, Marie, Pie Shops, 257
Calnetics Corp., 279
Campbell Hall, 219
Candle Corp., 207
Canon Communications, 275
Capener Matthews & Walcher, 182
Capitol Records, 235
Capp Care, 251
CareAmnerica Health Plans, 251
Carlson Travel, 303
Carol Little, Inc., 186
Carpenter Matthews & Walcher, 287
Carrier Johnson Wu, 190
Carsey-Warner Distribution, 235
Carson & Company, 285
Casanova Pendrill Publicidad, 181
Catalina Swimwear, 187
Cathay Bancorp, 194
Catholic Charities, 262
CB Commercial Real Estate, 289
CB Commercial Real Estate Group, 288, 290

Employers Index

CBS Entertainment Productions, 233
CBS-TV Channel 2, 201
Cedars-Sinai Medical Center, 249
Central Casting, 235
Century 21 Klowden-Forness, 290
Century Plaza Hotel & Tower, 256
Certified Grocers of California Ltd., 241
CH&A Corporation, 229
CH2M Hill, 229
Chadwick School, 220
Chamindale College Preparatory, 220
Chantal Pharmaceutical Corp., 214
Chapin Fleming & Winet, 270
Chapman Medical Center, 251
Chart House Enterprises, 258
Cheescake Factory, 256
Cherokee Group, 186
Chevron USA Production Company, 280
Chicano Federation of San Diego County, 262
Childhelp USA, 261
Children's Home Society of California, 262
Children's Hospital & Health Center, 253
Children's Hospital of Los Angeles, 249
Children's Hospital of Orange County, 251
Children's Institute International, 261
Chorus Line Corp., 186
Christensen White Miller Fink & Jacobs, 268
CIGNA HealthCare of California, 249, 251
CIGNA Preferred Provider Program, 253
Cinema Products Corp., 233
Cinema Ride, 295
City Design, 190
City National Corp., 194
City of Los Angeles Employment Opportunities, 247
City of San Diego, 247
CKE Restaurants, 257
Claremont Colleges, The, 218
Clark, Dick, Productions, 233
Classic Clothing, 186
Cliff & Associates, 284
Clifford Electronics, 191
Coast Citrus Distributors, 242
Coast Savings Financial, 194
Coca-Cola Bottling Co. of Los Angeles, 241
Coca-Cola Bottling of San Diego, 242
Cohn Wholesale Fruit & Grain, 242
Cohu, Inc., 225
Coldwell Banker Los Angeles, 288
Coldwell Banker Residential Brokerage Company, 290
Coleman/Caskey Architects, 189
Collins Fuller, 289
ColorGraphics, 284
Commercial Press, 285
Community Care Network, 251, 253
Community Health Group, 253
Community Health Plan, 249
Computer Sciences Corporation, 184
ComStream Corp., 225
Conrad and Associates, 177
Considine & Considine, 177
Converse Consultants West, 228
Cooksey Howard Martin & Toolen, 269
Cooper Iverson Marketing, 287
Coopers & Lybrand, 176, 177
Coopers & Lybrand Consulting, 205, 273
Copley Los Angeles Newspapers, 275
Corbin and Wertz, 177
Cortex Pharmaceuticals, 214
Corvas International, 215
County of San Diego, 247
Craft & Folk Art Museum, 277
Creative Artists Agency, 235
Creative Communications Services, 287
Creative Image Management, 235
Creative Teaching Press, 198
Crime Victims Fund, The, 263
Crossroads School for Arts & Sciences, 220
Crowell Weedon & Co., 298
Cruttenden Roth, 298
Crystal Cruise Line, 301
Cubic Corp., 184
Cushman Realty Corp., 288
Cytel Corp., 215

D

Dailey & Associates, 180
Daily Variety, 275

Daleco Resources Corp., 280
Dames & Moore, 228, 229, 238
Daniel Mann Johnson & Mendenhall, 189
Danielian Associates, 189
D'Arcy, Masius, Benton & Bowles, 180
DataWorks, 209
Datron Systems, 225
Datum Inc., 184
Davidson & Associates, 207
Davidson, Dennis, Associates, 286
Davis, Ball & Colombatto Advertising, 180
Days Inn Anaheim-Fullerton, 257
DDB Needham Worldwide, 180
Dean Witter Reynolds, 298, 299
Del Mar Race Track, 296
Delawie Wilkes Rodrigues Barker & Bretton, 190
Deloitte & Touche, 176, 177, 273
Delta Airlines, 301
Delta Lithograph Company, 284
Denton Design Associates, 284
Dep Corporation, 214
Department of Consumer Affairs, 247
Department of Housing and Urban Development, 247
Department of Labor, 247
Department of Parks & Recreation, 247
Department of Rehabilitation, 247
dGWB Advertising, 181
DH Technology, 225
DHL Worldwide Express, 301, 302
Di Zinno Thompson Integrated Marketing Solutions, 182
DiCarlo Highman D'Antony Dillard Fuller and Gregor, 269
Dinwiddie Construction Company, 211
Diodes Inc., 223
Disney Feature Animation, 236
Disney, The Walt, Company, 233
Disneyland, 296
Disneyland Hotel, 257
DMR Group, 273
Doheny, Carrie Estelle, Foundation, 244
Dole Food Company, 241
Dominguez Water Corp., 304
Donnelley Information Publishing, 198
Donnelley, R.R., & Sons, 197
Dot Printers, 285

Doubletree Hotel, 257
Doubletree Hotel at Horton Plaza, 258
Doubletree Hotel Los Angeles Airport, 256
Dow Corning USA, 203
Downey Financial Corporation, 195
Dreamworks SKG, 234
Driver, Robert F., Co., 266
Ducommun Incorporated, 184
Dudek & Associates, 230, 239
Duitch Franklin and Co., 176
Dura Pharmaceuticals, 215
Dworsky Associates, 189

E

E! Entertainment Television, 234
E&Y Kenneth Leventhal Group, 177
EarthLink Network, 205
Ecolab Inc., 203
Economic Research Associates, 273
Edelbrock Corp., 191
Edelman Public Relations Worldwide, 286
Edison International, 304
Educational films., 233
Edward White & Sooy, 270
Edwards, A.G., & Sons, 299
Edward's Theaters, 232
Eldorado Bank, 195
Eldorado National Corporation, 191
Elecktra Records, 235
Elexysys International, 224
Embassy Suites La Jolla, 258
Emery Worldwide, 301
Engineering Technology, 228
Englekirk, Robert, Consulting Structural Engineers, 228
Environmental Science & Engineering, 238
Equitable, The, 299
Ernst & Young, 176, 177, 273
Erwin Advertising & Design, 284
Evanson Design Group, 284
EVEREN Securities, 298
Excalibur Technologies Corporation, 209
Excel Realty Trust, 290
Executive Business Services, 209
Exxon Company USA, 280

Employers Index   311

F

F Fashion, 187
Family Fitness Centers, 295, 296
Family Restaurants, 257
Fancy Publications, 275
Farmers & Merchants Bank of Long Beach, 194
FCI Constructors, 212
FEC, 285
Federal Bureau of Investigation, 247
Federal Express, 301, 303
Federal Trade Commission, 247
FHP, 251
Fidelity National Financial, 265, 299
Fieldstone Company, 212
Filanc, J.R., Construction Company, 212
FileNet Corp., 208
Financial Network Investment Corp., 298
First American Financial, 265, 299
First Class Travel Management, 302
First National Bank, 195
First Pacific National Bank, 195
FirstFed Financial Corp., 194
Fisher Business Communications, 287
Fishking Processors, 241
Flamemaster Corp., 203
Flannery Group, 287
Fleet, Reuben H., Space Theater and Science Center, 278
Flintridge Preparatory School, 220
Flocke & Avoyer Commercial Real Estate, 290
Fluor Corp., 212
Fluor Daniel, 229
Food and Drug Administration, 247
Foodmaker, Inc., 258
Foote, Cone & Belding, 181
Forsythe Marcelli Johnson, 181
Foundation Health, 249
Foundations of the Milken Families, 244
Fountain Valley Regional Hospital, 251
Four Media Company, 234
Four Seasons Los Angeles, 256
Francis Parker School, 220
Franklin Stoorza, 182
Fremont General Corp., 264
Friction, 192
Friendly Hills Regional Medical Center, 252
Frye & Smith, 285
FSEC, 228
Furon Company, 280

G

G2 Advertising, 181
Gable Group, 287
Gallup Organization, 181
Garden Fresh Restaurant Corp., 258
Garden Grove Hospital & Medial Center, 252
GCI Spindler, 286
GDE Systems, 185, 225
Geffen, David, Foundation, 244
Geffen Records, 236
Gem Guides Book Company, 197
Gen-Probe, 215
General Devices, 228
General Dynamics, 185
General Instruments Corp., 225
Gensia, 215
Gensler & Associates, 189
Genvine Parts, 192
Geocon, 230
Geodynamics Corporation, 228
GERS Retail Systems, 209
Getty, J. Paul, Trust, 277
Gibson Dunn & Crutcher, 268, 269
Gilford Securities, 299
Gladstone International, 287
Gleason Industries, 281
Glencoe/McGraw Hill Education Division, 197
Glendale Federal Bank, 194
Golden Pacific Insurance Service, 264
Golden State Foods Corp., 241
Golden West Baseball Company (Angels), 296
Gold's Gym San Diego, 296
Goldwyn, Samuel, Company, 234
Goldwyn, Samuel, Foundation, 244
Golin/Harris Communications, 286
Good Samaritan Hospital, 250
Good Stuff Food Co., 241
Goodwill Industries, 261

Gore Graphics, 284
Graham and James, 268
Grant Nelson Group, 266
Grant Thorton, 176, 177, 273
Graphic Data, 285
Graphic Design Concepts, 284
Gray Cary Ware & Freidenrich, 270
Great Western Bank, 195
Great Western Financial Corp., 194
Great Western Forum, 295
Greater Los Angeles Council on Deafness, 261
Greenberg Flusker Fields Claman & Machtinger, 268
Greenfield Environmental, 239
Grey Advertising, 180
Greyhound Venture, 301
Greystone Homes, 212
Griffith Observatory, 277
Grill Concepts, 256
Grobstein Horwath and Co. LLP, 176
Grossmont Bank, 195
Grossmont Hospital, 253
Gruen Associates, 189
GTE, 223
GTI Corporation, 226
Guess?, 186
Guest Quarters Suite Hotel, 256

H

H&L Enterprises, 282
H&L Products, 192
Haagan, Alexander, Properties, 288
Hachette-Filipacci Magazines, 275
Haight Brown & Bonesteel, 268
Hamburger Hamlet Restaurants, 256
Hanna-Barbera Productions, 234
Hansen Natural Corp., 242
Harbor View Medical Center, 253
Harbor-UCLA Medical Center, 250
Harcourt Brace & Company, 198
Hargis & Associates, 239
Harmony Holdings Inc., 236
Harris, Sim J., Company, 212
Harvard-Westlake School, 220
Hay Group, 273
Health Fitness Corporation, 296
Health Net, 250, 252, 253

Heil Brice Retail Advertising, 181
Hellmuth Obata & Kassabaum, 189
Hensel Phelps Construction, 212
Henson, Jim, Productions, 234
Herbalife International, 292
Hewitt Associates, 273
Hewlett-Packard Company, 226
Hickory/Cal-Mart Travel Service, 302
Hicks, Roni, & Associates, 287
Higgins, A. Foster, & Co., 273
Higgs Fletcher & Mack, 270
Hill Brothers Chemical, 203
Hill Wynne Troop and Meisinger, 268
Hills Brothers Chemical, 203
Hillyer and Irwin, 270
Hilton & Towers, Anaheim,, 257
Hilton Hotels Corp., 256
Hinchy Witte Wood Anderson & Hodges, 270
HNTB Corp., 189, 229
Hoag Memorial Hospital, 252
Hobbs Trucking, 302
Holiday Inn Burbank, 256
Holiday Inn Crowne Plaza, 256
Holiday Inn on the Bay, 258
Hollywood Park Race Track & Casino, 295
Hollywood Records, 236
Hollywood Reporter, 275
Holmes & Narver, 190, 229
Home Savings of America, 194, 195
HomeTown Buffet, 258
Honvian, K., Companies, 212
Hood Corporation, 228
Hooker Industries, 191
Horizons Technology, 209
Hotel del Coronado, 258
House of Fabrics, 293
Howard Johnsons Hotel, 257
Hughes Aircraft Company, 184
Hughes Markets, 293
Hunsaker & Associates, 229, 230
Huntington Beach Hospital and Medical Center, 252
Huntington Library, Art Collections and Botanical G, 277
Huntington Memorial Hospital, 250
Hyatt Hotel at Los Angeles International Airport, 256

Employers Index 313

Hyatt Regency, Irvine, 258
Hyatt Regency Los Angeles, 256
Hyatt Regency San Diego, 258
Hybritech, 215
Hycor Biomedical, 214

I

ICN Pharmaceuticals, 214
IDEC Pharmaceutical Corp, 215
IHOP Corp., 256
Immaculate Heart High School, 220
Immune Response Corp., 215
Impco Technologies/AirSensors, 238
Imperial Bancorp, 194
Imperial Bank, 195
Incomnet, 223
Infotec Development, 184
Ingram Paper Company, 281
Inland Valley Daily Bulletin, 275
Insignia Commercial Group, 289
Insurance Services Network, 266
Interactive Group, 209
Internal & External Communications, 208
International Creative Management, 235
International Institute of Los Angeles, 261
International Lottery & Totalizer Systems, 296
International Technology Corporation, 228, 238
Interplay Productions, 208
Interpore International, 214
Intervisual Books, 198
Investor's Business Daily, 275
Irell & Manella, 268, 269
Irvine Medical Center, 252
Irvine Sensors Corp., 184, 224
Irving Group, The, 290
Isis Pharmaceuticals, 215
ISU Insurance Group, 264
IT Corp., 238
Ivy Hill Packaging, 281

J

J2 Communications, 198
Jacobs Engineering Group, 211, 238
Jalate Ltd., 186
Japan Travel Bureau International, 301

Jazzercise International Headquarters, 296
JB Oxford Holdings, 298
Jeffer Mangels Butler & Marmaro, 268
Jefferies Group, 298
Jerde Partnership, The, 189
JMC Group, 266, 299
John Wayne Airport, 302
Johnson & Higgins, 264, 265
Johnson, R.W., Pharmaceutical Research Institute, 215
Jones Day Reavis & Pogue, 268
Jones, Fletcher, Foundation, 244
Joni Blair of California, 186

K

K-Swiss Inc., 186
KABC Channel 7, 201
Kaiser Marquardt, 184
Kaiser Permanente, 250, 253
Kaiser Permanente Medical Care Program, 252
Kajima Engineering & Construction, 211
Karen Milliken, 273
Kaufman & Broad Homes, 212, 289
KBIG-FM (104.3), 200
KCAL Channel 9, 201
KCET Channel 28, 201
KCOP Channel 13, 201
Keck, W. M., Foundation, 244
Keenan & Associates, 264
Keith Companies, 229
Kelco, 203
Keldon Paper Company, 281
Keller Construction Company LTD, 211
Kellogg & Andelson Accounting Corporation, 176
Kelly Paper Company, 281
Kemper Securities, 299
Kennedy Cabot & Co., 298
Kercheval Engineers, 230
Kessler, Sander A., and Associates, 264
Kest, Sol and Clara, Family Fund, 244
Ketchum Los Angeles, 180
Kexhall Industries, 192
KFI-AM (640), 200
KFMB Channel 8, 201
KFMB-AM/FM, 200
KGTV Channel 10, 201

Kidspace Museum, 277
KIIS-FM (103.7), 200
Kimberly Clark, 282
Kinetics Technology International, 238
King World Productions, 235
Kirk Paper Company, 282
KKBT-FM (92.3), 200
Klages, Carter, Vail & Partners, 190
KLAX-FM (97.9), 200
Kleer-Vu Industries, 280
Kleinfelder Inc., 230, 239
KLVE-FM (107.5), 200
KMA Architecture & Engineering, 190
KMEX Channel 34, 201
KMKX/KYXY-FM, 200
Knapp Communications Corporation, 275
KNBC Channel 4, 201
Knobble Martens Olson & Bear, 269
Knott's Berry Farm, 296
Knowledge Adventure, 208
KNSD Channel 39, 201
KOGO-AM/KKLQ-FM/K102 FM, 200
Koll Construction, 212
Koll Real Estate Group, 289
Korean Air, 301
Korn Ferry International, 273
KOST-FM (103.5), 200
KPBS-TV Channel 15, 201
KPMG Peat Marwick, 176, 177, 178
KPMG Peat Marwick LLP, 273
KPOP-AM/KGB-FM, 201
KPWR-FM (105.9), 200
Kraco Enterprises, 192
Krause's Sofa Factory, 293
Kresser Stein Robaire, 180
KROQ-FM (106.7), 200
KRTH-FM (101.1), 200
KSDO-AM/KKBH-FM, 201
KTLA Channel 5, 201
KTTV Channel 11, 201
Kushner-Locke Company, 234
KUSI-TV Channel 51, 202

L

L&L Manufacturing, 186
La Costa Resort and Spa, 258
LA Fitness Sports Clubs, 296
La Jolla Country Day School, 220
La Jolla Pharmaceutical, 215
La Opinion, 275
La Reina, Inc., 241
Laguna Art Museum, 278
Lambesis, 182
Lanterman, Frank D., Regional Center, 261
Latham & Watkins, 268, 269, 270
Law/Crandall, 230, 239
Le Lycee Francais de Los Angeles, 220
Leavey, Thomas and Dorothy,, 244
Lee & Associates, 288, 289
Lee & Ro Consulting Engineers, 228
Lee Burkhart Liu, 189
Lee Pharmaceuticals, 214
Leesak Architects, 190
Leighton & Associates, 230, 239
LEK/Alcar Consulting Group, The, 273
Lenore, John, and Co., 242
Leventhal, Kenneth, & Company, 176, 273
Levitz Furniture Company, 293
Levitz Zacks and Ciceric, 178
Lewis D'Amato Brisbois & Bisgaard, 268, 269, 271
Ligand Pharmaceuticals, 215
Lintas Campbell-Ewald, 180
Lippin Group, 287
Liquid Investments, 242
Lithographix Inc., 284
Littler Mendelson Fastiff Ticky & Mathiason, 271
Litton Industries, 184
Lockheed Martin, 184, 185
Locus Computing Corp., 208
Loeb & Loeb, 268
Loews Santa Monica Beach Hotel, 257
Logicon Inc., 208
Loma Linda University Medical Center, 250
Long Beach Memorial Medical Center, 250

Employers Index

Long Beach Press-Telegram, 275
Long Beach Unified School District, 220
Lord Dentsu & Partners, 180
Lorenz Alhadeff Cannon & Rose, 271
Los Angeles Athletic Club, 295
Los Angeles Baptist High School, 220
Los Angeles Cellular Telephone, 223
Los Angeles Chemical Corp., 203
Los Angeles Children's Museum, 278
Los Angeles Clippers, 295
Los Angeles County Metropolitan Transportation Auth, 301
Los Angeles County Museum of Art, 278
Los Angeles County/USC Medical Center, 250
Los Angeles Daily Journal, 275
Los Angeles Daily News, 275
Los Angeles Dodgers, 295
Los Angeles Literary Associates, 198
Los Angeles Magazine, 275
Los Angeles New Times, 276
Los Angeles Paper Box and Board Mills, 282
Los Angeles Regional Family Planning Council, 262
Los Angeles Times, 276
Los Angeles Unified School District, 220
Los Angeles Weekly, 276
Lottery Enterprises, 296
Loyola High School, 220
LPA Inc., 190
Luce Forward Hamilton & Scripps, 271
Lucent Books, 198
Lusardi Construction Company, 212
LVI Environmental Services, 238
Lykes Brothers Steamship Company, 301

M

MacNeal-Schwendler Corp., 208
Maguire Thomas Partners, 288
Majestic Realty Company, 289
Manatt Phelps and Phillips, 268
Manufacturers Bank, 194, 195
Maples & Associates, 287
Marcor of California, 238
Marlborough School, 220
Marriott, Anaheim,, 258
Marriott Mission Valley, San Diego, 258
Marriott, Newport Beach,, 258
Marsh & McLennan, 264, 265
Marshall Industries, 223
Martin, Albert C., & Associates, 189
Marymount High School, 220
Maxicare Health Plans, 264
Maxwell Laboratories, S-Cubed Division, 239
MCA, Inc. and Universal Pictures., 235
MCA Records, 236
McCann-Erickson, 182
McCann-Erickson Los Angeles, 180
McCarthy Brothers Company, 212
McClellan Cruz/Gaylord & Associates, 189
McDonald Douglas, 184
McFarland Energy, 280
McGladrey & Pullen, 177, 178
McGraw/Baldwin Architects, 190
MCI Communications Corporation, 223
McInnis Fitzgerald Rees & Sharkey, 271
McKinsey & Company, 273
McLarand, Vasquez & Partners, 190
Mclaren Hart, 229
McQuerter Group, 182
MEC Analytical Systems, 239
Mendoza Dillon & Associates, 181
Mercer, William M., 273
Mercury Air Group, 301
Mercury General Corp., 264
Mercy Hospital and Medical Center, 253
Merisel Inc., 208
Merrill Lynch Pierce Fenner & Smith, 298, 299
Mesa Vista Hospital, 253
Metcalf & Eddy, 239
Metlife Health Care Network, 250
Metro Goldwyn Mayer, 234
Metrobank, 194, 195
Metrospace Corporation, 289
MICOM Communications Corp., 223
MicroSemi Corp., 224
Midnite Express International Couriers, 301
Milberg Weis Bershad Hynes & Lerach, 271

Miller Kaplan Arase and Co., 176
Mills, Timothy S., Insurance Services, 266
Mission Bay Memorial Hospital, 253
Mission Foods Corp., 241
Mission Hospital Regional Medical Center, 252
Mitchell Silberberg & Knupp, 268
Mitchell Web Press, 285
MK Centennial, 229
Molecular Biosystems, 215
Montclair College Preparatory School, 220
Montgomery Ward & Company, 293
Montgomery Watson, 228, 230, 238
Morgan Lewis & Bocklus, 268
Morley Group, 211
Morris, William, Agency, 235
Morrison & Foerster, 268, 269
Morton Electronic Materials, 203
Mossimo Inc., 187
Motorcar Parts & Accessories, 192
Mount St. Mary's College, 218
Muller, J., International, 230
Mulvaney Kahan & Barry, 271
Munger Tolles & Olson, 268
Murdock Inc., 184
Murphy, Dan, Foundation, 244
Murphy, P., & Associates, 273
Murria and Frick Insurance Agency, 266
Murtaugh Miller Meyer & Nelson, 269
Muscular Dystrophy Association, 262
Museum of African American Art, 278
Museum of Contemporary Art, 278
Museum of Tolerance, 278
Music Center of Los Angeles County, 232
Musick Peeler & Garrett, 268
Musil Perkowitz Ruth, 189
MVR Communications, 223
Mycogen Corp., 215

N

Nadel Partnership, The, 189
Nakano Foods, 241
National Bank of Southern California, 195
National Council on Alcoholism, 262
National Technical Systems, 228
Nationwide Papers, 282
Natural gas., 304

Natural History Museum, Balboa Park, 278
NBC Studios, 234
Neil Dymott Perkins Brown & Frank, 271
Neiman-Marcus, 293
Neptune Thomas Davis, 190
Netter Digital Entertainment, 234
Nettleship Group, 205
Newport Harbor Art Museum, 278
Neyenesch Printers, 285
Nico Insurance Services, 266
Nielsen, A.C., 181
Nielsen Construction Company, 212
Nigro Karlin and Segal, 176
Nissan Design International, 192
Nolte & Associates, 230
Norris, Kenneth T. & Eileen L.,, 245
North County Bank, 196
North County Times, 276
Northrop Grumman Corp., 184
Northwest Airlines, 301
Norton Lilly International, 302
Norton Simon Museum, 278
NTN Communications,, 234
Nucleic Acid Research Institute, 214
Nuffer Smith Tucker, 287

O

Oakwood School, 220
Occidental College, 219
Occidental Petroleum, 280
Office of Personnel Management, 247
Ogden Environmental and Energy Services Company, 239
Ogilvy & Mather, 180
Old Globe Theatre, 232
Oliver & Winston, 192
O'Melveny & Meyers, 268, 270
Omni Los Angeles Hotel and Centre, 257
O'Neil Data Systems, 284
Orange Coast Magazine, 276
Orange County Community Hospital, 252
Orange County Department of, 220
Orange County Performing Arts Center, 232
Orange County Register, 276
Orange County Transportation, 247, 302

Orange Foundation for Medical Care, 252
Orion Pictures Corporation, 234
Ortel Corp., 223
Osicom Technologies, 223, 226
Otis College of Art & Design, 219

P

P&D Consultants, 230, 239
P&D Environmental Services, 239
Pacer Technology, 203
Pacific Asia Museum, 278
Pacific Bell, 226
Pacific Enterprises, 280, 304
Pacific Printing Industries, 284
Pacific Scientific Co., 224
Pacific Southwest Realty Services, 290
Pacific West Communications Group, 287
Pacifica Hospital, 252
PacifiCare Health Systems, 265
PacifiCare of California, 252, 253
Packaging Advantage Corporation, 282
Paine Webber, 298, 299
Pairgain Technologies, 224
Palmieri Tyler Winer Wilhelm & Waldron, 270
Palomar Medical Center, 253
Panda Management Company, 257
Pankow, Charles, Builders LTD, 211
Paradise Valley Hospital, 254
Paramount Pictures, 234
Parker Publications, 198
Parsons Brinckerhoff, 230
Parsons Corporation, 228, 238
Parsons Engineering Science, 230
Parsons, Ralph M., Foundation, 245
Pasadena Star-News, 276
Patagonia, 186
Paul Hastings Janofsky & Walker, 269, 270
PCC Group, 208
PDT, Inc., 214
Peck/Jones Construction, 211
Peninsula Bank of San Diego, 196
Penn Lithographics, 284
Penny, J.C., 293
Pepperdine University, 219
Pepsi-Cola West, 241

Peregrine Systems, 209
Permanent Charities Committee of Entertainment, 262
Peryam & Kroll, 181
Petco Animal Supplies, 293
Petersen Publishing Company, 198
Peterson & Co., 178
Peterson International Insurance Brokers, 264
PharMingen, 216
Phelps, E.J., & Co., 266
Pico Products, 223
Pillsbury Madison & Sutro, 269, 270, 271
PIMCO, 299
Platinum Software Corporation, 208
Pleasant Hawaiian Holidays, 302
PMC Inc., 203
Polytechnic School, 220
Pomona Valley Hospital Medical Center, 250
Post Kirby Naonan & Sweat, 271
Powell, Charles Lee, Foundation, 245
Practice Management Information Corporation, 198
Precision Lithographers, 285
Preferred Health Network, 250
Premier Food Services, 259
President Global Corp., 242
Presto Foods Products, 241
Price Club, 293
Price Stern Sloan, 198
Price Waterhouse, 176, 177, 178
Price Waterhouse LLP, 273
Princess Cruises, 302
Private Healthcare Systems, 252
Procopio Cory Hargreaves and Savitch, 271
Project Design Consultants, 230
Project Independence, 262
Proxima Corporation, 226
PruCare of California, 250, 252
Prudential California Realty, 290
Prudential Healthcare Plan of California, 254
Prudential Securities, 299
PSI, 234

Q

Qualcomm Incorporated, 226
Quarterdeck Corporation, 208
Quicksilver Inc., 187
Quidel Corp., 216

R

Radian Corporation, 239
Rainbow Technologies, 208
Rampage Clothing Corp., 186
RAND, 228
Randall, E. Broox, and Son, 264
Randall Foods, 241
Rank Video Services, 234
RE/MAX Beach Cities Realty, 289
Red Lion Hotel, 257
Revel Travel Service, 302
Rhino Records, 236
Riccobon Business Forms, 284
Rice, George, & Sons, 284
Right Associates, 273
Ritz Carlton, 258
Ritz-Carlton Huntington Hotel, 257
Robinsons-May Company, 293
Rochlin Baran & Balbona, 189
Rohm & Haas, 203
Rohr, Inc., 185
Roper Starch Worldwide, 181
Rotonics Manufacturing, 280
Royal Caribbean, 302
RTKL Associates, 189
Rubin Postaer & Associates, 180
Rutan & Tucker, 270
Rykoff-Sexton, 241

S

Saatchi & Saatchi DFS/Pacific, 180
Saddleback Memorial Medical Center, 252
Safety Components International, 192
Saks Fifth Avenue, 293
Salerno/Livingston Architects, 190
Salvation Army, The, 262
San Diego Chargers Football Company, 296
San Diego Community Foundation, 245
San Diego Gas & Electric Company, 305
San Diego Harbor Excursions, 303
San Diego Magazine, 276
San Diego Museum of Art, 278
San Diego Museum of Contemporary Art, 278
San Diego National Bank, 196
San Diego Padres Baseball Club, 296
San Diego Paper Box, 282
San Diego Princess Resort, 259
San Diego State University, 219
San Diego Transit Corporation, 303
San Diego Unified School District, 220
San Diego Union-Tribune, 276
San Diego Zoo/Wild Animal Park, 296
San Dieguito Publishers, 285
Santa Ana Hospital Medical Center, 252
Santa Anita Racetrack, 295
Santa Monica Museum of Art, 278
Sanwa Bank California, 194, 196
Sav On Drugs, 293
Schumacher, J.C., Company, 204
Scripps Bank, 196
Scripps Clinic, 254
Scripps Community Health Network, 254
Scripps Memorial Hospital, 254
Sea World, 296
Sealright Company, 282
SEDA Specialty Packaging Corp., 280, 282
Sedgwick Group, PLC, 265
Sedgwick James, 265
Seeley Company, 289
Seiniger Advertising, 181
Seltzer Caplan Wilkins & McMahon, 271
Sentra Securities/Spelman & Co., 299
Service Craft Distribution Systems, 303
Seven-Up/ Royal Crown Bottling Co., 242
SGPA Architecture & Planning, 190
Shafer Advertising, 182
Shafer Public Relations, 287
Shapell Industries, 211
Sharp Cabrillo Hospital, 254
Sharp Chula Vista Medical Center, 254
Sharp Health Plan, 254
Sharp Memorial Hospital, 254
Shasco, Inc., 242

Employers Index

Shea Homes, 289
Sheppard Mullin Richter and Hampton, 269, 271
Sheraton Grande Hotel, 257
Sheraton Harbor Island Resort, 259
Shifflet Walters Kane & Konoske, 271
SHL Systemhouse, 205
Shorewood Realtors, 289
Sidley & Austin, 269
Simulation Sciences, 208
Sinclair Printing Company, 284
Six Flags Magic Mountain, 295
Sizzler International, 257
Skadden Arps Slate Meagher & Flom, 269
Skyska & Hennessy, 228
Small Business Administration, 247
Smartflex Systems, 224
Smith Barney, 298
Smith Micro Software, 209
Snell and Wilmer, 270
Social Advocates for Youth, 263
Software Dynamics, 208
Sony Electronics, 226
Sony Pictures Entertainment, 234
Sony Pictures Imageworks, 236
Sotheby's, 278
Source Consulting, 205
South Coast Communications Group, 287
South Coast Medical Center, 252
South Coast Repertory, 232
Southern California Bank, 195
Southern California Gas Company, 305
Southern California Graphic, 284
Southern California Water Company, 305
Southern Pacific Thrift & Loan, 194
Southland Envelope Company, 282
Southwest Airlines, 302
Southwest Museum, 278
Southwest Water Company, 305
Special Devices, 223
Special Effects Unlimited, 236
Specialty Paper Mills, 282
Specialty Restaurants Corp., 258
Spectrum Printing, 285
Spelling Entertainment Group, 235
Sperry Van Ness, 289
Sports Club Company, The, 295
St. Augustine High School, 220
St. Ives Laboratories, 214
St. John's Hospital & Health Center, 250
St. John's Knits, 187
St. Joseph Hospital, 252
St. Joseph Medical Center, 250
St. Jude Medical Center, 252
St. Margaret's, 221
Stac Electronics, 209
Standard Pacific Corp., 212
State Employment Office, 247
State of the Art, 209
Stater Brothers Holdings, 293
Steele, Harry and Grace, Foundation, 245
Stein, Jules and Doris, Foundation, 245
Stephens, P.W., Contractors, 238
Stichler Design Group, 190
STM Wireless, 224
Stock Alper & Associates, 287
Stoorza Ziegaus & Metzger, 287
Stradling Yocca Carlson & Rauth, 270
Strouds Inc., 293
Sullivan & Curtis Insurance Brokers, 265
Sumitomo Bank of California, 196
Sunclipse Inc., 282
Sundance Travel, 303
Superior Industries, 192
Superior Lithographics, 284
Sutro & Company, 298
Sverdrup Corp., 229
Swinerton & Walberg, 211
Syncor International Corp., 214

T

Tait & Associates, 229
Target Airfreight, 302
Target Stores, 293
Tarrant Apparel Group, 186
TBP/Blurock Partnership, 190
TBWA/Chiat Day, 181
TD Service Financial Corporation, 290
Team One Advertising, 181
Technical Directions, 206
TEG-The Environmental Group, 238
Temple Inland Food Service, 282
Tenet Healthcare Corporation, 250
Texaco, 280
Think Tank Inc., 182

Thomas Brothers Maps, 198
Thompson PBE, 192, 203
Three D Departments, 293
Thrifty Corporation, 293
Ticketmaster Corp., 295
Time, 276
Times Mirror Fund, 245
Tishman West Companies, 289
Tokai Bank of California, 194
Toshiba America Information Systems, 209
Towers Perrin, 274
Trader Joe's Company, 293
Trammel Crow Company, 289
Trans Western Publishing, 198
Trans-Box Courier Systems, 303
Travelodge Hotel on Harbor Island, 259
Tri Modal Distribution Service, 303
Tri-City Medical Center, 254
Trio Tech International, 223
TriWest Insurance Services, 265
TRW Technar, 192
Tucker Sadler & Associates, 190
Turner Construction Company, 211
Turner Home Entertainment, 235
Tutor-Saliba Corp, 211
TV Guide, 276
TV/COM International, 226
TWA, 302
Twentieth Century Fox, 235
Twentieth Century Fox Casting, 235
Twentieth Century Industries, 265

U

U.S. Department of Agriculture, Office of Food and, 248
U.S. Forest Service, 248
U.S. Immigration and Naturalization Service, 248
U.S. Maritime Administration, 248
U.S. Peace Corps, 248
UCLA Medical Center, 250
UCLA/Armand Hammer Museum of Art and Cultural Cente, 278
Union Bank, 196
Union Carbide Corp., 203
Unisource Corporation, 282
Unisys Corp., 209
United Airlines, 302, 303
United Health Plan, 250
United Parcel Service, 303
United Publishers Corporation, 198
United Restaurants, 257
United States Borax & Chemical Corp., 203
United Way, 262
Universal Care Health Plan, 250
Universal City Studios, 235
Universal Studios Hollywood Theme Park, 295
University of California, Irvine, 219
University of California Irvine Medical Center, 252
University of California, Los Angeles (UCLA), 219
University of California, San Diego, 219
University of California San Diego Medical Center, 254
University of San Diego, 219
University of San Diego High School, 221
University of Southern California (USC), 219
UNOCAL, 280
Urethane Technologies, 203
US Sprint, 223

V

VA Medical Center, 251
Vanard Lithographers, 285
Vans Inc., 187
Varco International, 280
Variety/Daily Variety, 276
Vernon Sanitation Supply Co., 282
Vestro Natural Foods, 241
Veterans Administration, 248
Viagene, 216
Vical Inc., 216
Viking Office Products, 293
Virgin Interactive Entertainment, 209
Virgin Records, 236
VisiCom Laboratories, 210
Vista Health Plans, 254
Vista-United Telecommunications, 224
Vitex Foods, 241
Voit Commercial Brokerage, 290
Vons Companies, 294
VTN West, 228

W

Warner Brothers Animation, 236
Warner Brothers Records, 236
Warner Design Associates, 182
Warner Group, The, 206, 274
Wateridge Insurance Services, 266
Watson Pharmaceuticals, 214
Watson Wyatt Worldwide, 274
WD-40 Company, 204
Web School of California, 221
Webtrend Graphics, 285
Weekend Exercise Company, 187
Weider Health & Fitness, 276
Weingart Foundation, 245
Wells Fargo Bank, 195, 196
West Anaheim Mecial Center, 253
West Turnquist and Schmitt, 178
Westco Products, 241
Western Atlas, 280
Western Digital Corp., 209
Western Financial Savings Bank, 195
Western Medical Center, 253
Western Outdoors Publications, 276
Westin Bonaventure Hotel and Suites, 257
Westridge School, 221
Wherehouse Entertainment, 294
White, Jack, & Co., 299
Whittaker Corp., 184, 203
Whittier Christian High School, 221
Whittier College, 219
Willis Corroon Corporation of Los Angeles, 265
Willis Corroon Corporation of Orange County, 266
Wilson, William, Company, 289
Wimberly Allison Tong & Goo, 190
Wonderware, 209
Wong, Joseph, Design Associates, 190
Woodward-Clyde Consultants, 230, 239
World Oil Company, 280
World Savings & Loan, 195
World Travel Bureau, 303
Wynns International, 192

X

XETV-Fox Channel 6, 202
XHTZ-FM/SLTN-FM/XHKY-FM, 201
XTRA-AM/91X -FM, 201
XXSYS Technologies, 212

Y

Yellow Freight Systems, 302
Yes Clothing Company, 186
YMCA of Metropolitan Los Angeles, 262
Young's Market Company, 242
YWCA of Los Angeles, 262

Z

Zellerbach Paper, 282
Zero Corp., 223
Zugsmith-Thind, 289

General Index

A

Accounting/Auditing, 175-178
Ads, classified, for jobs, 97
Advertising/Market Research, 179-182
Aircraft/Aerospace, 183-185
Apparel/Textiles, 185-187
Architectural Firms, 188-190
Automotive/Transportation Equipment, 191-192

B

Banking, 193-196
Better Business Bureau, 80
Biotechnology firms, *see* Drugs
Book Publishers/Literary Agents, 197-198
Books
    career strategy, 39-41
    corporate culture, 95-96
    for disabled job seekers, 41
    on internships, 160-161
    on interviewing, 153
    mid-life career change, 40
    on networking, 106
    on-line job search, 11, 74
    for recent graduates, 40
    on resumes and cover letters, 132
    salary negotiation, 93
    for senior job seekers, 40
    on small-company jobs, 74
    on temporary/part-time jobs, 163
    for women and minorities, 41
Broadcasting, 199-202
Business, small, *see* Small business
Business, starting your own, 35-38
Business trends in Southern California, 11-12

C

Career changing, 34-35
Career counseling, 25-34, 85
    at colleges and universities, 29-31, 85
    at social service agencies, 31-34

Career, creativity and success in, 168, 170
Career fairs, 86-88
Careers, how to choose, 21-25, *see also* Chapter 2
Chambers of Commerce, 20
Chemicals, 202-204
Computers: Consulting/Information Management, 205-206
Computers: Hardware/Software, 207-210
Consultants, career, *see* Career counseling
Consumer complaint agencies, 80
Construction, 210-212
Counseling, career, *see* Career counseling
Cover letters for resumes, 127-132
    samples of, 128-130
    WWW sites, 131
Culture, corporate, 95-96

D

Directories for use in job search, 57-65, *see also* under employment categories in Chapter 10
Drugs/Pharmaceuticals/Biotechnology, 213-216

E

Education and the job search, *see also* "Graduate school" and Chapter 3
    for additional skills, 43,51
    to change careers, 43
    continuing, 51-52
    income relationship, 44-45
    on-line, 52-53
Educational Institutions, 217-221
Electronics/Telecommunications, 222-226
Employer categories, list of, 173-174
Employers, *see also* Chapter 10
    10 fastest growing, 16-17
    10 best, 12-15
    10 largest, 18-19
Employers Index, 306
Employment agencies, 79-81, 162-163

Employment trends, 11-12
Engineering, 227-230
Entertainment, 231-236
Environmental Services, 237-239
Executive search firms, 81-82

F

Film production, 232
Financial Services/Stock Brokers, 297-299
Food/Beverage Producers and Distributors, 240-243
Food services, jobs in, 242
Foundations/Philanthropies, 243-245

G

Government, 246-248
Government agencies useful in job search, 84-85
Graduate school
  admission tests, 46
  application process, 45-46
  how to select, 46-48
  programs in Southern California, 48-49
  reasons for attending, 42-45
  WWW sites for information, 47

H

Health Care, 248-254
Hiring authority, contacting, 78
Homepages, corporate, 134-135
Hospitality: Hotels/Restaurants, 255-259
Hotel management, jobs in, 259
Human Services, 260-263

I

Information interview, 100-102
Insurance, 263-266
Internet, 7, *see also* World Wide Web
Internships, 29, 157-161
Interviewing, *see also* Chapter 7
  books on, 153
  15 toughest questions, 143-145
  for information, 100-102
  Internet tips, 134, 153
  9 interviewer styles, 146-150
  overview, 91-92, 133-143, 150-152
  rejection, reasons for, 150-151
  6-step system, 133
  thank-you letter after, 142

J

Job, *see also* Career
  adjusting to, 164-166
  boss, relating to, 166-167
  handling first day, 164-165
Job evaluation, 93-94
Job fairs, 86-88
Job hotlines, voice, 71-72
Job listings, 67-71, 83-85
Job search, *see also* Chapter 4
  on Internet, 9-11, 73, 88-90, 134
  10-step system, 54
Jobs, summer and part-time, *see* Chapter 8

L

Law Firms, 267-271
Libraries, for job research, 55-56

M

Magazines
  general business, 4-6
  professional, *see* under employment categories in Chapter 10
  trade, 65-67
Management Consultants, 272-274
Market Research, 179-182
Media, Print, 274-276
Minorities, small business resources, 37-38
Museums/Art Galleries, 277-278

N

Networking, *see also* Chapter 5
  assessment quiz, 103
  books on, 106
  etiquette in, 75, 104
  on Internet, 105
  overview, 75, 97-99, 103
  post-employment, 106, 171
  resource list of organizations, clubs, and trade groups, 107-114, *see also* under employment categories in Chapter 10

General Index

step-by-step guide, 99
women's groups, *see under* Women
Newspapers, as aid in job search, 2-4
Nursing, employment in, 254

O

Occupations, dictionary of, 24
Oil/Gas/Plastics, 279-280
Organizations, professional, 107-114, *see also* under employment categories in Chapter 10

P

Paper and Allied Products, 281-282
Part-time/temporary jobs, 161-163
Philanthropy, 243-245
Plastics, 279-280
Printing/Graphic Arts, 283-285
Public Relations, 286-287
Publishers, 197-198

R

Radio, 200-201
Real Estate, Developers and Brokers, 288-290
Real estate, jobs in, 291
Recreation/Sports/Fitness, 294-296
References, how to use, 142
Restaurants, 255-259
Resumes, *see also* Chapter 6
  basics of, 77, 116-119, 124
  computer compatible, 124, 127
  cover letters for, 77, 127-132
  on Internet, 131-132
  mailing, 78
  preparation of, 77, 116-119, 124
  professional preparers, 125-126
  samples of, 120-123
Retailers/Wholesalers, 292-294
Romance, office, 169

S

Salary negotiating, 93
Shipping, 300-303
Skills, transfering of, 34-35
Small business
  as employers, 74
  guidance in your own, 35-38
  resource centers, 36-38
  U.S. Small Business Administration, 35-36
Social service agencies useful in job search, 31-34, 82-84
Sports/Recreation/Fitness, 294-296
Stock Brokers/Financial Services, 297-299
Summer jobs, 154-161

T

Teaching, jobs in, 221
Telecommunications, 222-226
Television, 201-202
Temporary/part-time jobs, 161-163
Testing, vocational, 25
Travel/Shipping/Transportation, 300-303

U

Utilities, 304-305

V

Vocational schools in Southern California, 50-51

W

Women
  books for, 54
  business, small, resources, 38
  employment resources, 38
  networking groups, 110-114
World Wide Web sites pertaining to:
  career counseling, 28
  career fairs, 87
  coffee houses with Internet access, 106
  college courses, 53
  graduate schools, 47
  interviewing, 134, 152
  job listings, 67-71, 83-85
  job search, 9-11, 73, 88-90, 134
  networking, 105
  resumes and cover letters, 131-132
  Small Business Administration, 36
  Southern California, 8
  summer jobs, 156-157
  women, 38